Buster Keaton
in His Own Time

Buster Keaton in His Own Time

What the Responses of 1920s Critics Reveal

WES D. GEHRING

McFarland & Company, Inc., Publishers
Jefferson, North Carolina

ALSO BY WES D. GEHRING
AND FROM MCFARLAND

Movie Comedians of the 1950s: Defining a New Era of Big Screen Comedy (2016);
Genre-Busting Dark Comedies of the 1970s: Twelve American Films (2016);
Chaplin's War Trilogy: An Evolving Lens in Three Dark Comedies, 1918–1947 (2014);
Will Cuppy, American Satirist: A Biography (2013); *Forties Film Funnymen:
The Decade's Great Comedians at Work in the Shadow of War* (2010); *Film Clowns
of the Depression: Twelve Defining Comic Performances* (2007); *Joe E. Brown:
Film Comedian and Baseball Buffoon* (2006); *Mr. Deeds Goes to Yankee Stadium:
Baseball Films in the Capra Tradition* (2004)

Frontispiece: Film and baseball were Buster Keaton's "two great loves." The game is often referenced in his movies such as fleeting self-defense batting away of objects, pretending to play poorly in *College*'s (1927) baseball sequence, and *The Cameraman*'s (1928) tour de force solo performance at Yankee Stadium. Plus, crews had to be proficient in *either* film or baseball, since periodic games helped Buster brainstorm.

LIBRARY OF CONGRESS CATALOGUING-IN-PUBLICATION DATA

Names: Gehring, Wes D., author.
Title: Buster Keaton in his own time : what the responses of 1920s critics reveal / Wes D. Gehring.
Description: Jefferson, North Carolina : McFarland & Company, Inc., Publishers, 2018. | Includes filmography. | Includes bibliographical references and index.
Identifiers: LCCN 2018007457 | ISBN 9781476666808 (softcover : acid free paper) ∞
Subjects: LCSH: Keaton, Buster, 1895–1966—Criticism and interpretation.
Classification: LCC PN2287.K4 G44 2018 | DDC 791.4302/8092—dc23
LC record available at https://lccn.loc.gov/2018007457

BRITISH LIBRARY CATALOGUING DATA ARE AVAILABLE

ISBN (print) 978-1-4766-6680-8
ISBN (ebook) 978-1-4766-3326-8

© 2018 Wes D. Gehring. All rights reserved

*No part of this book may be reproduced or transmitted in any form
or by any means, electronic or mechanical, including photocopying
or recording, or by any information storage and retrieval system,
without permission in writing from the publisher.*

Front cover: Buster Keaton as Rollo Treadway in *The Navigator*, 1924
(Metro-Goldwyn Pictures Corporation/Photofest)

Printed in the United States of America

*McFarland & Company, Inc., Publishers
Box 611, Jefferson, North Carolina 28640
www.mcfarlandpub.com*

In memory of my mother
Marilyn McIntyre Gehring

Table of Contents

Preface and Acknowledgments	1
Prologue	3
1. Working Towards the Feature Films of 1923–1929	15
2. The First Two Features: *The Three Ages* (July 25, 1923) and *Our Hospitality* (November 20, 1923)	37
3. *Sherlock, Jr.* (April 4, 1924): John Bunny and Fatty Arbuckle Factors	59
4. *The Navigator* (October 14, 1924): Arguably Keaton's Greatest Film	74
5. *Seven Chances* (April 22, 1925)	88
6. *Go West* (November 23, 1925)	102
7. *Battling Butler* (August 30, 1926)	118
8. *The General* (December 22, 1926): Groundbreaking Dark Comedy but Keaton's Greatest Film?	132
9. *College* (September 10, 1927): Punishment by Way of Harold Lloyd Land	148
10. *Steamboat Bill, Jr.* (June 2, 1928)	161
11. *The Cameraman* (September 15, 1928): A Visit to Yankee Stadium	172
12. *Spite Marriage* (April 22, 1929): Somewhat Saved by Silence	184
Epilogue: Period Material Provides a Modern View	192
Filmography	205
Chapter Notes	207
Bibliography	220
Index	231

Preface and Acknowledgments

"Nowhere to Run" (1965)—Martha and the Vandellas

By time-tripping back to 1920s Buster Keaton material, many forgotten but fascinating and often provocative items have been discovered about this pioneering existentialist. Not surprisingly, given his trailblazing "Theatre of the Absurd" world, his screen persona was frequently driven to run from something, be it the police (*Cops*, 1922), or wannabe brides (*Seven Chances*, 1925). Yet, with his cultish anticipation of today's dark comedy mindset, most succinctly showcased by his tombstone endings, the message was clear—there was "Nowhere to Run." Thus, if Buster were to be given a belated theme song, à la Charlie Chaplin's composition "Smile," or Groucho Marx's "Hurray for Captain Spalding," nothing could be more quintessential Keaton than "Nowhere to Run." Indeed, even in one of his last movies, 1965's *Film*—fittingly a silent short subject by *Waiting for Godot* playwright Samuel Beckett—Keaton's character is pushed to run.

With *Film*, first screened mere months before his death, and the release of "Nowhere to Run," the world had finally caught up with his once other worldly prophetic figure—from a nightmare to the norm. Pertinently, for a comedian who had more faith in mechanical consistency than mankind, the song's video even had the Vandellas singing in an automobile factory amidst the construction of a single car. Keaton might have masterminded the short subject from what he called his postcard-sized "scripts."

Regardless, by the 1960s Keaton seemed more contemporary than Chaplin. And in the 1980s no less a figure than the BBC's most important broadcasting gift to America, Alistair Cooke, reported that British critics were calling Keaton a "resurrected god." Be that as it may, the following pages examine this "resurrected god" *in his own time* … when he was nickname "Zero."

Nevertheless, the real task at hand here is to thank the many people who helped make this book possible. At this point, no matter how the text fairs with readers, most conscious authors feel like the director François Truffaut played in his film within a film from 1973's *Day for Night*: "Shooting a movie is like a stagecoach trip. At first you hope for a nice ride. Then you just hope to reach your destination." This exhaustion can sometimes even make a writer feel like one of *Star Wars*' (1977) bar scene characters. (Note there is no text photo of the author.) Anyway, as the acknowledgments begin, there is always the fear that someone has been missed. So if anyone is overlooked, my *profound* apologies. Let me start with a heartfelt thank you for my department chair, Tim Pollard. He has once again been ever so generous in every way to make this book happen. And as with all my writing, Janet Warrner supplied valuable editorial help, while Kris Scott was responsible for the computer preparation of the manuscript. Chris Flook once again was especially helpful with all technology questions and needs. Ball State emeritus professors David L. Smith and Conrad Lane provided valuable discussions about the project, and often obscure Keaton-related articles. Former BSU endowed chair (and award-winning filmmaker) Robert Mugge was also an excellent and patient sounding board. And given the text's focus on 1920s film criticism, BSU's interlibrary loan staff was *especially* helpful: Kerri K. McClellan, Elaine S. Nelson, Jodi L. Sanders, Lisa R. Johnson, and Karin Kwiatkowski. Plus, BSU's James Shimkus, from Information Services, always went beyond the extra mile on the odd questions.

Away from home, the New York Public Library's main branch at Fifth Avenue and Forty-Second Street is always an invaluable source, with its two marble lions, "Patience" and "Fortitude," standing guard at the entrance. At this location, my focus is on the "tombs" section—looking at New York's many seminal dead newspapers on microfilm. (Of special importance here was Diane Serrano.) The city's Performing Arts Library at Lincoln Center is also a necessary stop, with its period clipping files of film artists and individual pictures.

Bowling Green University's (Ohio) Jerome Library, a popular culture mecca, was an invaluable source of period movie magazines. I was especially indebted to the ongoing assistance of special collection librarian Mary Zuzik. Even after two research trips, she would contact me with updates on lingering questions.

I cannot thank enough New York's Liz Kurtulik, from Art Resources' Permissions Department, for her invaluable help in tracking down and helping to arrange permission for the reproductions of Edward Hopper's *Automat*, and Gerald Murphy's *The Watch*.

My family has always been most encouraging and helpful—especially my film-loving daughters Sarah and Emily. Along related lines, this was a most challenging project *but* not just because of the added difficulty of keying on 1920s literatures. I lost my mother, my greatest cheerleader, shortly after Christmas, and the book took on an increased mission to be a tribute to all she meant to me.

Prologue

In James Agee's watershed 1949 essay, "Comedy's Greatest Era," he suggested a special silent comedy hierarchy of four "eminent masters: Charlie Chaplin, Harold Lloyd, the late Harry Langdon and Buster Keaton."[1]

James Agee essay jump-started the serious study of silent comedy and forever established, at least for a time, an era's pantheon four: Chaplin (1889–1977), Keaton (1895–1966), Lloyd (1893–1971), and Langdon (1884–1944). Chaplin, of course, is arguably also the greatest auteur (silent or sound) in movie history. His ability to write, direct, perform, and compose the music for one groundbreaking picture after another is unprecedented. Moreover, his alter ego Tramp is often considered film's most well-known icon, with the possible exception of Mickey Mouse.

Ironically, nonetheless, while Agee has randomly listed Keaton last in his self-proclaimed celebrated foursome, the comedian is now considered Chaplin's only critical rival of the era; this will be expanded upon shortly. However, a further paradox is that during the 1920s, Lloyd was the box office champion for several obvious reasons. While Chaplin let years pass between productions, Lloyd was the most prolific funnyman in the business. In addition, his cinema was the most gag-saturated of the group—greatly assisted by an army of idea men. Moreover, his persona of an underdog mama's boy that makes good perfectly matched the world of success-driven Babbitt America. Plus, while not having the brilliant comic intuition of Chaplin and Keaton, Lloyd had a firm handle on the innate boundaries of his screen persona, which is obvious in his 1928 memoir, *An American Comedy*.[2] This is no small accomplishment, because it is not enough to just be funny. Consistency allows the comedian to create a singularity viewers come to expect and return to see again in a variation of the same pattern.

Indeed, this lack of an undeviating constancy was what contributed to the decline of Harry Langdon's short high-profile career even before the coming of sound. Moreover, while Chaplin and Keaton were capable of wearing several creative hats (indeed, the creator of the Tramp was a whole haberdashery), and Lloyd was good at delegating authority, Langdon caught what film historians have come to call "the Chaplin disease." That is, after Frank Capra helped create a very successful Langdon baby persona who survived only by the grace of God, the comedian unsuccessfully attempted to go it alone.[3] But unlike Lloyd, Langdon did not fully understand his persona's perimeters. With the end of his "A" picture career, Langdon returned to vaudeville and met a talented comedian on his way up, Bob Hope. In one of Hope's many later memoirs, *The Road to Hollywood* (1977), he shared: "One day between shows, Langdon told me: 'Young man, if you ever go out to Hollywood and become a star—and I think you could—don't make my mistake. Don't try to convince

Harry Langdon, as a poor man's Chaplin, did not fully grasp his persona. It was pathos, not "whoopee," that drove his alter ego.

yourself that you're a genius.'"[4] Just as Keaton has jumpfrogged over Lloyd to essentially parity with Chaplin, a serious examination of period literature suggests Agee would best have kept his silent film deity to the trio of Chaplin, Keaton, and Lloyd.

Regardless, Agee's essay had the greatest impact upon Keaton. It helped resurrect his career, and begin the slow process of reclaiming his inspired silent film legacy. Keaton's vocation would never again approach the momentous movies of the 1920s, except for the brief but electrifying sequence he shared with Chaplin in the latter's last stimulatingly personal picture, *Limelight* (1952, in which they comically struggle their way through a musical duet). Yet, Keaton brought his gifts to an ongoing venue of projects, with 1950s television being the most frequent setting for his laughter showcase.

The decade also produced a mediocre movie of his life, *The Buster Keaton Story* (1957, with Donald O'Connor in the title role). While short on facts, it gave the comedian both increased public exposure and added financial security. Allegedly lost Keaton pictures kept being rediscovered and shown, culminating with two pivotal decade-ending events. On April 4, 1960, the Motion Picture Academy ceremony, with perennial host Bob Hope helping honor 1959's best pictures, took time to pinball its way back to silent cinema and present Buster Keaton with an honorary Oscar "for his unique talents which brought immortal comedies to the screen."[5] Appropriately, he received a spontaneous standing ovation. The timing seemed fitting, too, given the fact that the epic *Ben-Hur* (1959) took home eleven Oscars—the long overdue statuette for Keaton had stumbled onto the perfect year. That is, *the* money *Ben-Hur* sequence was the chariot race, and the funniest image in Keaton's first feature film, *Three Ages* (1923), was the comedian decked out in Roman garb with chariot problems of his own.

The second key event of 1960 was the publication of Keaton's autobiography, *My Wonderful World of Slapstick*, written with Charles Samuels. Receiving glowing reviews, what is most striking about the book, besides a life story that rivaled any of his amazing movies, is the gentle forgiving tone it presents of a man who was severely wronged in so many personal

Keaton spoofs *Ben-Hur*'s chariot sequence in *The Three Ages* (1923).

and professional ways after the silent era ended. As stoic as his signature "Great Stone Face," the memoir is devoid of any bitterness. In his last remaining decade, there would be more memorable moments, from starring in Samuel Beckett's *Film* (1965), to making a personal appearance that same year at the Venice Film Festival. Of the latter honor, he was said to have received "the loudest and longest ovation ever accorded any artist."[6] Though he would die just a few months later, Buster Keaton was back.

Since that time many books have been written about Keaton's life and/or his films. And his current revisionist elevation to a position on par for many with Chaplin, a station to which this then cultish figure was not even remotely considered during the 1920s, is the catalyst for this book. *However*, I wanted a new twist. I would closely examine his twelve silent features (done between 1923 and 1929) keying in-depth upon *period* reviews and other 1920s material on Keaton and his contemporaries. What had these critics missed and/or seen which had gone underappreciated by the masses? Moreover, what had fallen through the cracks of time that contemporary critics and/or fans were not aware of which could now further decode and/or elevate his silent features. Furthermore, what had changed about society in general? Let me hasten to add that other Keaton authors had often made excellent though more limited use of period materials, such as Edward McPherson's admirable *Buster Keaton: Tempest in a Flat Hat* (2005).

For that matter, even the most pedestrian Keaton study would cite how his allegedly most momentous movie, 1927's *The General*, was his greatest critical failure during the Jazz Age. Yet, did *everyone* get it wrong in 1927? Moreover, since *The General* has now been held in lofty status longer than Keaton was so decidedly placed behind Chaplin, who is to say it should still be granted this August status? To paraphrase an old Russian proverb, "the past is ongoingly unpredictable." And I was going to attempt to submerge myself in *the* Keaton decade more than anyone had before.

Though this text is predicated upon a rabbit hole to the past, that does not mean more contemporary perspectives will not also be addressed. How could it not? While there is always a door we don't have a key to, one cannot properly gauge bygone days without whatever is Keaton's current Rorschach test. Regardless, it could even be said that this time-tripping is metaphorically taking a page from Keaton. That is, late in his career he starred in the 1961 *Twilight Zone* episode "Once Upon a Time," in which he managed to be a time-traveler between 1890 and 1960—which eerily almost duplicated the bookend years of his existence (1895–1966), while actually matching the length of his life—70 years.

Be that as it may, one cannot play at being a revisionist to the past of a specific artist without being a witness to his contemporaries. As with anything remotely connected to biography, the chronicle studies an era as much as an individual. Thus, by closely excavating 1920s Keaton documentation, discoveries and insights about his fellow comedians have also been made.

The joy of this cinematic search *back* to the 1920s is that while it will often reinforce some of the status quo originally augmented by Agee, many provocative new perspectives have been uncovered. And there is a simplistic humor to the process because it is merely a modification upon that old joke about the definition of a filing cabinet: "a place where you lose things alphabetically." More precisely, the cinematic game changers discovered in the following pages have unambiguously been found by patiently plowing through 1920s film documents day by day. Happily, many once obviously known facts and period patterns of comedy have been uncovered, providing a fresh look at the decade. History provides perspective which explains why Keaton's comedy stock has increased. Yet, history's weight often also smothers details and/or explanations, making them almost irretrievable, like the proverbial lost keys.

Consequently, the motivation for this book was to create a Keaton feature criticism text which might have been largely written in the 1930s. Tweaking what obituary writers are known to say, I wanted the first last words of a period, as it relates to Keaton, that has been more than neglected. Of course, this sets up a domino effect. First, as previously noted, one must document this against Keaton's current critical framework. Second, new information and interpretations will sometimes rescramble what passes for today's revisionism. And third, this reevaluation of his critical wheelhouse is also applicable to new perspective on his comedy contemporaries, and on the Jazz Age in general.

One might best demonstrate how this plays with the corners of one's mind by returning to Agee's designation of a pivotal four comedians. As earlier suggested, without trying to commit cinema blasphemy, *the* film comedy pantheon of the 1920s revolves around Chaplin, Keaton, and Lloyd. In features Langdon was *briefly* important but as he was more of a late artistic blip on the decade's radar, with little auteur talents. He starred in three excellent features in less than two years, *Tramp, Tramp, Tramp, The Strong Man* (both 1926), and *Long Pants* (1927). The features which he orchestrated after this trio are not without interest, but they hardly compare to the aforementioned Capra-connected works. Indeed, history bears this out. Langdon is now a character for silent film aficionados, while Capra is cinema's Norman Rockwell. As John Cassavetes, the father of American independent filmmaking, once observed, "Maybe there really wasn't an America. Maybe it was only Frank Capra."

Langdon was a gifted comedian but without the behind the scenes feature film orchestration of people like Capra, and before that, the short subject contributions of Mack Sennett, Langdon does *not* merit Agee's lofty perspective. Robert E. Sherwood (1896–1955), arguably *the* 1920s film critic for *LIFE* (the humor magazine, *not* the later pictorial publication), whose writing would win him four Pulitzer Prizes—and an Oscar—best explains the *why* behind Langdon's false elevated status in his 1928 review of the comedian's *The Chaser*:

> Every critic who pans Harry Langdon's new picture ... (and every critic should pan it), will probably experience an acute sensation of personal guilt. For it is apparent even to the most discreetly clad eye that Langdon has fallen from grace—and the blame for his tumble is largely attributable to the critics (myself, I am compelled to admit, included). Langdon read what the reviewers said about him—that he was the logical successor to Charlie Chaplin—and promptly developed a Young Pretender complex. He decided that if Charlie could write ... and direct as well as act, then so could he. "The Chaser" is one result of this decision, and a sad, and ineffably sad result it is.[7]

Though many other 1920s critics are quoted in this text, Anderson is most frequently the one who best capsulized the situation. Whether it is a foreshadowing of his future Pulitzer Prizes, his window to the 1920s reminds one what it means to be embraced by good writing. However, to put a cap on the question of silent comedy revolving around three figures, one might close the subject with another 1928 article by the frequent *Photoplay* contributor Louis E. Bisch, M.D., Ph.D. In an essay entitled "What Makes You Laugh?," he provides the following practical advice for what ails you: "Nothing can possibly benefit you more than to go see Charlie Chaplin or Harold Lloyd or Buster Keaton. Often have I, as a physician, recommended that kind of prescription for brain fog [sleep-related complaints], the blues or just jaded nerves."[8]

Regardless, during this decade, the comedy pecking order, as defined by period critics, is best described thus: Chaplin is God, Lloyd is Mr. Consistency, and Keaton is a roller coaster ride of brilliant oddity, or disappointment. The Chaplin 1920s hosannas could fill a set of encyclopedias and might best start with Keaton's own observations from a 1923 *Picture-Play* magazine article: "I dread the day when we won't find another new wheeze [gag].... That's what a comedian has to guard against, running out. That is why Charlie Chaplin makes his pictures so slowly. I know as a matter of fact that he takes thousands of feet of film on every picture, only to destroy it when he sees it in the projection room. And this carefulness is just what makes him a great artist."[9] In a 1927 *Photoplay* article, Adele St. Johns all but deified Chaplin:

> To those of us working to make motion pictures, he is the way-shower, the trail-blazer. He is the master. Almost every new stop in motion picture technique, every advanced step in motion picture art has come from Charlie Chaplin. He is the creator of the new forms, the new ideas. To the greatest directors and the greatest stars his pictures are like a text book. I know directors, for instance, whose names stand at the very head of the list, who went ten and twelve times to see "The Gold Rush" [1925]. And when I asked them why, they explained that it was the greatest example of perfect motion picture timing ever seen, and that it opened new fields in that direction [of personality comedy] just as "A Woman of Paris" [1923] opened new dramatic and directional fields.[10]

Granted, today *A Woman of Paris* is credited with being a precursor to the celebrated sophisticated comedies of Ernst Lubitsch, whose subtle oeuvre is now simply described as the "Lubitsch Touch"—to which he fully credited Chaplin. But because Chaplin did not appear in the film, it barely broke even at the box office. And neither the comedian nor later historians have fully embraced what a huge *critical* success it was in the 1920s, frequently referenced *throughout* the decade. Upon its initial release the *Los Angeles Times* critic stated: "With a brain that is colossal, a magnificent perception of uncanny understanding of human nature, Chaplin rises in his artistry above his [personality comedy] art. There is not one medium [genre] through which his infinite genius can be expressed, though comedy, or rather tragedy, laughingly distinguished comes nearest to an adequate channel for his expression."[11] Three years later (1926) *Photoplay*'s Ruth Waterbury was still raving: "One day Chaplin produced 'A Woman of Paris.' The next day there was a new screen type. He was the sophisticate, the gentleman whose heart is not necessarily made of gold nor as big as all outdoors; the gentleman who does not necessarily marry the poor girl nor who is not unusually fond of his dear old mother; but a gentleman, nevertheless, and gifted with sex appeal."[12] Still, leave it to *Life*'s Sherwood to best sum up this vision of Chaplin greatness near the close of the decade. When someone had the audacity to criticize the broad humor of the comedian's *Circus*, he responded: "It may well be (and is) contended that the laugh-getting stunts in "The Circus" are gags—old gags, some of them—of a type that might be used by Harold Lloyd, Buster Keaton or even Larry Semon [with no reference to Langdon]. There's only one answer to that, and it happens to be a sufficient answer: in 'The Circus,' these gags are performed by Charles Spencer as Chaplin only Charles Spencer Chaplin could perform them."[13] Consequently, Chaplin was film's prodigy, with no less a figure than Nobel Prize (1925) winning British playwright George Bernard Shaw (1856–1950) pronouncing him cinema's only genius as of the 1920s.

So what of Lloyd? If the rare Chaplin film was greatness guaranteed, the much more prolific Lloyd was just as dependable for always producing something mind candy funny. For example, a 1923 *Los Angeles Times* article on *Grandma's Boy* noted that the public "has become so used to seeing each one [of his films] better than the last, that they have faith in his being able to keep it up."[14] The *Los Angeles Times*' 1923 review of Lloyd's *Why Worry?* even opened by punning the title about guaranteed laughs: "Yes—'Why Worry?' There isn't the least need to when it comes to considering the supply of entertainment that Harold Lloyd has to offer."[15]

Of course, the reviews of this dependable funnyman were frequently footnoted with the reminder that the film was not artistically fueled but was rather a clever collection of gags and direction driven by others for Lloyd's boy-next-door "Glasses Character" (wearing horn-rimmed eyeglasses). For instance, the *New York Sun*'s 1925 "Very Funny" verdict of his most critically and commercially successful film, *The Freshman*, added: "Harold Lloyd is, of course, no Chaplin, which means that he is not a tragically comic figure ... [moreover] less credit goes to him than to the authors [gag men John Grey, Sam Taylor, Tim Whelan, Ted Wilde] and directors [Fred C. Newmeyer and Sam Taylor]."[16] Still, Lloyd was wise enough to create the character and know its parameters, and never attempted to do it all, à la Langdon's failure. Thus, once again *LIFE*'s Robert Sherwood best summed up Lloyd's lengthy filmography of guaranteed entertainment in his witty 1928 review of the comedian's last silent film, *Speedy*:

Glasses were central to Harold Lloyd's mainstream screen character.

"[Lloyd] maintained a record of consistency that has not been equaled in the up-and-down-and-gone-tomorrow history of the movies ... 'Speedy' carries no message.... Its only object is to provoke laughs, loud laughs, and that object is accomplished with admirable efficiency."[17]

Before leaving Lloyd's Everyman "Glasses" character, which almost sounds patterned upon President Warren G. Harding's 1920 campaign theme of a "Return to Normalcy," it is important to underline how much Lloyd publicized his regular guy persona. This is significant for several reasons. First, it further reinforced his go-getter, *anything is possible* persona, which would help hasten his decline with the devastating Depression. Second, just as a record of the 1920s, it is important to demonstrate the multiple ways he kept his surrogate name persona before the public. Third, *Mr. Average* so clashes with Keaton's other worldly cinema alter ego that it better helps explain the later revisionist take on the "Great Stone Face." Finally, because of Lloyd's relentless mainstreaming PR push, it further spotlights Keaton's eccentric to surreal persona. There were so many Lloyd print campaigns to accent his 1920s mainstream image, he might have used 1930's Nobel Prize–winning novelist Sinclair Lewis as his press agent ... minus the satire. In fact, from today's vantage point, Lloyd's main street overkill does seem satirical.

Therefore, the text will limit itself at this point (see Chapter 1) to just a few typical examples, which will work their way through the decade. For instance, many pieces appeared under what might be called a "No Ego Umbrella," such as a 1923 *Los Angeles Times* article titled "Swelled Head Not Funny."[18] Noting Lloyd's "utter lack of conceit," the article quoted the comedian himself spouting this nice guy mantra: "Any actor who lets vanity get the better of him is bound to suffer for it. It leads him into the belief that audiences are looking to him for their fun, when the fact is they are looking rather to situations as he may contrive them, express them or bring them out."[19] In 1924 *Screenland* magazine contained a sort of "I want you to like me plea" essay whose lengthy title is self-explanatory: "Harold Lloyd Offer $500.00 in Prizes for Your Letters: He wants to know 'Which of His Films You Liked Best.'"[20] (Keep in mind that today this would represent well over $5,000.)

There was also a "Pep Talk" category. With 1920s Hollywood producing more than three-fourths of the world's movies, thousands of youngsters were flooding filmland. Not surprisingly, the industry was doing everything it could do to deter this movie migration. Thus, in a 1925 Lloyd-authored *Picture-Play* piece called "Don't Be Discouraged!," he confessed that like many movie people, he had been encouraged to write articles dissuading youngsters.[21] Yet, he always "declined," claiming: "If you combine luck with ability, you stand a splendid gamble of making good, in my opinion."[22]

Next, one could move on to a Lloyd denomination nominally labeled "virtuous." This is fittingly showcased in a 1926 *Brooklyn Eagle* review of Lloyd's *For Heaven's Sake*. The critique opens by calling the comedian: "pre-eminent as an exponent of clean, wholesome screen comedy."[23] Finally, one must add a Lloyd component of "going *beyond* no ego." This is initially exhibited in the 1926 *Picture-Play* piece "Yes Men Need Not Apply": "Harold Lloyd says that he had neither desire nor room for an employee who will not voice an opinion and on occasion differs with him."[24] But he seems to be even more self-deprecating in *Time* magazine the following year (1927): "Mr. Lloyd always examines his gag staff to be sure no drop of marrow lingers in their funnybones. He asks the continuity men if they have achieved the highest possible pitch of acceleration."[25] Though Lloyd obviously contributed comic bits, the *Time* essay oddly adds a rare footnote which suggests otherwise. It says, in part, Funnyman Lloyd, "gag connoisseur, exhausted the combined efforts of three expert gagsters in making *The Kid Brother*."[26] Plus, the collective number of other more generic newspaper "plants" far outstretched his comedy contemporaries. The phenomenon might best be exemplified by two more 1923 *Los Angeles Times* articles. One piece, titled "Harold Lloyd Does Marathon to Studio," chronicles his decision to start jogging to work after his recent marriage resulted in a weight gain.[27] The other essay is career-related to the release of his building-climbing movie, *Safety Last* (1923): "New Disease Hits Harold Lloyd Fans." But the story almost suggests a Jazz Age Chubby Checker has introduced "The Twist": "If you see someone walking down the street with a broad grin on his face and observe him chuckling to himself, and then all of a sudden see him stop and gaze fixedly up at one of our skyscrapers in an awed fashion, you rest assured that said person is suffering from a new disease, which has been called Lloydisteria."[28]

All in all, one could infer that Lloyd's attempt at being the exemplary nice guy in the movies, as well as in real life, is a reverse variation of Shakespeare's line about a character who "doth protest too much." That is, he worked too hard to somehow elevate his good pop culture comedy beyond its innocent weightlessness. As yet another 1923 *Los Angeles Times* article condensed it, after a fashion: "Youth is the element that ensures pep. Lloyd is still under 30, and he has surrounded himself with men whose eyes view life through their enthusiasm. Youth has not time to be serious."[29]

Lloyd's "enthusiasm"—epitomized persona could not have been further from the image of the third 1920s comedy pantheon player—Buster Keaton. This disconnect between Lloyd's happy mainstream movie microcosm with Keaton's often disturbingly funny film oeuvre is best boiled down to the latter comedian's signature screen visage—the "Great Stone Face."

Keaton's expressionless crestfallen mask clearly suggests the world is a preposterously senseless place, which behooves the individual to minimize any display of emotion which could put him at risk. Period adjectives used to describe this countenance included: sad, pessimistic, frozen, sour, and gloomy. And given this was during Prohibition, there were also axioms like "sober as a preacher in a dry town." Keaton's "mask" had been created by his vaudevillian father Joe when the youngster teamed on stage with his parents as "The Three Keatons." The seemingly indestructible "Buster" (thus the name) had been used by his parents—particularly his dad—in the most physically violent of acts, like the Three Stooges on steroids. There was much hitting and breaking of objects, particularly furniture, between father and son. However, the pièce de resistance core of the act involved throwing the boy about, with the key to the routine's humor being Buster maintaining that seemingly unnatural resistance to pain symbolized by that stone face. This forerunner to a theatre of the absurd environment is best explained in a 1927 *Photoplay* article by Joe: "His mother and I had a burlesque acrobatic set in which my wife and I threw Buster about the stage like a human medicine ball. [This sometimes involved literally tossing young Buster into the crowd, especially] if there was a heckler. One night in Syracuse, Joe told Buster:] "Stiffen yourself, son." Catching him by a valise-handle-like contraption we had fastened between his shoulders, I gave him a fling. The next instant Buster's hip pockets flattened the nose of that troublemaker in the front row."[30] As a footnote to this article, an attached handle with which to throw a person, albeit a small one, at other people might sound like a fabrication. But in college football of this late 19th and early 20th century period quarterbacks were also outfitted with handles with which to gain yardage by being thrown over the line of scrimmage. (The forward pass had yet to be invented—or had it?) Regardless, it was not until President Theodore Roosevelt convened a 1905 White House conference on college football to address the rising number of gridiron *deaths* that the "handle" practice was phased out. However, this did not apply to vaudeville, and the undersized Buster would continue to be a human projectile for another decade.

An unusual pause in the action/violence for vaudeville's "Three Keatons" (circa early 1900s).

A year prior (1925) to his father's article, Buster himself had authored an essay on both the Three Keaton's and his lack of a smiling persona in the *Ladies Home Journal*.[31] This father-son order has been reversed to provide both Buster's broader perspective on Joe's creation/description of this strange routine, as well as afford an added insight from the younger Keaton on not smiling: "In this knockabout act, my father and I [also] used to hit each other with brooms ... if I should chance to smile, the next hit would be a good deal harder.... When I grew older, I readily figured out for myself that I was not one of those comedians who could jest with the audience and laugh with it. My audience must laugh at me."[32] Ironically, the closest facsimile to this brutal act which was preserved on film, at least during Keaton's young adulthood, occurs in *Doughboys* (1930), the second sound film during his escalating years of decline at MGM. Since the film was about World War I, and the comedian was a veteran of the conflict, he was seemingly allowed a modicum of input on the picture. The fact that he and Chaplin were the greatest comedians on the planet did not seem to enter into the equation for the studio, whose lion logo roared for all the wrong reasons. Regardless, Keaton felt it was the best of his early sound features— largely because of the sequence. The scene approaches the brilliance of his silent independent pictures, and this involves a loose variation upon his old theatre days—when it was essentially father versus son. The *Doughboy* sketch has Buster in drag as part of the most ferocious tango duo on any stage. Keaton's partner, like his father before him, throws him around like a proverbial rag doll. The big finale has Keaton's collaborator swinging Buster around and around before launching the comedian into the audience. Imagining it as an emotionless child projectile would have had to be in the running for the ultimate bit of dark comedy vaudeville.

Despite Keaton later poo-pooing much subtextual thought being put into his stone-faced films, such as in his aforementioned memoirs (whose very title acts as a misdirection, *My Wonderful World of Slapstick*), these and other Keaton quotes from the 1920s suggest at least an intuitive anticipation of existentialism.[33] For example, in a November 25, 1922, interview with Britain's *Picture Show*, Keaton observed, "If you want to make people laugh you must weep, or at least be in enough trouble to make you entitled to weep."[34] Keep in mind that in Albert Camus' later existentialistic primer, *The Plague* (1948, with its title acting as a modern metaphor for the individual isolation of man), the novelist/philosopher wrote that with this isolation "no one had hitherto been seen to smile in public."[35]

Moreover, it is not enough to link Keaton to Samuel Beckett and the theatre of the absurd, à la 1952's *Waiting for Godot*, by noting that the playwright cast the comedian in his only movie—the 1965 silent short subject *Film*. Significantly, Keaton's character is named 0 in Beckett's short subject. The Beckett biographer, James Knowlson, has noted that since the dramatist's youth he had been impacted by Keaton.[36] Moreover, there is another possible beguiling Beckett and Keaton connection, most befitting figures connected to absurdity. In the comedian's later years he had a small part in 1949's *The Lovable Cheat*, an adaptation of Honoré de Balzac's play *Mercadel Le Falseur*. Keaton is a creditor forever kept waiting for a figure named Godeau. This figure may or may not arrive at the close—but he is never seen. Could Keaton fan Beckett, well versed in Balzac's work, have seen *The Lovable Cheat* before writing the similar *Waiting for Godot*?[37] Be that as it may, the reason Beckett was attracted to casting Keaton in an early *Godot* production was a misdirection diversion effort at "holding the terrible silence [of an unresponsive God] at bay."[38]

Regardless, Keaton's theatre of the absurd existentialism is expanded upon further in the following pages. However, the links are peppered throughout the 1920s Keaton literature. For example, in the aforementioned *Ladies Home Journal* article, the comedian appears to be headed towards a comically whimsical close by chronicling some of the worldwide nicknames attached to his screen persona. Though amusing, it seems rather self-serving, more like Lloyd's PR tendencies. Yet, then comes the existentialistic-like payoff: "No one as yet has given me authentic translations but I imagine that most of these [character] names of endearment signify null and void, and their combined meaning, if totaled up, would equal zero."[39] Boom! There it is! Keaton's feelings/curiosity towards his persona were as emotionless as his *dead*pan face. In Camus' *The Stranger* (1946, a name which could be applied to sphinx-like Keaton), the novelist's title character is executed not so much for having killed someone, but rather for having shown no sentiment.[40] One is immediately reminded of Keaton's seemingly heartless murder of a cowboy early in *The Frozen North* (1922), his short subject parody of Western star William S. Hart. This is especially apt here, because it is not readily apparent the Keaton killing is a spoof. In contrast to the comedian's "Zero" perspective, Chaplin affectionately named his Tramp "The Little Fellow," while Lloyd's alter ego go-getter was just as demonstratively called "Speedy" (the comedian's actual childhood moniker). With Keaton essentially seeing his screen character as a cipher, it does not get more existentialistic than that.

Yet, one can even push the Beckett-Keaton validation one step further. The playwright had greatly admired Buster entering the screen in *Sherlock, Jr.* (1924). And Beckett biographer Linda Ben-Zvi reminds one that the dramatist had not only cast the comedian in *Film* for all Buster's pioneering existentialistic characteristics: "[Beckett] creates a film about film, depicting the unique property of the form. The audience is not, as in conventional films, lulled into forgetting the manipulation of the camera eye."[41] And while Buster's minimalist face was his trademark, Beckett does him one better in *Film*—Keaton's face is never seen until the short subject's conclusion. Granted, the playwright's movie is not for everyone, yet there is no denying yet another link between the two artists.

Keaton was often too far ahead of his time. To rehash, Chaplin was on high. In film after film critics invariably embraced words like genius. Indeed, in *Picture Play* magazine's June 22, 1922, critique of *Pay Day* (1922), now considered one of Chaplin's lesser works, critic Alison Smith wrote that comparing him to any other comedian was "like drinking soda pop after a glass of Mum's extra dry [champagne]."[42] Lloyd's reviews were invariably positive, too. But his pictures were an acknowledged assembly-line collection of clever gags, which like Henry Ford's 1920s mechanical assembly-line Model-Ts, were all consistently good but no one was popping their cork over a Ford. As *Photoplay*'s January 1928 review of Chaplin's *The Circus* (1928) observed, "[Comedy is] a gag, of course, but a typical Chaplin gag [is] touched with humor and humanness ... that is the secret of ... [his] human interest plot, which will hold your attention to the end of the story."[43]

To the credit of the 1920s, Keaton was linked to the greatness of Chaplin and the popularity of Lloyd, too—but at a distance. Moreover, most of the decade's criticism, however, was likely to pigeonhole him within the clever gag category of a Lloyd ... only without the latter's consistency and *normalcy*. An updated introduction to Lloyd's 1928 memoir, though written in the subject's lifetime, actually called Keaton a "Frozen man from Mars."[44] What has made Keaton grow in stature through the years, however, is how modern he now seems. He cerebrally speaks to the existentially black humor of today, surrealism, and hitting establishment targets with demandingly dark reaffirmation parody—all of which are addressed in the following chapter.[45]

Critics from the 1920s struggled with Keaton's greatness and often avoided a universal thumbs-up to any of his features, as was the norm (for different reasons) with Chaplin and

Lloyd. Keep in mind Keaton was still bucking, and even pushing beyond, the American literary movement known as "The Revolt from the Village"—which was a strike on small-town hypocrisy and emptiness. And most fitting for Keaton, was their attack on the sentimental norm of the American village mentality. The catalyst were the provocative poems of Edgar Lee Masters' *Spoon River Anthology* (1915), and the prose of Sherwood Anderson's *Winesburg, Ohio* (1919)—written just as Keaton was entering the movies. One might even couple the comedian's sometimes film-ending tombstones with Masters' haunting collection of free-verse poems—each one spoken from the grave by a different individual whose life had been wasted. Yet, on occasion period publications had fleeting insights, such as *The New Yorker*'s period review of *Battling Butler* (1926), which credited the comedian as appealing "to your sense of the ridiculous."[46] But one 1920s critic, over *all* others, understood what was at the core of Keaton's modern appeal—*LIFE*'s Robert E. Sherwood. Plus, if one were forced to save just one critique of the comedian, either from the Jazz Age or today, it would by *LIFE*'s November 16, 1922, issue, in which Sherwood observes: "Buster Keaton is a distinct asset to the movies. He can attract people who would never think of going to a picture palace to see anyone else. Moreover, he can impress a weary world with the vitally important fact that life, after all, is a foolishly inconsequential affair."[47]

1

Working Towards the Feature Films of 1923–1929

> In pantomime, strolling players use an incomprehensible language … not for what it means but for the sake of life. [Writer, actor, director Leon] Chancerel is quite right to insist upon the importance of mime. The body in the theatre…
>
> —Albert Camus[1]

> The meaning of life is that it stops.—Franz Kafka[2]

Immersion in 1920s Buster Keaton criticism and commentary first necessitates putting up a time-tripping periscope for perspective. Thus, to best sketch a brief pre–1923 Keaton biography, one should build upon the underpinning outlined in the Prologue. For me, this means succinctly playing a game which draws in the two other pantheon film comedians of the 1920s: Charlie Chaplin and Harold Lloyd. A solid starting point is to demonstrate how the nicknames applied to their screen alter egos reflects the world view of three novelists important to each of them, more fully explaining what each comedian is all about, as well as broadening one's perspective on the interconnectedness of the arts. The Prologue has already coupled Keaton's self-described "zero" character to the writing of Camus and Beckett, though Kafka provides an excellent 1920s bridge. Yet, Keaton's memoir provides an earlier American writer who provides a fitting foundation to Kafka, Camus and on to Samuel Beckett. However, before pursuing this Keaton connection it would be advantageous to start with Chaplin and Lloyd.[3]

Chaplin, referring to his Tramp figure as "The Little Fellow," is synonymous with the sentimental yet often cause-driven world of 19th century Charles Dickens. Chaplin came from such a setting and openly acknowledged the influence. Indeed, his *Charlie Chaplin's Own Story* (1916) is a book the comedian took off the market when critics found his life history a bit too close to Dickens' *Oliver Twist*.[4] Yet, Chaplin's deprived childhood could have been a rough draft for a sequel to *Oliver Twist*, a volume Chaplin's 1964 autobiography tells us he was moved to buy when he could "hardly read," noting he "felt like Oliver Twist."[5]

Regardless, it seems unfair to overly criticize the first book, because the sometimes street urchin Chaplin survived a London not so different from that of Twist's own London. Moreover, the filmmaker brought that same fine line of pathos to his films as well as achieving that unlikely Dickens tale of rags to riches in real life—the millionaire "Tramp." Both

Dickens and Chaplin tell the most entertaining of stories without sliding into bathos. And the victimized early Chaplin was recreating a "theatre of the real cinema," with or without his affinity for Dickens.

In contrast, American heartland-born Lloyd's memoir found him relating to Mark Twain's Tom Sawyer (1876) as "an average American boy."[6] But given Lloyd's lifelong nickname of "Speedy" (also the title of his last silent film, 1928) and his cinematic success-driven "Glasses Character," his image of Tom Sawyer must have fixated upon the crafty business-side of Twain's figure. This was the boy who could con his friends into "buying" the privilege of doing Tom's punishment task, à la whitewashing Aunt Polly's fence. Consequently, being a sly "entrepreneur" often fits Lloyd, both on the screen and off.

Keep in mind, his 1923 *Safety Last* figure never planned to scale the skyscraper for his promotional scheme. But his climbing friend was wanted by the police, thus forcing Lloyd's business-first character to risk all for additional sales. And as touched on in the Prologue, filmmaker Lloyd was an even more serious example of business boosterism. For example, his hemorrhaging, self-serving PR articles included a 1926 issue of *Screenland* with the endless title "Harold Lloyd Football Costume from 'The Freshman' [1925] to the Fan Who Writes the Best Harold Lloyd Letter."[7] The essay went on to explain what the correspondence was to address: Write a letter about the lad (Lloyd) who made "'The Freshman'—why you like him and what effect Harold had on you ... the best letters will be awarded prizes in the order of their excellence."[8] If one remembers the Prologue, this is the same comedian who often underlined the dangers of ego. Moreover, Lloyd's real life promotional addiction better suggests the Babbitt-like character so driven for "Main Street" success satirized by America's most popular 1920s novelist, Sinclair Lewis. This was the writer who had previously, with tongue firmly in cheek, been offered up as a potential Lloyd agent.

Though Lloyd's films do not embrace the biting small-town narrow-mindedness of Lewis' books, the comedian's character's ongoing push to prevail now often suggests the superficiality of American life inherent to these novels. And Lloyd the filmmaker seems the embodiment of Babbitt. Regardless, Lloyd and Lewis so captured the decade's details that arguably their greatest accomplishment might now be defined as preserving an era in amber. Indeed, Lewis' Nobel Prize citation praised, in part, his "vigorous and graphic art of description." Even a 1924 *Motion Picture Classic* article described the novelist's attention to minutiae as if he had a "photographic mind."[9] Consequently, in literature Lewis is now frequently scrutinized not as a great novelist but more of a fascinatingly non-traditional period sociologist, like Robert and Helen Lynd's 1929 landmark inquiry, *Middletown: A Study in Contemporary Culture*.

The Lynd's zeroed in on Muncie, Indiana, as America's average "Middletown," a setting most simpatico with Lewis' *Main Street* (1920), or any number of Harold Lloyd boy-next-door "Speedy" adventures—for instance, the aforementioned *Safety Last* as a clever "climbing" metaphor for going up the proverbial corporate ladder. Paradoxically, Lewis saw this left-handed compliment early when he turned down a Pulitzer Prize for his 1925 novel *Arrowsmith*, largely because, as reported in a 1926 *Literary Digest* issue, "he dislikes any prize going to a book 'best presenting the wholesome atmosphere of American life and the highest standard of manners and manhood.'"[10] His refusal said, "Did the Pultizer people read the book?"

Strangely enough, Lloyd never seemed to understand either the similar implications of his persona, or more precisely, of the hypocritical "reading" one could make of his calculated spotlighting of himself as a regular guy. (In comparison, modest Keaton was like a man holding a small candle.) Thus, Lloyd later gladly accepted a 1952 honorary Oscar during the McCarthy era, which doubled as a backhanded slap at the forever controversial Chaplin. And this perspective was *baldly* stated in Lloyd's citation: "Master comedian and *good citizen*" (italics mine). Unlike Lewis, Lloyd allowed himself to be used by another prestigious (so-called) institution.

Regardless, despite Lloyd's unquestioned 1920s popularity, one could argue he was not so much a great comedian but rather a competent actor playing at being funny. There is even a later precedent in Ernst Lubitsch's explanation on why he cast Jack Benny in *To Be or Not to Be* (1942). Benny had been shocked at the invitation: "It was always impossible for comedians like me or [Bob] Hope to get a good director for a movie ... and here was *Lubitsch* for God's sake, calling to ask if I'd do a picture with the greatest comedy director that ever lived."[11] An insecure Benny queried Lubitsch during the *To Be* production on why he had hired a comedian (Benny) instead of an actor for the lead. German-born Lubitsch, a former comedian and clown, provokingly answered: "You think you are a comedian. You are not even a clown. You are fooling the public for thirty years. You are fooling even yourself. A clown—he is a performer what is doing funny things. A comedian—he is a performer what is saying funny things. But you, Jack, you are an actor, you are an actor playing the part of comedian and this you are doing very well. But do not worry, I keep your secret to myself."[12]

If one applies this perspective to Lloyd, there is ample period proof in Lloyd's tidal wave of PR material, especially when he is playing his modesty card. Two 1924 *Los Angeles Times* articles provide a sort of one-two punch for this argument. First, Edwin Schallert capsulized Lloyd's work as "mechanically devised pictures."[13] One might call it red meat for the masses. However, the second essay best embellishes the Lloyd situation initially noted in the Prologue: "Every member of the technical staff surrounding the comedian has been with him from five to eight years and it is indeed one harmonious working body. Harold invariably refers to his comedies as 'our pictures' and speaks of 'our difficulties' [and] 'our successes.'"[14] This does not suggest Keaton was without a great deal of support, as is so effectively demonstrated by Lisle Foote's excellent *Buster Keaton's Crew* (2014).[15] Yet, unlike Lloyd, Keaton directed or co-directed the majority of his 1920s features, and while modest about taking writing credits, it is obvious the films closely follow his character's oeuvre. And of course, Chaplin essentially did it all. Regardless, as film historian David Thomson has suggested, Lloyd is less a personality than "the budding executive of Comedy Inc."[16]

In any case, though a less gifted comedian, his "Comedy Inc." machine was very lucrative and not cheap in buying the best gagmen, or as 1920s slang would word it—"He did not have alligator arms." For example, a 1925 *Los Angeles Times* piece reported Lloyd added to his staff a longtime Keaton man, Clyde Bruckman, to better help him knock "audiences off their seats."[17] Still, Lloyd's funny fluff was stuffed too tight, like those cigarettes in hard packs so often advertised in 1920 movie magazines. Lloyd's pictures had neither a thinking man's space for Keaton's often withering view of humanity, or Chaplin's embrace of a similar perspective, yet poignantly sending the Tramp forward anyway, because it was the right thing to do. For instance, Chaplin's alter ego helping *City Lights'* (1931) blind girl to see, even if it would lead to losing her, given her expectations of a young rich gentleman—not a Tramp. While Lloyd material was a comically pleasant dead-end diversion, both Chaplin and Keaton subtextually challenged the viewer. Thus, what 1921 *Picture-Play* critic Agnes Smith said of Chaplin's *The Kid* (1921) was equally true of Keaton's dark world view—though Chaplin consciously seemed to be creating the duality, while Keaton had a certain intuitive instinctual ballast. Nevertheless, Smith's insight applied to both comedian's: "[Their cinematic] fun is knock-about enough to catch the loud ha-ha of the vacant mind ... but it is also subtle enough to make the intellectual pause and connect with ... classic humor."[18] However, if one wanted to make a distinguishing contrast between the elevated bar to Keaton and Chaplin's 1920 work it would be old school art appreciation versus postmodern shock. Chaplin's traditional tidy approach suggests art is where one gets it right, because life is ultimately an unfinished rough cut. In contrast, Keaton's work wants to constantly remind you of life's no-exit (save death) chaos.

However, to best sketch a mainstream 1920s, one must again briefly link Lloyd's pictures to Lewis' novels as beguiling Jazz Age freeze frames, not to mention anticipating a conservative Motion Picture Academy awarding the comedian an Oscar three decades later. In a 1920s Will "Deacon" Hays' speech, Hollywood's censorship czar made one of his "most emphatic statements" about political correctness by using Lloyd's work as a template.[19] The *Los Angeles Time*'s coverage of this cinema sermon was simply titled "Lloyd Clean Films Win."[20]

Moreover, what is often forgotten today is that conservatism was given a boost by a Red Scare after World War I, too, precipitated by Russia's Czarist reign being toppled by the Bolshevik Revolution. In this coming attraction for the Red-baiting 1950s, thousands of leftist Americans were jailed. These chaotic conditions for African Americans who had come North to work in industry added to the conflict. Though this will be expanded upon shortly, Hollywood did not go untouched. Nothing as extreme as the 1950s McCarthy Era Blacklist occurred. But a rarely noted "Doom Book" made the rounds of studio chiefs, defaming allegedly questionable film community individuals.

For example, when Chaplin's 2000-plus page FBI file was finally made accessible after his 1977 death it contained, to recycle another 1920s phrase, "a whole lot of nothing." Yes, the comedian had held a 1919 function for the left-wing political activist William Z. Foster, later chairman of the American Communist Party.[21] (During Chaplin's long residency in the United States, ending in 1952, it was never illegal to belong to the Communist Party.) Regardless, Chaplin's voluminous file revealed *no* evidence the comedian had ever been a member.[22] Granted, Chaplin had hosted that Foster reception. Yet, what follows is a typical comic example of Chaplin's so-called "radical" comments to Foster: "'We [Hollywood] people are against any kind of censorship.' Laughing, [Chaplin] led Foster to the men's toilet and pointed out a pennant with the words WELCOME WILL HAYS that was tacked to the door."[23]

As a further footnote to the subject, while Lloyd forever attempted to curry an *average guy* image with the public, Chaplin seemed to enjoy courting controversy. For example in his 1922 book, *My Trip Abroad* (which started as a series of *Photoplay* articles), a reporter asked him if he was a Bolshevik. The comedian replied, "I am an artist. I am interested in life. Bolshevism is a new phase of life. I must be interested in it."[24] (This chronicle of his 1921 European vacation appeared in England under the title *My Wonderful Visit*.) The provocative public Chaplin also merits an addendum. The artist's sexual scandals, which first began appearing in the 1920s, always seemed to be forgiven because of the phenomenal popularity of his "Little Fellow," and the game-changing sophistication he brought to the screen with *A Woman of Paris* (1923), whose adult man of the world was beginning to be associated in modern circles with the real Chaplin. (For instance, see Ruth Waterbury's 1926 *Photoplay* piece, "Why Woman Like Sophisticated Men," or the revisionist critique of the picture in the January 27, 1924, *Los Angeles Times*.[25]) Still, the Tramp was his special talisman and as long as he periodically produced a "Charlie" picture, Chaplin was like Teflon—scandals which would bring down almost any other silent star just did not stick. If truth be told, Chaplin's McCarthy era problems were more about additional sexual scandals then communism—because by then "The Little Fellow" was long retired, and Chaplin had "essayed" a dark film comedy bluebeard in *Monsier Verdoux* (1947).[26]

Chaplin's Teflon '20s are best demonstrated by his quickie 1924 marriage to Lita Grey, his pregnant leading lady for the Tramp's icy Yukon travails in *The Gold Rush* (1925; and then replaced by Georgia Hale). At first there were a few disconcerting headlines that the bride was only sixteen years of age (Chaplin was thirty-five), which the Los Angeles school district accented by ruling that she must still comply with required school attendance. Yet, the marriage circumvented most of the criticism. And then the picture became the most popular silent comedy ever made. Indeed, Chaplin later called it the movie for which he wanted to be remembered. Moreover, even before its release, Will Rogers, then America's favorite print humorist, put it in 1920s' chauvinistic perspective, via his widely syndicated newspaper column: "This girl don't need to go to school. Any girl smart enough to marry Charlie Chaplin should be lecturing at Vassar College on 'Taking advantage of your opportunities.'"[27]

Playing upon *The Gold Rush* reference, plus the fact that Chaplin was the 1920s critical darling, and that Lloyd was box office consistency, "Stone Face" Keaton's roller coaster relationship with period critics and audiences might sound like he had been named second in command of the Donner Party. While that was not the metaphorical case, his darker cinematic subtext did make him the odd man. For instance, this might not be readily apparent given the literary figure with which Keaton most associated his screen alter ego—Twain's Huckleberry Finn, the title character of his 1884 novel.[28]

While Lloyd's choice of Tom Sawyer and Keaton's embracing of Huckleberry Finn are characters forever intertwined in Twain's canon, the duo are not remotely close in social significance. One can easily imagine Sawyer growing up as part of the local Chamber of Commerce and some special men's club, positions to which Lloyd's Speedy obviously aspires, as well as Lloyd himself—who later became a high ranking Shriner. Both Twain tales are set in a fictional St. Petersburg, Missouri (based upon Twain's Hannibal, Missouri, childhood). The time period falls between Congress' Missouri Compromise of 1820, and the American Civil War (1861–1865). The Compromise essentially mandated that the number of free and slave states be kept in balance. Thus, when the rapidly growing country added a state in which slavery was illegal, or one in which it was legal, a counterbalancing state needed to be annexed. Plus, if a slave managed to escape to a free state, federal law mandated that this "property" be returned to its owner.

However, 1876's *Tom Sawyer* is a charming and buoyant white boyhood tale of playing pirates, getting out of chores, young romance, and multiple adventures, including bank robbers, being lost in a cave with fears greater than darkness (yet with his sweetheart), to further excitement involving Twain's beloved Mississippi River. The novel is essentially a non-controversial classic driven by a spunky youngster with whom Lloyd and generations of boy/men have identified. Like a Lloyd picture, Twain's novel is entertainment-focused and the reader/viewer relishes the feel-good escapism.

In contrast, Keaton's *The Adventure of Huckleberry Finn* is now taught as an iconoclastic coming-of-age blueprint for J. D. Salinger's later novel *The Catcher in the Rye* (1951), narrated by rebellious teenager Holden Caulfield. Both texts are funny yet scathing attacks on the entrenched phony values of the adult world delivered in first-person colloquial voices.

Caulfield is hatched with full-blown coming-at-you comic anger. In contrast, Huckleberry is a laid back persona slow to come to the same realization—he simply cannot live with the absurd real world status quo. More to the point, he inadvertently finds himself hiding out with a runaway slave (Jim). Unlike Caulfield, Huckleberry has had little formal education. Yet, he is aware that the establishment Bible and the State condone slavery, and the law says helping Jim would mean jail and hell. Though without Caulfield's anger, he acknowledges society's demented rules, *but* so be it. He will just have to follow his *own code* to free Jim. Is it any wonder that Ernest Hemingway said American fiction begins here?

Like Huck, Keaton's character is often slow to recognize the inherently illogical "rules of the game," and yet tries to survive life on his own terms, too. For instance, in *Our Hospitality* (1923), the 1831 main story is set roughly around the time of *Huckleberry Finn*. Keaton finds himself in a darkly comic spoof of the legendary Hatfield–McCoy feud, in which two families ongoingly attempt to kill each other over differences going back decades. Renaming the crazy clans Canfield-McKay, Keaton's picture opens with a brief prologue in which young John McKay (Edward Coxen) is killed by a Canfield and his widow and baby, Willie McKay (Buster Keaton, Jr.), escape to the North.

Flash forward twenty years and the somewhat effeminate young Willie (Buster Keaton) receives a letter informing him he has inherited the family mansion. With his mother long dead, and not fully cognizant of the still ongoing feud, he returns south by a comic-looking but historically accurate early train whose engineer is played by Joe Keaton, the comedian's father. (A detailed examination of *Our Hospitality* occurs in the following chapter.) On the train he becomes infatuated with a beautiful young woman (Natalie Talmadge Keaton, the comedian's wife), and she with him. Unfortunately, her name is Virginia *Canfield*.

Neither party realizes what this means. Consequently, when the train is met by her father, Joseph Canfield (Joe Roberts), and her two brothers (Ralph Bushman and Craig Ward), Buster is in immediate danger when he asks directions to the McKay mansion. As the brothers lead him to what turns out to be a dump, they plot his death by attempting to get a gun from any of the shops they pass. The duo are so focused on their murder mission that they lose track of Buster. In the interim, Virginia has asked Willie to supper, though her brothers are now prepared to kill the young man, given their family arsenal. But the father will not allow it ... as long as Buster's character is at their home—because of "our hospitality." Yet, any time Willie steps outside, it's open season. And thus begins a killer cat and mouse game of epically deadly Tom and Jerry proportions. Though only Keaton's second feature film under his direction, *Hospitality* is arguably among his most beloved full-length pictures during the 1920s. Many of its basic components occur again and again in his "what's the point" features to follow. Moreover, this inherit absurdity was not out of place in the comedian's bizarre childhood. Keaton's youth points towards Twain's tangential late work, like the posthumously published *The Mysterious Stranger* (1916), with links to Kafka, Camus, Beckett, and the surrealism of Salvador Dalí. Keep in mind, however, that the key word in telling Keaton's early story is *hyperbole*.

Keaton's father essentially doubled as his son's Boswell, whose biography of Samuel Johnson set *the* bar for the genre. Joe Keaton's perspective went under that bar, and straight to tall tales. Even the hard facts, such as the nature of the "Three Keatons" vaudeville act, first described in the Prologue, still seem like a cross between Beckett and Paul Bunyon. Buster's birth in Pique, Kansas, on October 4, 1895, was a completely random event, since the family just happened to be there while working in the lowest rungs of vaudeville, and they were gone in days—a vaudevillian's vagabond life.

Joe's many myths of his son's birth and early days, all dutifully recycled by his son, had the location being Pickway, Kansas—with the town either simultaneously, or shortly thereafter, exiting by way of a tornado. Joe even christened his son "The Cyclone Baby," and later wrote a 1927 *Photoplay* article with that title.[29] And like the Western loner who would be so popular in print and pictures during the heyday of Buster's 1920s movie career, Joe also dubbed him a homeless "Wanderer." No matter that this term also applied to all of vaudeville itself. Regardless, the "wandering" did impact Buster's future in many ways, most tangibly in his wanting to get off the road and broaden his comedy base. In a 1923 *Los Angeles Time* interview, he shared: "In the first place, working in the movies gives me a chance to be at home with my family. Why, for years I hardly knew what home meant. My domicile was always a hotel room. In the second place, in the making of motion-picture comedies I have a much greater chance of trying out new schemes to make people laugh and forget their troubles. And there's a lot of satisfaction in that and a lot of fascination as well."[30]

The "Wanderer" moniker no doubt also contributed to Keaton's loner screen persona, eventually a child star among vaudeville adults, as well as a life-long fascination with trains—the major means of transportation between play dates. Because of this, locomotives are central to many of his later films, from his best short subject, *One Week* (1920), to such pivotal later features as *Our Hospitality* and the title character of his celebrated *The General* (1927). However, for Keaton and comedy, trains are part of a greater insight into his comedy. In Luis Buñuel's 1927 review of *College*, which followed the release of *The General*, the surrealist critic perceptively wrote, "Keaton arrives at comedy through direct harmony with objects," which paradoxically meshes with the acting technique of the later minimalist physicality of action star Steve McQueen.[31] That is, both men have an organic connection with giant mechanical props, be it Keaton's trains, or McQueen's interaction with the huge gunboat engine in *The Sand Pebbles* (1966), for which he received an Oscar nomination.

Central to both individuals is that these mechanical props are an extension of their characters. For each one, human relationships are undependable, whereas a cared-for mechanical object is stable and unfailing. And note that the title character for both *The General* and *The Sand Pebbles* is that mechanical companion, which echoes Buñuel's "harmony with objects." Like the neglected period paintings of Gerald Murphy, such as *The Watch* (1925, which fittingly for Keaton shows the interior workings of a *railroad* watch), mechanical-connected subjects suggest a sanctuary from some human hurt ... an individual damaged from failed personal relationships—which was especially true of Keaton and McQueen.

A final point fueling Keaton's love of trains was driven by the fact that the professional athletes he admired were also nomadic fellow rail passengers, especially when they supplemented their income by periodic forays into vaudeville. For example, a 1926 *Motion Picture Classic* article reveals that a prized memento of Keaton's youth was an autograph album which included signatures *and* notes from three almost mythic boxers—then America's favorite sport. Thus, John L. Sullivan (1858–1918), the first heavyweight champion of gloved boxing (1882–1892), as well as the last bare-knuckle champion, "wrote in gigantic letters" to the seven-year-old, "'Little Buster, you may be a big Buster some day, May 21, 1903.'"[32]

Gentleman Jim Corbett (1866–1933), who defeated Sullivan, "predicted" in the parlance of the ring, "Buster, you're a knockout."[33] Yet, the famous knockout king Jack J. Sharkey paradoxically waxed the most poetic to the youngster: "To my little friend, Buster, from his old fried, Tom Sharkey. And after all, life is but one sweet dream. Let us be blithe and gay, for tomorrow is another day. Yours truly, Thomas J. Good Boy!"[34]

Gerald Murphy's railroad *Watch* (1925) painting perfectly matched Keaton's period mindset.

One cannot read these sweet axioms to an admiring boy without thinking that they helped influence Buster to do his popular boxing picture, *Battling Butler* (1926). However, since the comedian also grew up to be a great baseball fan and amateur player, maybe his most intriguing autograph is that of songwriter Jack Norworth (1879–1959), who co-wrote "Take Me Out to the Ball Game." Like fellow vaudeville friend Joe E. Brown, Buster was a serious New York Yankee fan, and one of Keaton's most memorable movie sequences occurs on his "loner" visit to an empty Yankee Stadium in *The Cameraman* (1928). Indispensable period critic Robert E. Sherwood's 1928 *LIFE* review called the one-man game in "the house that Ruth built" as "beautiful and true and infinitely touching. It is typical Buster Keaton at his best."[35] (See Chapter 11.)

Nevertheless, these moments anchored in reality detour one from the exaggeratingly colorful imagination of Joe Keaton, even before Buster's addition made their vaudeville act a hit—which allowed the youngster to meet many turn-of-the-century personalities. However, Joe's greatest gift of chutzpah was concocting the "Buster" story—because it was essential to what would become the headlining Three Keatons, and Keaton's later screen persona. The child known as Joseph, named after his father and his father's father, was said to have taken a bad fall down a roominghouse flight of steps. The boy was allegedly only six months old and his parents feared the worst. But after young Joseph came up smiling (a component soon to be jettisoned), a fellow vaudevillian said, according to a 1923 entry in the text *The Blue Book of the Screen*, "What a Buster."[36] (In period stage parlance a "buster" was someone who could take a fall.)

Though there are innumerable variations of the story in print, one should backtrack to a 1922 *Picture Show* article aptly titled "BUSTER KEATON'S Tumbling to Success," in which his father immediately explained, "'Why that's a good name! I just believe,' a grin of inspiration spreading over his face, 'that I'll call the kid that.'"[37] Yet, a raconteur is a showman who always wants to tell a better story. Consequently, Joe Keaton credited the famous illusionist and stunt performer Harry "Handcuff" Houdini (1874–1926) as having witnessed the accident and coining the term "Buster." Now, while Houdini had yet to achieve international fame, he was not then performing in Kansas.

Little Keaton might have taken the fall, though most likely it was at an older age. Moreover, if another performer saw the tumble and pronounced him a "Buster," prominent Keaton biographer Edward McPherson, among others, suggests it was comic George Pardey.[38] Of course, having it be Houdini makes for a better story. In examining four different Houdini biographies, the Keaton story has little basis in fact.[39] Two of the texts make no mention of Keaton; none of the books chronicle a fall, and only one credits the nickname "Buster" coming from Houdini—but places it later in the 1890s, and merely as a term of endearment, not a fall.[40]

Ironically, when "The Three Keatons" became a successful act, after the addition of a son billed as "The Human Mop," the trio is said to have gotten to know Houdini while appearing on the same vaudeville bills. By the 1920s, however, the tall tale stories of a little Buster had been in circulation for years, especially fueled by the PR talents of Joe Keaton. Not surprisingly, they became newsworthy again after Buster became a film star, especially when the myths helped fuel his films, like the cyclone of *Steamboat Bill, Jr.* (1928, see Chapter 11). The myth also assisted in underlining that Houdini was a definite component of his later screen alter ego.

There are also additional variations of the Keaton story that seem to anticipate the cartoon character Snoopy's "dark and stormy night" phrase from Charles Schulz' *Peanuts* strip. It was always evoked whenever America's favorite dog "author" started to write a fictional story. Yet, it is long predated by Buster's 1926 *Ladies Home Journal* article, in which he claims to have "arrived" under a medicine show tent during raging storm while his father and Houdini were away on a one-day road engagement.[41] Other tellings ranged from being born in a church during yet another bout of torrential rain, to the quintessential whopper—a cyclone snatches up Baby Keaton and later safely deposits him in a tree.[42] Kansas' Frank *Wizard of Oz* Baum certainly had nothing on the imagination of Joe Keaton, or maybe there was just something about being in this land (Kansas) of wonderfully outlandish fables.

A provocative footnote to the falling and/or flying Buster is that the boy's beloved autograph/notebook included no signature and mini-tribute to Buster from the great Houdini, especially since the *Motion Picture Classic* article had gone out of its way to mention the *many* then famous personalities noted in Buster's book. This seems a rather amazing omission, given Houdini's purported central associations with the family.

Of course, maybe the name is not there because Joe Keaton did occasionally tell the whole truth. In his "Cyclone Baby" article Joe had related that one night when "The Three Keatons" were on the same bill with Houdini, the artist was late. To kill time and probably because Joe felt an impatient audience would be more easily calmed by a cute youngster, a delaying distraction was concocted until the great escape artist appeared. Thus, in Joe's words, "Buster, still a boy, was sent on [stage] to hold the audience with some imitations.... [Alleging Buster had no intention to be funny, his son announced:] "Mr. Houdini may not be able to appear tonight. He lost the key to his dressing room." The audience howled and Harry burned up [was angry when it was related to him]."[43] Since this literary connection to the comedians has Keaton linked to Huckleberry Finn, one might better have that text help explain Joe's style. The novel opens with Huck introducing himself and Twain: "You don't know about me, without you have a read a book by the name of 'The Adventures of Tom Sawyer,' but that ain't no matter. The book was made by Mr. Mark Twain, and he told the truth, mainly. There were things which he stretched.... That is nothing. I never seen anybody but lied, one time or another."[44]

Conscious or not, these literary foundations found their way into the later film work of each comedian—the pathos of comic sentimentality over the cerebellum in Chaplin, Lloyd's seemingly bright corner-cutting boy/man headed for Main Street doldrums (as later demonstrated by Preston Sturges' sideswiping of Lloyd's 1920s persona in *The Sin of Harold Diddlebock*, 1947), and Keaton anticipating the theatre of the absurd done up in surrealism, à la his *Sherlock, Jr.* (1924) projectionist stepping into a movie.

However, before leaving Joe Keaton's gift for embellishment, one must say his son remained a lifelong disciple. Decades before he was replicating this marvelous malarkey in his memoirs, or even repeating it in his 1920 interviews, he was pushing bizarre into pure surrealism, from his aforementioned entrance into a projected movie, or the otherworldly house he creates in *One Week*, to the occasional PR piece. Thus, while Lloyd was cranking out print blather ad nauseam, Keaton would let maybe a year go by between "news" befitting a Salvador Dalí. For example, in a 1922 *Photoplay* piece, he orchestrated an interview with his baby son, also named Joseph, which also manages to shish kebab Keaton's strained relations with his wife's control-conscious family, including his star sister-in-law Norma Talmadge. What follows is an excerpt from Adela Rogers St. Rogers' "interview":

> ADELA: "Hello," I said casually—you can never tell about babies—"do you know you've got a nose exactly like your Aunt Norma's...?"
> JOSEPH: "That may be but you'd better not let her hear you calling her my Aunt Norma," he said, twiddling his toes merrily. "She told me herself yesterday that I was to call her Norma."
> ADELA: "How do you like it here?" I asked, "how does it seem to be a film prince and be related to screen royalty like this?" [His Aunt Constance Talmadge was also a stuffy film star.]
> JOSEPH: "If there's one thing I'm not," said Joe firmly, "it's a snob.... I can get along with very little sleep and I like things going on. [Two traits Buster prided himself on having.] Of course I've upset the household a good deal. I reckon they had an idea I was going to be a [girl] doll for them to dress up.... One thing I am, is independent. I won't let anybody ... walk over me [wishful Buster]. I've got a will of my own and I thought they might just as well get used to it now as later.... I'm a baby with ideas and I'm going to be considered around home."[45]

One more of these rare but ever so delightfully outlandish stories merits telling. The following year (1923) the *Los Angeles Times* ran an article on the "Great Stone Face" with its playful absurdity summarized in the title "Buster Would Write Book on 'How to Smile.'"[46] But the copy is just as funny: "Buster has smiled so seldom in his life he remembers each instance minutely, and recounts each with all the dramatic fervor a polar explorer or soldier of fortune might impart to his risky adventures. A book on the subject of smiling by Keaton should be as breath-snatching as the wildest penny-dreadful [cheap sensational fiction printed on cut-rate pulp paper]."[47] What makes this piece doubly fascinating is that Keaton also draws a parallel between himself and Edgar Allan Poe and his comic writing—someone seen as solemn but who also wrote comedy ... at a time when Poe was seldom related to comedy. Indeed, that is still true today for many people.[48] However, Poe was an American pioneer in black humor, and the fact that Keaton was both aware of that and saw his work in somewhat the same vein further underlines just how far ahead of the times Keaton was. (In Keaton's later groundbreaking dark comedy *The General*, 1926, he ironically named his leading lady Annabelle Lee, after Poe's poem.) And while Keaton's approach to black humor was then different than that of Chaplin, another dark comedy trailblazer, it makes for a connection between the two which is seldom if ever made.

That is, by the 1940s, Chaplin pictures like *The Great Dictator* (1940) and *Monsieur Verdoux* (1947) had finally reached Keaton's 1920s death-equals-comedy perspective.[49] For example, Chaplin's early dark comedy *The Gold Rush* was inspired by the Donner Party tragedy of 1846–1847, in which real-life American pioneers are snowbound in the Sierra Nevada mountains and resort to cannibalism to survive. Thus, Chaplin's film has his Tramp and prospector Mack Swain snowbound, with hunger driving the latter character to hallucinate that "Charlie" is a chicken. For a brief time Swain attempts to have the Tramp for supper. *But* the film never uses an actual death for comic purposes, à la the aforementioned Chaplin films. In contrast, the 1920s Keaton seemed to do just that for most of his *The Frozen North*. Moreover, there is *no* qualifying of this death-equals-comedy in his *The General*. For example, at one point the comedian draws his sword but the saber comes off at the hilt, with the wayward blade comically skewering an approaching enemy—which did not play in the 1920s (see Chapter 7). From the beginning Keaton had anticipated George Carlin's axiom that the duty of a comedian was to find society's line and then cross it deliberately.

One might metaphorically liken Joe Keaton's creative imagination to a farmer turning over the soil in a minefield in order to better prepare the mad mind which created "The Three Keatons." Prior to three-year-old Buster's addition to the "act," a term which should be used loosely, Joe and wife Myra were struggling medicine show performers— the doormat of troupers. Buster's mom played the cornet and his dad sometimes sang Irish songs and fluctuated between a blackface Sambo bit and his specialty—a crude car wreck sort of sketch in which he combined seemingly self-destructive dancing and acrobatics on, into, and over a table, for a sort of Tasmanian Devil riff of cartoonish violence. One could definitely trace Buster's later ability to take a pratfall to his father's wherewithal to do any sort of physical shtick for a laugh. Joe's pièce de résistance was to place one leg on the table, or the nearest horizontal object, and attempt to seemingly defy gravity by lifting his other leg to a parallel position with the table. Amazingly, Joe would seem to momentarily break the rules of science (by simultaneously being horizontal to said table) before taking one of his surreal patented falls. Years later Buster mentored Red Skelton at MGM, and taught his protégé a winning rendition of this tour de silly for the hit movie *Bathing Beauty* (1944).[50] If done effectively, little is new in comedy.

Regardless, since his father's comedy repertoire included bits like this, Buster soon realized he was born to be sort of a "clockwork orange" (part human, part unfeeling) projectile, because it was verboten for him to register any pain, thus the dark humor. And voila—"The Great Stone Face" was created. The Prologue provided a period description from Joe's pitcher perspective, but how did Buster's ball of "harmony with objects" feel about literally being part of vaudeville's most unusual thrown whatsit? Buster provided the answer in the 1923 text *The Blue Book of the Screen*: "'My father used to carry me on the stage and drop me. After explaining to the audience that I liked it, he would pick me up and throw me at a piece of scenery, sometimes knocking the scenery down with me and sometimes not. He would often throw me as far as thirty feet.' When in England, the management of the theatre insisted that Buster must have been stolen, or adopted, or something. He said that no parents would treat their own child as his father and mother treated him."[51] Surprise, their brief tour of Britain failed, and the trio successfully returned to the more violence-sanctioning United States. Still, it had never been, nor would it ever be, easy for "The Three Keatons" to avoid questions about little Buster. Thus, Joe was often dodging and/or addressing issues including child abuse, educational requirements required for a youngster, and simply vaudeville laws banning juveniles of varying ages from performing.

Joe usually got around these obstacles in assorted ways. He routinely lied about Buster's age and/or claimed that the boy was a midget. To embellish the gnome fable, the youngster's traveling clothes were tailored upon adult male fashions. Even when they became a vaudeville sensation and he performed as a boy, his age was still usually padded. Indeed, young Buster often joked, with mock incredulity, at how his age differed in so many cities. And any semblance of a traditional tutored education was seldom attempted, with any literacy help provided by his mom. Consequently, if their stage act was not absurd enough, little Buster had an equally ludicrous long childhood, since his diminutive size allowed this hammer throw routine to be played out for years. When it was later less effective, though the teenage Buster had only grown to be approximately five foot four, father and son would largely "entertain" by stage fights involving much breaking of furniture and props on each other which sometimes went beyond an act.

Still, as the very popular routines' expiration date approached, fueled by a growing son, entertainment inroads being made by pioneering film, and the dangers of Joe's growing anger and alcoholism issues—the latter invariably driven by the coming changes—Buster left "The Three Keatons" in 1917. The perspective of Joe, whose routine once included Irish ballads, might best be summarized by the darkly comic axiom of the contemporary author and activist, William Butler Yeats (1865–1939): "Being Irish, he had an abiding sense of tragedy that sustained him through temporary periods of joy." Sadly, this would one day ring true for Buster, too. Still for a time Buster seemed to have escaped. However, one is reminded of a haunting memoir of philosopher Jason Stanley: "My mother's most frequent advice was about knowing when to get out of a dangerous situation. The moment where one must accept that a situation is genuinely dangerous is usually well past the time when one can exit."[52] In point of fact, Buster's delayed tipping point was even worse than that of Joe's—because his signature professional component was to express no emotion, something that frequently bled into Keaton's real life. For Buster it was only a matter of time.

Regardless, as a former child star of vaudeville, Keaton almost immediately had a lucrative New York offer to join the annual musical comedy edition of *The Passing Show*. In the lingo of baseball-loving Buster, this was Triple-A entertainment, just a notch below the Majors, à la the *Ziegfeld Follies*. Buster would be paid well over two hundred dollars a week (in excess of two thousand dollars in today's currency). However, a funny thing happened on the way to being a solo Broadway clown. Keaton met Roscoe "Fatty" Arbuckle, the film comedian whom Hollywood film producer Mack Sennett, of Keystone Kops fame, had made into a superstar between 1913 and 1916.

The sandy-haired, blue-eyed "Fatty" Arbuckle came by his nickname honestly, weighing in at over two times Keaton's 120-odd pounds. But with the 1915 death of America's first international film comedy star, John Bunny, Charlie Chaplin was the only cinema funnyman to top Arbuckle's world-wide fame and market value. While Sennett always did his best to keep his stars' sticker price potential from them, Arbuckle had finally seen the dollar signs and that was what he was doing in New York.

The first meeting of Keaton and Arbuckle is the stuff of hyperbole. But whether it was a chance encounter in Times Square, or a meeting arranged by a mutual friend, Buster's visit to Arbuckle's Comique Colony Studio changed his life. The place was on East Forty-Eighth Street, a seedy area near some train tracks near Manhattan's First Avenue—not exactly the Great White Way. Granted, Arbuckle was friendly, enough. Though, why not? He recognized the vaudeville star he had stolen some material from the previous year. And the atmosphere was pleasantly casual, with this dainty, on-his-feet comedian, despite that weight, even offering to put Keaton into the short subject then being shot.

However, Buster was wary. Was he being used again? At the same time, he was curious about this new medium. Moreover, the soon-to-be "Great Stone Face" of stage *and* screen had been studying films for some time. The initial catalyst might have been his father's hatred of them—after all, they were killing vaudeville. Indeed, that was where Buster started watching "the flickers," because short films were appearing on vaudeville bills. Plus, Buster had sought out movies, being impressed by the scope of *Birth of a Nation* (1915) and fascinated by Chaplin. Most importantly, however, Keaton could not keep his eyes off the camera. Movie magic for him was all about the technical side of filmmaking. Thus, he decided to appear in his first movie that day—*The Butcher Boy* (1917). In a grocery-store set that might have doubled for a later W. C. Fields routine (preserved, after a fashion, in the potato-nosed comedian's film *It's a Gift*, 1934), Buster is a customer in the market for a bucket of molasses.[53]

Shockingly, Buster smiles twice but arguably just as shocking, he is wearing his signature porkpie hat in his first film. If you were a 1910s movie comedian, you wore a derby. If it was good enough for Charlie, Fatty, and an army of copiers into the 1920s, such as Laurel & Hardy, why not Buster. Yet, as suggested in the Prologue, "The Great Stone Face" just did things differently. Keaton leaves both his bucket and hat on the counter, with a quarter for the sticky stuff in the can, and wanders off.

When Arbuckle asks for his payment, a preoccupied borderline rude Buster replies it is in the bucket. Well, two could play this cheeky game, so Arbuckle fills Keaton's hat with molasses, before retrieving the two bits, and then also filling up the bucket. When Buster goes to exit, with fake politeness Fatty tips his hat. When Keaton attempts to reciprocate, what is now essentially a molasses pie hat will not budge. A comically displeased Buster is now assisted by prankster Fatty. Naturally, the bucket of molasses spills and Keaton is stuck to the floor. A "helpful" Fatty sees a chance for more revenge, and rescues his statue customer with boiling water to Buster's feet. Once freed, Fatty picks him up and tosses him outside. Keaton enjoyed the largely improvised bit, and later even received some delayed payback for Fatty stealing some of his material. That is, in later years, Keaton himself periodically recycled a variation of the sketch. (Interestingly, though the narrative is different, Fields' aforementioned grocery sketch also uses a molasses floor for a close.)

Undoubtedly, both Buster's pleasure over this introduction to film, as well as an easy rapport with Arbuckle made the oversized comedian's offer to come join him at Comique Colony tempting. Of course, the pay would be decidedly less. But just as John Bunny had walked away from a better paying stage career in 1910, money was not really an issue for Buster. The more telling catalyst was Keaton's desire to borrow a camera so he could take it apart that evening. The next day he was part of the Arbuckle team, with another pre-molasses *Butcher Boy* shoot. Buster recalled the sequence for his 1926 *Ladies Home Journal* article, a heavy- with-slapstick routine he would tone down in his later work: "The two principal comedians were just then exchanging bags of flour with one another, across the store. I intercepted one with my head and was knocked out. Those early screen comedians aimed true and threw straight! I can [still] remember that blow now."[54]

Joining Arbuckle's company would *impact* Buster in several other life-changing ways. Fatty's independent producer Joseph M. Schenck, who had arranged Arbuckle's lucrative exit from Sennett while giving the comedian carte blanche creative powers—if he stayed in budget—would soon essentially do the same for Keaton. Moreover, he would later become Schenck's brother-in-law. Schenck married and orchestrated the melodrama stardom of Norma Talmadge the same year Buster joined the team (1917). Keaton wed Norma's sister Natalie in 1921, though her undistinguished film career, if one can even call it that, came to an end after she appeared in his *Our Hospitality*. Indeed, she was working in Arbuckle's office at the time Keaton made his game-changing visit.

There was yet another Talmadge sister, Constance, who was the youngest and most talented of the three Brooklyn girls who were pushed into the movies by a stage door mother. Both Constance and Norma were, for a time, major silent film stars. But the coming of sound would essentially end the duo's acting careers. Buster's wife had never been in their league, and is now more a footnote to her famous sisters and first husband. The Talmadges, however, would be a constant bane to Buster's existence—to be addressed shortly, and later in the text. Yet, given that Norma and Constance had both worked earlier with John Bunny at Brooklyn's Biograph Studio, it is quite possible the sisters inadvertently contributed to Buster's celebrated walking into a movie-within-a-movie sequence in *Sherlock Jr.* (1924, see Chapter 3).

The short subjects Arbuckle and Keaton made between 1917 and 1919 in New York, and then in Long Beach, California, would be a happy, very successful time for both comedians. It was an increasingly well-paying apprenticeship for Keaton, and his presence helped make the films more inventingly clever. And while Keaton was briefly off the screen for 1918 military service, Schenck made sure Buster's parents were financially taken care of. Then in late 1919, when it was deemed time for Arbuckle to move onto feature films, producer Schenck made it possible for Keaton to take over Fatty's lucrative and free-wheeling operation. The only major difference would be that while Arbuckle's films would continue to be released through Paramount Famous Players-Lasky, Keaton's short subjects would be distributed through Metro (where Schenck's brother Nicholas had ties) and later First National.

What would follow between 1920 and 1923 would be the most inventive uninterrupted series of shorts to appear in Hollywood since Chaplin's 1916–1917 Mutual Films, including such Tramp classics as *Easy Street* and *The Immigrant* (both 1917). And fittingly, Keaton's own production unit was to be housed in the old Lone Star Studio, where Chaplin had made those pictures.

The fully polished Keaton porkpie-hatted persona arrives in this series of darkly comic shorts which anticipates the theatre of the absurd, and parallels Europe's growing fascination with surrealism—with Buñuel and Dalí fully embracing the comedian by the time of *College* (1927). What better preparation could a comedian have had than being a "cyclone baby" starring for well over a decade in that most bizarre tall-tale like vaudeville act "The Three Keatons." But Buster's own films were his first chance to show a mass audience—ready or not—a progressive new face on comedy which the aforementioned period critic Robert E. Sherwood had so adroitly articulated: "[To] impress a weary world with the vitally important fact that life, after all, is a foolishly inconsequential affair."[55]

Instead of the Tramp's poignant artistically conscious art standard, or Lloyd's box office nerd, Keaton's self-described "O" or "little bit of nothing" character had cornered the cult market—with a disturbing subtextual message that would gradually grow into the thinking individual's theatre of the real. Is this as good as it gets? Keaton's little man, like a universalized Hitchcock "Wrong Man," is just trying to get by in a world of 35 mm topsyturvydom. From this it is easy to morph into Kafka's chapter-opening quote: "The meaning of life is that it stops." Moreover, does not the term zeitgeist come to mind when one realizes Keaton's mesmerizing short subjects were being made at a time when Kafka, a fan of American comedy was writing *The Trial*—a novel about a "Mr. K" waiting for a tribunal to judge him on something of which he is not aware, and never comes to pass? In the 1950s Vladimir and Estragon, from Samuel Beckett's *Waiting for Godot*, will get in line behind Mr. K. waiting for a God who never comes. And by the 1960s life had come full circle back to Keaton playing the figure "O" in Beckett's silent short *Film* (1969), which is largely just a camera following Buster from behind in New York. Keaton's simple take on the subject might just as well have come from Kafka, Camus, or Beckett: "A man may keep away from everybody but he can't get away from himself."[56]

While none of Keaton's career-establishing shorts are to be missed, I would bookend the best as the first, *One Week* (1920), and the late entry *Day Dreams* (1923). One of the latter film's strong *Los Angeles Times* period reviews provides a broad generalization of what one might expect of the series: "There is a clever basic idea to 'Day Dreams,' but no plot, thank heaven ... it's about a boy who loves a girl ... and promises to make good or come back and shoot himself.... Don't ask me how [he continues]. I don't know, except that it is via his smileless face, his pathetic smallness, [and] his constant failure."[57] Written and directed by Keaton and Eddie Cline, *Day Dreams* received another enthusiastic review from the *Los Angeles Times* in 1923. The review boiled the comedian's explanation for its success down to a variation upon the previous article's "constant failure" close. After this second piece describes *Day Dreams* as having "a settled look of sadness, as from a secret sorrow ... something.... Buster attributes to the fact that audiences want to laugh at him and not with him."[58] Arguably, the film also contains Keaton's career-defining treadmill of life image. During a chase scene on a ferryboat, the engine starts up while he happens to be in the ship's side wheel—reducing him to "a squirrel in a wheel."[59] Like Alice in *Wonderland*, he must run as fast as he can to stay in one place. The scene is not as famous as comparable signature sequences for three pivotal Keaton contemporaries, but it sends the same message years earlier. That is, in Laurel & Hardy's *The Music Box* (1932, an Oscar winner for Best Live Action Short Subject), Stan and Ollie replicate the "Myth of Sisyphus" in trying to get a crated piano box up a hill via a lengthy flight of steps. And Chaplin metaphorically plays a comparable game when he is swallowed by the machine in *Modern Times* (1936).

Keaton was aware that the short length of his films allowed them to become untethered from a narrative, or a more earthbound reality ... often becoming like the title of the short itself—*Day Dreams*. Mark Sennett best articulates this in a 1925 *Los Angeles Times* article nicely summarized by its title, "Two Reels Are Enough for Comedy."[60] To best paraphrase this Sennett/Keaton perspective, "For twenty minutes an audience will accept nearly anything from what might best be called *pure comedy*."[61] This helps explain why avant-garde-like two-reelers were frequently given equal status with silent features. For example, as a private collector of original posters, I own several 1920s "full sheet" or "one sheet" posters (still the standard size found in today's movie lobbies) of 1920s re-issued short subjects well into the silent era.

Consequently, the Buster Keaton known today fully emerges, with neither the smiles and even laughter seen in Arbuckle's *Coney Island* (1917), nor the overly broad slapstick of the aforementioned bag of flour to the face in *Butcher Boy*—the fun but often primitive slapstick of his collaborations with Fatty. Interestingly, Keaton's Huck Finn factor emerges again. One of Buster's fellow 1920s artists from another medium, painter Grant Wood, of *American Gothic* fame (1930, the pitchfork father/daughter duo painting so often an object of parody), also had a loner's affinity for Twain's satirical attack on hypocrisy. The subject is all the more moving given R. Tripp Evans' brilliant biography which for the first time frankly but sensitively acknowledges Wood's homosexuality.[62] For Wood, and obviously Keaton, Twain's book had also "cured" him of the sentimentality of the Victorian/Dickens era: "Having been born into a world of Victorian standards I had accepted and admired the ornate, the lugubrious, and the excessively sentimental naturally and without question. And this [novel] was my first indication that there was something ridiculous about sentimentality."[63]

Sentimentality is not in Keaton's playbook—especially in these shorts. Indeed, there is a haunting Cat Stevens observation that frequently describes Keaton's zero character: "Death's disguise hangs on me"—not exactly the stuff of most comedians. Yet, dark comedy's favorite subject is frequently present in Keaton, such as Buster's seemingly casual gunning down of a cowboy in the aforementioned *Frozen North*, or the porkpie hat-adorned tombstone "end" of *Cops* (1922). And like the gravestone innuendo, Keaton title cards often broach death, too. When he does undercover work in *The High Sign* (1920), such thoughts are casually stated: "Guarding a man from danger and killing him at the same time is SOME job."

In *Convict 13* (1920) Buster is supposed to be hung. The rest of the inmates sit in bleachers, as if they are at a ball game, anxiously awaiting the start, while food vendors fan out among them. At the last minute what would now double as a bungee cord replaces the noose and he is saved—but Keaton bounces enough that unless Wile E. Coyote had doubled for Buster—it would have been broken-neck burial time. Underscoring the dark comedy, his fellow inmates are so upset that the warden has to promise then, via another title, "We'll hang two tomorrow to make up for this." Oh, and for good dark comedy measure, a few others are shot dead, too.

Keaton's *Hard Luck* (1921) continues dark comedy's use of death by being a study of the genre's favorite variety—suicide. Thus, Keaton anticipates Bud Cort's litany of suicidal possibilities in *Harold and Maude* (1971)[64] by fifty years. Buster's movie begins with the title "Fired from his job, jilted by his girl, down on his luck...." What follows is an inventory of suicide attempts, beginning with a botched effort to lie down in front of a trolley, managing to be missed by a descending safe, attempting to hang himself but being thwarted by an undersized tree, standing in front of a speeding nighttime car—which turns out to be two motorcycles ... which zoom by on either side of him, and getting drunk instead of dead by drinking poison from a Prohibition-labeled bottle. (Keep in mind that when the boy-next-door Lloyd went through a similar lost love in 1920s *Number, Please*, "Speedy" merely went to an amusement park for a distraction.) Regardless, *Hard Luck* continues with the film card "Night falls—he wants to do the same." Yet, just when things seem to improve for 1920s cultist Keaton, another romantic partner seems to appear, and the jilting comes full circle.

This results in an ambiguous suicide situation. He proceeds to an adjacent swimming pool and attempts a very dangerous high dive. Does this represent a macho display of what she will miss, or a death wish? Ironically, if the former plan was the goal, he fails by missing the pool ... and seemingly dies by disappearing through the concrete crack he has created. Regardless of his original plan, for once his deathly ineptitude appears to have not worked, because the film seems to be slowly heading to the punning anticipation of the inevitable "The End." Maybe there will not be a Wile E. Coyote close. But suddenly a title tells us, "Years later"—and Buster surfaces from said crack with a Chinese wife and two children.

While there are more dark comedy death scenarios peppered throughout these short subjects, his "dive" to China and return with a family foreshadow the propensity for surrealism in these same films, too. However, before exploring some of the more imaginative examples, a crucial point needs to be made about Keaton and his fearlessness in casually using death in dark comedy. For example, there is a scene in *Cops* when Keaton accidently finds himself navigating a horse-drawn wagon of soon-to-be mangled furniture in a large parade contingency of New York policemen.

Thinking the applauding crowd is actually directing their parade attention at him, he soon becomes blasé and decides to light a cigarette. But real life heavy smoker Keaton, finds he is without a match. Suddenly, there is a cutaway to an anarchist with a melon-sized bomb and a lit fuse. The next edit finds that the terrorist, in attempting to shot-put said bomb among the cops, has managed to land it next to Buster on his wagon seat. For Keaton's character, it is like manna from heaven. He still needs a match and nonchalantly uses the fuse to light his cigarette. And then just as indifferently he throws this oversized "lighter" into the street among the cops.

Not surprisingly, it seems to blow up several policemen. Of course, when the smoke clears, they seem more like Mack Sennett's indestructible Keystone Kops. Now granted, it serves a purpose in Keaton's thin story—it disrupts the parade and Buster now has an army of comic cops after him. (This was also the inspiration for all the policemen chasing the Beatles in Richard Lester's celebrated *A Hard Day's Night*, 1964, sometimes now known as the *Jukebox Citizen Kane*.) Regardless, where is the fearlessness of Keaton using a scene like that?

After Russia's Bolshevik Revolution and the 1918 end of World War I, high inflation, pay cuts, and industrial layoffs caused race riots, strikes, and acts of violence towards foreign-born workers. In early 1919 a series of bombings attributed to followers of socialist leader Luigi Galleani led to the Red Scare of 1919, as much of America became hysterical over the socialist/communist dangers of "hyphenated-Americans." But the bombings only increased, with an unsolved 1920s Wall Street explosion (in a horse-drawn wagon) killing 84 and wounding 141 people. With the targeting of political figures like Attorney General A. Mitchell Palmer, what became known as the "Palmer Raids" were instituted by the Department of Justice to capture and deport radical leftists. Though initially championed, it was soon seen as overstepping civil liberties.

While periodic bombings occurred throughout the decade, a liberal backlash occurred around the case of Nicola Sacco and Bartolomeo Vanzetti. These two Italian-born United States anarchists were convicted and sentenced to die in 1921 over the murder of two individuals during a robbery to help fund terrorist activities. Guilty or innocent, the trial was quickly seen by many as a gross miscarriage of justice based on ethnic and socialist profiling—becoming one of history's first international cause cèlèbres. Appeals delayed their execution until 1927, with protests from such high profile people as H. G. Wells, Dorothy, Parker, John Dos Passos, future Supreme Court Justice Felix Frankfurter, George Bernard Shaw, and Edna St. Vincent Millay. Following the execution, riots occurred in cities around the world.

Keaton's *Cops* had seen fit to use the anarchist joke in early 1922, when the Sacco and Vanzetti case was first becoming very controversial. Buster's setting (New York, scene of the worst violence), a wagon-based delivery system, and the victims (policemen), heightened, for the time, the questionable use of the joke—though as Keaton intuitively knew, the message of dark humor was that there was no message. It proved problematic to some distributors, but Keaton was unapologetic and just a few year later *Photoplay*'s review of his Civil War opus *The General* (1927) criticized Keaton because the film's deadly "basic incidents ... actually happened."[65] Which, one wants to scream, is the pivotal point of black humor. Of course, one could return to the 1926 *New Yorker* reviewer who seemed to better understand Buster and the genre when, in discussing the boxing ferocity in *Battling Butler*, observed the comic violence called upon "your sense of the ridiculous."[66] The human comedy has always been tragedy plus time.

Keaton mentor, Fatty Arbuckle, had a persona so grounded in innocence, there was no recovering from the 1921 sexual scandal and manslaughter trials.

Regardless, Keaton's *Cops* sequence could have turned into a 1920s minor version of what got Bill Maher fired from ABC when, shortly after 9/11, he stated, in part, that terrorists "staying in the airplanes when it [sic] hits the building [sic], say what you want about it, [was] not cowardly." The timing and "act of war"-like nature of Maher's situation made it more volatile. Yet, today's P. C. police can and do attempt to wet-blanket dark comedy. Nonetheless, neither Maher nor Keaton avoided dark comedy. Moreover, the black humor directed at legendary screen cowboy William S. Hart is much more ongoingly harsh in *The Frozen North*.

Today references to the situation, if it is referenced at all, generally merely state that Hart was so upset he would not speak to Keaton for two years. But period literature suggests that the rape scandal that essentially ended Fatty Arbuckle's on-screen career played a major part in the savaging of Hart. Keaton's mentor had hosted a wild 1921 Labor Day weekend party in which many people, including would-be actress Virginia Rappe, had attended. She later died of a ruptured bladder and acute peritonitis. But soon after the actress' death her friend Maude Delmont would claim that Arbuckle had raped the ironically named Rappe.

Unfortunately, the party had taken place in San Francisco, a city which then looked down upon upstart Hollywood and its nouveau riche, allegedly uncultured picture people. The ugly allegations against Arbuckle would eventually be proven false. Yet, the mismanaged case necessitated three trials to fully exonerate Fatty, which took the proceedings well into 1922. And despite the final jury apologizing to Arbuckle for what the case had put him through, his on-screen persona of a sweet innocent fat man/child could never be restored. Indeed, a public boycott of his films had started almost from day one, forcing distributors to pull his pictures.

Moreover, even if there had been some second-chance hope, the Hollywood powers to be, fearing the scandal would kill its cash cow industry, created a censorship office, headed by the aforementioned Hays, even before the case was settled. And to prove it had teeth, after Fatty had been proven innocent, he was still banned for a time from the screen. Now, even his acquittal was questioned. Thus, when the ban was eventually lifted, there was no hope for a recovery.

Keaton's depression over what was happening to his friend no doubt added to the darker nature of *Cops*, which went into production when Arbuckle's court proceedings were still ongoing. No doubt, the railroading which Keaton saw his friend going through made him feel like an anarchist himself. So how does this further impact *The Frozen North*? While industry leaders essentially used Arbuckle as a sacrificial lamb, working Hollywood largely supported his innocence. One exception was Hart, who came down viciously on Arbuckle. It hardly seems a coincidence that Fatty's greatest champion, who donated a large portion of his future profits to Arbuckle, was responsible, as noted before, for dark comedy directed at Hart in *The Frozen North*. Though the story is credited to Keaton and Cline, it is assumed to be largely the work of Arbuckle.

If so, Fatty would have been drawing from his earlier affectionate spoof of Douglas Fairbanks in *The Sheriff* (1918, now lost). However, here Keaton/Arbuckle play dark comedy rough. Hart's Western alter ego would never shoot someone in the back, or steal. Keaton's cowboy relishes both. Hart's screen character was a gentleman with women, whereas Buster's take on Hart is misogynist—which is a more personal dig at period implications of abusive behavior in Hart's short marriage to actress Winifred Westover—coincidently ending during the year of Arbuckle's trials. (Was the real Hart attempting to distract from his own problems?) Finally, Hart's realistic cowboy was becoming passé, versus silent film's new desire for the Western flash of a Tom Mix. Thus, Keaton plays Hart as wooden as a log cabin ... something Keaton, as "The Great Stone Face," could really milk. And though Keaton's dark comedy here is harsher than normal, it is neither inconsistent with other examples of his black humor, nor his style components in general.

In fact, Keaton's shorts have some of the most surrealistic gags, and one of the best opens *The Frozen North*. One reads the subway sign "Last Stop," and cowboy Keaton emerges in a snowy Alaskan landscape "Nanook of the North" would have found troubling. However, the fantastic imagery of Keaton films comes in all shapes and sizes. In *The High Sign* he solves hanging up his hat by merely drawing a hook on the wall. *The Scarecrow*'s (1920) opening title reads, "Slowly and majestically the sun steals gradually over the hill-tops," then one cuts to a sun on steroids zooming up in the sky. *The Haunted House* (1921) begins with a door lock that has a bottle cap over it, necessitating one pop it open like a beer bottle before using one's key—anticipating the apparent bank door which Buster must open with a combination that turns out to be merely his front door in the later *Sherlock, Jr.* And in a variation of the earlier drawn hook gag, *The Haunted House* also allows Buster to simply throw his cane at the wall in order to once again hang up his hat on it.

Indeed, *The Haunted House* is a one-joke surrealistic compendium. For example, the oven also doubles as a record player. At the kitchen table an overhead string system has various food attachments which one can swing back and forth, as well as basic spices. A tub of water can easily be flipped over to become a sofa, while the liquid pours through an outlet for a place in which ducks can paddle, if one has farming in mind. Indeed, the agricultural perspective is further encouraged when the top of the aforementioned table lifts up and one's leftovers go through a trap door for your pigs. There are additional inventive devices for the farmer doubling as Salvador Dalí, but this should suffice for any ad selling the farmhouse of the future.

While the surreal touches abound throughout Keaton's short films, an especially significant one occurs in *The Blacksmith* (1922). The noteworthiness is grounded in two reasons. First, many period publications praised it in detail. *Moving Picture World* observed: Buster Keaton ... keeps up his good record for turning out snappy comedies. [For example,] the way in which Buster "sells" a fancy pair of shoes to a beautiful work horse, going through exactly the same stunts as a shoe salesman would do for milady [a woman of fashion] is a scream."[67] Second, treating the horse like a special customer is an obvious precursor to Buster finding love, or at least companionship, with the brown-eyed cow in *Go West* (1925, see Chapter 6). Of course, one could say that the Sacco and Vanzetti bomb-reminding *Cops* sequence distracted viewer memories from Buster communication by phone in this earlier film with another beautiful horse in that film, as well as taking her to the dentist! Just as these films foreshadow *Go West*, several of his surrealistic short subjects anticipate classic later pictures by other filmmakers. The best example would undoubtedly be Keaton's *The Playhouse* (1921), a watershed work from what emerged from a fortuitous accident—breaking his ankle during the production of *The Electric House* (1921, another picture on the lines of *The Haunted House*—with its Rube Goldberg stamp, à la complicated gadgets that do simple tasks).

Regardless, the frustrated Keaton was stewing over being unable to work because of his injury. However, his fascination with the technical side of filmmaking, as well as his dislike of egotistical artists, provided a way around his injury. The *Playhouse* has Buster attending a minstrel show in which he plays the orchestra and everyone in the show. The surrealistic trick which necessitated no movement from the hobbled Keaton, was made possible by a special matte box in front of the camera lens, with nine metal shutters which would be moved one at a time up and down. By the careful metronome movement of Keaton, and the even more difficult same speed handcranking of the camera as the film was constantly rewound to record a new section of film stock, there is a theatre full of Keatons.

The movie fascinated and bedeviled Hollywood for years with its Keaton-cloning comedy. Eventually a variation of the procedure was used in the Oscar-winning Best Picture *An American in Paris* (1951), in which Oscar Levant's character daydreams he is performing George Gershwin's *Concerto in F for Piano and Orchestra* for a concert audience. Gradually the sequence reveals he is also the conductor, members of the orchestra, and a demonstrative member of the audience. Younger viewers are also entertained by comparing Keaton's *Playhouse* program with the menu in *Being John Malkovich* (1989); both are limited to countless repetitions of the two actors' names—though by then special effects had an easier time creating multiple Malkoviches. As a footnote to Keaton's inspiration, he is said to have been spoofing period producer Thomas Ince's tendency to give himself hordes of credits on each of his films. However, a careful reading of Keaton's literature past and present also provides a case of the comedian kidding egotistical Chaplin, too.

Ultimately, coming full circle back to that *first* Keaton short post–Arbuckle, *One Week*, one could even argue that he was doing tour de force work immediately as a solo comedian. Certainly, the bizarre home which he constructs from the mislabeled boxes of his pre-fab house is classic Keaton oeuvre, complete from its Kafkaesque result to its train track obliteration, after one passing train seems to give it a momentary reprieve. Indeed, that second demolition train is a standard Buster gag throughout his career, either metaphorically or literally—all seems okay and then chaos happens—to remind one life has no happy endings. Keaton actually recreates a variation of this delayed train demolition, only with a car, in his early sound film, *Parlor, Bedroom and Bath* (1931, one of the only bright spots in a picture largely dictated by MGM).

Moreover, as with most of these short subjects, Keaton's clever gags often seem to distract viewers from that darker subtext. Many of the period reviews for the picture *The Electric House* bear this out. For example, a 1923 *Los Angeles Times* review, under the title "'Electric House' Worth Laughing At," stated: "[It was] being held over for a third week at the Symphony [Theatre]. Buster invents many labor-saving devices in this comedy, which the public accepts with applause."[68] Another more pointed example occurs with the *New York Times'* pocket review of the much darker *High Sign*: "a riotous Buster Keaton comedy ... ingenious and irresistibly funny."[69]

Without addressing all of his first independent shorts, two cannot be omitted—two which come from radically different points of interest. There is the triumph of *The Boat* (1921), and the now provocative inside look at Keaton's real life strained marriage in *My Wife's Relations* (1922). The first has the brilliance of *One Week*—only this time the random destruction of a split-level house occurs because Buster has created a boat too large to be taken out through some massive basement doors. The surrealism is a boy/man who cannot grasp the size differential between the boat and the exit—with the craft's name underlining the point with the almost profane moniker, "DAMFINO" (a boat title recycled in Keaton's *College*, 1927).

The Boat also opens with one of the comedian's favorite gags—the mistaken visual. Inside the craft Keaton is being rocked back and forth, as if caught in a major storm. But then an exterior shot reveals an unfinished boat's balance being messed with by his son. One is reminded of Chaplin's *The Immigrant* (1917), and a different take on a similar gag. That ship *is* suffering from rough seas but the gag involves passengers trying to eat at a table across from each other and inadvertently sharing the same plate as it slides back and forth in front of them. (Probably Keaton's signature example of this visual misrepresentation, at least in these shorts, is the opening of *Cops*. Buster appears to be speaking to his snobbish girlfriend from behind bars, which is actually where he will ultimately end up. Yet, the next shot reveals they are just talking through a large gate.) Be that as it may, *The Boat* will close as does *One Week*, with a catastrophe; the house is destroyed by a train, the boat sinks.

My Wife's Relations, which will be fleshed out further in the following chapters (as it relates to Keaton's actual marriage), is about the comedian being wed to someone with whom he has little in common, and whose family is dominatingly negative towards him. This premise is not that far from Keaton's relationship with his matriarchal mother-in-law Margaret L. Talmadge and her three daughters, two of whom were the aforementioned film stars, Norma and Constance. Mother Talmadge's sense of self-importance can be capsulized with the title of her 1924 family biography, *The Talmadge Sisters: Norma, Constance, Natalie: An Intimate Story of the World's Most Famous Screen Family, by Their Mother*.[70]

No family member treats him pleasantly in the film until a letter is discovered implying he has come into a large amount of money. Then the film title appears: "Kate's husband is rich—now we must be nice to him." However, once that is discovered to be false, a title card appears: "Let's murder him first and then kill him later." And the family immediately looks at him with such coldness, that he puts up his collar as if he is chilled. Soon he goes on the lamb and is only safe when he just manages to catch one of his beloved trains. As he stretches out on the tail end of the caboose and puts his feet up, one sees that the train is named the "Reno Limited"—with Reno then synonymous with getting a divorce.

Keaton's 1921 marriage to Natalie has always been something of a mystery. Though they had met and briefly dated as early as 1917, the union always had the feel of a business arrangement between Natalie's mother (marry off the untalented daughter) and Buster's producer/advisor Joe Schenck (trying to further solidify a powerful industry family—Norma then being his wife). Keaton did nothing to encourage the union as a love match when an October 1921 *Motion Picture* magazine quoted the comic thus: "It's too soon yet to say anything, I've only been married three weeks. [after a pause] Marriage is fine as an institution but bad as a habit.... [Moreover,] I shall never join the 'Why, dear' club. You know how it is. A man comes home late. [His] wife asks him where he was. He starts to stammer an explanation. 'Why, dear, you see I—' No I shall never join the 'Why, dear' club."[71] The only sure thing to be said about Keaton at the time was movies totally consumed him. In 1923 he would be rewarded for his efforts.

2

The First Two Features

The Three Ages *(July 25, 1923)* and Our Hospitality *(November 20, 1923)*

> We just wrap up a little hokum. We build up a little story on some sure-fire idea, throw in a dozen gags, if we can think of 'em, and let 'er ride. The scenario we use is written on a … picture post card. If it's lost it's no great matter.
> —Buster Keaton, *Picture-Play Magazine*, March 1923[1]

Though Keaton's above quote is too modest, the interview is more aptly titled "Low Comedy as a High Art."[2] Buster had actually wanted to jump to features at the beginning of the decade, riffing comedy like the jazz artists did to their music—giving their name to the age. More than anything, Keaton had wanted to follow the ill-fated Fatty to the next level. But Buster's boss of a brother-in-law (Joseph M. Schenck) wanted to make sure the comedian was ready.

By 1923, however, the critical and commercial success of Keaton's post–Arbuckle films had prominent period critics recognizing it was time for Keaton to move to features. For example, arguably the era's most significant reviewer, the aforementioned *LIFE* humor magazine critic Robert E. Sherwood, had suggested just that in his pioneering collection of film critiques—1923's *The Best Moving Pictures of 1922–1923*.[3] In a special section on "Short Subjects," Sherwood had placed Buster number one, with the implication it was only a matter of time before he graduated to longer pictures: "The undisputed leader has been Keaton. He has taken the place held first [in the two-reel market] by Charlie Chaplin and subsequently by Harold Lloyd—both of whom are now definitely committed to a policy of feature pictures. Keaton, whose incredibly solemn visage is not the least effective of his comic attributes, has made a number of pictures this year that have been distinctively and individually his own."[4]

Ironically, Fatty Arbuckle might have been included with Chaplin and Lloyd in Sherwood's two-reeler graduate category, had it not been for the scandal. Indeed, he had already completed three yet to be released features for Paramount—making them back-to-back. Paradoxically, that had been the catalyst for the ill-fated Labor Day party. Interestingly, however, shortly before this all came to pass, Fatty had articulated why so many comedians wanted to move to features, despite how two-reeler comedies often carried equal weight with the 1920 features. It was all about the pressure and expense of minutes of pure comedy. In a 1919 article for *Picture and Picturegoer* titled "Nothing to Laugh At" he observed:

It's no joke—making 'em! Nothing to laugh at when you consider ... [everything]. The getting of laughs is the biggest gamble in the world, for while the veriest beginner in a drama line knows almost to a T what will touch the hearts of his audience and the toughest writer of "sob stuff" is so well primed with traditional wisdom anent [concerning] "good situations" that can't go very far wrong, the comedian and the inventor of comedy stories are always, more or less, in the dark—now and ever often have been.... And not only that. The public's sense of humor changes continually ... when we came to run the film off in the studio projection room, before an assembly of stage hands, costumers—anyone within reach—the expensive scene went without a giggle [or] murmur ... the second time the joke came off—by a subtle manipulation of clothes and stunts. But it was quite a chance [worry]....[5]

Plus, it was not so much that comedians wanted to coast a bit in features. There was also a subtextual tone to last chapter's 1925 *Los Angeles Times* article by Mack Sennett which suggested that twenty minutes of comedy was about all an audience could take without a break—quite a change from today's frequent nonstop saturation comedy.[6]

Key Early Film Factors

Be that as it may, four key subjects must be addressed prior to zeroing in on Keaton the feature film auteur. First, he had appeared strictly as an actor in the 1920 feature movie adaptation of the 1913 Broadway hit *New Henrietta*. The film was entitled *The Saphead*, and while Buster was well-received, the picture only garnered mixed reviews. For example, while *Moving Picture World* called it "first class entertainment," *Photoplay*'s *Saphead* critique was mediocre at best.[7] Indeed, one is reminded of the joke from several years ago when a number of formerly "lost films" were found in an old frozen Alaskan dumping site. (At that time the then-territory was the end of the viewing circuit, and instead of shipping worn prints back to the studio, the movies were simply buried.) Regardless, to paraphrase the crack, "Great lost films not so great once found."

However, *The Saphead* has a certain Rosetta Stone quality for Keaton features. That is, it anticipates some of his basic comedy components to follow. Most significantly, unlike the typical personality comedian of the silent era, it provides Keaton with another screen alter ego—the wealthy and pampered milquetoast type. Indeed, the always insightful Robert E. Sherwood even did a later piece on the dangers of the stuck-in-amber persona for a 1925 *Photoplay* article titled "The Perils of Monotony."[8] Not surprisingly, there was one exception: "Chaplin is the only star in the filmy [sic] way who has been able to do this, who has established one distinct character and maintained it, unchanged, over a period of years. And even Chaplin has not put the thing to a real test, as his appearances of late have been regrettably few and far between."[9] Though only noted fleetingly, Sherwood also referenced Buster on this subject: "Keaton is also mixing 'em up, having even discarded his celebrated pancake hat in his last two pictures [*Seven Chances* and *Go West*, both 1925]. He knew that there can always be too much of a good thing."[10]

The Saphead also showcased other Buster basics familiar from the shorts but possibly highlighted more by being in a feature. For example, drawing from his vaudeville background, Buster enjoyed spoofing other people and/or popular trends. Thus, his little Saphead character is driven in part, by his reading of the book *How to Win the Modern Girl*. And with a growing 1920s middle class, the era would see an explosion of interest in "how to" books. Plus, parody was hardly limited to the screen; many popular print humorists embraced the phenomenon, too. For example, Will Cuppy's *How to Be a Hermit*, or James Thurber and E. B. White's *Is Sex Necessary?* (both 1929).[11]

Other Buster fundamentals found in *Saphead* include: a girlfriend's father hating him, the need to make good for her, and being not unlike the title implies—a real saphead. This is done in multiple ways, including a trip to a gambling house and being told the playing chips cost $2,000 a piece. He answers, via a title card, "What are they made of?" And a personal favorite simply has him going to the wrong railway station to meet his girl—which allows Keaton to include yet another of his train talismans to the picture. However, maybe *Saphead*'s most elemental Keaton characteristic is the inertia he brings to the beginning of those films in which he plays the wealthy boy/man. Thus an early title in the picture states, "Bertie [Keaton] had been in love for years and [finally] decided something must be done about it." Said title would not be out of place at either the beginning of his later *The Navigator* (1924), or *Seven Chances* (1925). Of course, in all these pictures, Keaton's character helps resolve whatever the issue by the speedy grace of his athleticism.

The latter factor can not help but remind one of the early Douglas Fairbanks persona, whose pre–1920s swashbuckling feature films were as an athletic comic, too. Moreover, he had even starred in the aforementioned Broadway production of *The Saphead*. Plus, when Fairbanks had been approached about repeating his part in the film adaptation he had recommended Keaton, possibly because of their similar physical grace in enhancing comedy. In addition, the year Keaton entered films (1917), Fairbanks had already mastered what would become a Keaton staple—the misleading opening gag. For example, in Fairbank's Western parody, *Wild and Woolly* (1917), one first sees the comic actor seemingly seated around his campfire. But as the camera pulls back, the wannabe cowboy's elaborate encampment is really a detailed facsimile in his New York apartment. Moreover, the offer to Fairbanks for the *Saphead* adaptation would have come precisely when he was creating his brilliant screen persona makeover to playful swashbuckler in *The Mark of Zorro* (1920).

The Importance of Parody

After *The Saphead* the second pivotal component of which to be aware, prior to a period examination of Keaton's features, involves the nature of parody.[12] American film parody is a comic, yet generally affectionate and distorted imitation of a given genre, auteur, and/or a specific work. The genre has been a mainstream part of film comedy since the beginning. It was, in fact, a pivotal ingredient in the works of Mack Sennett, the father of American film comedy. For instance, Sennett's *Teddy at the Throttle* (1917) is a winning takeoff on D. W. Griffith's propensity for the last-minute melodramatic rescue, such as the close of his cinematically groundbreaking yet racist *Birth of a Nation* (1915). Indeed, this chapter will soon examine Keaton's first feature, *The Three Ages*, and how it spoofs both D. W. Griffith's epic *Intolerance* (1916) and his short subject, *Man's Genesis* (1912).

There are, however, three vital parody details of which to be cognizant. First, the genre should be funny even without viewer knowledge of the subject under affectionate attack. Obviously, however, the parody is progressively more entertaining the greater one's familiarity with the subject. Second, though the fundamental goal of parody is to be *funny*, the genre is also an educational guide, sometimes referenced as "creative criticism." To construct an effective parody, one must be thoroughly versed in the subject—like framing a house to see what goes into a given genre structure and/or auteur vision. And besides better defining the subject through laughter, it can also provide a historical tenor of the time. In the case of Griffith, Sennett's and Keaton's period parodies demonstrate the initial popularity of this serious artist and also anticipate how Griffith could become passé during the Jazz Age's Roaring '20s, when he seemed incapable of moving beyond the nineteenth-century melodramatic structure that was being spoofed.

A third parody principle is that there are two kinds of spoofing—the broad and obvious puncturing of a genre and/or an auteur, and a more subdued approach that manages comic deflation with an eventual reaffirmation of the subject being blitzed. Again, one might think of Sennett as a personification of the first and most mainstream of parody types. Sennett spoofs, and those of rival silent comedy producer Hal Roach, were sometimes so broad one need not go beyond their titles. For instance, both men produced short parodies of James Cruze's 1923 epic Western *The Covered Wagon*. Sennett's version was *The Uncovered Wagon*, and Roach countered with *Two Wagons, Both Covered* (both 1924).

Parodies of reaffirmation are not so obvious. They are often confused with the genre being undercut. The aforementioned Fairbanks transitional *The Mark of Zorro* would be a pioneering example of the reaffirmation approach. This is reflected in *Zorro*'s period reviews. After the *New York Times* first calls title character Fairbanks an "athlete comedian" in a narrative which switches between "intermittent fun and thrills," the review switches gears and acknowledges the film "is different ... from the usual Fairbanks picture."[13] The publication then struggles to define Fairbanks' changeover to swashbuckler by noting a sometimes more serious, "somewhat tamer" pace when the lead plays his aristocratic cover character.[14] *Variety*'s critiques do not much accede to a persona change but atypically, from previous Fairbanks reviews, keys less on the star and more on the love story—"Here is romance and into the bargain a commercial film ... [with co-star Marguerite de la Matte providing] romantic charm."[15]

This parody distinction is especially important in differentiating the hit critical and commercial response to *Our Hospitality* and the mediocre reaction to *The General* (1926, see Chapter 8), part of Keaton's Southern trilogy, with *Steamboat Bill, Jr.*, 1927). Though obviously this will be expanded upon greatly later in the text, suffice it to say the public readily recognized and applauded the broad spoof of *Hospitality*'s Hatfield–McCoy feud. But *The General*'s dark close-to-the-vest reaffirmation parody of the Civil War was largely missed by critics and the public alike.

Battling Philosophies of Arbuckle and Chaplin

The third issue to be clarified prior to examining Keaton's features involves Arbuckle and Chaplin. Despite the close friendship Keaton had with the mentoring Fatty, the two differed greatly over their attitudes toward the viewing public. Arbuckle anticipated a now comically celebrated H. L. Mencken axiom paraphrased from his September 19, 1926, *Chicago Daily Tribune* column: "No one ever went broke underestimating the intelligence of the American public."[16] Keaton felt otherwise, and it would cost him as time progressed and his 1920s work would become artistically more darkly demanding, such as working towards *The General*'s reaffirmation parody on war.

Ironically, this was something Chaplin, for all his differences from Keaton, also bought into until the mid–1920s. Paradoxically, this would start to unravel for Chaplin in 1923, the year Keaton finally began making his own features. The agent of Chaplin's change would be the perceived commercial failure of *A Woman of Paris* (1923; though a box office bust for a Chaplin film, over time it eventually made a slight profit). Yet earlier, the whole film community, except for Douglas Fairbanks, had said Chaplin could not make a popular dark comedy about World War I—but *Shoulder Arms* (1918) had been a huge critical and commercial success.[17] Then *The Kid* (1920) was thought to be pushing "Charlie" too close to tragedy, and it became an even greater triumph.

Consequently, well into 1923 Chaplin believed he could push the envelope again with the general public by bringing to the screen for the first time a story of sophisticated realism which also doubled as a simple slice of life. The movie was *A Woman of Paris*, about a country girl's (Edna Purviance) poignant misunderstanding and a move to Paris in which she becomes a wealthy older man's (Adolpho Menjou) mistress. However, Chaplin seems to have underlined all the more how much he was going to follow the audience's will when it was

Arbuckle (bottom), Keaton (second from top) and unnamed "friends" unwind at the beach. Note the *smiling* face and toned body of the athletic Buster.

briefly revealed, almost as an aside, in a brief July 1923 *Los Angeles Times* article, that the working title of the yet to be released picture had been "Public Opinion."[18] Chaplin had agonized over the decision, and his hope that the public would follow him yet again for some time—which is best revealed by the title of an early 1922 *Current Opinion* article: "Charlie Chaplin, As a Comedian, Contemplates Suicide."[19]

All this is more fully mapped out in an October 1923 *Los Angeles Times* article: "[The film] is his Magna Carta, in which he feels he has obtained the right to go ahead and be vital…. If the public accepts his first dramatic venture, then Mr. Chaplin feels justified in making more pictures in which he can show them the reverse side of the custard pie … 'I [Chaplin] hope the public will like this new way, for if they don't I'll be very badly disappointed. And yet I think they will.'"[20] However, for the first time, Chaplin did not have a huge cinema commercial success, though this would not have been immediately apparent for two reasons. First, this was decades before the huge saturation bookings of today, in which movies open simultaneously on thousands of screens across the nation. In the 1920s it took months before major movies reached the smaller secondary markets. Second, *A Woman of Paris*' reviews were almost universally lionizing in a way which, according to *Picture-Play Magazine*, had been "lacking since the early days of D. W. Griffith."[21]

Yet, this was actually a modest appraisal compared to the major metropolitan critiques, which could often be gleaned from just the review titles. For example, the *Los Angeles Times* banner announced, "Chaplin Opens New Epoch," and stated: "The caviar of picture entertainment—that is Charlie Chaplin's "A Woman of Paris." It is so full of novelty and subtlety that it will perhaps open a new epoch for the photoplay technician, and intrigue and mayhap [perhaps] delight the taste jaded by too much routine."[22] There was more of the same on the East Coast: "Probably no motion picture ever exerted as much comment as Charlie Chaplin's "A Woman of Paris" in New York this week.... Everyone hailed the picture as a masterpiece of direction—as a great advance in technique.... The highbrows declared that this picture is great art. Because it treats its characters naturally and does away with posturing and grimacing.... They believe that it is the beginning of a revolution in screen art. I hope it is. It is the first picture I have ever seen that was apparently devised by an adult mind for people of intelligence."[23] *LIFE*'s seminal 1920s film critic Sherwood, after equal high praise, has, however, best painted the picture into the mosaic which is Chaplin: "'A Woman of Paris' is not a [personality] comedy, and Chaplin himself does not appear in its cast of characters. But for all that, it is as essentially Chaplinesque as 'A Dog's Life,' or 'The Kid.' In it, he has merely reversed his usual formula; instead of introducing a querulous note of tragedy in a sympathy of laughter, he has equipped his orchestra with sorrowful music, with a comic counterpart assigned to an in-conspicuous soprano saxophone."[24]

Why belabor this *A Woman of Paris* comparison with Keaton, with regard to an audience's ability to grow with an artist? Because Chaplin ultimately tallied up the vote of his audience expectation level. Keaton would not. Thus, while Chaplin retreated to his delightful "Little Fellow," even to the point of returning to a "custard pie"-like moment in his underrated *The Circus* (1928), Keaton still felt the audience would be able to keep up. Arguably, his refusal to change, especially as it related to going extremely over budget on his now celebrated *The General*, was a major contributing factor to his fall from grace by the late 1920s.

Why did Keaton not lower his expectations? Besides starting with the always legitimate explanation of being stubborn, a genuine factor for this fellow nicknamed "Buster," one could return to the *A Woman of Paris* factor. Though seen as a commercial failure at the time, its 1923 critical acclaim continued to pile up throughout the decade—a fact lost on film history. As one closely studies 1920s film literature, the movie continues to be acclaimed and/or referenced for the duration of the decade, especially by power players within the industry. Before quoting an elegantly articulate 1924 celebration of the film by Douglas Fairbanks, probably the most influential artist in the 1920s film community, one must note that its source, the *Ladies Home Journal*, was then a preeminent source of significant period film criticism—another fact forgotten by history. Regardless, Fairbanks wrote: "Before very long philosophy and certain abstract subjects, such as futility, will find their way to the screen.... If Charles Chaplin had done nothing else in his picture, 'A Woman of Paris,' he has demonstrated that there is a subtler use of the screen than had before been attempted. He has proved that everyday life, touched by imagination and not ruled by exaggeration, can be made compelling."[25] Thus, maybe this ongoing praise of *Paris*, or film's potential in general, encouraged Keaton to still believe in an enlightened public—not to mention an unrelenting competition with Chaplin. Other potential factors actually bleed into the final Keaton cornerstone to be aware of before examining his 1920s features.

Anticipating Theater of the Absurd

If one were to choose any artist from this era as a poster child for what would come to be called existentialism, or theatre of the absurd, Keaton would be a ready candidate. At its most basic level, the existential attitude is a feeling of disorientation in a meaningless world. Consequently, maybe a more compelling reason for Keaton not following the "Public Opinion" vote was he just did not care. His absurd youth built upon an absurd vaudeville act was his existentialist foundation.

Plus, though Buster's uniformed World War involvement did not include combat, his tour was lengthened to entertain troops. And as a student of that war, many of the injured soldiers for whom he performed would have been the most mutilated victims (thanks to advances in medicine and war) of any armed conflict to that point in time. Already a confirmed atheist, this would hardly have contributed to finding religion. Just like the Army, both before and after his duty, he had essentially allowed others to direct his life, from his dysfunctional family, to his later eventual brother-in-law, Joseph M. Schenck. Though this family "boss" essentially allowed Keaton to do his comedy with little interference, Buster could have made more money on his own. Plus, Schenck probably helped orchestrate the comedian's loveless marriage, and was later responsible for what Keaton felt was the biggest mistake of his life—signing with MGM and losing his artistic control.

Moreover, during 1921–1922 two overlapping trials would have no doubt further contributed to Keaton's sense of absurdity in the world. As has already been documented, baseball and film were essentially on almost an even keel for Keaton. But then came the "Black Sox Scandal," when the Chicago White Sox threw the 1919 World Series. Through a series of additional questionable actions before and during the trial, the eight accused ballplayers, including "Shoeless" Joe Jackson (the Pete Rose of the 1920s), were acquitted. But Major League Baseball, afraid of how the public would respond, had already appointed "Judge" Kenesaw Mountain Landis as the First Commissioner of Baseball—with dictatorial powers. Landis promptly banned the eight players for life. For many, this was and continues to be, an overly harsh act, especially given the acquittals.

Then, when Keaton's best friend was involved in his scandal, the Motion Picture Producers and Distributors of America followed Major League Baseball's lead and hired Will Hays as its first president and censorship czar. And as previously noted, after Arbuckle's third trial acquittal of rape and murder charges—with the jury going out of its way to express what a miscarriage of justice had occurred, Arbuckle was also banned. Though later reinstated, his film career was ruined, which meant his life was over.

During this time Keaton threw himself into his work even more, while helping Arbuckle as best he could and ignoring the controlling family into which he had married, though taking time to satirize their reluctant dollar sign acceptance of him in *My Wife's Relations* (1922). Again, this was made during the baseball/Arbuckle period of lost innocence and compound absurdity. Plus, while it was hardly an era in which a public figure could be open about being an atheist, an existentialist given, it was all over his dark comedy films and his private life. For example, the Talmadges were strong Catholics, but Keaton had refused a church wedding.[26] Plus, there were occasional innuendo-laden Keaton cracks about religion in the *Los Angeles Times*, if one read between the lines. For example, his wife was always wanting a bigger house, so in a 1924 *Times* article titled "Buster to Build If He Can Find a Hill," the comedian sarcastically observed, "It's going to be a difficult task to get a hill top, however. Most of them are reserved for sunrise Easter services."[27]

The absurdity and death in Keaton's films, sometimes softened later by being just a dream, à la *The Frozen North* (1922), or other times being the real deal, as in *The General* or *College* (1927), occasionally feel like documentary evidence of the unknowable—is it a Keaton "quotation" of "I just don't care," or "It doesn't make any difference anyway"? One is reminded of this by yet another Robert E. Sherwood quote, but this arrives far from the world of Keaton and films. In versatile Sherwood's Pulitzer Prize-winning joint biography of President Franklin Delano Roosevelt and Harry L. Hopkins, the author describes a character as "having humor and gaiety arising out of deviation from the ordinary pattern of man, which is fear of death."[28] (Keep in mind, dark comedy is the bravest of all genres because it does *not* allow for any establishment crutches, such as religion, to soften the finality of death.) Plus, Keaton's comedy fearlessness, as with *Cops*' casual use of a terrorist bomb as a cigarette lighter, sometimes anticipates what George Carlin much later brought to "satirizing American blood lust."[29] (Keaton borrowed the bomb-lighting gag from George Herriman's equally absurdist period newspaper comic strip, *Krazy Kat*. See Chapter 5.) Sadly, however, Keaton was too far ahead of his time, and audiences were not always, as Robin Williams once chided spectators' difficulty following his warp-speed absurdity, able to "keep up!"

The Three Ages: Finally His Own Feature

Early in the chapter of Sherwood's book *Best Moving Pictures of 1922–1923* he announced it was time for Keaton to move into features. Yet, he was just one of many critics suggesting the upgrade. An early 1923 *Los Angeles Times* article praising Buster's three-reeler *Day Dreams* (1928) observed: "We knew Buster would have to make bigger comedies. His previous [two-reeler] efforts satisfied so much they didn't satisfy—if it can be put that way. 'Day Dreams' [three-reeler] is Buster's first enlargement of a kind of screen entertainment that never wears out its welcome."[30] By making the six-reel *Three Ages*, however, Keaton played it safe by essentially interconnecting three stories which could be broken down into separate two reelers if his first feature did not jell with audiences. It essentially plays upon D. W. Griffith's 1916 *Intolerance* as a model; the film examines bigotry through four eras: contemporary, Judean, a French tale of the 1572 St. Bartholomew's Day massacre, and a Babylonian story. Most period reviews did not mention Griffith's critically acclaimed picture, possibly because it had been shot seven years before, and as an early art house film was a commercial disappointment. In 1916 a message of charity had not played well at a time when acts of World War I (1914–1918) German atrocities, real and fabricated, would soon (1917) pull America into the conflict.

When *Intolerance* was mentioned, such as in the *Los Angeles Time* review of Keaton's picture, other films and/or filmmakers were often also noted, such as "Cecil De Mille's prehistorical cutbacks [early pictures]."[31] In fact, both De Mille and Griffith were high-profile filmmakers that year. First, though Keaton's movie would be released earlier, much attention throughout 1923 was focused upon De Mille's epic feature *The Ten Commandments*, which was broken into two parts: a prologue of the biblical Exodus story, and a contemporary tale of how two brothers interpret the Ten Commandments. Second, Griffith's controversial opus *Birth of a Nation* was re-issued with much fanfare on Broadway in March of 1923, a 12-real saga broken into two parts, covering both the Civil War and Re-construction, with a *Los Angeles Times* overview essay stating: "It has been a long time since this wonder production has been seen, and the offices of Mr. Griffith ... have had thousands of requests from all parts of the country for a revival showing ... and after months of re-editing, retitling and rearranging of scenes under the personal supervision of Mr. Griffith, it is now a better picture than when first released ... [and] started on the road to fame."[32] Of course, *Birth of a Nation* brings one full circle back to *Intolerance*, since it was made in direct response defense of the controversial and often violent retort to *Birth*.

Of course, if one addresses *Three Ages* as a parody of *Intolerance*, it is in terms of a historical format instead of subject matter, since Keaton's chronicle looks at love in various eras. *Three Ages* opens with an image of Father Time, and a book which provides a two-page Preface:

> If you let your mind wonder back through History you will find that the only thing that has not changed since the World began is—LOVE—Love is the unchanging axis upon which the World revolves.
> There is no better way to prove this than by comparing the love stories of three widely separate periods of Time.
> As appropriate examples we have selected the Stone Age, the Roman Age, and the Modern Age.

The film then cross-cuts through the three ages over a four-part criteria. First, Buster and a bully/brute each simultaneously fall for a pretty girl. Second, the two males each attempt a courtship, with things going badly for Buster. Third, this results in a challenge and/or a contest with Keaton's character again falling short. Fourth, through what will become something of a template miracle in most of the comedian's features, he will win. However, as these victories pile up, each becomes more comically questionable.

Recent research has also suggested that Griffith's short subject, *Man's Genesis* (1912), quite possibly influenced the Stone Age portion of *Three Ages*.[33] The former film also features a prehistoric battle between "Bruteforce" and a weaker caveman over the girl "Lilywhite." (The name also suggests Griffith's racism.) The underdog wins by discovering that his club has a donut-sized hole large enough to hold a rock, which a title states, in part, "[Is] the first weapon that could hurt others." Keaton makes a similar discovery in *Three Ages*, but it is dealt with only briefly. Victory for the more gadget-driven Keaton necessitates creating the first catapult. The comedian initially uses rocks but then literally catapults *himself* to a romantic triumph.

Man's Genesis is not the only unmentioned period picture which might have influenced *Three Ages*. In 1907 there was a two-reel version of *Ben Hur*, which probably impacted the Roman Age of Keaton's comedy—since the chariot race is central to both. One cannot underestimate either the impact of Lew Wallace's 1880 novel, whose full title is *Ben Hur: A Tale of the Christ*, nor a multitude of theatrical adaptations after its 1899 Broadway opening. With the novel being arguably the best-selling book of the 19th century, the play had that sort of impact during the first two decades of the 20th century. While the 1907 film focused on the chariot race, the major stage productions were most celebrated for the spectacle each one brought to the race—live running horses and real chariots moving on a treadmill, with a rotating backdrop, galloped at the audience. The Broadway production, with only a few brief breaks, essentially played from late 1899 to the spring of 1920!

Keaton found time for some *Three Ages* golf.

Moreover, traveling versions of the play, as well as a national tour that ran for twenty-one years, meant millions of Americans had been mesmerized by the epic chariot race. And if one had somehow managed to miss this *event*, the 1907 film *Ben Hur*, boiled down to the race, played upon thousands of vaudeville bills across the country. Any American, especially a vaudeville act as a popular as "The Three Keatons," would have had a hard time missing the national hoopla centered around the pop culture phenomenon. Thus, it would have been a natural for the parody-oriented Keaton to use such a broad target.

Lastly, there is a final short subject which had a definite impact upon *Three Ages*, Winsor McCay's 1914 animation, *Gertie the Dinosaur* (1914). This favorite of Keaton's had also played in the vaudeville houses of the day. Keaton wanted a big entrance in his film, so he arrives in his first feature on the back of a Max Fleischer stop-motion animated dinosaur. After all, he had to top the earlier elephant-riding appearance of his nemesis through the ages (future Oscar winner Wallace Beery, for Best Actor in *The Champ*, 1931).

Modern historians and critics tend to not give *Three Ages* a lot of ink. And granted, it is the weakest of the Keaton-controlled features, though it did well enough not to be chopped into three short subjects. Thus, it has the clever gag-laden feel of the two reelers but without any of the surrealism and/or dark comedy which Buster often added to elevate a short film into the pantheon status of a *One Week* (1920), or *The Boat* (1921). Consequently, like a Lloyd picture, it has funny entertaining bits which are an end in themselves, nothing for the ages. For example, it is funny that Keaton's *Three Ages*' chariot has a license plate, or that a jumbled sign is suddenly translated to say "no parking"—but this is mind candy, not mind-provoking, like his treadmill take on life in *Day Dreams*.

However, often a positive comes from a pedestrian work by an evolving genius. One can more easily watch the wheels go by, and see how small pieces of action will later be embellished into either more inventive gags, or incorporated into a more creative whole. For example, at one point in *Three Ages* he briefly learns some basic courting lessons from watching Beery woo the girl. This will be brilliantly expanded upon and essentially reinvented the following year in *Sherlock, Jr.* (1924), when Keaton takes his romantic cues from watching the screen lover in his film within a film.

On another occasion, during a Stone Age scene, a rock is thrown at him and he uses his club like a baseball bat and slugs it right back at his rival—a funny one note joke. In contrast, the best sequence in 1928's *The Cameraman* is a prolonged visit to an empty Yankee Stadium in which the comedian dazzlingly put on a workshop of all possible baseball nuances. This includes every appreciable peculiarity known to a pitcher with men on base, to an equal number of quirks facing the hardest task in sports—being a hitter (see Chapter 11).

Still another precursor to a Keaton classic occurs in the Roman story, in which Buster finds himself in a dungeon with a lion. Via a title the comedian amusingly remembers a mythic survival involving removing a thorn from a lion's paw. Unfortunately, Buster's lion is in fine shape. However, his nails could use some polishing, and soon Keaton is acting the part of salon owner, just as he played shoe salesman to a horse in *The Blacksmith* (1923). Both such actions anticipate his feature-length love for a cow in *Go West* (1925).

It turns out that while *Three Ages* is a rickety feature, it is a wholly neglected compendium for the inspired shape of things to come. Even the underrated *College* (1927) owes a major narrative note to the film. In the later picture Buster has been a failure at every university sport he tries. Yet, when his girl is in trouble, the big finish finds him suddenly mastering all his past able-bodied defeats, including the coup de grace close to these athletic achievements—a pole-vaulting rescue into her second story sorority houseroom. (This was long considered the only time Keaton needed a stunt double—USC's Lee Barnes, who won the gold medal in the event at the 1924 Paris Olympics.) While it is a masterful conclusion to a drawn-out routine in *College*, this is just a random gag in *Three Ages*, in which Keaton's use of a Roman spear is reminiscent of a vaulting pole.

Three Ages does, however, have one pivotal signature scene which represents an exceptional summation of a key difference between Buster and Harold Lloyd. Keaton is back to receive a football kick in the film's Modern Age, not unlike a similar sequence in Lloyd's later *The Freshman* (1925). Naturally, given Harold's persona, he will catch the ball and score the most unlikely of winning touchdowns. In contrast, after Keaton receives the pigskin, he sees a wall of hurt heading his way and flips the ball to another running back, who is immediately creamed. Lloyd's success represents the oversold American dream; Keaton is selling self-protection reality. Twenty-odd years later, writer/director Preston Sturgis will satirically use *The Freshman* football finale to open Lloyd-starring *The Sin of Harold Diddlebock* (1947), and second Keaton's message.

Recent critiquing of *Three Ages* generally give short shrift to the fact that Keaton was stuck with a rank amateur for a leading lady (Margaret Leahy), if it is mentioned at all. Keaton producer Schenck had hatched a PR plan that the winner of a British beauty pageant would receive a prominent part in his wife's (Norma Talmadge) next picture. Sadly, after Leahy had been hyped as England's greatest beauty, it was discovered she was theatrically challenged. Fearing a lawsuit if Leahy did not appear in something, Schenck and Talmadge foisted her off on brother-in-law Buster's *Three Ages*.

Keaton was not happy about the situation, especially since his other sister-in-law (Constance Talmadge) would have been perfect parody fodder for the picture, since she had played the "mountain girl" in the Babylonian episode of *Intolerance*! Yet, the comedian owed Joe a favor for giving him his first feature. Plus, in Schenck's defense, Buster had always said comedy heroines needed little talent. He was wrong, at least in Leahy's case, because she needed retake after retake. Plus, Keaton had never required so many sneak previews—to double-check the effectiveness of all the reshot scenes.

If the rare modern analysis of the movie even mentions the Leahy factor (in her first and last movie), no one seems to have noted the industry kidding Keaton and company received. For example, while the *New York Tribune* liked the comedian's work, critic Harriette Underhill had more time and fun shredding everything about Leahy: "Miss Leahy was chosen as England's most beautiful. When we saw ... [her] we felt that there was a mistake some where, for she was only mildly pretty. And then when it was announced that, instead of playing Angie Lynch in 'Within the Law' [1923], as Miss Talmadge had planned, it was found that Miss Leahy had 'such a particular aptitude for comedy' that she would play opposite Buster Keaton in 'Three Ages.' It seems to us, after seeing the picture that Miss Leahy's aptitude for comedy just about equals her beauty."[34] Given that *Three Ages* was something of an experiment—three two-reelers as a feature—it was not as broadly reviewed as Keaton's other 1920s features. For example, the *New York Times* did not critique it, though contrary to popular belief, the publication often championed Buster's 1920s work. The reviews it did receive were often positive, but the contemporary sense that it was universally praised by period critics is false. For instance, the November issue of the high profile magazine *Photoplay* complained: "BUSTER KEATON testifies that love goes unchangingly on through the years.... There are some good moments but as a whole the picture is dull and stolid. Margaret Leahy, the Talmadges' English importation, is as wooden as a chubby little blonde girl can be. And Wallace Beery is wasted as the comedy villain. No chance for uproarious laughter!"[35]

If the extended reference to Beery is surprising, since one sees few comments about the actor's part today, the title of a June 1923 *Los Angeles Times* article puts the subject in perspective: "Public Demand Puts Beery Back in Villain Class."[36] Despite being universally praised as King Richard in the previous year's epic Douglas Fairbanks critical and commercial mega-hit *Robin Hood* (1922), "which proved conclusively that Beery could act any type of role," the public and producers preferred him as a villain.[37] (Ironically, opening shortly after *Three Ages*, Beery would again co-star with Fairbanks in the *Robin Hood* sequel *Richard the Lion-Hearted* [1923, now a lost film].)

So what was it about Beery's crooked characters which *Photoplay* felt had not been present in *Three Ages*? A 1924 *Picture-Play* magazine article entertainingly describes it, besides reminding one that Beery remains a neglected figure in contemporary literature about *Three Ages*: "It is the comedy of Beery's villainy that really triumphs. And the tricks by which he achieves the comedy ... the devilish twinkle that he gets in his eyes, the way that his fingers tap his cheeks when he contemplates some mischief, and occasionally, too, the manner in which he sticks his tongue in the corner of his mouth when he is evading punishments."[38] It is a solid assessment. As a child of the 1950s, I fell under his spell watching many of his early sound films on TV, such as 1934's *Treasure Island*, and his good yet simultaneously nefarious pirate Long John Silver.

Regardless, as stated earlier, the *Three Ages* reviews were generally good but unlike Harold *Mr. Consistency* Lloyd, or the on-high critiques of Chaplin's work, Keaton films usually met with some nit-picking. For example, the *Los Angeles Times* stated: "Buster has burst out in his first five-reeler, and he's a regular shooting star. Were it not that the real plot of his feature is so seedy he might make the other five-reel specialists look to their laurels, and at least force them to have said laurels preserved with some sort of tincture [elixir] so that they will last good and long."[39] *Moving Picture World* gave it high marks but closed its review with a summation which suggested the cultish-like status with which several of Keaton's future features would also be met: "The comedy is apart from the ordinary, has the virtue of not seeming effortful, and will cause special comment among a great number of fans."[40]

Not surprisingly, *LIFE*'s Sherwood also praised *Three Ages*. Yet, again, applauses were not without strings: "Although one has considerable difficulty in following the weird meandering of Buster's plot (if any), one has no trouble whatever in greeting his antics with a hearty laugh."[41] Yet, strangely enough, the close to his generally glowing review almost sounds like *anything* happy in troubled times is to be commended: "[Keaton] has helped to keep this much-molested human race in good humor, at a time when it has nothing but high taxes, banana shortages, wrong numbers and Signor Mussolini to think about."[42] (Ironically, with regard to Sherwood's quandary over Keaton's plot problems, the following year the comedian would hire the critic to write an original story for him ... and the gifted *LIFE* writer could not come up with a close for a story about Buster and a skyscraper![43]) More problematic was the all-important film industry insider publication *Harrison's Reports*: "It would possibly have been excellent in three reels. Scattered through the picture are some highly amusing situations but there is too much mediocre action intervening to keep the spectator keenly interested. And had a player more experienced than Margaret Leahy been entrusted with the leading feminine role, the picture would have been the gainer."[44]

One publication whose enthusiastic review was Lloyd-like in its absence of qualifiers was *Variety*: "'Three Ages' is a continuous laugh for nearly an hour ... and for amusement stands in a class by itself."[45] That being said, the critiques for this Keaton film, and for the majority of his other silent features, might best be likened to the later pocket review of kindred spirit Edward Albee's 1959 play "The Zoo Story," which opened on a Berlin double bill with Samuel Beckett's "Krapp's Last Tape." The distilled critique observed, "[The work is] consistently interesting and illuminating—odd and pithy."[46] Moreover, like Keaton's artistic perspective, whether conscious or intuitive, Albee also felt viewers "should be challenged to confront situations and ideas that lie outside their comfort zone."[47] (The Keaton–Albee connection is addressed further in Chapter 6, when the comedian's 1925 *Go West* screen alter ego's affection for a cow is compared with the playwright's 2002 Tony-winning work *The Goat, or Who Is Sylvia?*—in which an architect falls in love with a goat.)

Regardless, my most interesting period discovery about *Three Ages* involves a hitherto unknown tongue-in-cheek PR interview Keaton conducted with an unknown member of his staff for the *Los Angeles Times*. However, before addressing it, one must establish a context for Keaton interviews during the silent era—he often stayed in his "Great Stone Face" character, with only the occasional smile, and was often even taciturn about any subject, unless the question especially caught his interest. For example, at the time of *Three Ages*' 1923 release, critic Margaret Werner did an interview with him for *Movie Weekly*.[48] Though she would eventually crack the signature frozen face, Keaton's initial mood here and in most other sit-downs could be capsulized from a Werner excerpt: "'Mr. Keaton, tell us something of your career.' Had we asked him to do a nose dive from the window, the poor dear could not have looked more horrified. The blue eyes grew wide as a frightened child's and he looked so imploringly that we were tempted to say: 'There, there, sonny. Mamma won't spank.'"[49] Though part of Buster's public frozen face was just PR for staying in character, he did tend to be reserved, unless he was with buddies. Then, as his friend, the iconic and ephemerally sensual Louise Brooks, later said of Keaton, "Buster was always 'on.'"[50]

Even the comedian's mother-in-law, Margaret L. Talmadge, who, like her daughters, was usually less then kind to him, had to admit in her pretentious and self-serving 1924 family biography with the mile-long title, *The Talmadge Sisters: Norma, Constance, Natalie: An Intimate Story of the World's Most Famous Screen Family By Their Mother*: "[People] should see him with his young sons! Or, hear him tell an amusing story in his imitable way. I've seen him keep a whole roomful of [known] people entertained for hours, when he does original songs and dances to his own ukulele accompaniments, or juggles phonograph records, or imitates 'wild movie actors I have known.' But Buster never smiles to ingratiate himself with anyone. He looks straight at strangers out of his serious eyes in an almost disconcerting fashion."[51] Given this comic background in a friendly setting, New York Yankees fan Keaton must have also been on good terms with Babe Ruth. In 1921, after arguably the greatest baseball player in history had his career season as a hitter, even better than the 1927 season in which he hit 60 home runs, Ruth put together a lucrative vaudeville act. Among the many 1921 Western Union Telegrams he received before the tour, now safely stored in the Baseball Hall of Fame (Cooperstown, New York), is one from Keaton.

Most of the telegrams meet general expectations, and are from a broad range of people, from legendary Philadelphia Athletics manager Connie Mack writing: "Best wishes for your success/expect you to be as great a star in vaudeville as you are in baseball," to even Helen Keller sending: "Tremendous success/may you make a home run from the stage into every heart in America."[52] However, Buster's telegram kidded: "Don't let Duke [vaudeville backstage person] cross you/hope you are a bigger hit in vaudeville than you were in baseball."[53]

Now, as the old stand-up comic line goes, "I told you [all] that to tell you this." Having established that Keaton was always "on" in a secure setting, the comedian—working with an in-house staffer—provided the 1923 *Los Angeles Times* with a parody cave man interview during the production of *The Three Ages*. Entitled "Mr. Keaton Believes!," it addresses how the transmigration of souls was assisting his ability to feel comfortable acting in three ages of history:

> PRESS AGENT: Do you believe in the transmigration of souls?...
> KEATON: Certainly.... Who said I didn't? Look around here. Do you see that stone age cave for the "Three Ages"? Well, why does it give me great pleasure to see my bride, Lizzy Stonehatchet [because Ford's inexpensive Model-T was often called a "Tin Lizzy," the term "Lizzy" often found its way into period jokes], cooking an ichthyosaurus for my evening meal inside that [cave] reproduction of an H. G. Wells prehistoric interior? [The previous year Wells' bestseller, *A Short History of the World*, had been published.] I'll tell you. It's because in a former transmigration I was a missing link. Now, look over there. Don't let that Roman coliseum fall on you. [The Los Angeles Coliseum had just been completed, allowing Keaton some impressive "Roman" backdrops for little cost.] Why is it when I stand in the arena of your blood-stained gladiator's den, that I feel perfectly at home slaying lions, tigers and Roman emperors? Why? Because I once was a Roman gladiator. I have slew many a bull in my earlier history.... Again, I ask you, why is it, when I wander over to Norma Talmadge's "Ashes of Vengence" [1923] set that I can strut around.... Simply because in a former transmigration my hangout when off duty was in ... the Louvre. My favorite sport used to be spearing rivals on my rapier [saber]. When I got them lined up on a row with one thrust I used to get three and four on the same rapier—clean up to the hilt. Then [sic] was the days.[54]

Shirley "reincarnation" MacLaine could not have said it better, or more comically. Plus, as noted in the previous chapter, the "interview" played to the parody and mimicking skills with which the young Buster had so entertained his adult vaudeville co-stars over a decade before. Moreover, his ability to shish-kebab enemies three to four thick on his sword is an ideal example of Keaton's dark sense of humor. Indeed, his black humor-based joke about killing a soldier with a wayward saber in *The General* (see Chapter 8) was one reason period critics were troubled by the film now often called Keaton's most significant picture.

Before, however, moving on to what many saw in the 1920s as essentially Keaton's first feature—*Our Hospitality* (1923)—there is one more Babe Ruth-directed telegraph which merits noting. Earlier in the text much was made of Keaton's anguish over the mistreatment of mentor Fatty Arbuckle by the Hays Office—which was modeled after the censoring template established by the Black Sox scandal. Baseball had given dictatorial powers to Judge Landis. Though Hollywood's diamond duplication of such questionable condemnation was clear hypocrisy for all to see, especially for someone like Keaton, who lived and died both pastimes, one of the telegrams superbly made a direct connection between the sport and show business. The Chicago White Sox team which remained after Landis had banished the eight players who had allegedly thrown the 1919 World Series had sent the following telegram to the new vaudeville star, Babe Ruth: "Glad to hear of success in present profession and may your blows sting as on ball field/Chicago fans interested to see you be at your best and hope Judge Landis does not strike you out/Best wishes and many happy returns of the day."[55] A final addendum to *Three Ages* concerns two different period milestones attributed to the picture. First, according to a 1923 *Los Angeles Times* piece, Keaton was seen as pioneering in taking personality comedy into historic costume-land, with a second *Times* articles underlining that the clown genre had "held off a little bit longer than anyone else."[56] Second, yet another 1923 *Times* essay stated: "'Keaton is the most popular comedian in the American Navy,' says Lieut. J. H. Seifert, who is in charge of all the film programs shown on board Uncle Sam's men-o'-war.... Seifert added that perhaps Buster's war record had some influence with the gobs [sailors], who take a keen personal interest in the lives ... of their favorite stars and comedians. "Keaton's 'Three Ages' is now [successfully] being shown on the [Navy's] ships."[57] It bears noting that while

Keaton upon his return from World War I.

Chaplin's groundbreaking war comedy *Shoulder Arms* (1918) had been a great critical and commercial success, prior to its release he had received letters with chicken feathers enclosed—given that he never served in the armed forces.[58] (Yet, he was undoubtedly more valuable to the World War I effort in his bond tours, which raised, in today's figures, well over a billion dollars.)

Our Hospitality

For all the *Three Ages'* positives, the 1920s essentially saw Keaton's feature film career beginning with *Our Hospitality*. And as previously noted, while clown comedy is more character-driven than plot-driven, *Hospitality* was obviously not three cobbled-together short subjects, however funny some sequences were. Moreover, Keaton had made a gargantuan artistic leap from *Three Ages*. This first film in his Southern trilogy has several parallels with his next installment of the series—the *now* much acclaimed *General*. Both inventingly use Keaton's favorite prop (a steam engine), are laced with dark comedy, and utilize serious subjects to anchor their parody. However, the burlesque of the former picture was both broader and more accessible to a 1920s audience, managing to not slip into the often-oblivious-to-many world of reaffirmation parody ... the phenomenon that so hurt the 1920s appreciation of *The General*.

Ironically, while the now seemingly almost flawless *Hospitality* was appreciated at the time (*Variety* calling it "probably the best thing Keaton has been identified with"), there was a great deal of 1923/1924 critical quibbling, too.[59] Its exclusive period sin was it ran long. For example, *Screenland* said, "'Hospitality' has one serious weakness. It is entirely too long, running over six reels. Yet, the opus has amazing humorous qualities in spots."[60] Even *the* 1920s film critic, *Life*'s Robert Sherwood, felt "there is plenty of it that is terrifically funny, and plenty that is exciting—but there is too much of everything."[61] Once again this was an era when the concept of saturation comedy was a negative.

Paradoxically, however, when one reads the reviews of this Hatfield–McCoy spoof, with Keaton renaming the feuding families of this Southern *Romeo and Juliet* tale Canfield and McKay, the greatest praise goes to an extended sequence which would be the most logical place for an editor to do some cutting. This involves New Yorker Willie McKay's (Keaton) extended 1831 train trip to the South, some twenty-one years after he was spirited out of this danger zone as a baby (played by Keaton's son Joseph in *Hospitality*).

Off to reclaim his inheritance and unaware of the hazards ahead, Keaton's long rail journey involves a mode of transportation one might imagine boarding in Willy Wonkaland. Yet, the fun factor here is that Keaton was doing everything possible to exactly recreate Britain George Stephenson's historically watershed 1829 "Stephenson Rocket." The hilariously diverting toy train-like engine from yesteryear included a tall smokestack chimney at the foot of a cylindrical boiler attached to train cars which were essentially stagecoach-like in appearance. A 1923 *Los Angeles Times* article amusingly celebrated historian Keaton from word one:

> [Paging Mr. Stephenson.] It was George Stephenson who electrified England 100 years ago by building the world's first railroad train. If the inventor could be induced to abandon his trumpet in St. Peter's jazz orchestra long enough to come back to earth and see what Buster Keaton had done he would blink in amazement.... Praise for the faithfulness of the reproduction was given by a distinguished countryman of Mr. Stephenson, the Rev. M. J. Haggerty ... who is in Los Angeles for a visit ... [and]

A Keaton lobby card for *Our Hospitality*.

saw Buster's train at his studio.... The original "Rocket" is still intact and is on exhibit on the station platform of Darlington [England], the chief town of Haggerty's diocese.⁶²

After affirming the meticulousness of Keaton's reproduction, the "Rocket"-enthusiastic reverend launched into a series of Stephenson stories. For example: "When Stephenson first applied for a permit to lay his rails he was summoned before Parliament [and asked,] 'Do you mean to say people could ride in that contraption without danger to their health? Would it not be injurious to travelers' hearts to travel through the air that way [at approximately thirty miles as hour]?'"⁶³ Though not without interest, the "Rocket"-zealous minister becomes rather long-winded with more stories. One notes this only to set up a little boy-like interruption by Keaton to tell what he knows about early trains, too. Since, as previously noted, Keaton could be rather taciturn in these sorts of situations, the filmmaker's charmingly shared comments engagingly reveal a single-minded eagerness not so different from his boy/man screen persona. Plus, the comments have been lost to time until now:

> I'll tell one now, said Buster. My scenario staff dug down into a lot of historic data about the first American railroad train ... [and] the conductor was called a "captain." The captain sat at the end of the train and communicated with the engineer by a string running forward into the engine and tied to a piece of wood. When the captain pulled the string the wood fell at the engineer's feet. The engineer, however, served a warning that he would not heed the signal. On the first run the captain pulled the string but the engineer kept right on. The captain crawled forward and ordered him to stop. "I'm running this train and I'm not going to take orders from anybody," said the engineer. They decided then to use their fists. The engineer stopped and they climbed down and went to it. The captain won. After that the engineer obeyed when he pulled the string. And that's why conductors and not engineers direct the starting and stopping of trains today, said Buster.⁶⁴

Keaton had considered an American train from that era, too. But besides Stephenson being considered the "father of the modern locomotive," his "Rocket" had a more comically entertaining appearance. An added plus to this equation was that the "Rocket" was reminiscent of Keaton's more surrealistic short subjects, despite being based in fact. With Jazz Age pundits thinking that longer comic films needed to be more realistic, versus the anything-goes nature of short subjects, there was an exquisite logic to *Hospitality*'s having it both ways. Indeed, there was a lessening of Keaton absurdity in his later features, especially *the* other train picture—*The General*. The latter Civil War era engine is also painstakingly accurate but just not funny.

Regardless, period critics could not get enough of *Hospitality*'s comic train trip to Kentucky. For example, the film industry-focused 1923 *Harrison's Reports* review was mesmerized by the subject. Besides the appearance of the "Rocket," there were:

> many scenes of the narrow-gauge [track] "Limited" ... showing it crawling to its destination so slowly that the hero's dog has no trouble in trotting along under it.... The sequence of scenes that picture the trip ... is the most delightful novelty seen in months. In one scene a mule is shown standing beside the track. Unable to cajole the beast away from danger, the engineer ... jumps out of his place, moves the track, and then the train goes on its way. In another scene part of the locomotive is shown entering a tunnel, and then backing out; it happens that a farmer is driving three cows through the tunnel and evidently has the right of way. There are many other [train] scenes equally amusing.[65]

Moving Picture World's 1923 critique added: "The introduction of a reproduction of one of the very first railroad trains, with a dinky little engine like the modern [toy] stationary engines and coaches that resemble old-fashioned horse-drawn carriages, is a decidedly novel idea and gives opportunities for many original and highly amusing comedy touches."[66] Putting the November 1923 *Hospitality* release in period parody context, *Picture-Play Magazine* observed: "Buster Keaton, like a true artist, [is] following closely the trend of the times in picture play productions. Now that the historic picture, such as 'The Covered Wagon' [the epic hit released in March 1923], with its famous train of prairie schooners ... [and] the reproduction of the [Robert] Fulton's [development of the first commercially successful steamboat, the] 'Clermont,' has come into vogue, Buster will show us ... [the historically accurate but comic 'Rocket']."[67]

Of course, while Keaton was riffing upon a 1920s circumstance, he was also simply utilizing a trait common to all nomadic 20th century film clowns and beyond—have fun with the means of transportation, too. It is not merely different locations providing new comic backdrops and characters for the focus funny person to exploit; the entertainment can begin with the conveyance. For example, Laurel & Hardy always had visual fun with Model-T Fords, especially the still drivable one compressed like an accordion in 1930's *Hog Wild*. And Steve Martin and John Candy so effectively employed the same phenomenon in a 1987 Laurel & Hardy-like teaming it inspired the film's title—*Planes, Trains & Automobiles*.

Though Keaton's interest in trains and historical accuracy was at the heart of *Hospitality*'s extended rail outing, another factor was undoubtedly at play, too. This is revealed, appropriately enough, in a 1926 article/interview during the production of *The General*. *Los Angeles Times* critic Alma Whitaker stated: "Buster does not consider all his pictures a success. He knows, for instance, exactly why 'The Three Ages' ... [was] less successful ... [there] was too much burlesque [of all the periods]."[68] Consequently, the factual freshness of "The Rocket" almost does not seem like spoofing so much as a mirthful time machine distraction back to the real focus of *Hospitality*'s parody—an infamous family feud. The fact that this goofy transport is also period appropriate is merely a bonus. Otherwise, the "Rocket" diversion is like those trick birthday candles which flicker on and off.

Another winning diversion for the popular film was the fact it featured three Keaton generations—the comedian, his father Joseph as the train engineer, and Buster's baby son, who briefly appeared in the film's prologue. Moreover, his leading lady was wife Natalie Talmadge. Indeed, one newspaper ad campaign played this up, including caricatures of all four, and billing Buster's father as "Daddy Joe Keaton."[69] Moreover, when possible, the comedian's brother-in-law boss, Joe Schenck, who represented the general family, had these print ads run next to ones for Constance Talmadge's *The Dangerous Maid* (1923), which was then also in general release. (For example, see the *New York Herald Tribune*'s movie section for December 11, 1923.[70])

Naturally, such an unusual cinema situation sometimes dominated period reviews. For instance, the *Los Angeles Times* critique opened thus: "Looks as if there's a lot of genius lying around loose in the Buster Keaton family, to judge from 'Our Hospitality,' the comedian's newest picture, which packed the house at Loew's State [theatre] yesterday. There are Papa Buster and Mamma Natalie and Baby Buster, [and] Grandpa Joseph Keaton. The fans loved it, and were particularly crazy about Baby Buster even if they did see only a glimpse of him."[71] This goes on and then comes back to more celebration of that "one wild wow in all its meanderings" of that "wildly funny" train ride.[72] Even poet and *Chicago Daily News* critic Carl Sandburg was taken with *Hospitality*'s family perspective in his early 1924 review: "Not often do we have a chance to see a Hollywood married couple performing in the same film ... this is a case where we see one of the Talmadge sisters yoked with her husband in a photoplay cast. Not only child and heir, Buster Keaton II, is also in the cast, playing a part designated as 'The Baby.' Also, there is [Grandfather] Joseph Keaton playing a railroad engineer.... [The comedian] and his family shall not suffer so long as they can put out pieces of this kind. We can see families going to see this picture and coming away saying, "what a family!"[73] This review, especially in its latter portion, also indirectly reminds one that *family* would be a major selling point for a film industry still recovering from multiple scandals, best symbolized by the Arbuckle case. Regardless, Sandburg much preferred this picture to *Three Ages*, in which he described "the star players, as some people will figure it, are the mammoth [ridden by Wallace Beery] and ... [Keaton's] dinosaur."[74]

Be that as it may, what about Keaton's *Hospitality* destination in this Kentucky version of Romeo and Juliet meet the battling Hatfield–McCoy feud? Well, the *New York Sun*'s review drops a pivotal observation, after also largely focusing on both the picture's family affair nature, and the train trip, which it labels "the funniest thing" in the film.[75] Regardless, the insight, which is largely just airlifted in and dropped, with no set-up, really demands already having seen the film: "[Keaton] does not, as do Chaplin and, in only slightly lesser degree, Lloyd, make a situation funny by merely being in it but given a funny situation he can make you shriek out unexpectedly."[76]

What the critic fails to first establish is that Keaton's true dark comedy cognition—the theatre of the absurd meat of the story—occurred only *after* his sweetheart has innocently invited him to her home. His surreal supper begins with the realization that death would follow departure, since twisted Southern "hospitality" negates killing guests ... even inadvertent victims of a senseless feud. Thus begins the cat and mouse game of not leaving this safety zone, because to just step outside means his personal Armageddon. What a brilliant premise for Keaton; since the 1920s demands of feature length films had added a degree of difficulty in sustaining his Kafkaesque parables. Ironically, *Our Hospitality*, essentially Keaton's first feature, remains one of his consummate dark comedies, and arguably a rare instance in which there was some degree of cognizance by period audiences.

Why was this Keaton's most 1920s acceptable, and accessible, presentation of dark comedy? First, by this time, the 19th century Hatfield and McCoy feud had been laughed at for so long that period audiences embraced its ridiculousness. Indeed, it had become so asinine, in part, because both before and during the feud the two families had occasionally even intermarried and/or changed loyalties. Like the cockamamie-looking "Rocket," this deadly discord was surrealism grounded in historical truth. Moreover, any time a noteworthy event and/or a genre has been around long enough, the final stage is a predisposition to parody. For instance, after the significant run of American Western films between the late 1930s and the early 1960s (a genre so often couched in violence and racism), it essentially succumbed to spoofs, such as *Cat Ballou* (1965) and *Blazing Saddles* (1974). Even pictures like Sergio Leane's 1960s "Spaghetti Westerns," or George Ray Hill's 1969 *Butch Cassidy and the Sundance Kid*, were a more sophisticated form of spoofing entitled "reaffirmation parody."[77]

A second reason Keaton's *Hospitality* could succeed so well with period audiences, without the comedian compromising core values of dark humor and absurdity, were the presence of some crucial components which differentiated it from his otherwise often bellwether-like *General* (see Chapter 8). For example, in *Hospitality*, Keaton's character neither kills anyone himself (as was the accidental case in the former film), nor are on-screen death scenes used for humor, à la *The General*. To illustrate, beyond Keaton's deadly wayward saber, *The General*'s coup de grace example was the collapsing railroad bridge, which sent the title character train into a river gorge. The most expensive sight gag in history up to that proved more shocking than funny to most viewers. Indeed, spectators who had gathered to see the actual shooting shrieked when a conductor appeared to go down with his engine. (It was merely a realistic dummy.)

The third reason fueling *Hospitality*'s popular period flirtation with what could be called "dark comedy lite," is implied in the *New York Times*' 1923 review.[78] That is, the fleeting movie murder opening prologue anchors the harmless dangers which will occur twenty years later. Just as Billy Wilder included a realistic gangland shooting near the start of the darkly comic *Some Like It Hot* (1959) to provide a catalyst for why two male musician witnesses would go "underground" by joining an all-girl band, *Hospitality*'s opening almost ephemeral murder of Keaton's screen father also imparts a minimal fear factor ambiance for Keaton's later comic concerns.[79] One is reminded of comedy theorist Neil Schmitz's observation that humor "transfers the effect of error [such as the feud], the result of wrong, and reformulates pain as pleasure."[80]

Ironically, the critical and commercial success of *Hospitality*—with its cornerstone in historical detail and framed by dark comedy—would set Keaton up for future failure in *The General*. While this is expanded upon later in the text, suffice it to say that the comedian's growing addiction to the increasing expense of factual authenticity (without the forgivingly obvious guaranteed laughter of historical humor—such as the goofy-looking "Rocket"), would eventually cut into his profits and artistic freedom. Moreover, this situation, with regard to *The General*, would further be exacerbated by his making dark comedy more explicit, without the distracting surrealism which seemed to innately radiate from *Hospitality*. The latter film's triumph could be capsulized in an earlier high water mark review line from *Moving Picture World*'s 1922 critique of Keaton's classic *Cops*: "His personality, a somber blue note in a bedlam of jazz, had seldom been capitalized to better advantage."[81] In contrast, his *General* "blue note" had not provided enough obvious organized chaos jazz for period audiences to appreciate.

Paradoxically, a 1923 *Los Angeles Times* piece had expounded upon how inexpensively Keaton normally worked. In a rail trip with his cameraman to get some pre-production location shots the comedian had turned in a bill of $7.84.[82] The article's description of the trip, which Keaton later described as a "great time," captures the simple pleasures of this film-focused comedian: "On the way up ... Buster played pinochle with his cameraman. When they tired of that the cameraman brought out a pocket chess board with stick-in pawns. Then they reminisced for a while, bought oranges from the train butcher [food vendor] and finally went to sleep on each other's shoulders."[83] The piece concluded with a further bit of irony, with regard to future expensive Keaton shoots. That is, his studio general manager Lou Anger had sarcastically said, "Save it, Buster, and show it to [Eric] von Stroheim and Mr. [Cecil B.] De Mille."[84] Both directions were already known for their expensive epics. Indeed, von Stroheim's extravagant shooting schedules would actually end his directing career prior to the coming of sound, though he would remain in demand as a actor until his 1957 death.

Of course, Keaton, the most athletic of daredevil comedians (a later hero to Jackie Chan[85]), added a thrill comedy waterfall rescue conclusion to the picture which was praised in conflicting ways by period reviewers. The *Los Angeles Times*' critic saw it as "a delicate kidding of [D. W.] Griffith in 'Way Down East'" (1920, with its melodramatic Niagara Falls close).[86] In contrast, the 1923 *New York World* saw it more as "taking a leaf from Harold Lloyd's [thrill-seeker] book."[87] Consequently, these two variations on the rescue (more inventive spoofing of Griffith, versus being entertainingly derivative of Lloyd) brings one full circle back to the opening critical quibbling about *Hospitality*'s length.

Interestingly, the immediate broad impact of *Our Hospitality* can, in part, be demonstrated by its popularity with Soviet poet and playwright Vladimir Mayakovsky (1893–1930), a leading figure in the surrealistic *Russian Futuristic* movement. With his first important poem titled "A Cloud in Trousers" (1915), one can see how he would enjoy Keaton's often absurdist pictures. This was underlined in 1926 when he was having difficulty getting some of his work adapted to film—his experimental writing was meeting censorship from a state now embracing Soviet socialist realism. In a script proposal that year to a Moscow studio, this celebrated author underlined the enchantment of Keaton's *Our Hospitality* train in his submission:

> FIRST QUESTION: Why do foreign films beat ours, both generally and in artistic quality?
> ANSWER: Because the foreign film finds and uses special means that derive from film technique, and cannot be found in any other medium of expression. (The train in *Our Hospitality*, the transformation of Chaplin into a chicken in *The Gold Rush*, [and] the lights of the moving train in [Chaplin's] *A Woman of Paris*.)[88]

Mayakovsky had already established his American silent comedy pantheon of two.

Regardless, there was no debate about the movie being both an often funny film, as well as an impressive gauge of Keaton's leap in creative growth since *Three Ages*. Engrossingly, the most appreciative praise for the picture came from *LIFE*'s theatre critic, Robert Benchley, who was fast becoming arguably America's favorite sophisticated print humorist. (In a few years he would double-down on this talent by also becoming an Oscar-winning film comedy star.[89]) In a 1925 review of a now forgettable stage production, Benchley added an aside about the impressiveness of the previous year's still internationally celebrated German film, *The Last Laugh* (1924). He then pivoted to also grant the two-year-old *Hospitality* equal praise: "We had much the same ominous feeling about written humor after seeing Buster Keaton in 'Our Hospitality.' If the [silent] movies can capture humor as it was captured in that picture, and, with no evident effort, express it as it was there expressed, then we old writing-boys had better pack up our leaden words and wooden phrases and learn a new trade. Following our experience at that picture, we secretly began learning glass-blowing, and are ready any day now to duck."[90]

In the spirit of Benchley's inspired praise of Keaton, as well as a chapter which closes with an extended reference to Soviet surrealist poet Mayakovsky, one is tempted to spoof the historical ballyhoo of the Soviet's "Kuleshov effect." Allegedly somber footage of the same actor was juxtaposed with shots of a plate of soup, a person in a coffin, and a child playing with a toy. When shown to an audience—and it was the same footage of the actor—the viewers claimed to have noted subtle nuances of performing for each scene. Ah, the power of editing … so called. However, they never tried it on Keaton. Then it would have been known as the "Kuleshov catastrophe"—because the "great stone face" would have given them "a whole lot of nothing" … surrealism indeed!

3

Sherlock, Jr. (April 4, 1924)
John Bunny and Fatty Arbuckle Factors

> Do not try to do two things at once and expect to do justice to both. This is the story of a boy who tried.
> —first subtitle of *Sherlock, Jr.*

Before exploring how the above axiom applied to Keaton's personal life, too, as well as some historical bombshells about this picture, one needs to address a few *Sherlock, Jr.* related carryovers from the previous *Our Hospitality* (1923) chapter. First, as with the aforementioned fact that the 1920s media never seemed to stop referencing Charlie Chaplin's *A Woman of Paris*, to a certain extent a somewhat similar phenomenon seemed to occur with *Our Hospitality* (both 1923). For example, the *Hospitality* praise with which *LIFE*'s Robert Benchley closed the previous chapter came from an extended aside in a 1925 *Theatre* review. Of course, this should come as no surprise, because as with fellow *LIFE* critic Robert E. Sherwood, Benchley believed that visual comedy should accent the cerebral (as exhibited by the thought-provoking Keaton), over the mere slapstick of Harold Lloyd.[1] Coupled with this was another trait Benchley shared with Keaton—a fondness for dark humor. For instance, one of Benchley's popular 1920s comic essays "Fascinating Crimes 1," later collected in the humorist's book *The Early Worm* (1927), observed: "[a certain doctor] was found ... hanging from the top of the flag-pole ... of the Masonic Lodge. The mystery was even more puzzling in that Dr. Meethas was not a Mason."[2]

Second, a now obscure film short subject, *The Iron Mule* (1925), might also have contributed to *Hospitality*'s ongoing period acknowledgment, with the two-reeler also having ties to *Sherlock, Jr.* Keaton had perpetually been attempting to help his former mentor and close friend Fatty Arbuckle since the 1922 sex/murder scandal which had ended the latter comedian's on-screen film career. Besides pledging a percentage of his salary to Arbuckle's future livelihood, Keaton was always brainstorming for ideas to keep him active. One such gesture was to give Arbuckle access to *Hospitality*'s zany-looking "Rocket" train after the feature's release. The goal was to provide Arbuckle with a surefire prop as a centerpiece for a short subject the portly comedian could direct.

The resulting *Iron Mule*, whose name also spoofs the title of John Ford's epic *Iron Horse* (1924, about building the transcontinental railroad), is an entertaining short which keys upon the zany journey south portion of *Hospitality*. Many of the same comic bits are effectively reused, such as the engineer cooking his dinner on a skillet in the train's boiler, while the wonderfully wacky appearance of the "Rocket" once again succeeds as a continuous gag. Plus, Arbuckle effectively uses a breathtaking mountainous backdrop every bit as spectacular as the original feature. Since the comedy is essentially all journey, with no set destination, *The Iron Mule* ends rather abruptly with an arbitrary comic Indian attack. However, while random conclusions are usually a short subject given, this one includes an uncredited but unmistakably superb cameo by Buster Keaton as one of the acrobatic Indians.

Third, what links these factors to *Sherlock, Jr.*, is that the forever thoughtful Keaton had hired the depressed Arbuckle to co-direct this picture. But multiple sources, starting with Keaton's memoirs, have documented how the gesture failed, via Arbuckle's attitude, and the arrangement ended within days.[3] Yet, there are several contradictions here, and the timeline for these statements do not match. Moreover, several hitherto before unnoted period articles would seem to offer a better big picture explanation on the film's ultimate story, Arbuckle's involvement, and a potential inspiration from America's first international screen comedian—John Bunny (1863–1915).

The story as it now exists has Keaton working as a film projectionist but obsessed with studying a book on *How to Be a Detective*. Thus, the comedian has immediately established his parody métier. After work he takes a modest box of candy to his girlfriend, but Buster has a romantic rival who steals her father's watch and pawns it—to buy a more impressive present for the girl. Worse yet, he plants the pawn ticket on Buster. When the wannabe detective attempts to solve the theft, the ticket is discovered in the comedian's pocket and he is forced from the girl's home in disgrace.

Though the parody focuses on the detective genre, most burlesques apply a scattergun effect to spoofing. Thus, Buster returns to his theatre job. The movie he is projecting also parodies melodrama and is the perfect catalyst for *Sherlock, Jr.*'s most celebrated sequence. However, let a quote from the *New York Sun*'s 1924 positive review set the scene: "When I tell you he is running a picture called 'Hearts and Pearls,' or 'The Lounge Lizard's Love,' you will not be surprised that he went to sleep. The dream is a most gorgeous concoction ... with lions chasing him and an automobile skidding along.... [Eventually] In his dream Mr. Keaton gets the film mixed up and he is the hero, a famous criminologist, who brings to justice the villain."[4] What the critic neglects to note is that Buster's dream double manages to enter the film within the film and create one of silent cinema's most memorable sequences. This then watershed film development of entering a movie, which will be further addressed shortly, was later celebrated by Woody Allen's 1985 *The Purple Rose of Cairo*—except in this case the process is reversed and a character (played by Jeff Daniels) steps out of a projected movie. Variations continue to occur, such as Lauren MacMullan's inventive Disney cartoon, *Get a Horse* (2013).

Regardless, Keaton is soon booted from said screen by the villain, only to have his dream double dive back into the picture and execute several tour de force sequences. For example, each time an edit occurs in *Sherlock, Jr.*'s internal film, Buster's unscripted interloper finds himself in a scene change which invariably places him in comic danger. For example, retreating from a lion's den, he is suddenly in a desert in which one of the comedian's beloved speeding trains threatens to make a substance resembling guacamole out of him. In another instance he finds himself on an island. But when Buster attempts to dive into the ocean, he piles into a *Nanook of the North* (1922) snowbank, with only his kicking legs visible, as if he is a bit of abstract Eskimo art blowing in the wind. And so it comically goes.

Up until this point the viewer has been watching Keaton's surrealistic dilemma in long shot, from the vantage point of a theatre audience watching the movie within the movie. Now Buster's imaginary screen takes over our screen and pulls us into the comedian's dream. And as so often occurs during sleep, the young projectionist's problems pour themselves into this alternate world as he ponders a problem. However, in this case, the setting is a mansion in which a necklace has just been stolen, and several characters from Buster's reality occupy this upscale world. The twist, however, is that the girl's father has sent for the world famous detective, Sherlock, Jr. (Keaton). And for the first time since *The Saphead* (1920, see Chapter 1), a stylishly dressed and more pointedly handsome Keaton is suddenly on display. Only this dapper dream double is no "saphead," and the movie is now under the comedian's auteur control. Moreover, it should be known that the filmmaker realized he looked strikingly debonair, and relished future cinematic opportunities to revisit this look ... though his mental acuteness often retreated to that of the "saphead" template.

With another parody thrust one is immediately aware that the butler is involved in the theft—a plot device hoary with age even then. Indeed, if this were a straight detective mystery, one would be justified in recycling *New Yorker* critic Anthony Lane's recent observation about another ancient paint-by-number thriller: "Does it matter that the plot is so full of holes that you could use it to drain spaghetti?"[5] Yet, this is what parody builds upon, having "creative criticism" fun with a genre under *affectionate* attack—revealing an out-of-fashion component.

Regardless, the villain and butler of *Sherlock, Jr.*'s film within a film quickly devise various ways in which to kill the now worldly Keaton. Naturally, this allows the comedian to tap into his gift for clever dark comedy gags. Thus, he will soon survive a pool game with a booby-trapped (exploding) billiard ball, endure the grizzled gambit of choosing a non-poisoned drink, and avoid a sabotaged seat which triggers a seemingly innocuous wall decoration (a medieval battle axe) to swing down and shish-kabob whoever plants his keister in said seat.

Besides surviving these dream dangers, Keaton will comically lead his adversaries on the most ingenious chase, which will also naturally include retrieving the necklace and his kidnapped girl. His most innovative trick involves recycling an old vaudeville routine the comedian would recreate on *The Ed Sullivan Show* three decades later. It involves leaving a flat hoop-like getaway box in an open window which, unbeknownst to the viewer, contains an elderly woman's skirt and bonnet. When cornered, young Sherlock dives through said window and container—with a brief cinematic cutaway of a wall so that the viewer can fully see and enjoy the reality of the seeming sorcery to come. Then presto! With a running jump through this special portal Buster is abruptly disguised as an old woman. It reminds one that Houdini was part of Buster's past, even if he did not nickname him.

Another wizardly-like sequence incorporates a second enchantingly real leap involving this Sherlock's version of a Watson. This aide is dressed as a woman street peddler holding her sales case open. She is standing against a wall obviously obscuring an opening with her body and fake upper torso and legs—which are unseen and held up horizontally behind her. Still being chased Buster leaps through her case lid and "tummy" for another escape. Finally, another brilliant bit has nonstop Buster on the handlebars of a speeding motorcycle, after his assistant, unbeknownst to Buster, has fallen off from the seat. Reshooting, after an exchange of clothing, Buster actually plays both parts. (A motorcycle sidecar variation of this misadventure was replicated in Howard Hawks' 1949 *I Was a Male War Bride*. And while not played for comedy in John Sturges' 1963 *The Great Escape*, the Keaton-like daredevil Steve McQueen briefly escapes motorcycle-riding Nazis on his own motorcycle, only to goose-up the excitement by reshooting parts of the sequence by having risk taking McQueen then playing some of the pursing Germans.[6])

Regardless, the highlighted *Sherlock, Jr.,* scenes are just the most inventive of a host of amazing Keaton "dream" routines, culminating in a close reminiscence of how his classic short subject *The Boat* (1921) concluded—the sinking of the wonderfully christened craft *Damfino*. Our projectionist wakes up attempting to swim and his girlfriend soon bursts into the booth begging forgiveness for believing he had stolen her father's watch. Ironically, while he slept she had actually been playing an amateur detective herself and proved his innocence.

Fittingly, however, the movies do finally come to Keaton's rescue. No longer the cultivated Sherlock, he does not know what to do when his loyally loving leading lady (Kathryn McGuire), a situation rare to his movies, expects her boyfriend to be romantic. As luck would have had it, however, the film then being projected within the movie has come to a love scene. Thus, with her back to the screen, Buster can take cues from the more experienced movie male. One is reminded of Peter Sellers' character in *Being There* (1979), when Shirley MacLaine expects loving awareness. He too is at a loss but is rescued by a similar situation—aping the action of a romantic male on a TV in the background. Of course, while Buster is not the cipher which best defines Sellers' *Being There* character, he is somewhat mystified when his censorship era movie screen actor's closing love scene dissolves from kisses to kids.

Be that as it may, if Keaton's films remain ever more timely by way of their *Waiting for Godot* absurdity, arguably the best representation of that is *Sherlock, Jr.* And this watershed picture is driven by Buster entering a film within a film, solving a mystery, and then returning to what Albert Cumus' existentialist *The Stranger* would call "the gentle indifference of the world."[7] The touchstone nature of *Sherlock, Jr.*, influencing today's greatest auteur, Woody Allen, and his aforementioned *Purple Rose of Cairo*, might best be measured by an Allen admission in a recent *Hollywood Reporter* interview.[8] He maintained that he could easily erase most of his nearly 50 movie filmography, save for a handful of pictures, starting with *Cairo*. As an addendum, the Camus quote about "gentle indifference" could also serve as an existentialistic couplet to the title of the *Reporter* interview: "No, Woody Allen Won't Read This Interview."

Without taking anything away from the film magic of Keaton's brilliant shtick during the movie within a movie, it is time to address the first of the historical bombshells referenced earlier. The first question to be asked might sound petty, but it leads to a provocative re-examination of *Sherlock, Jr.*—where did the idea for entering the screen come from? (And this bit of detective work on a detective movie goes much beyond the old adage—"Success has many fathers but failure is an orphan.")

After becoming part of "The Three Keatons," Buster was soon obsessed with Houdini's magic tricks, whenever the two acts shared the same vaudeville bill. Thus, as with so much about *Sherlock, Jr.*, the most basic answer to the question would point towards his stage work. Yet, this must be linked to his immediate fascination with film artifice when mentor Fatty Arbuckle gifted him with a camera. However, returning to the point, a *Los Angeles Times* article from April 25, 1924, vaguely states: "Buster Keaton has made 'a picture.' In 'Sherlock, Jr.' ... Buster shows filmdom something new. He has long had the idea for his latest comedy in the posterior part of his cranium. And now he has dragged it forth and has made a reality of it. Buster starts out as a projection-machine operator in a hick-town.... And then one night Buster floats off on the beam of his projector and jumps right in the Hollywood stuff himself."[9] Another 1924 *Los Angeles Times* essay from the following month further fleshes out the inspiration: "Buster got the idea of using the projector operator for a hero while attending premieres of his own pictures. He is a modest soul and when he goes out in public to see how his comedies are going over ... in small towns around Los Angeles, he invariably heads for the projectionist's booth and peeks out through the peephole at the screen. [Moreover,] Keaton has a projector in his own home and knows all the troubles which can beset an operator from personal experience."[10] Yet, in a 1958 interview Keaton gives considerable credit for his dream double entering the screen to a member of his technical staff—Elgin Lessley.[11]

All this is well and good but it somehow misses the legacy of the aforementioned pioneering film comedian John Bunny. The rotund 260-pound Bunny quickly became known around the globe during his 1910–1915 screen career. His 1915 *London Times* obituary stated: "[He] enjoyed remarkable popularity during the last four years, and it is said that the people of five continents have laughed at his face."[12] In fact, the previous year, London's *Saturday Review* observed: "Not to know Mr. Bunny argues oneself unknown.... Mr. Bunny is a universal friend, and the most famous man in the world."[13]

Though seldom credited for it today, Bunny helped elevate at the time what was still often considered a second-class medium to a level of artistic significance. For example, the March 1915 issue of *World's Work* equated him with the celebrated French stage actor/comedian Benoit Coquelin (1841–1909).[14] Bunny was cinema's first unofficial world ambassador. Years before the globetrotting Douglas Fairbanks and Mary Pickford, Bunny was received like royalty abroad. For instance, the August 1914 issue of *American Magazine* reported: "In Paris, Berlin, and St. Petersburg the cry, "There goes Bunny!" in as many respective languages, always greeted his appearances in public and was the tune that made of him a modern Pied Piper with a throng clamoring at his heels."[15] Bunny's status as international film star was accented further by shooting several popular movies in England and Ireland during a 1912 visit to Europe. In fact, his work was in such demand that he even made a film while on board a ship to the continent, *Bunny All At Sea* (1912).

Bunny's persona could be called a template for the later screen character of W. C. Fields, since both entertainers had a gift for playing the henpecked husband, such as the latter's extraordinary *It's a Gift* (1934) and *The Bank Dick* (1940, a film in which Fields' title character even claims to have known Bunny). A comparable Bunny marital dilemma would be a *Cure for Pokeritus* (1912), in which he attempts a secret boys' night out of smoking, drinking, and playing poker, only to run afoul of his domineeringly Olive Oyl–thin wife Flora Finch. Their groundbreaking team as cinema's first visually funny fat-skinny contrast came to be known as "Bunnyfinchers," establishing a screen tradition of physically mismatched comedy twosomes well over a decade before Laurel & Hardy.

Also, the popularity of Finch's controlling wife anticipated George McManus' revered period newspaper comic strip *Bringing Up Father*, which first appeared in 1913 and was later known as *Jiggs and Maggie*, with the latter figure often wielding a rolling pin. As a personal and professional link to Keaton, Bunny was also a huge baseball fan, a fact he sometimes incorporated into his movies, just as the younger comedian would. Thus, in Bunny's *Hearts and Diamonds* (1914), he featured several period stars, including the amazing New York Giants pitcher Christy Mathewson—"The Gentleman Hurler," posthumously elected into the Baseball Hall of Fame in 1936 as one of five inaugural members.

Having Bunny get away from Finch for a baseball game was a perfect scenario for his antiheroic screen relationship, and undoubtedly other such "Bunnyfinchers," that once existed. However, the comedian's filmography is incomplete, with many missing titles and movies. (Besides the passage of time, early nitrate films often were recycled to save on costs.) Regardless, Bunny enjoyed the adulation he received as a celebrity at the Giants' Polo Grounds. For

An early example of Keaton spoofing period "How to" books.

instance, period accounts noted that during a 1914 game against the Boston Braves "at which fully 20,000 people attended, where dozens of men famous in political, civic [and] literary affairs inspired but passing comments as they entered the grand stand, thousands of people rose and cheered when Bunny made his appearance."[16]

This Bunny mini-biography is belabored here for a reason, though he might now simply be considered fat, funny, and forgotten. The performer was a mega-star at the dawn of motion pictures, which means his short subjects would no doubt have appeared on vaudeville bills with the live action acts like "The Three Keatons." Yet, whether this happened or not, his meteoric career would have been impossible for young Buster to be unaware of. After all, poet Vachel Lindsay, the extraordinary trailblazing film theory author of 1915's *The Art of Moving Picture*, considered cinema's Bunny an exceptional founding father of funny.[17] Even Helen Keller was aware of the entertainer billed as "the man who makes more than the president!"[18]

So what if Keaton is cognizant of Bunny? How does that relate to *Sherlock, Jr.* It gets better. In 1914–1915 the older comedian, to capitalize on his immense popularity, put together an epic three-hour touring road show entitle *Bunny in Funnyland*. A cornerstone of the opus would seem to have been the inspiration for Keaton's much-honored entry into the screen-within-the-screen from *Sherlock, Jr.* Again, without taking anything away from the extended nuances Keaton later brought to the phenomenal sequence, as already demonstrated, credit for this comic revelation usually has rested upon the younger comedian. Of course, as Paul Murray Kendall notes in his 1965 *Art of the Biography*: "The biographer can only answer that biographical truth is not and can never be absolute truth.... What he engages to tell is the best truth he can find, to the best of his abilities."[19]

Bunny in Funnyland seems to provide the "best truth" possible. As the French would say, here is a *concourse de constances*—a confluence of circumstances. Moreover, *Funnyland* was a multimedia stage production at a time when Keaton still was appearing in vaudeville. It would have been most improbable for the young comedian, a real student of all stage acts, not to be aware of Bunny's touring three-hour epic—seemingly a precursor cross between the zany disjointed Olsen & Johnson's *Hellzapoppin* (1941) and television's *Rowan & Martin's Laugh—In* (1968–1973).

And as with these later productions, *Funnyland* was very commercial. For example, when Bunny's show made its first Indianapolis appearance in November 1914, an *Indianapolis Star* article later reported that it "played to the biggest three days' business of any similar attraction that has ever appeared [here, and] hundreds were turned away at every performance."[20] The original *Star* review stated: "The opening of the performance shows the famous comedian in moving pictures. These give way and the comedian himself steps out of the frame [screen] and then the fun begins."[21] The sketches which follow include a reproduction of Bunny's Vitagraph Studio, and presumably more movie/magic chicanery. Other period newspaper accounts, such as an October 1914 *Chicago Tribune* review, also praised Bunny's participation as an "actor, singer, dancer, raconteur, mimic and celebrity."[22] Following accounts of the tour, however, it is clear that while material often changed, a *Funnyland* centerpiece was Bunny opening and/or closing his extravaganza by appearing to do a film flimflam by entering or exiting a seemingly projected movie.

Keaton would seem to have borrowed this screen shenanigan from Bunny's stage career, and the younger comedian's description—in David Robinson's 1969 *Buster Keaton*—of how the *Sherlock, Jr.,* film-to-film hoax was conceived would have been a bit of comic trickery known to a theatrical veteran like Bunny: "We built ... a stage into that frame but lit it in such a way that it looked like a motion picture being projected on a screen ... the lighting effect gave us the [movie] illusion, so I could go out of a semi-darkness into that well-lit screen."[23]

Again, Keaton did so much more than Bunny with his screen shell game. Yet, history is made not only by major players but by those whom time seems to have forgotten. Moreover, if film scholars do not peer into shadowy corners, a sense of historical continuity is lost, and one puts art into an intellectual coma.

John Bunny: Fat, Funny, and Forgotten.

Plus another potential link between the crafty screen stratagem of *Funnyland* being known to Keaton involves the increased awareness of all things Bunny which should have come from his sister-in-law—silent film star Norma Talmadge. Her first modest contract part came in Bunny's 1911 *Neighboring Kingdom*. While the comedian's filmography is incomplete, the one compiled by silent film historian Sam Gill has Talmadge surfacing in at least two other Bunny pictures: *The Troublesome Stepdaughter* and *Lovesick Maidens of Cuddleton* (both 1912).[24] Moreover, Keaton's other sister-in-law, silent film star Constance Talmadge, was also under contract to Bunny's home studio (Vitagraph) at the beginning of her career, which paralleled the comedian's heyday.

In addition, the Talmadge sisters' mother's autobiography/family biography, which was published the same year (1924) that *Sherlock, Jr.* was released, implies a family friendship with the comedian.[25] This would hardly seem unusual, given the relatively modest size of the Brooklyn-based studio. And if this was the case, it was no doubt fueled by the more comedy-minded Constance. Her mother credited her with having "two favorites—Maurice Costello, the great film lover of those early days, and jolly old John Bunny, whose kindly face and comic antics captivated the hearts of thousands."[26] Another thing which no doubt would have endeared Constance to Bunny was that the talented youngster was an excellent mimic, and she enjoyed imitating Bunny's shrewish screen wife Flora Finch at the studio. What would have made this especially entertaining was Constance ironically riffing "Finch in the throes of ... tender passion."[27]

Are all these links a smoking gun, with regard to Bunny's possible influence on *the* scene in *Sherlock, Jr.*, or arguably Keaton's complete oeuvre? If nothing else, it at least merits an added reason to re-examine or at least just remember the faded film pioneer. One might draw an analogy from Chaplin and Fatty Arbuckle. Probably Charlie's most charming sketch in a career of charming sketches, is the "Oceana Roll" in *The Gold Rush* (1925), when those fork-driven fanciful dinner rolls suddenly become the delightful dancing feet of a foreshortened Tramp. Yet, Arbuckle had already done the routine in *The Rough House* (1918). Still, Chaplin essentially owns the sketch, because his version simply is inspired, topped off with pathos. Then again, Arbuckle deserves some recognition, both for historical continuity's sake, and sheer creativity.

Bunny largely has been forgotten, while Arbuckle now is remembered for a scandal in which he was innocent. History, like art, is where we constantly should attempt to get things right. Yet, as Pulitzer Prize-winning author Joseph Lelyveld suggests: "Reading History Backward, as we mostly do, we bring our knowledge of destinies and outcomes its actors could scarcely have imagined in the midst of all their striving."[28] Thus, to paraphrase the aforementioned Paul Murray Kendal, all one can strive to find is "the best truth possible." Be that as it may, reintroducing Arbuckle brings one to another of the chapter-opening promised *Sherlock, Jr.*, bombshells.

That is, when the thoughtfully loyal Keaton had attempted to assist the screen-banished Arbuckle by having him direct and/or co-direct (depending upon one's source) *Sherlock, Jr.*, it had not panned out: With that in mind, many sources have documented how Keaton gently eased Arbuckle out in mere days by orchestration his mentor's direction of Marion Davies' feature film *The Red Mill* (1927). However, one does not have to be a mathematician to see that the numbers do not add up. How could Keaton orchestrate such a volatile situation so quickly? And even if he had, the implication was that Fatty had just smoothly moved from directing one film to the other—yet *three years* separate the productions!

If Keaton had juggled any substitute production to Arbuckle, would it not have made more sense that he promised his friend he could use *Our Hospitality*'s cockeyed choo choo in a future two-reeler, which the chapter's opening chronicled as coming to pass with 1925's *Iron Mule*? By then the market for *Hospitality*, in those non-saturation booking days, would have had a chance to play itself out. Moreover, it would suggest that Arbuckle had worked on *Sherlock, Jr.*, longer than has previously been suggested. Yet, there is no question that some incident occurred during the production which resulted in Arbuckle's exit.

An essay by graphic designer and Keaton/Arbuckle aficionado David B. Pearson in film historian Andrew Horton's anthology, *Buster Keaton's Sherlock, Jr.* (1997), has offered three hypotheses on Arbuckle's involvement.[29] The first *short scenario* has been suggestively negated. The *second option* was put forward by Fatty's companion and future second wife, Doris Deane: her husband wrote and directed it all.[30] Though seldom given credence, Pearson is wise to keep this choice in play … but for a reason never before on the table. Yet, in order to better flesh this explanation out, the *third perspective* needs clarification.

The Arbuckle-Keaton production tradition was always to think in terms of a story's opening and closing; assuming the middle would take care of itself. Both physicality and dreamscape stories were Arbuckle staples, and Keaton inadvertently gives credence to the first in British film historian John Montgomery's 1954 study *Comedy Films: 1894–1954*: "while making *Sherlock, Jr.*, he [Keaton] had to ride a motorcycle while sitting on the handlebars. [During an accident, one of several on the production] He hit both cameras, knocking down *the director* [italics mine], and colliding with a car."[31] Since Arbuckle started out sharing a director credit with Keaton, though history now acknowledges only Buster's name in that category, is it not fair to assume Fatty's involvement on *Sherlock, Jr.*, was far move than a few days?

As a footnote to the last quote, one of the accidents during this production was arguably Keaton's worst during a lifetime of taking dangerous risks. At one point during the film he is seen running along the top of several freight cars—more beloved train stuff for the railroad-loving Keaton. The payoff joke involves the comedian jumping onto the overhead waterspout for the *steam*-driven engine, with the comedy theory approach of *anticipation*—a Keaton drenching—generating a big laugh. The ultimate funny sequence merits a mission accomplished. However, the comedian had miscalculated the force of the cascading water—which forced him to the tracks below with such force that he broke a vertebra in his back. Though true to his tolerance for pain, he was not aware of the seriousness of the accident until years later, when a doctor told him he had essentially broken his back. Still, though at times suffering through the proverbial blinding headaches, he kept working on the production. Coming full circle, even this injury might also merit consideration for, at least temporarily, needing a second director (à la Arbuckle), to help stay on schedule.

The second Arbuckle legacy passed on to Keaton, the aforementioned propensity for utilizing dreams in a narrative, has several important potential links to *Sherlock, Jr.* The closest likely connection to a Buster-Fatty collaboration, after the Arbuckle scandal, but prior to *Sherlock, Jr.*, occurred in the extreme dark comedy parody of William S. Hart— *The Frozen North* (1922, see Chapter 1). With Arbuckle's screen career ruined, Western star Hart had been one of the few faces of Hollywood (versus the studio money men) who had contributed to this travesty. Besides comic revenge directed at Hart, *The Frozen North* has other pertinent ties to Fatty and *Sherlock, Jr.* The dark comedy pièce de resistance of the earlier film has Keaton mistaking a woman kissing a man as his wife and shooting them both—only discovering later it was a dream he had *while at the movies*. The short subject is also reminiscent of Arbuckle's 1916 film *He Did and He Didn't*, when the oversized comedian also thinks his screen wife (Mabel Norman) is being unfaithful, only to eventually discover it had also been a dream.

However, to pull all these parts together, in order to make a stronger case for a major Arbuckle involvement in *Sherlock, Jr.*, would necessitate an attack within the picture on the puritanical public who pushed for the comedian's ban after the film industry eventually promoted his reinstatement. Most specifically, this meant the narrow-minded, small-town America so strikingly showcased in Sinclair Lewis's 1920s novels. However, I would posit that was the original thrust of an earlier version of *Sherlock, Jr.* What would seem to be irrefutable validation of this interpretation occurs in a January 28, 1924, article from the *Los Angeles Times*. Entitled "HICK-TOWN CENSORS—LOOK OUT!: Buster Keaton on War Path With New Comedy, Showing Gang at Work," it posited: "Hick-town moving-picture censorship boards had better look out! Buster Keaton is now making the funniest satire of their methods that ever came out of Hollywood. In "Sherlock, Junior" ... Buster shows the average small-town "board of cinematographic censorship" at work. Two short-haired women as well as a long-haired male reformer are on Buster's board. And, boy, what fights they stage! The [brutal 1923 World Heavy Weight Boxing Championship Jack] Dempsey—[Louis Angel] Firpo first round was nothing compared to the rows in which Buster's board of censorship engage. A perfectly harmless motion-picture is clipped, cut and sheared down until nothing is left of it except the tag reading 'Passed by the Hickville Board of Censorship.'"[32] This was *not* a sneak preview but rather a private screening for Producer Joseph M. Schenck and Lou Anger, the general manager of the Keaton studios.[33] The article carries

How far Arbuckle had fallen. He's seen here with Chaplin in *The Rounders* (1914).

neither a by-line, nor an explanation of how the press got hold of the story. But the account seems to have been immediately suppressed for two obvious reasons. First, satirizing small-town blue-noses would have no doubt been toxic to any box-office chances for the picture. Second, and even more importantly, closely linking the verboten Arbuckle to Keaton would threaten to ruin Buster's lucrative money-making future. Keaton's earlier attempts to publicly help his friend during the trials had been shot down by Schenck for the same reason.

The aforementioned Pearson's theory on what had precipitated the Arbuckle split from *Sherlock, Jr.*, after a longer involvement with the production, played upon the only possible clue Keaton had inadvertently given—his mentor would have been upset directing leading lady Kathryn McGuire in one particular scene. Pearson's proposal was that the film within the film, after her kidnapping finds: "The butler carries her off to a deserted shack and implies that he is going to rape her. If Roscoe Arbuckle, a man banned from Hollywood because he was falsely accused of rape/murder, had to direct this scene, it is easy to see how it could have caused him to crack. And I believe that is what happened."[34] Pearson is to be praised for contributing to the argument that Arbuckle was involved with *Sherlock, Jr.*, longer than Keaton was prepared to admit. Yet the historian's explanation as to what was the mainspring for Arbuckle suddenly being difficult with whom to work and needing to be phased out seems thin. After seemingly contributing a great deal to the story, giving greater validity to Doris Deane's case that Arbuckle was involved throughout the production, why would a single sequence, to which Fatty would no doubt have even contributed, so upset him as to make his involvement with the production no longer feasible?

While the nature of Arbuckle's full involvement with the production will no doubt remain yet another Hollywood mystery, or more broadly embellish the army of riddles which constitute life, please indulge another possibility. My proposition is that the "HICK-TOWN CENSORS—LOOK OUT!" movie was suppressed and destroyed and that was why Arbuckle lost it. Fatty's last chance for a measure of revenge, via his loyal friend's assistance, was crushed.

This conjecture gets a boost from the calendar, too. Keaton's loose time management formula for a year meant spending roughly two months a piece on two films, with several weeks of vacation between each, and always working around an October trip East to take in the World Series. Based upon the publication date of the "HICK TOWN" article, the implied first version of *Sherlock, Jr.* would have been in theatres sometime in February 1924. Yet, there is not word one about a newly described *Sherlock, Jr.*, until April—roughly matching Keaton's two-month time schedule. Plus, the often repeated stories of this picture having been his most difficult to edit could likely have been caused by attempting to salvage as much of the first shoot as possible.

Though the full story of *Sherlock, Jr.*'s production will probably remain something of an enigma, period reviews of the film can at least *correct* a contemporary misperception that the final film only received poor reviews. Indeed, even Marion Meade's much praised *Buster Keaton: Cut to the Chase*, went so far as to claim "most of the notices were not so good."[35] In fact, just the opposite is true. Other than the aberration of *Variety*'s dislike of *Sherlock, Jr.* "as unfunny as a hospital room," review after review said just the opposite.[36] For example, fully a dozen mainstream critiques were full of kudos. A healthy sampling should start with America's most prestigious and most frequently misrepresented as a non-sympathetic-to-Keaton publication—the *New York Times*. Moreover, the 1924 *Times* even zeroed in on the factor which is now more fully celebrated as the picture's groundbreaking sequence—when Keaton enters the screen within the screen: "you realize that something has happened—one of the best screen tricks ever incorporated in a comedy—and laughter starts, and for the balance of the picture you smile, snigger, chuckle, grin and guffaw.... This is an extremely good comedy which gives you plenty of amusement, so long as you permit Mr. Keaton to glide into his work with his usual deliberation."[37]

The *Los Angeles Times* also both celebrated the film and pinpointed its singular sequence: "The picture seems to be funnier than 'Our Hospitality' [which would hold an especially unique place among 1920s viewers.] Trick gags, of course, are the very backbone of a Keaton picture. The comedian hit upon an excellent one (and incidentally it determines the success of this picture) when he had the character of the projectionist step out of the booth and onto the screen.... The rapidity with which the scene changes as our hero stumbles over one obstacle after another is one of the funniest bits of business Keaton has ever offered."[38] The newspaper also used the *feature*'s relatively short length (45 minutes) to underline the period's belief that humor was not as effective when pushed past an hour. *Photoplay* said of *Sherlock, Jr.*, "Comedies are like oases in a celluloid world, rare and refreshing, and you don't want to miss Buster with his immobile face and unique composure in his new settings."[39] The magazine also seconded an abbreviated length as superior for comedy: "it is short, snappy and amusing."[40]

The *New York American* review raved: "'Sherlock, Jr. ... is this week's piecé de resistance ... [and] Buster has relied on no old-time gags or jokes to get across his detective comedy. He uses his own ideas with the result that there are no forced situations and the whole comedy is one continuous series of laughs."[41] Plus, while today's historians point towards his following feature, *The Navigator* (1924), as his first return to the elegant wardrobe of *The Saphead*, period critics immediately noted it in his detective's finery regalia. Indeed, the *New York American* caught another aspect of the attire missed by modern critics. While today the elegant clothing is merely treated as a handsome natural extension of Keaton in a well-to-do setting, in the 1920s it was special because of its comic contrast with his normal pork pie hat get-up. Thus, the *American* reviewer added: "Buster in evening clothes, with a silk hat, cane, and spats, is funnier to me than Buster with his eccentric clothes and trick hat. His high and mighty manner as the criminologist is enough to make a stone image laugh."[42] In fact, the *New York American* was so taken with *Sherlock, Jr.*, that a second critic did a combination critique/Keaton homage the day after the initial review that ultimately flirts with poetry in its praise:

> the rare clown Buster Keaton ... [is] in a humorous slapstick comedy, "Sherlock, Jr." The framework on which he is permitted to hang his wares is a dream movie—patterned in a vague way after the Kaufman-Connelly [1924 play] "Beggar on Horseback," and it offers the opportunity for any number of wild and extravagant stunts—such as ... a wild ride ... on the handlebars of a shaky and sputtering motorcycle ... done in more than the approved Sennett [and Arbuckle] manner. But it is Mr. Keaton—Mr. Keaton who sets fire to the picture.... Volumes could be written on Keaton's intriguing lack of expression ... which seems to say a great deal and say it with laughter. It is blankness raised to the dizzy heights of great comedy, a blankness that is completely a thing of the spirit.[43]

As an important footnote to the *Beggar on Horseback* reference in the previous quote, famed critic and period personality Alexander Woollcott provides a telling Keaton connection to the production in his 1924 Preface to the opus in book form: "[It] is a dream play, an honorable descendant of "Alice in Wonderland."[44] Woollcott might just as well have been speaking of *Sherlock, Jr.*

Time magazine's 1924 review of the film almost seems to be an extension of this *Beggar* preface: "the unexpected, fantastic dream situations lend themselves to some remarkable trick effects, including one of which Buster walks right out of an audience and into a picture on the screen."[45] *Harrison's Reports*, which addressed its review to 1920s theatre owners, observed: "Very good indeed; it is the broadest sort of farce ... under any circumstances it should prove enjoyable to all these who will see it."[46] *New York Herald Tribune* critic Harriette Underhill most enjoyed its thrill comedy characteristics: "His game of billiards [with one ball ready to explode on contact] and his threats to sit down in the [booby-trapped] death chair are as exciting as anything we ever saw. [And] the part of his dream where the scenery changes so quickly that he hasn't time to adjust himself is more than mildly amusing, too."[47] *Moving Picture World* said: "we never saw so many gags and such original ones as are unfolded in 'Sherlock, Jr.' It is an unusually cleverly constructed comedy film ... it is ... very amusing all the way through and will keep any audience in smiles and chuckles."[48] One could go on indefinitely with these superlative period *Sherlock, Jr.*, reviews. Yet the perfect close would be to note the observations of the decade's pivotal film critic, as well as the 1920s' most insightful Keaton interpreter, *LIFE*'s Robert E. Sherwood: "Like all Keaton comedies, 'Sherlock, Jr.,' is constructed with amazing ingenuity ... [Buster is] honesty and artistic integrity."[49]

Coming full circle back to Arbuckle and the shooting and/or multiple shootings of *Sherlock, Jr.*, and whatever reason removed Keaton's mentor from the picture, the two remained close friends. Indeed, Buster would be the best man the following year (1925) at

Though Buster's screen character struggled with film, filmmaker Keaton was one of the greats.

Fatty's marriage to second wife Doris Deane. And Arbuckle, thanks to industry ties with people like Buster, would periodically find directing work under the alias "William Goodrich," after his father's full name of *William Goodrich* Arbuckle. There is, however, a hyperbolic belief, sometimes attributed to the pun-loving Keaton, that Arbuckle did actually megaphone several pictures under the credit line of "Will B. Good."

Most of these "Goodrich" pictures were low-budget short subjects, like the aforementioned *Iron Mule* gift from Keaton. Also, Arbuckle's protégé no doubt had something to do with getting Arbuckle the directing job on the previously noted Davies' "A" feature *The Red Mill*, despite the mismatch of the 1927 date. Plus, Fatty also megaphoned another 1927 "A" feature with the popular Eddie "Banjo Eyes" Cantor, *Special Delivery* (co-starring future mega star William Powell). While the former picture was a hit, both movies were bathed in irony.

The Red Mill was lavishly produced by newspaper magnate/powerbroker William Randolph Hearst and even was celebrated for its title writing. Yet, Hearst's publications had done the lion's share of damning Arbuckle during the 1922 scandal trials. In fact, Hearst (the later title character inspiration for Orson Welles' still extraordinary *Citizen Kane*, 1941), would often brag that he had sold more newspapers throughout the Arbuckle case than during his pioneering "Yellow Journalism" goading of 1898's Spanish American War. Moreover, an added Hearst paradox was profiting from and fueling the Arbuckle travesty while living openly with his mistress Marion Davies on the West Coast, while his wife maintained their New York residence.

The irony is then doubled by Paramount hiring "William Goodrich" to direct future sound star Cantor because Arbuckle had been under contrast to that studio when the scandal hit. Indeed, Paramount had three unreleased Fatty features in the can—a workload that was actually the catalyst for the ill-fated party which Keaton had almost attended. After just one hung Arbuckle jury, it was Paramount, then Hollywood's most powerful studio, which decided to throw their star under the proverbial bus to safeguard Hollywood turnstiles. The studio was a leading force in setting up the censorship office which eventually ended the comedian's on-screen career. Paramount was so afraid of a public backlash that it was willing to eat the cost of those three Arbuckle features.

Making a further mockery of this situation is a 1926 *Photoplay* article which seems to be returning to the satirical edge of the piece noted earlier about an advance version of *Sherlock, Jr.*—"HICK-TOWN CENSORS—LOOK OUT!" Despite historical evidence that Arbuckle had been directing prior to 1926, the *Photoplay* essay states, with a backhand to small-town America: "Fatty Arbuckle is to have a chance to earn some money at last. Metro-Goldwyn has engaged him to direct a new picture…. However, the film company is playing it safe. Fatty's name will not appear on the credit list. For directorial purposes he has taken the name of William Goodrich. Thus, all those towns which are still barring Arbuckle pictures will have no kick coming against showing the works of Mr. Goodrich."[50] Blowing Arbuckle's cover here makes no sense … if he required one. Plus, it needs saying *one more time*, he had been working prior to this. The February 24, 1924, *Los Angeles Times* even announced he was co-directing *Sherlock, Jr.*[51]

Regardless, flash forward to 1932 and a major studio was willing to put Arbuckle back on the screen. Warner Brothers signed him to do six short subjects, with such strong comedic supporting players as Shemp Howard and Lionel Stander. The pictures proved popular enough to have him ink a 1933 contract for a feature. However, a comeback was not to be. He died of a heart attack that night at the age of 46. The significance of his return is iffy, since the new work is sometimes as primitive as his early days with Mack Sennett. He had been frozen in comedy amber for over a decade. Yet, just as his banishment was unfair, it is equally unfair to judge what he still might have done from such a small sample.

The only time Keaton's amazingly upbeat memoir, after all his travail, really flirts with sadness is the chapter on his friend and mentor. Keaton's heading for that section would later be recycled by David Yallop for his excellent coverage of Arbuckle and the trials that essentially began his slow death—*The Day the Laughter Stopped*.[52] While one is haunted by what Arbuckle's career might have been, a healthy portion of his enigma for the Keaton fan aches for a peek at their original version of *Sherlock, Jr.*

4

The Navigator (October 14, 1924)
Arguably Keaton's Greatest Film

"The real circle of life, Charlotte reminds us, is not so much a circle as a chain."[1]

—Author/teacher/*New York Times* critic Adam Gopnik, in writing about the E. B. White children's fable *Charlotte's Web* (1952)

This quote is an especially fitting opening for this chapter for three reasons. First, Buster Keaton's intuitive tendency to pepper his pictures with variations upon existialism's dark comedy treadmill has never been so pronounced as in *The Navigator*. As will be expanded upon shortly, the examples vary from a brilliantly choreographed extended run/race around and around the ship's promenade deck, to an out-of-control, spinning submarine close.

Second, *Charlotte's Web*, like so many children's (so-called) fables, is described by White scholar John Griffith as a work which, despite its bedtime story style, concerns alienation, the sense of not belonging, the feeling of oddness in a world where the patterns of normalcy do not seem perfectly relevant.[2] One could not coin a better pocket capsulation of Keaton's character. Griffith insightfully notes that while the one-time *New Yorker* regular White would never have placed himself among the high modernism of a "Lost Generation" Ernest Hemingway or an F. Scott Fitzgerald: "there is no avoiding the fact that White's writing, in its less ponderous way, shares in the [dark] moods and assumptions that colored "serious" literature in the years between the two world wars."[3]

Third, *The Navigator* is forever hailed as Keaton the auteur's first return to portraying the title role he played for hire in 1920's *The Saphead*—the handsomely attired but dimwitted aristocrat. Sadly, *The Navigator*'s opening title does not help that misperception: Rollo Treadway—Heir to the Treadway fortune—living proof that every family tree might have its sap. Buster Keaton." Both period critics and later Keaton biographers, such as pioneering Rudi Blesh, continued this perspective. Yet even his text later inadvertently describes Rollo and his poor little rich girl heroine (Kathryn McGuire), adrift on an empty ocean liner, as "two lost children"—a much better gauge of Keaton's *boy* persona.[4]

That is, one of the best takes on Keaton's only silent comedy rival, Charlie Chaplin's Tramp, really applies more to Keaton having a child persona, complete with even his dream/fantasy component—something most synonymous with youth. This credit goes to Budd Schulberg (1914–2009), Oscar-winning screenwriter of *On the Waterfront* (1954). In his exceptional yet neglected autobiographical novel *The Disenchanted* (1950), Schulberg has Manley Halliday, a character based upon F. Scott Fitzgerald, observe: "Know the secret of Charlie? Not a man at all. [He] sneaks up in [the] attic, puts on father's clothes ... anything he happens to find lying around then he pretends he's grown up. But it's all a dream."[5]

As the 1920s progressed, however, the Keaton persona as dimwit assumed a more negative perspective, with some critics complaining that it was unbelievable that he could move from cluck to clever. For example, in a 1927 *New York Times* article on the comedian's Civil War opus *The General* (see Chapter 8), a pundit complained that Keaton, "who has difficulty in crossing a road, is supposed to be crafty enough to outwit the Northern General."[6] This duality has even bothered some modern critics, though theorists like Robert Knopf have devised honorable but strained defenses. For instance, Knopf's justification for Keaton's sudden metamorphosis was merely a fan expectation of the comedian's screen alter ego, especially when it also involved his Douglas Fairbanks–like athleticism: "audiences [often] come to expect spectacular acrobatics from Keaton, the [conversion/clever] endings of the film's become almost a convention—extended sequences that draw attention to Keaton's extra fictional [unbelievable] reputation as physical comedian."[7]

While I applaud Knopf's provocatively edgy justification, it seems like verbal slapstick reminiscent of a cartoonish scene in Frank Tashlin's Martin & Lewis movie *Artists and Models* (1955).[8] Jerry is in need of a chiropractor, which results in the comedian's legs being twisted like so many pretzels. With that, the specialist comes full circle in what might be called "octopus therapy," by physically becoming intertwined with Jerry the human pretzel. In other words, Knopf's defense of Keaton involves too much metaphorical heavy lifting.

Keaton's persona is just that of a little boy, helped along by the name "Buster." Moreover, even in his Rollo roles he is not so much dumb but a spoiled rich kid who has had everything done for him. *However*, before addressing the thin *Navigator* narrative (essentially two pampered preteen-like figures on an ocean liner), one might note some pivotal examples of Buster the boy. My favorite is the brilliant aforementioned baseball sequence in *The Cameraman* (1928, expanded upon in Chapter 11), when he goes to Yankee Stadium to film possible highlights, only to discover the team is out of town. But finding himself alone in the "House That Ruth Built," one of the most storied fields in the history of all sports, is the kind of thing many little boys fantasize about. And one could change "many" to "most" in the Jazz Age, when few if any other person better symbolized that era of excessive fun more than Babe Ruth. Plus, the Yankees were Keaton's favorite team, and baseball his favorite sport.

Thus, going even beyond Keaton's little boy alter ego, when his *Cameraman* character takes the time to brilliantly pantomime every detail of being first a pitcher and then a hitter on that diamond, one can feel comfortable that every fiber of his being is delicately clinging to childhood like dust on a cobweb. Moreover, in that so much of Keaton's oeuvre is parody-driven, like a youngster, he is constantly playing at being someone else. Not surprisingly, he often takes this childhood make-believe into the dream world, as in *The Frozen North* (1922) and *Sherlock, Jr.* (1924). In the former short subject he catnaps into playing a cowboy so tough he entertainingly skewers the sentimentality of old school screen cowhand William S. Hart as only a child might (aided by Hart having maligned his best friend, Fatty Arbuckle).

Even better, *Sherlock, Jr.,* invites a double-dose of childhood parody. Boy/man Keaton wants to be a detective, and like a ten-year-old, he studies a "how to" book on the profession. But Buster is also spoofing this type of publication, which was then coming of age, including a series by Douglas Fairbanks (with Kenneth Davenport), with titles like *Laugh and Live* and *Making Life Worth While*.⁹ Often geared towards youngsters, like the Fairbanks books, and including pictures from his films, having Buster reading his "how to" book further underlines the persona of a boy. Regardless, like most youngsters he fails his assignment. However, thanks to his projection booth siesta, he spoofingly dreams of being the Junior to literature's greatest traditional detective—Sherlock Holmes. As chronicled earlier, he masters every nuance of the gumshoe genre, as well as including a healthy dose of Harry Houdini–like magic. No off-ramp behavior is capable of tricking him. Plus, both Keaton's cowboy and detective characters further validate his comedian-as-child persona by being products of the "Hollywood Dream Factory" era, during the film capital's golden age. That is, each of Keaton's cinema snoozes occurs in a neighborhood movie theatre—a special 1920s sanctuary for escapist youth. For example, future multiple Oscar-winning director/producer Robert Wise remembered a time paralleling the release of *Sherlock, Jr.* when his movie obsession got him in trouble at his small-town Indiana theatre: "when I was nine or ten…. I went that evening to the movies to see … [a Fairbanks picture]; I decided to stay through and see it again. I was half-way through it when I felt a heavy hand on my shoulder; my older brother had been sent to drag me home."[10] Fittingly, another hand has to grip Buster's shoulder to bring him out of one *Sherlock, Jr.* reverie—another "boy" so caught up in his movie dream demeanor that he fights it as if he is clutching a ghost.

The more detailed the examination of Keaton's filmography, the further one sees him locked into a childhood alter ego. Consequently, he usually seems asexual towards his obligatory childish heroines. The comedian often knows he is supposed to like this girl/woman, yet there is neither the stereotypical romance of a Harold Lloyd picture, nor the placement of them on a pedestal, à la Chaplin. Indeed, like a little boy, there is almost an indifference. And when he wins the girl in *College* (1927, see Chapter 9), and they are seen exiting a church, he quickly defuses a Harold Lloyd affectionate close. Instead, a series of negative dissolves has one questioning the very institution of marriage and life in general.

Moreover, similar to a lad, Keaton forever seems to be running (which is what little boys do), such as the previously mentioned multi-deck chase. Also, being "stone-faced" is another form of expression. The same movie also displays a typical litany of his little boy hijinks, such as endlessly taking risks, with no sense of their possible consequences, such as his swashbuckling Fairbanks-like *Navigator* high dive into the ocean. There is also his propensity to create elaborate Rube Goldberg toy-like gadgets—best exemplified on this ship called *The Navigator*, by redesigning a huge galley to serve just two people. Indeed, everything has the proclivity to be a toy … even a dangerous one. For instance, at one point in the film he becomes entangled in the rope of a miniature cannon (normally used on such a ship for a ceremonial firing/salute). But in this case he cannot become unentwined and nearly becomes a target. (The gag is reworked with a real-sized cannon for even bigger laughs in *The General*.)

Clothing also suggests Keaton as a childhood character, such as *The Navigator* bedtime sequence when much is made of the duo finding just the right attire—two cute sailor outfits—reminiscent of junior jammies. And when he is later frightened that night, he assumes a child's number one defense—Buster hides under the covers. And his pork pie hat, while not surfacing in *The Navigator*, is a child's, or young dandy's hat. In fact, it was originally conceived as a woman's hat. Thus, if one is used to seeing him wear schoolboy head gear, early *Navigator* scenes of a top hat-attired Buster make him seem all the more like a child playing daddy. Such a mindset can further snowball in various ways. At one point in the picture Buster must don an old-school deep water diving suit. Granted, there is a certain humorous component inherent to this outfit, rather like yesteryear's rendition of a spacesuit.[11] However, seeing Buster in this nautical gear conjures up images of Halloween and an elaborate little one's costume.

Be that as it may, an overview of *The Navigator*'s story begins with a child's catalyst. Getting up late in the morning, Rollo looks out the window and sees a just married couple who seem overjoyed; thus, he immediately decides this seems like an entertaining play activity for the day. With the choice made, he asks his helicopter parent-like man servant to make all the arrangements for a honeymoon in Hawaii. Of course, he has neglected the key ingredient in this plan—asking a prospective bride.

However, it seems that Keaton's character finds a young woman living in his tony Nob (slang for noble/nobility) Hill, San Francisco neighborhood (also known as Snob Hill) attractive. (As a footnote to this shooting location, given that there were already many big-ticket homes in Los Angeles, including Keaton's, San Francisco was the site of Fatty Arbuckle's career-destroying party. At that time, this city had a great deal of resentment towards nouveau riche Hollywood. Then, and now, there was a strong feeling among film historians that there would have been no Arbuckle scandal had the party occurred in the more protective confines of Hollywood. Consequently, one could argue that by locating wealthy Rollo in Knob Hill, and calling him a sap, Keaton was knocking the "snobs" that contributed to his best friend's tragedy.)

Regardless, the film's first inspired gag has chauffeured Rollo driven *all the way* across the street to propose. Moreover, the scenario anticipates Charlie Brown's idealized "Little Red-Haired Girl." Though she is never actually seen in the comic strip, timid "Chuck" periodically sees her beyond the strip's panels, and wishes they could somehow connect. Along the same lines, when Rollo proposes, Kathryn McGuire's Betsy O'Brien acts as if she too has, at best, only seen Buster's alter ego in the distance. Not surprisingly, she turns him down. And shy Rollo, just like Charlie Brown, takes defeat lying down, gives up and politely leaves. Then, like any good comedian, he indirectly references a previous solid laugh, and tops it. That is, a sad Buster tells his chauffeur, via a title card, that he will dissipate his disappointment with a "long walk," and simply plods home across the street.

The sudden randomness of Keaton's need to marry, coupled with his lack of social skills in preparing for a proposal, somewhat anticipates his *Seven Chances* (1925, see Chapter 5). Moreover, while there is no set *Navigator* limit placed upon when the ceremony occurs, à la *Seven Chances*, there are two other parallels with the film. First, the initial girl is who Rollo seemingly always wanted, and with whom he ultimately ends up. Second, in time it appears that the *Navigator* heroine, like his *Seven Chances* co-star, has always harbored some feelings toward her neighbor but was simply put off by Keaton's man/child haphazard lack of romance in popping the question.

That being said, a serious early sequence in *The Navigator* is also reminiscent of the somber opening to *Our Hospitality* (1923, see Chapter 2). While no murder occurs, a solemn series of events prepare one for the comedy to come, as well as possibly casting further aspersions upon San Francisco, since the events take place at the city's famous harbor. Regardless, no less than two sets of spies are present in order to keep their foreign rivals from stealing a certain ship and supplies from the dock. Betsy's father owns the unmanned *Navigator*, the ship on which Buster has mistakenly already bedded down on his bizarre solo honeymoon. Yet, this is also the vessel one group of foreign agents plans to set adrift in order that it does not fall into rival hands. Unfortunately for her father, he has left some private papers aboard, and goes back to retrieve them. At this point the spies abduct him and unmoor the boat to keep it out of the wrong hands. The dutiful daughter, however, has become concerned about her father. Unknown to the agents, she boards the supposedly empty vessel just as it has begun to drift away. Naturally, she is not cognizant of the goal for the ship to sink. This is how it comes to pass, that, once again to borrow a line from Charlie Brown's novelist dog Snoopy, "One dark and dreary night," Buster and Betsy find themselves at loose ends somewhere in the Pacific.

To take the title of a then future science fiction/fantasy television show on which Keaton would one day guest star, his *Navigator* character now finds himself in a kind of *Twilight Zone* (1959–1965) world. What could better hone in on *The Navigator*'s study in existentialism? That is, it is also a *Samuel Beckett Zone*. Is there a better modern man metaphor than being *adrift*, seemingly alone, and asleep no less, in a natural haunted house? This is emphasized by the fact that the most lonely, isolated locations are vacuous empty settings designed for people. Plus, Keaton's later use of long shots to visually log his increasingly manic movement around and around the vacant multiple level decks is like a frenzied rat in a treadmill existence. Plus, the lengthy distance from the camera reduces his size and significance. Arguably, this void of a vessel is Keaton's greatest prop metaphor for life. To recycle that popular 1920s phrase noted earlier, he is trapped in a "whole lot of nothing."

Nevertheless, the following morning Rollo will have several amusing near miss moments with Betsy's "girl Friday." His toss of a cigarette from a deck above is her first proof that she is not alone. Her discovery is also the basis for their inadvertent track meet around multiple decks. Still, it is not until she goes below and he accidently falls down one of the ship's large air vents—spectacularly crashing down beside her—that they finally meet. And anew, as if his complete set of socials skills is reduced to surprise arrivals and proposal, he asks again.

With the same consistency, she turns him down, yet leaves the door open by adding she is hungry and tired. Thus, to the galley they go. However, it is a challenge and a half, given their child-like nature and a food operation established to serve hundreds. In fact, this oversized galley accents a look of preteen size for the duo. Of course, this thought is further underscored by kiddie decisions, like Buster trying to open an immense can with an ax. He is no more successful than when W. C. Fields recycles the gag during a 1934 *It's a Gift* picnic. In addition, *Navigator* coffee cannot be improved by using salt water, though Buster adding huge amounts of sugar is childishly charming.

While their meal proves a failure, when the two return to the deck their luck seems to have changed. A ship is spotted in the distance, while Buster loses yet another hat to the wind—a variation of a gag he employed earlier. (This bit possibly influenced an ongoing comic loss of headgear at sea in a 1925 Charlie Chase short subject *His Wooden Wedding*, 1925. The film's director, future multiple Oscar-winning director/writer Leo McCarey, will return to this ship gag with Jack Oakie in 1930's *Let's Go Nature*. Yet, in both cases, script doctor McCarey further tweaks the fun by having the hat boomerang back to each comedian.[12])

Be all that as it may, Rollo and Betsy are frantic to get the attention of the nearby ship. So the couple decide to run up a flag. Again, playing to their child-like nature, Betsy wants to use a bright yellow one—which is accented in the film by being tinted in the otherwise black and white picture. Unfortunately, this is the international symbol for a ship being under quarantine. Thus, their potential rescuers flee.

This pushes Buster into a plan which results in the most surreal of images. Lowering a lifeboat attached to the ship, he attempts to row them to safety. Besides being naturally unsuccessful, his small craft begins to sink. In need of rescuing, Betsy practically drowns

4. The Navigator (October 14, 1924)

Rollo by hitting him with a life preserver. Ultimately, this results in the back and forth saving of each other, since she finds herself in the drink, too. The sequence is unique for two reasons. First, she faints at the base of a long sea ladder which has been put over the side of the ship. When Buster realizes he must now somehow carry her up this endless ladder, his eyes, both here, and in another sequence involving cannibals, have arguably never been so demonstrative—registering somewhere between extreme disgust and an almost Eddie Cantor banjo-eyed size. Second, trying to carry the comically comatose Betsy up the long ladder modestly reminds one of Buster's brilliant later drawn-out *Spite Marriage* (1929) sequence with Dorothy Sebastian, when he must tote the actress' drunkenly inert body back to their room and somehow put her to bed.

The couple's shipping shenanigans carry on for some time until the following title appears: "Weeks later—still drifting, we now find the crew with a safe and quiet place to sleep." Buster and Betsy have now adapted to their setting. For example, the galley has been modified to an elaborate Rube Goldberg series of gadgets which bizarrely take care of their every need. One is reminded of earlier Keaton short subjects such as *The Electric House* (1920), in which the complicatedly comic dwelling was the parody point of the whole movie. These elaborate contrivances no doubt had the same result on his public. Because well before the 1924 *Navigator* production had even started, a *Los Angeles Times* Keaton article reported on some of the gifts his second son had received from fans the previous Christmas: "Some of the baby buggies have mud guards and four-wheel brakes. Another had pneumatic [moved by air pressure] tires and built-in features including milk bottle receptacles, teething ring hooks, a floating rubber ball suspended from the ceiling."[13] In the same 1924 article Keaton deadpanned about why his public would have responded in such a manner: "It's all a mystery to me."[14]

Regardless, *The Navigator*, which poet and sometimes *Chicago Daily News* critic Carl Sandburg described in 1924 as "a series of vaudeville 'gags' strung on a thin line of a story that often breaks and gets lost but which hurts nothing or nobody," is mainly now comprised of cannibals and dazzling diving suit dilemmas.[15] With regard to the cannibals, this part of the tale involves a substantial-sized tribe of natives which emerge when Rollo and Betsy once again think they are saved, after spotting an island. The sizable tribe embellishes an irony attached to the picture. Here is a story about two loners lost at sea, yet the *Buford* (renamed *The Navigator* for the film), was really a floating studio. A May 1924 *Los Angeles Times* article stated of the 450-foot long (a length of one and a half football fields): "In addition to the crew of 110 men the "Buford" has room for 500 actors and artisans in the first-class section and 150 in steerage. It is estimated that when Buster sails there will be more than 1100 persons on board the ship."[16] The article's title said it all: "DEEP SEA COMEDY: Buster Keaton Collects Shipload For Next Film."[17]

Moreover, the *Buford/Navigator* numbers said nothing of the many visitors to the floating set, especially since the ship was mostly anchored off the coast of Catalina Island during the approximately ten-week shoot. Even then, the island, located 20-odd miles off the southwest coast of Los Angeles, was attracting tourists. The sea around Catalina, an island 22 miles long and eight miles across at its greatest width, was becoming Hollywood's favorite area in which to shoot maritime movies. (For example, portions of the later Oscar-winning Best Picture, *Mutiny on the Bounty*, 1935, were shot off Catalina.) Regardless, among the various visitors to Keaton's nautical shoot were his family, a visit best summarized by an October 1924 *Los Angeles Time* article title: "Keaton's Ship Was Lure for Whole Family": "All of Buster Keaton's relatives dropped in to see him.... Norma Talmadge and Joseph

M. Schenck were the first.... A few days later, Constance Talmadge arrived. Then came Buster's wife, Natalie Talmadge Keaton, with the two Keaton babies, Joe and Bob. Mrs. Keaton was accompanied by her mother, Mrs. Margaret Talmadge. Buster's father came over from the mainland by hydroplane."[18]

Regardless, with cannibals near, the *Navigator*'s anchor is thrown overboard and yet more danger occurs—an underwater rock formation causes a leak. When his playmate innocently asks, "Can't you fix it?" they happened to be almost sitting on an elaborate diving suit. What results is a wonderfully drawn out sequence in which he immediately but reluctantly realizes what this means and hopes against hope, with those expressive eyes, that Betsy will not. Her slow recognition that he could attempt a dangerous repair mission is brilliantly milked, with Buster displaying a more realistic trepidation than a Chaplin or Lloyd ... unenthusiastically realizing he must don the suit. Period critics found this the highlight of the movie, as do many contemporary viewers. An exceptionally positive *Los Angeles Times* review will chronicle this underwater adventure in detail:

> Down there Buster uses one swordfish as a weapon to fight a dual with another swordfish. It is all very scientific—thrusts, parries, and all, and we wonder how he managed it. That is, if we can stop to think for laughing. He puts up a sign down there—"Dangerous, Men at Work." When the job is done, while he's still at the bottom ... he fills a bucket with water and washes his hand:—and then empties the bucket! He uses a lobster which catches his leg to cut a wire, and he does other things equally funny. But there's an eerie minute full of thrills when he has a fight with an octopus down there in the shadowy sea depths. I'll bet Buster didn't have any make-believe in that look of seriousness he wore when he put on the diving suit and went down into the ocean.[19]

The critic was so taken with Keaton's character, his description was reminiscent of the random twists of fate to be found in the near-contemporary dark comedy short stories of Irish writer William Trevor (1928–2016). Trevor said of his tales: "Each character is somebody that I know very well—as myself. You become very interested in that person. You become immensely inquisitive and immensely curious. I'm sort of a predator, an invader of peo-

No doubt, Buster would have preferred his heroine go into the deep.

ple."²⁰ Keaton's Rollo further encouraged the "invader" quality of the 1924 *New York Sun* reviewer, who was equally fond of the underwater sequences. The critic's amusing description might also be that of a swashbuckling underwater Douglas Fairbanks: "A swordfish happens along and spears him in the rear. Buster captures it. Another one, a few sizes larger, swims up. Keaton holding his captive fish in his hand as though it were a foil, engages in a fencing dual with the new-comer. Original, don't you think?"²¹

Jazz Age reviewers were so impressed with these adrenaline-rush sequences they were even willing to forgive that it was "possible that the underwater scenes were made in a tank ... [because] they are fearfully thrilling."²² In contrast, today's viewers often only seem

Underwater, Buster's mood still has not changed.

impressed because Keaton *did* put himself at risk. Plus, it took shooting attempts at three different locations to get the footage. First, the water off Catalina was too murky. Next, the added weight to a combination tank/swimming pool destroyed the latter structure. Finally, mixing danger and frigid working conditions, Keaton and his cameraman were forced to lengthen the shoot by moving to the icy waters of Lake Tahoe, Nevada. Ironically, the one diving suit incident which might have killed Keaton occurred on land. The gag involved Rollo continuing to smoke when his helmet was attached. But Betsy accidentally latched it, and it was not immediately apparent that Keaton was suffocating. This was a blindside paradox, given the countless times the comedian had *knowingly* risked his life in this and other films.

Keaton's diving suit dilemmas are soon linked to the cannibal threat in one of the most brilliant uses of surrealism ever filmed—even surpassing dueling with a swordfish and metamorphosing a lobster into a wire cutter so nonchalantly one might assume it was standard gear for any underwater tool kit. The natives had come onboard while Rollo was underwater, severing his lifeline, and kidnapped Betsy to their island. However, just when it looks most dicey for the girl/woman, Buster manages to walk out of the surf in his seaweed adorned diving suit, like a cross between a soggy spaceman and the *Creature From the Black Lagoon* (1954). The cannibals freak out, not knowing whether to run for protection, or worship what might be some futuristic Neptune.

As a brief addendum to this seemingly otherworldly rescue, one must note that this scene is no doubt what inspired the Keaton-loving surrealist Salvador Dalí to wear a deep sea diving suit, just like Buster's at London's 1936 "International Exhibition of Surrealism." There have been past tangential references sometimes vaguely linking Keaton's film and Dalí's stunt—but it had to have been *this* beyond-bizarre exit from the sea which would have so inspired Dalí to also attempt a lecture in such a suit at the June conference. And accidently borrowing another page from Keaton, Dalí almost suffocated during his talk, with his diving helmet having to be pried off. Indeed, even Dalí's 1936 artwork seems to ape this film, such as his *Lobster Telephone* from that year—which was a box cradle and a lobster for a receiver. Of course, as a whimsical tongue-in-cheek observation from a student of the absurd, maybe lobsters open-for-comic-transformation tendencies make them a sub-textual existentialistic basic. For example, when Jean-Paul Sartre tried mescaline, he believed he was being followed by lobster-like beings. Regardless, *The Navigator* natives soon realize Buster is just a man in a weird wardrobe and again come after the couple. Yet, Keaton then doubles down on his back and Betsy hops on this unconventional dinghy and begins to row him towards their ship.

One should also pause to note that the chief is played by the African American film pioneer Noble Johnson (born Mark Noble, 1881–1978), who had founded the Lincoln Motion Picture Company (1916–1921), an all-black company which was a trailblazer in portraying African Americans as real individuals instead of demeaning stereotypes. He worked in mainstream films, like *The Navigator* and sometimes also played Latinos and Native Americans, to help fund the Lincoln Company. The studio had been founded the year after D. W. Griffith's groundbreaking yet racist 1915 epic, *The Birth of a Nation*, providing a Southern artist's warped perspective on the Civil War and Reconstruction. Griffith's picture had reinvigorated both the 19th century hate group the KKK (Ku Klux Klan), as well as the NAACP (National Association for the Advancement of Colored People), which was established in the 1909 centennial of Abraham Lincoln's birth.

Sadly, American films well past the silent era often depicted people of color in a degrading

4. The Navigator (October 14, 1924)

manner. Indeed, before the late 1920s advent of "talkies," these parts were often even played by whites in blackface. As a reflection of the times, most silent comedians, save the British-born Chaplin, used the occasional racial sight gag. For instance, in Keaton's *Seven Chances* (1925, see Chapter 5), the comedian' character is under the briefest of time constraints to marry someone in order to qualify for an inheritance. And at one point he approaches a possible partner from behind, only to discover she is black. Unfortunately, this was typical of the 1920s, and a conscientious critic/historian must factor in the norms of the era in which the work was made. However, while Keaton was seemingly no racist, he did seem to have a greater preponderance for this sort of material, including a blackface sequence in *College* (1927, see Chapter 9), in which the "gag" involved being discovered when some of his shoe polish rubbed off.

Regardless, on a more positive note, when Keaton's mystifying deep sea creature had first emerged from the waves, this Chaplin fan had seemingly borrowed a bit from his comedy contemporary's 1917 *Easy Street*. In the Tramp's atypical role as a policeman, he had finally bested the bully (Eric Campbell, his perennial Mutual film nemesis, 1916–1917) from the ironically named street. Thus, when Charlie asserts himself by strolling in the neighborhood with his signature east-west feet, there are still gang members lurking about. Thus, when individuals venture out from the buildings on the right-hand side of the street, Charlie does a sudden single pirouette, and scares them diving back inside. And again the process is repeated on the left side of the street.

Keaton's take on the routine is not as elaborate as Chaplin's but just as amusing. Immediately realizing both the danger Betsy and he are in, yet aware of having, at least briefly, taken the cannibals aback by his baffling unexpected appearance, he temporarily asserts some comic power. While not a pirouetting Chaplin, or what W. C. Fields liked to describe as a "Goddam ballet dancer," Keaton manages a series of quirky jerks, with the same amusing results as Chaplin's.

However, you can only fool a cannibal in search of supper so long and Rollo and Betsy are soon escaping via Keaton the improvised boat. The duo manage a last stand of sorts back at *The Navigator*, but soon the couple find themselves back in the water sinking. Both are physically spent. Not at all curious about how they will appear on some metaphorical menu, they spontaneously decide to drown like two good existentialists. Yet, no sooner do Rollo and Betsy disappear below the waves than they magically start to resurface.

Filmmaker Keaton has delivered a "deus ex machina"—essentially Greek for a god from a machine in the sky—rescue. This is an ancient theatrical exit device when a playwright had painted himself into a corner. However, in this case it was a salt-water savior from an underwater machine—a submarine has randomly saved them by surfacing. Since the brilliantly intuitive but barely schooled Keaton was probably not up on classic Greek literature, the catalyst for this sequence probably came from another Chaplin—Charlie's brother Sydney.

Though now greatly neglected, "the other" Chaplin was a popular gifted silent comedian and superior businessman, who largely helped orchestrate 1919's birth of United Artists, the company which brought together his brother, Douglas Fairbanks, Mary Pickford, and D. W. Griffith—the first time, to paraphrase period publications, "The inmates were running the asylum." That being said, a February 1924 *Los Angeles Times* article on Sydney, which appeared nearly a year before *The Navigator* opened, had critic Grace Kingsley writing: "If you are in a fortune-telling mood you might sit down with Syd Chaplin and try to figure out what the young genius is going to do next in his profession. Charlie's brother has so many offers that he is finding it hard to make up his mind as to his future. The recrudescence [renewal] of Syd's fame is brighter even than his original success."[23]

This increased awareness of Sydney dated from the 1910's when he did both solo work and often co-starred with his brother, such as appearing in Charlie's groundbreaking World War I darkly comic mega-hit, *Shoulder Arms* (1918). Ironically, Sydney had actually beaten his brother to a film about what was then paradoxically called "The Great War," though the United States had not yet been drawn into the conflict, 1915's *A Submarine Pirate*. This then rare comic use of a ship now often known as simply a sub, was a logical catalyst for Keaton's close to *The Navigator*. (Years later Jerry Lewis would mine Sydney's picture more thoroughly in 1952's *Sailor Beware*, particularly in drawing comedy from using the wrong end of the periscope.)

Regardless, shortly before the October 1924 New York premiere of *The Navigator*, the *Los Angeles Times* ran an article on the modern young independent film heroine, à la "the flapper." Not surprisingly, given Keaton's habit of casting more traditional secondary leading ladies, the comedian had strong views on this new fad: "The flappers are flapping ... the American public is tired of flappers flippety flipping around the screen. We need more old-fashioned American mamas in screen comedy. ["American mamas" is possibly a reference to Elmer Harris' popular earlier musical comedy play, *Poor Mama*.]"[24] The 1924 article closed by saying *The Navigator*'s comic heroine "Katharine McGuire ... is his ideal type of a screen actress."[25] Ironically, in next to no time after this article appeared but still before the Eastern opening of Keaton's nautical comedy, the comedian's studio was inundated with American mamas, flappers and every other category of womanhood. Plans were already underway for Keaton's next feature, the before-mentioned *Seven Chances*, in which the comedian's character is in desperate straits to find any bride as soon as possible. Thus, an ad had been placed in a local newspaper for women to appear at the studio in bridal regalia. Almost immediately the *Los Angeles Times* reported on a near riot: "Eleven hundred or more showed up at the studio gates in all kinds of white gowns, and carrying all sorts of flowers. The Hollywood police finally had to clear the streets around the studio but even at that traffic was tied up for more than an hour until Buster's casting staff had finally selected the women they needed."[26] Luckily for Keaton's safety from the mob gathering, and/or angry flappers masquerading as wannabe actresses, Buster was safely in New York for *The Navigator*'s October premiere. It was also nicely timed to enable him to take in his beloved World Series, which in 1924 also conveniently involved the New York Giants versus the Washington Senators.

The Navigator turned out to be Keaton's greatest 1920s commercial success, and in later years he would frequently go on record as listing this film and *The General* as his most significant features. Today, and for decades, the nod invariably has gone to the latter picture (please see Chapter 8). Yet, despite the now illustriously renowned tradition of *The General*, there are strong revisionist arguments to be made for bestowing this most eminent status on another Keaton film, particularly either *Sherlock, Jr.*, or *The Navigator*. This subject will be addressed further later in the text. It is only noted here to state that during the 1920s because of its great *commercial* success, *The Navigator* was often considered *the* Keaton picture. Though, as stated earlier, *Our Hospitality* (1923) was fondly referenced throughout the decade. Given the nature of the movie business, especially until film as art became a more accepted mainstream norm, beginning in the 1950s and 1960s, the initial disappointing box office returns of *Sherlock, Jr.*, and *The General* had largely kept them out of any "most important Keaton feature" discussions.

Consequently, since money was the measuring stick, and *The Navigator* is a legitimately exceptional film, modern Keaton studies have either assumed the film was also a runaway critical hit, or done shallow research on that point. For example, Marion Meade's *Buster Keaton: Cut to the Chase* states, "The picture received almost unanimous praise."[27] But a thorough examination of period reviews finds this was not the case. Besides setting the record straight, this is meant as no Keaton slight. Instead, as this text has consistently demonstrated, he was regularly the odd man out of the silent comedian pantheon status he shared with Chaplin and Harold Lloyd. Yes, he was generally recognized as a substantial funnyman but period critics seldom if ever uniformly praised his features, even with a signature Keaton classic like *The Navigator*.

In contrast, as this book has just as unchangingly chronicled, during the Jazz Age Lloyd could do no wrong, and Chaplin was in a stratosphere all his own. Indeed, the latter superlative merits referencing a 1924 *Los Angeles Times* article which appeared under the title "Chaplin Shows Art of Pictures Century Hence," months before *The Navigator* was released: "Charles Spencer Chaplin has murdered the chances of immortality for every film actor who will follow in his footsteps.... Lots of people can tell you what motion pictures will be like in a hundred years. Charles Chaplin can show you ... we have the actor who reached perfection without ever traveling along the road of imperfection."[28] Be that as it may, the praise for Chaplin and Lloyd was piled double-decker high for their pinnacle pictures. For instance, good luck in finding any remotely negative period commentary of Chaplin's *The Gold Rush* or Lloyd's *The Freshmen* (both 1925). Keaton's more cerebral touch, with its distinctively surrealistic nuances and a dark comedy unsoftened by the pathos which Chaplin brought to his streaks of black humor, made the "Great Stone Face" an acquired taste. No *Navigator* review better captured this dichotomy than *Time* magazine's opening comments: "Buster Keaton is like President Coolidge. You either like him or you do not. If you are one of the latter, you will stay away from the box-office polls. Otherwise, you will watch him on shipboard, attacked by cannibals, prodded by swordfish."[29]

Granted, the *New York Times* praised much of the picture: "'The Navigator' is an excellent panacea for melancholia or lethargy, as it is filled with ludicrous and intensely humorous situations.... While there is no denying the jocular and farcical action of this picture, there are stretches which should be cut, as some of the humor is just a bit overdone. Nevertheless, Mr. Keaton deserves untold credit for his originality."[30] Unfortunately, because of the easy accessibility of the prestigious *New York Times*, its singular status is what often passes for a summary of period critiques of a given film. Such an apparent approach also resulted in the sadly misleading film career overview of Keaton's special protégé, Red Skelton, in Arthur Marx's biography of the latter comedian.[31]

Regardless, a further exploration of *The Navigator* reviews represents the same back and forth tone previously suggested. For example, *Variety*, American's entertainment bible, opened its critique stating: "Keaton's latest and extended comedy is spotty. That is to say it's both commonplace and novel, with the latter achievement sufficient to make the picture a laugh getter ... while Keaton himself has done better work ... the gag bits will uphold the picture beyond a flop classification."[32] *New York Herald Tribune* critic Harriette Underhill's critique was somewhat more upbeat. But its opening was an expanded variation on the *Time* magazine perspective: "No critique of a Buster Keaton picture ever need be written. If you like Buster and his methods you like his pictures, otherwise not. To us he seems fairly amusing in everything he appears in.... Other critics will say it is not so good, and others will say that it is the best thing he ever made; but for us it contains just the same amount of merit."[33] Maybe the *Tribune*'s review subtitle capsulized the newspaper's almost neutral position most succinctly: "Buster Keaton Is Just Himself in 'The Navigator.'"[34]

A more diverting back and forth commenting on the merits of the film came from a mystified but comically honest *New York World* critic who unintentionally credited Keaton's attitude with a maybe surrealistic touch: "The fair thing to do is to say that Buster Keaton's new picture was not only a success with the crowd but that it was a landslide of merriment. And not once did I see him do a thing which seemed to be either imaginative, novel or truly witty. He is a comedian who does not care at all what I think of his slapstick [compare this with the ad nauseam periodic public polling of Harold Lloyd], and he is a wise young man. He is getting rich ignoring me."[35] Additional *Navigator* comic commentary, but of a sardonically positive note, came from the *Harrison's Reports*: "It should appeal to anyone who has any sense of humor whatever, no matter how latent it is."[36] And the *New York Sun* reviewer was equally jocular about the movie's positives—yet halfway through the critique was yet another without-warning jack-in-the-box qualifier: "If you like Keaton and his genius for maintaining a complete and fascinating lack of expression you will want to wrap up 'The Navigator' and take it home."[37]

Pocket reviews in publications like *Picture-Play Magazine* and *Photoplay* were brief but cheerleadingly perky, such as the former magazine's summary: "An uproarious farce, with Buster Keaton and Kathryn McGuire supplying most of the fun. It is all action and pure nonsense."[38] Of course, this was bracketed in the journal's "Second Choice" film category.[39] One might best close this back-and-forth horse race of reviews with two which elicited comparisons to Keaton's top competition—Chaplin and Lloyd. Fittingly, given the fluctuating nature of what has preceded it, the oscillation continued here, too. Syndicated columnist Louella O. Parsons, writing in the 1924 *New York American*, also includes a fascinating footnote to a stage routine by one of the country's greatest and most enduring clowns (Ed Wynn): "[Keaton's] adventures are numerous and hilarious. They include such things as ... inventions to make cooking easy that are as humorous as Ed Wynn's gags on how to eat a soft boiled egg without soiling one's wearing apparel.... It would be absurd to try to unfold the plot, because you must go to the Capital Theatre yourself to enjoy Mr. Keaton. 'The Navigator' is by far the best picture he has ever made—not only the best he has ever made but a comedy that puts him in a class with Charlie Chaplin."[40]

Paradoxically, a closing critical divergence from such lofty praise came from the cinema pundit this text has put forth as both the silent film era's premier critic, as well as the decade's most insightful Keaton interpreter—*LIFE*'s Robert E. Sherwood. Unlike the previous Parsons comment about it being "absurd to try to unfold the plot," Sherwood's complaint was that *The Navigator* does not have a plot: "Keaton has some gloriously comic material, and some that is just plain stupid. He has developed his points with amazing ingenuity but he has not been able to figure out the shortest distance between them."[41] Sherwood does have a point about the picture's rambling nature, especially since Keaton admits as much with his deus ex machina close. Yet, the very nature of personality comedy makes it, as previously cited, one of the few genres in which plot is not particularly important. Fans essentially come to enjoy a new variation of their favorite clown's standard comedy shtick. Sherwood went on to embellish his lack of a plot problem: "'The Navigator' [is] worthy of your attention—and you will have occasion to be devoutly grateful for the laughs that it affords. Still, I can't help wishing that Buster Keaton possess the architectural [narrative] skill of that shrewd craftsman, Harold Lloyd. Though Buster Keaton, in his own right, is twice as funny as Harold Lloyd."[42]

Yes, this is the same 1922 Robert E. Sherwood who previously was quoted for recognizing Keaton as being ahead of his time with intuitively recognizing comic absurdity: "[Keaton] can impress a weary world with the vitally important fact that life, after all, is a foolishly inconsequential affair."[43] (At best this would imply a rough cut life, with no promise of either a given straight path, or promises in general.) One could alibi, of course, that while Sherwood also anticipated that eve of nothingness upon which *Waiting for Godot* (1953) ends, as a future multiple Pulitzer Prize-winning playwright, maybe he wanted a more discernibly direct narrative to the abyss.

Of added interest to a plot, or the lack thereof, is that Keaton's memoir reveals he had hired Sherwood to write an original story for him in the summer of 1924, prior to the fall release of *The Navigator*.[44] Though Sherwood was not yet a playwright, Keaton had recognized the inherent humor and insight in the critic's reviews. One might yell conflict of interest—a reviewer mingling with filmmakers. Decades later the award-winning *New Yorker* critic Pauline Kael would receive condemnation for just that sort of thing. However, her recrimination was for a much greater involvement, versus this vacation blip on the radar during the infancy of film criticism.

Regardless, quite possibly Keaton just recognized that Sherwood simply understood the comedian's sense of the absurd. The attempted Sherwood story was not unlike *The Navigator*, in that Buster's character and the heroine are again trapped alone in an isolated setting. But this time finds them cut off atop an unfinished skyscraper during a winter walkout strike, with no one on the ground recognizing the ongoing desperation of their situation. According to Keaton, it was "the perfect situation" for his "indomitable little man facing what seem impossible odds."[45] Yet, Sherwood could not come up with an acceptable close for Keaton. Thus, it is possible that *The Navigator*'s sudden submarine rescue, given the recent almost-collaboration between the two, in which the frustrated critic could also have fallen back on a deus ex machina solution, contributed to pushing even Keaton's most knowledgeably loyal critic to quibble about arguably the comedian's greatest picture, notwithstanding *The General* (see Chapter 8).

Here again, though never more strikingly, it has been demonstrated that in his own time, Keaton was just too far ahead of many critics and/or audience members. Neither group, based upon a thorough examination of period literature, ever gave him a joint blanket endorsement. It is enough to yell that quintessential haunting line from Arthur Miller's 1949 *Death of a Salesman*—"Attention must be paid." Yet, even today as he is recognized by many as on a par with Chaplin, still not enough attention is being paid. This less than full endorsement of such a cerebral comedian might best be explained by a period poem which Keaton no doubt would have appreciated, especially since its sense of absurdity is set upon one of the comedian's beloved trains. Entitled "Limited," this 1916 Carl Sandburg public domain poem appeared on the eve of Keaton's entry into film, at a time when this equally cerebral poet was also not yet fully appreciated by the public:

LIMITED

I am riding on a limited express, one of the crack trains of the nation.
Hurtling across the prairie into blue haze and dark air
   go fifteen all-steel coaches holding a thousand people.
(All the coaches shall be scrap and rust and all the men and women
   laughing in the diners and sleepers shall pass to ashes.)
I ask a man in the smoker [car] where he is going and he answers: "Omaha."[46]

5

Seven Chances (April 22, 1925)

> If speech, as suggested by writer Shirley Hazzard, "can crucially suggest what is not said," a human face, especially one reduced to a frozen mask, à la Buster Keaton, is even more succinct with its message.[1]

A film adaption of the play *Seven Chances* was not something Buster Keaton wanted to make. Plus, it was not a film he should have had to do. The comedian was just coming off his most commercially successful picture, 1924's *The Navigator*. Moreover, though not receiving the universal superlative period reviews often suggested by modern film historians (see previous chapter), today one could legitimately create criticism heresy by suggesting it and/or *Sherlock, Jr.* (also 1924) as superior to *The General* (1927). With that being said, and even having a small studio with his name on it, Keaton was still under the thumb of his brother-in-law and independent producer, Joseph M. Schenck. While Keaton was largely left to his own artistic whims, Schenck periodically called in favors. *Seven Chances* was one such favor. Moreover, Schenck was assuming an ever more powerful position, after becoming United Artists' chairman of the board in 1924.

What had especially upset Keaton, however, was that the rights for this picture had been purchased without consulting him. Granted, Schenck could argue that since he was also producing pictures for Keaton's two movie star sisters-in-law, Schenck's then wife, Norma Talmadge, and Constance Talmadge, *Seven Chances* had been purchased merely as a possibility for one of the three. Yet, as will be shortly addressed, it is definitely a male-driven story—but more along the lines of a *Harold Lloyd* normal "Glasses Character."

There are also other reasons sometimes given for Keaton reluctantly doing the picture. Two examples: his loyalty to Schenck for so quickly giving Keaton his big film break, or covering expenses for the comedian's parents when Buster was in World War I. However, the most repeated tale is simply Keaton owed Schenck money. On face value that might seem strange, since Keaton was paid handsomely, received bonuses, and was given a raise after *The Navigator*. But because he was still essentially working for his brother-in-law, Keaton never saw the huge payouts pocketed by the solo Chaplin and Lloyd. Plus, unlike that duo, Keaton was a bad businessman, spent freely, and allowed his wife Natalie to all but burn her way through the comedian's cash. If she could not be a movie star like her sisters, she could shell it out as lavishly as they did. For example, an early 1926 *Los Angeles Times* article on Constance and Norma nicely sets the tone for Natalie to match their needs. Constance observes: "Although many of my new gowns and costumes were designed in New York, and some came direct from Paris, plenty of others were created right here in Hollywood ... Paris and New York recognize that Southern California women are as well dressed as any in the world.... The French capital, the American metropolis and Los Angeles are the three big style centers."² And clothes need a setting, so Buster's $30,000 plus surprise home for Natalie (worth well over $346,000 in today's dollars), was considered too modest. Eventually, his wife was unhappy until she had what the movie colony called the comedian's "Italian Villa"—which translates to nearly five million dollars today. In later years, one could paraphrase the various ways Keaton reluctantly referenced the Hollywood palace, "It took a lot of pratfalls to build that place." His 1922 short subject, *My Wife's Relations*, had never been so prophetic.

Along related lines, part of Keaton's gift was a curse. That is, he lived to create comedy—sublimating himself so much into his art that he often avoided and/or was passive in confrontational situations. It was a trait which only became worse as the decade progressed, culminating in 1928, when Schenck convinced Keaton to give up his own studio and work for what was becoming the Cadillac of film companies—MGM. The case for the change was that besides providing him with a much more lucrative salary, MGM could supply Keaton with the best and most of anything a filmmaker could want. However, buried in the fine print was a loss of control.

This situation begs another reference to master magician Harry Houdini. Earlier this text established that the master magician's allegedly early association with nicknaming baby

Though Keaton, flanked by Ray Barnes (left) and Snitz Edwards, is angry about marrying *anyone*, his expression better reflects his mood about making this film. (This is the first of three memorable teamings with Edwards.)

Keaton "Buster" was pure hyperbole. However, the "Three Keatons" would later get to know Houdini when they played on the same vaudeville bills. And young Buster was obsessed with watching and attempting to emulate Houdini tricks. Yet, one wonders, given Keaton's personal and professional vulnerabilities with people, if an early 1920s *Los Angeles Times* review of a Houdini appearance might also have tapped into a metaphorical attraction the comedian had for the magician: "Imagine ... a man so imbued with power as to be enabled to free himself or escape from any form of restraint ... a man capable of extricating himself from places and situations from which none other has ever been able to free himself."[3] The later surrealist photographer Rodney Smith (1947–2016), whose whimsical work was often compared to Keaton, addressed this topic of escaping into absurdity directly: "I wanted to get as far away from the world that I was familiar with."[4] Yet later, as if he was channeling the core of a Keaton picture, Smith wrote that underneath the quixotic joy of his photography "is a loneliness, a slow whiff of sadness and an everlasting melancholy."[5]

This is reminiscent of an observation by Keaton contemporary and champion of the avant-garde, painter/writer/filmmaker Jean Cocteau: "Whatever it is about you that disturbs people, cultivate that, because that is who you really are."[6] Keaton had an often disconcertingly passive nature in real life, starting with a controlling, aggressive father, later a managing brother-in-law, and marriage into the domineering Talmadge family. Nothing demonstrates this more than his "Great Stone Face," or movie endings from *Cops* to *College* which suggest "What's the point?" Yes, the "Stone Face" was his *movie* mask, but the "mask" behind it was increasingly similar as the 1920s progressed. To paraphrase an old Woody Allen bit, "In my family we didn't discuss things, we just grew tumors."

Be that as it may, as previously noted, the execution of Camus' title character in the appropriately named existentialistic primer *The Stranger* was more for lack of emotion than a crime. And like Vladimar and Estragon contemplating suicide near the close of *Waiting for Godot*, are not the dispatchers of "the stranger" doing him a favor, like the brutal police Keaton's character gives himself up to at the close of *Cops*? After all, the film's final image is Buster's grave. Moreover, it could be argued that he accidently yet unfeelingly killed one or more people when he casually threw a bomb into a police parade, after nonchalantly lighting his cigarette with its fuse.

Now before any Mr. or Ms. Front Porch readers accuse me of crediting Keaton, via a whiplash maneuver, of consciously creating a pre–Camus-like example of existentialism, with kamikaze enthusiasm, one needs to deconstruct the phenomenon. Buster, like many artists, was an intuitive master. This evokes an observation by art historian David Raskin on the work of sculptor/writer Donald Judd: "[He] wrote to figure out what he believed in."[7] That is to say, Keaton filmed to find funny, and answers were a sometime bonus. Indeed, even countless artists who have had preconceived templates found their metaphorical palettes had a mind of their own.

Regardless, getting to the task of unspooling *Seven Chances*' paper-thin synopsis, one must say it suffers from an auteur/author danger suggested by *New Yorker* critic Pauline Kael, with regard to this most collaborative of art forms—cinema. She did 1960s criticism battle with *Village Voice* auteurist Andrew Sarris, who had introduced the theory to American audiences from its 1950s origins in the groundbreaking French publication *Cahiers du Cinéma*. With the passage of time, seemingly her most significant warning is that even if an agreed-upon auteur (synonymous with director) exists, their disciples might elevate *all* of this artist's work over possibly a brilliant picture by an otherwise journeyman filmmaker. For example, if presented with two untitled and unfamiliar films, one of which was directed

5. Seven Chances *(April 22, 1928)*

by Alfred Hitchcock and the second of which was megaphoned by an unknown—would there not be a tendency to go with Hitchcock?

In the end Sarris' auteurism won the war, yet Kael's above potential concern is a hazard with which most film pundits still struggle. Moreover, that would seem to be the case with *Seven Chances*—an often entertaining picture but second-tier Keaton. As will be demonstrated later in the chapter, that was precisely the position taken by period critics. Yet, with modern cinema's important elevation of Keaton to near and/or par status with Chaplin, devotees of the deadpan director/comedian have sometimes anointed everything he has done. For example, see Daniel Moew's lengthy chapter on *Seven Chances* in *Keaton: The Silent Features Close Up*.[8] That being said, the picture's prolonged second half chase sequence, which includes playing dodge ball with seemingly every rolling rock in the solar system merits comparison with Keaton's extraordinary short subject *Cops* (1922).

Regardless, now on to *Seven Chances*' story. It was an old tale even when it had been a surprise Broadway hit ten-odd years before. Buster had disliked it then, and his opinion had not changed in the ensuing decade. Keaton plays a junior partner in a failing brokerage firm. Jimmy (Buster) and his partner might even see jail time if a money miracle does not occur. This time Keaton's deus ex machina Greek rescue from the sky essentially opens the movie, rather than its submarine close to *The Navigator*. That is, his grandfather's grizzled little old lawyer (Snitz Edwards), a wonderful character actor who later enhances such Keaton pictures as 1926's *Battling Butler* and 1927's *College*, appears with a will worth seven million dollars. But there is a catch. Gramps must have been aware of Jimmy's romantic fears, because the will stipulates that to receive the money grandson Jimmy must be married by seven p.m. on the day of his 27th birthday. Since this vehicle is anchored in comedy land, Snitz's character manages to arrive precisely on that day.

However, a lengthy preceding prologue suggests that should be no problem. That is, like the calendar-year classic *Meet Me in St. Louis* (1944) on steroids, four seasonal tableaux are presented in a lovely early version of Technicolor. Each one has Mary (Ruth Dwyer) and Jim standing at the gate of her picket-fenced home with the girl's pet dog. They affectionately talk and Buster always pets the dog. As appealing as these static tableaux are, they are still static—never a positive posture for stonefaced Buster. This is a Chaplin set-up, perfect for the poignant emotional pull of the Tramp's expressive face. Keaton's blank visage is built for an amazingly athletic figure forever in long shot movement.

Seven Chances is further detrimentally drawn out by a series of seasonal titles, starting with "One beautiful summer day, when fragrant flowers were in bloom, Jimmie Shannon met Mary Jones, and he wanted to tell her he loved her." We then see the aforementioned setting and action, with the pooch being a Dalmatian puppy. Then the picture moves to the next seasonal set-up. "When Autumn had cast its golden glow and the flowers had faded and died [the words briefly stop] he still wanted to tell her he loved her." Again, it is the same camera set-up, the same couple, with only an older dog (which Keaton accents by petting each time), a different season, and the season-appropriate clothing having changed.

This *slowly* proceeds through the course of a year, more than fully establishing that Jimmy loves Mary but has woefully inadequate romantic skills. Granted, these are important plot points for later in the story, yet this is an extremely down-tempo pace, especially for a Keaton picture. Plus, keep in mind, this is a time in film history when 1920s German cinema was credited with elevating silent cinema to near perfection by almost *eliminating titles*. The still celebrated F. W. Murnau German film *The Last Laugh* (1924, starring Emil Jannings) had become the cause célèbre of this mid–1920s cinema advancement. For example, before the release of Keaton's comedy, America's prestigious *Literary Digest*, which limited its film commentaries to special events, ran a February 28, 1925, *Last Laugh* essay called "A Movie Without Headlines [Titles]."⁹

Consequently, adapting a by now warmed-over play better suited for Harold Lloyd, and beginning with multiple titles, which further antiquated the film movement in comparison to Germany's cutting-edge cinema development, *Seven Chances* begins with decided disadvantages. Was there anything Keatonesque about the opening? There was one obvious item—beyond the Technicolor—which demonstrated Keaton's ongoing interest in new cinema developments. (Ironically, he would later be anxious to try sound, which, with his MGM loss of control, would further hasten his rapid decline.)

Regardless, the need for tape-measure exactitudes in *Seven Chances*' repeated seasonal tableaux represents a Keaton meticulousness which hearkens back to being able to play all the parts in the 1921 short subject *The Play House*, or enter the movie within the movie in *Sherlock, Jr.* Paradoxically, however, the prologue also includes a *personal* Keaton footnote which seems to have been acknowledged neither in the silent era, nor in modern Keaton literature. It is also antithetical to Keaton's *professional* persona—sentimentality. As previously noted, things were hardly simpatico in the comedian's household. Indeed, the previous year something as simple as naming his second child had created a battle royal that made the newspapers. For instance, a March 1924 *Los Angeles Times* article reported: "And now peace reigns once more in the Talmadge-Keaton clan [note the order]. Ever since February 3, last, and as a matter of fact, prior to that, the battle over what Buster's second baby should be named has been raging. Constance and Natalie had their opinions and so did 'Peg' Talmadge, mother of the three Talmadge sisters. And when Norma got home from New York recently new fuel was added to the flames of controversy. After hours of discussion, the list finally was narrowed down.... And Bob it is."¹⁰

In any case, during the following fall another child-related Keaton article appeared with future ties to *Seven Chances*. Titled "Films Tell the Story of Keatons," the October 1924 *Los Angeles Times* essay revealed:

> Buster Keaton already has put in twenty months on a motion picture of his [oldest] son.... And soon he will start another film of his second son.... Each week a photographer [cinematographer] from the Keaton studio visits and photographs [films] little Joe, Buster's eldest son. Buster intends the two films to show the growth of his children from babyhood to manhood.... Each time the moving pictures are taken young Joe is placed in the same spot.... The film for Buster's second son will be started in a week or so.... The Keaton film will be shown only to members of the family.¹¹

The prologue of *Seven Chances*, his next film, plays upon this same principle. The central but modest developing joke is the comic growth of a tiny Dalmatian puppy—within the exactly placed and posed seasonal tableaux—into a rambunctious and seemingly Shetland pony-sized pet. As an addendum, this side of Buster the loving 1920s father is rarely addressed. Plus, it adds another layer to his depression and alcoholism in the early 1930s, when, among many almost simultaneous problems, an ugly divorce cost him *all* access to his boys—with his wife even changing their last names to Talmadge. (This is addressed further in the Epilogue.)

That being said, how did Keaton make an unwanted *Seven Chances* into a semblance of a Keaton picture? Indeed, this speaks directly to the pure nature of the aforementioned auteurism, as expounded by *Caheirs du Cinéma* critic and founding member French New Wave filmmaker, François Truffaut. That is, auteur critics were often greatly interested in how a filmmaker might be handed an assignment *not* of their choosing, and still manage to personalize it with nuances of their own.

5. Seven Chances *(April 22, 1928)*

Buster and Natalie Keaton in semi-happier times, with sons James (left, "little Joe") and Robert (circa late 1920s). An ugly divorce in the early 1930s would have Natalie changing the boys' surname to Talmadge.

Beyond Keaton's modest tweaking of *Seven Chances*' prologue, his major decision was to tell much of the story in the movie's first half—thus allowing the picture's long extended finale to be a throwback to the comedian's celebrated early short subjects. Consequently, how did he "Keatonize" the original play? First, it gave the handsome, sometimes private-life clotheshorse Keaton a chance to dress smartly, à la the cinema phenomenon which began with *Saphead* (1920). Second, it allowed economical filmmaker Keaton some brilliant moments. For example, arguably the comedian's greatest example of minimalism, eliminating one to two extra shots, occurs with one of his ongoing failures to find a bride. Keaton goes to his country club with his business partner—a romantic player who has written down the name of seven *sure thing* potential brides, thus the title "seven chances."

The highlighted example of cinema efficacy occurs when the ever more desperate Keaton is quite literally proposing to everyone, after the *without fail* list fails. Consequently, he sees a pretty woman (unbilled Jean Arthur) in the country club balcony. (She is sometimes also credited with being an office receptionist.) Buster pens a proposal and tosses it up to the balcony. Returning to the one-shot of Keaton below, after a short pause, he receives his answer without moving—the torn-up note comes fluttering down upon him, like so much snow. Keaton then cleverly complements the (cold) tone of the response by putting his collar up and walking away.

With both his partner and his grandfather's lawyer continuing to help him with his bridal quest, other distinctly Keaton touches occur. After yet another failure, the baseball-loving comedian turns to the duo and via a title card observes, "Who bats next?" Still, while the less-than-romantic Buster is miles from what Woody Allen would describe as a "boudoir mechanic," he is persistent. Thus, a Keaton given—the partly obscured sign—is used for another bridal failure. For example, he goes by the side entrance of a theatre with a poster of a pretty woman as the current attraction. He tips the quasi-guard at the side entrance and attempts yet another proposal. After his entrance, boxes in front of the advertisement are moved, revealing that the attractive performer is Julian Eltinge (1881–1941), at that time the world's most famous female impersonator, and with whom "The Three Keatons" might even have shared a vaudeville playbill.

While this joke is usually lost on modern audiences, period patrons would have also enjoyed a comic topper to Buster's mistake. That is, though no encounter is seen between the comedian and Eltinge, soon a roughed-up Keaton comes flying out of the theatre's back-stage door. If one merely knew Eltinge was a woman impersonator, the viewer might just laugh because Keaton was getting some gender error payback. However, there is more humor here for a 1920s theatre fan. They would also have been aware that bachelor Eltinge attempted to play down any question of being gay by exuding an overly macho public persona, including even starting bar fights. (Though his romantic interests still remain a mystery, one is reminded of a celebrated British routine co-created by Keaton fan Marty Feldman, of later "EYE-gore" fame in 1974's *Young Frankenstein*. Reminiscing after the funeral of a longtime elderly friend, Feldman slowly reveals certain telltale signs about the deceased, with the periodic tagline, "Funny he never married.") Regardless, for Keaton's period audience the Eltinge bit was a multi-layered gag. Buster, though still without a bride and now beaten up, then manages to squeeze one parting laugh from the scene—he takes his doorman tip back.

Keaton further tweaked *Seven Chances*' unsolicited story by peppering it with more of his patented short subject surrealism. Thus, at one point he spots an attractive woman in a hair salon. As Buster contemplates another proposal the stylist matter-of-factly lifts the woman's head off—he had been working on the wig of a fake noggin. Keaton, the comedian from absurdity, is only modestly taken aback. Noting another possible bride at the beauty parlor, he is soon at her side. But given what has just happened, and that this next seeming beauty has a blank expression reminiscent of Lillian Hellman's line, "Her face is unclouded by thought," the practical Keaton gives the new noodle a twist. This one turns out to be real—normally good news for the wannabe groom Buster. Yet, head twisting tends to guarantee one's proposal will be refused.

Another Keaton touch evocative of his surrealistic shorts later comes from his frantic need to know just how much more time he has before the seven o'clock deadline. (The following event actually occurs after the play's original chase by a multitude of sudden wannabe spouses.) Regardless, in Buster's harried rushing about the city for a bride he comes upon a clock store, but the million and one assorted watches displayed therein all have different times! It is funny but telling, since surrealism mocks middle class values—so full of schedules and due dates—all driven by clocks.

Maybe this is what Salvador Dalí is suggesting in his signature painting, *Persistence of Vision*, but often referenced as *Clocks*. One sees three melted clocks in the desert, all of which resemble pocket watches—that period's most prevalent time taskmaster. With no people in the picture, the clocks have done their duty, providing demanding diversions until death's escape. Along related lines, in a previous text I used a photo of Richard Dupont's sculpture *Going Around By Passing Through* as a frontispiece for a study in dark comedy.[12] Resembling a shrouded tree trunk-like figure, the sculpture and its title captured the essence of the book—we pass through life going in circles ... killing time ... until time kills us— my eternal take on Buster.

As a supplement to surrealism-meets-Keaton films, "persistence of vision" is actually the phrase which describes how films work. Pictures projected at twenty-four frames a second appear to move because of the ever so brief "persistence of vision" of the previous image on one's brain. Thus, it is very fitting that Houdini fan Keaton would so relish the magic of the movies after Fatty Arbuckle lent him a film camera following their first meeting. Regardless, Buster's confused clock shop sequence *seems* to end with a modest gag topper. When he asks the store owner what time it really is, the proprietor/repair man's own watch has stopped. Other cinematic examples, from various artists, include a broken clock, à la one without hands, in Ingmar Bergman's coffin carriage sequence from *Wild Strawberries* (1957), or the conscious breaking of a pocket watch in Guillermo del Toro's *Pan's Labyrinth* (2006), both symbolizing death.

Do I think Keaton willfully meant this when the gag was added? Of course not. However, I am not just chasing shadows here. It can easily be seen as a fault line conduit to the darkly comic absurd world Buster regularly inhabits, especially when it involves romance.

With Buster's almost immediate need for a bride, no timepiece was too obscure to check.

Plus, daft clocks even play a part in *Seven Chance*'s conclusion. The watches of both his partner and his grandfather's lawyer find him arriving too late. Yet, when the disgruntled Keaton trudges outside the door of a now willing Mary's house, in which a thrown-together wedding was to have taken place, he spots a church steeple clock that has not quite reached seven o'clock. All these timepieces, and by extension, time itself, seem as disturbingly random as the clock store sequence itself. Such flawed *pieces of time* actually represent a further doubling down on absurdity. That is, as noted earlier, Buster always has more faith in the mechanical than in mankind, believing it to be more predictable than the mercurial minions. Yet, while this may well be true, given that man makes the machinery, even here there are no guarantees.

In any case, *Seven Chance*'s wedding ceremony is completed just as the church bells begin to ring. Then coming full circle back to the film's prologue, the final has the new couple denied a closing kiss—the now giant Dalmatian suddenly comes between them and is the accidental recipient of their smooches. Yet, had it not been for the late "foghorn in a fog" nature of the clocks, to borrow a line from writer Stephen Spender, *Seven Chances* would have been ripe for *College*'s cemetery closing dissolve, which pricks the hope of another last minute-marriage.

Moreover, speaking of dissolves, before going to *Seven Chance*'s pure Buster additions to the film, one must note two more technical tweaks the comedian further Keatonized from what he had been stuck with by Schenck. Early in the film Buster twice gets in his car and the scene dissolves to his destination. Providing his own variation to what period Soviet filmmakers would call a "form" cut—editing to a similarly shaped object—once again the comedian provides a distinctive auteur touch. A later form cut example which still evokes this Keaton sequence occurs in Oscar-winning editor turned director Hal Ashby's 1971 *Harold and Maude*. Also fittingly a dark comedy, the scene involves Bud Cort's Harold opening a hearse car door for Ruth Gordon's Maude at a cemetery. This then cuts to him doing the door opening action at their destination—her railroad car home, subtextually reminding us that she is a holocaust survivor ... and prompting viewers, if thinking of Keaton, how often he used trains as symbols of instant destruction. Indeed, there is a moment late in *Seven Chances* when a crane accidently drops the comedian behind a high fence and a steam engine suddenly rushes by, temporarily suggesting his death. In fact, the aforementioned *Harold and Maude* segment could literally be called "Keatonesque."

Returning to Keaton's need for a bride, his partner finally takes extreme measures by placing an ad in the local paper:

> **WANTED, A BRIDE**
>
> James Shannon, Prominent Young
> Banker Falls Heir To $7,000,000
> If He Is Married Today
>
> **ALL HE NEEDS IS A BRIDE**
>
> Girl Who Appears At Broad Street
> Church In Bridal Costume By
> 5 O'Clock Will Be The Lucky Winner

As with the original cattle call casting for these extras during the film's production (see previous chapter), all chaos soon breaks out at the designated church, as hundreds of wannabe rich brides pack the place. They appear in all sizes, shapes, and ages. Plus, if one pays attention, the woman impersonator theme returns, after a fashion—with a few potential Buster brides looking like truck drivers in drag. Of course, if these extras had appeared with the realistic feminine daintiness credited to the gifted Eltinge, the sight gag would have gone missing.

Buster had arrived early to an empty church and promptly fallen asleep in the front pew—a day of denied proposals can be grueling work. But he soon awakens to a packed surreal church of possible brides. Once recognized, the women start to fight over him. But soon a minister appears, and after being taken aback by this matrimonial mob, he tells this sea of white that this is undoubtedly some sort of practical joke and "you must leave the church as quickly as possible."

Keaton somehow manages to briefly escape the multitude of now mad women. But soon he is oblivious to a frightening fact: the horde has found him and is quietly beginning to follow behind him as he slows to a walk to catch his breath. *But* the race is soon on again, and Buster somehow shifts into a speed comparable to a character in George Herriman's (1880–1944) period comic strip, *Krazy Kat*, which first appeared as a focus cartoon character in 1916, and continued until Herriman's death. The reference is not made randomly. Krazy Kat is universally acclaimed as the greatest comic strip in newspaper history. And there are many parallels with Keaton, from not being as fully appreciated by the period masses, to having a decidedly surrealistic bent. In a nutshell, the strip was an absurd love triangle—Kat loved Ignatz Mouse, Offissa (police dog) Pupp loved Kat, and Ignatz loved no one. Moreover, the ongoing signature scene forever repeated was Mouse creasing the romantic Kat's cranium with a brick—which "Krazy" took as a sign of love. (It also underlines the Keaton basic that relationships do not work.)

Intellectuals had, however, fully embraced *Krazy Kat*, especially after Gilbert Seldes' groundbreaking 1924 pop culture text, *The Seven Lively Arts*, and the character had influenced many period artists. Indeed, Michael Tisserand, Herriman's definitive biographer, credits a *Krazy Kat* strip with inspiring the aforementioned *Cops* scene in which Buster casually lights a cigarette with the fuse from an anarchist's bomb, then casually tossing it aside, blowing up several policemen.[13] Moreover, Herriman was a close friend of Clyde Bruckman, a former fellow New York newspaper colleague, and the co-scripter of Keaton's *Seven Chances*. Herriman was much admired in the Hollywood film community, especially among film comedians—often hanging out at one of Buster and Fatty Arbuckle's favorite "watering holes"—Joe Winkel's Temecula, California, bar. Indeed, the previously noted Arbuckle-directed Marion Davies picture *The Red Mill* (1927), a position Keaton had orchestrated for the blacklisted comic, included a mouse named Ignatz.[14]

So what brings to mind Herriman, with regard to *Seven Chances*, beyond another twisted romantic scenario, in which Keaton also wants out? Well, as the legion of "ladies" chase Buster, they come upon a poor bricklayer with a half-finished wall yet to have hardened. Many of the women stop, grab a brick, and like Ignatz, commence bombarding Buster. Soon the wall is all but gone and a darkly funny—potentially lethal—situation is again more comically nuanced for a Herriman-knowledgeable 1920s audience. In fact, arguably the *Krazy Kat* connection enhances Keaton's black humor situation by mere association. This is best described by a former newspaper cartoonist who, for a time, was a major silent comedy star—Harry Langdon. In a May 1924 interview with the *Los Angeles Evening Herald* Langdon observed: "You don't have the elbow room [in a newspaper] that you have in screen comedies. On the other hand, you can get away with jokes that would be censored as too violent and brutal on the screen. Somehow the public does not think of it as brutal when they see a ton of coal fall on a fat policeman in a comic strip, but they would send you to jail, or have you burned alive or something if you tried it on the screen."[15]

Silent comedy seems to have had a special affinity for gathering former newspaper cartoonists into their ranks, such as Bruckman working on the majority of Keaton's features. Indeed, several cartoonists achieved on-screen popularity, too. The latter would range from the just quoted Langdon, to the now largely forgotten Larry Semon, whom film historian Gerald Mast described as "one of the strangest-looking comedians of the silent era.... [He] looked as if he ran a ... delicatessen on Mars."[16] The newspaper cartoonist pipeline to film lessened in the sound era, though prominent examples periodically appeared, such as *My Man Godfrey* director (1936) Gregory La Cava, to writer/director Frank Tashlin's work with a host of major comedians in the 1950s.

Herriman was an odd case, however, in that while he supervised a few *Krazy Kat* film shorts during the 1910s, he simply enjoyed doing his newspaper strip on a movie lot. For example, in another May 1924 article from the *Los Angeles Evening Herald*, the local press which carried his strip, entertainingly describe this eccentric situation. Accompanied by a picture of the cartoonist holding a live cat and the ironic title "Noted Comic Artist Leads a Strenuous Life," the *Herald* read, in part, "Here's George Herriman sitting on the steps of 'Bean' Walker's [a gag writing former cartoonist] office comforting Krazy Kat [the live cat in his lap] after a strenuous day at Hal Roach studios where he does his daily strip.... Ignatz has evidently been sent home to his ink bottle.... Herriman declares there is no better place to think of daily [newspaper strip] "gags" than a comedy lot."[17] Regardless, once the race continues, *Seven Chances* brings to mind a June 1923 *Los Angeles Times* article baldly titled, "Comedian Has to Be [an] Athlete."[18] Buster as track star soon manages to zoom through a football game in progress. However, the ever-growing number of stampeding brides so trample over the two teams they all but disappear, like cowboys lost in a cattle drive gone wrong. Suddenly, one has a film image which might double as newspaper cartoon strip panel—twenty-two players seemingly flattened on the field. And one is reminded of Langdon's warning about cinema needing to somewhat censor its comic violence, since one does not really see the smooshing but rather its aftermath.

The gag works on several levels, beginning with its steamroller-like tableaux aftermath. Second, there is the delightful surrealism of these big tough football players being obliterated by a "team" of brides in full wedding regalia. Third, period audiences would have gotten an added darkly comic bonus from the fact that just a few years earlier President Theodore Roosevelt (1858–1919) had threatened to ban the sport, unless new rules were created to eliminate the actual deaths that were occurring in college football. However, no one at his special White House conference had thought to consider the danger of runaway wannabe brides. Fourth, another period point lost on contemporary audiences was that because of the mobility created by the automobile, the 1920s was the first decade in which football became a viable subject to be spoofed. (This was the era in which the first large stadiums were built.) In fact, Harold Lloyd's football conclusion to *The Freshman* actually used real footage of that year's Rose Bowl game, shot in nearby Pasadena, California.

Buster's prolonged running to escape the results of his partner's newspaper ad takes him through the city and eventually into the country, where his misadventures involve everything from running through a beehive sanctuary to swimming a river, nearly being shot in a hunting preserve, and climbing a giant fir tree just as it is being cut down. Eventually he comes near the dunes close by the Pacific Ocean, just outside of Los Angeles. The almost Western setting is reminiscent of the desert backdrop for many of the *Krazy Kat* comic strips, as well as anticipating Keaton's next film, *Go West* (1925, see following chapter).

Before, moreover, leaving that Buster *Go West* reference, two interesting Keaton-

5. Seven Chances (April 22, 1928)

Herriman connections cannot wait until the next chapter. First, while Keaton's character is a struggling ranch hand, one of Herriman's early comic strips is about the cowboy *Lariat Pete*. Second, and even more significant, is that while there are various links between the cartoonist's work and *Seven Chances*, the central *Go West* plot twist is pure *Krazy Kat*. That is, as previously stated, the strip keys on the comically peculiar love of a cat for a mouse, and a dog for a cat. In Keaton's cowboy picture, he falls in love with a cow—*Brown Eyes*! While this film oozes parody pathos, it also spoofs the traditionally odd romantic link between the cowpoke and his horse.

Regardless, the original cut of *Seven Chances* peters out with Buster still being chased by the women; this involved running down a steep dune incline and arguably taking some of the most amazing and largely accidental pratfalls of his life. Still, Buster was upset with this picture which had been forced upon him. A lackadaisical sneak preview merely confirmed the comedian's fears. Was this to be his first semi-failure in a feature in which he had been in charge? Perhaps if one discounted the jerry-rigged *Three Ages* (1923), which might have been better released as a trio of short subjects.

Yet, like many gifted filmmakers, Keaton could double as an inspired script doctor. For example, he would later comically embellish several Red Skelton pictures during the 1940s and early 1950s when this older artist's glory days were over.[19] Thus, at the close of *Seven Chances*, Keaton had noted some modest but genuine titters during the sneak preview when he dislodged some rocks which chased him during his pratfall down the dunes.

That was all the catalyst needed to have 1500 fake (papier-mâché) rocks constructed, ranging in size from basketballs to eight-foot boulders. Then they were trucked to another sandy ridge which had a more steeply angled descent. This time Buster seemed to co-star with the Rocky Mountains ... piecemeal, as he tried to outrun a smorgasbord of stones. Shot in long shot and long take, sometimes reality can be pushed to surrealism, like the cart being pulled sans people through a bombed out courtyard in Roberto Rossellini's *Paisan* (1946). Periodically, Keaton found temporary safety, from climbing a tree—soon flattened—then taking refuge behind a large boulder that had somehow become anchored. Yet, the quick build-up of stones soon dislodged his safely net and it was back to running like a future Jesse Owens.

Once Keaton the comic athlete has completely milked every laugh out of his downhill adventure, or to borrow the title of Keaton fan Richard Lester's Oscar-nominated surreal short subject, *The Running, Jumping, and Standing Still Film* (1960), Buster runs into that brigade of brides squared off at the bottom of the hill. Well, what could now be funnier than turning around and trying to play metaphorical dodge ball—attempting to run back up the steep incline while seeking to evade this slapstick avalanche of assorted stones? One was now completely in Keaton country.

Buster was still not happy overall with *Seven Chances*, but his tour de force elongated conclusion, from the expanded chase to the astute addition of the multi-faceted rock slide, much improved both his and the public's perspective on the film. Indeed, Keaton's attempt to go back up that tsunami of a rock avalanche anticipates arguably the comedian's signature walk against the wind in the later *Steamboat Bill, Jr.* (1928, see Chapter 10). Thus, one might have labeled a review of *Seven Chances*, then, or now, by recycling the title of a previously noted hyperbolic 1922 *Picture Show* article about how the comedian received his nickname: "Buster Keaton's Tumbling to Success."[20]

Today the amazing conclusion to the picture has somewhat elevated the picture's importance. But at the time, especially following *The Navigator*, the reviews were often disappointing. And if that were the case, the criticism usually came down to his using serviceable but yet older material. Granted, in Keaton's defense, this dusting of *Seven Chances* with some familiar Buster bits was to make this more Harold Lloyd–like story doable for him. Still, Keaton did not help his cause by reminding viewers of this looking backward perspective. For example, the *New York World* review opens thus: "In a forenote on the program at the Capitol this week there is a brief interview with Keaton, the star of this week's picture. It begins: 'Screen comedy, for the most part, has been traveling along in the same path it started on back in the early days of the industry.' I am inclined to think Mr. Keaton was in earnest when he said this, and furthermore "Seven Chances" would indicate that he is having a hard time striking out down a fresh road."[21] Not surprisingly, the *World* reviewer felt the picture "simply wasn't funny."[22] In fairness, there were many positive critiques such as the *Chicago Daily News*' poet/critic Carl Sandburg reporting much laughter during his viewing of the film. Yet, even he felt the need to add, "The story is not so new but they have certainly put new wrinkles, ruffles and curlicues on an old-timer."[23] And while the *New York Times* felt "there are some humorous scenes," the critique's beginning echoed the beginning of the *World*'s review: "After viewing Buster Keaton's latest comedy, *Seven Chances*, one is justified in assuming that there is a slump in the fun market."[24] Worse yet, critic Mordaunt Hall used part of this crack as the critique's title: "A Slump in Fun."[25]

Variety said Keaton "isn't so effective in the early parts of the film," and also felt the lengthy chase was rather retro.[26] But then the publication turned the tables and credited Keaton's marathon of a run as having a "novelty touch which makes the picture stand up as something exceptional."[27] This was the most contemporary-sounding of *Seven Chances*' period reviews. *Harrison's Reports*, which was geared more for theatre owners, labeled it a "pretty good farce-comedy" but it does not get to the "roars of laughter" generated from the chase sequence until later in the review.[28]

Time magazine's capsule review of *Seven Chances* was nothing more than a synopsis, while the *New York Daily News* clocked 82 laughs in the picture.[29] But then the latter publication defuses its positive *Seven Chances* critique with a near-closing comment which again suggests recycled material: "Strangely, the climax is almost identical with the climax of 'Introduce Me' [a now lost 1925 film starring the then popular Douglas MacLean]. In 'Seven Chances' boulders chase Buster down a mountainside, and in the other farce it's snowballs. It goes to show all the great minds in Hollywood think of the same thing at the same time."[30]

Seven Chances' most problematic period critique ironically comes from the 1920s' best film critics, *LIFE*'s previously praised Robert E. Sherwood. Regrettably, it documents another of the era's blind spots towards comments on race, gender, age, and appearance. What starts out sounding like budding feminism dovetails into something disturbing—though his overriding point is what most period pundits had complained about—old material:

> BUSTER KEATON has made one bad mistake in 'Seven Chances': he has based his main appeal for laughter on that most questionable of all comic properties, feminine unloveliness. You have viewed many scenes wherein a young man starts out after a shapely young woman ... only to find, on catching up with her that she is 100% African ... [though Keaton, like most silent comedians, had a weakness for the racist gag, this is sadly broader in its offensiveness]. Keaton uses that, and many others that are closely akin to it. Thus, the laughs ... are not honest laughs. They are tinctured with a certain amount of shame on the part of the audience.[31]

Sherwood grants that there is "plenty of good stuff in 'Seven Chances' ... [but it] is not Keaton's best comedy, primarily because it is concerned more with external activities than with the highly individual drollery of Buster Keaton himself."[32]

5. Seven Chances *(April 22, 1928)*

Here was yet another distinct difference between a period *Seven Chances* critique and commentary on the film today. First, in the 1920s, the movie's uniquely absurd conclusion, in which Buster seems trapped in a cosmic penny arcade machine, attempting to avoid being pinballed into oblivion, was not fully appreciated. Second, though initially worded awkwardly, the sage Sherwood eventually calls out the racist material that sometimes surfaces in the film. Today's historians rarely, if ever, give more than short shrift to the subject.

Granted, to write about the past one needs to operate, as much as possible, in the context of the times—one of the most difficult demands made of a historian, and one which, in all honesty, can never be fully embraced. Still, pieces of time asterisks need be noted. In fact, such admissions invariably lead to potential insights into the absurdity of life. For example, only recently has it been discovered that *Krazy Kat* creator George Herriman was black, yet secretly passing for white, or as one review title of the aforementioned Tisserand's *Krazy*/Herriman biography phrased it, "Invisibly Black."[33] No wonder the strip is caught up in Ignatz the mouse forever throwing bricks at the amorous Kat. Yet, to maintain his cover, even Herriman sometimes trafficked in racially stereotyped drawings. (This subject will be addressed further in Chapter 9, given Keaton's comedy in *College* is most marred by racial typecasting, despite the many brilliant moments he managed to create in yet another picture, like *Seven Chances*, he was not happy about making.)

Before closing, *Seven Chances* is also a catalyst for discussing Buster's timing. No, not in comedy, which was invariably exquisite, but rather the release date competition of Chaplin and Lloyd. For example, Keaton's first real feature, *Our Hospitality* (disregarding the short subject accordion hodgepodge which was 1923's *Three Ages*), opened in December 1923, after the fall releases of Harold Lloyd's *Why Worry?* and Charlie Chaplin's *Woman of Paris*—two pictures which metaphorically sucked most of the critical acclaim out of the room. *Our Hospitality* remained one of Keaton's most ongoingly beloved 1920s pictures, something lost on many contemporary historians. Yet, it no doubt would have generated more modern attention if these other pictures, particularly Chaplin's game-changing opus—which resulted in reams of newspaper ink both before and after its release, had not been in direct competition with Keaton.

Along similar lines, while *Seven Chances* has been upgraded by contemporary historians, period critics tended to include it in some sort of comedy malaise for late 1926 and early 1927. Yet, within months, arguably the signature pictures for both Chaplin, *The Gold Rush*, and Lloyd, *The Freshman*, appear to momentous critical and commercial acclaim. Suddenly the comedy year has been saved, and Keaton is now even more old school. Yet, in the midst of his competitors, Keaton then releases maybe the comedian's oddest picture to define, *Go West* (see the following chapter).

One is reminded of Keaton dark comedy print contemporary, Will Cuppy (1884–1949).[34] When the Depression was just beginning, his book *How to Be a Hermit* (1929) appeared. And as America readied for World War II his essay collection *How to Become Extinct* (1941) was published. Possibly the giftedly cynical Cuppy began to believe what he had always kidded about—that there was a "Hate Cuppy movement" out there—because he later committed suicide. While thankfully Keaton never went that far, as the 1920s progressed a series of events and choices resulted in a darker Keaton attitude which might have been his primer for his own real "how to become a hermit."

6

Go West (November 23, 1925)

> "Fans know how the hero in dreams of the ... [West] flicks a little tobacco into a cigarette paper, gives it a little dexterous roll between the fingers of his right hand, lights a match with his thumbnail and puffs away ... [Buster Keaton recently] wasted a couple of pounds of tobacco and reams of paper trying to master the trick. He's still smoking 'tailor-made.'"
> —*Los Angeles Times* (November 26, 1925)[1]

Period reviews for *Go West*, which will be addressed later in the chapter, generally matched the same evaluation he received for learning how to roll a cigarette. This must have proved especially hard for such a perfectionist, especially, as noted earlier, this gifted filmmaker was also a four-pack a day smoker. Regardless, there is something of a disconnect between *Go West*'s initial reception, and later implied commentary on period criticism. For example, pioneering Keaton biographer Rudi Blesh later labels it a "great" film, while three decades further on another respected biographer of the comedian, Larry Edwards, calls the movie one of his [Keaton's] most beloved silent films."[2] Daniel Moews' revisionist Keaton text is kind but closer to the period's puzzled and usually disappointed perspective on this ripe-for-spoofing genre.[3] For instance, even before *Go West* went into production, John Ford's epic but traditional Western *The Iron Horse* had already celebrated its 400th performance at Broadway's Lyric Theatre.

However, given a thorough immersion in the period, Keaton's fundamental creative tendencies, and both the production background and reception of the comedian's previous picture, *Seven Chances* (1925), it is hard to comprehend how anything but a wicked parody under *his* authorship would result with *Go West*. This is based upon obvious period points—always there but never fleshed out."

First, Keaton's last picture was forced upon him (see previous chapter). Worse ... it was based upon a popular 1916 stage play which obligated him to adapt at least a semblance of a narrative he found inconsistent for his screen persona. Not surprisingly, therefore, *Go West* is a rare Keaton picture in which he takes solo story credit, though the script in attributed to Raymond Cannon. Moreover, Keaton returns to his métier—cheeky parody, a subject which will be expanded upon shortly.

Second, after personality comedies, arguably the most popular 1920s film genre open to parody was the Western. Despite Jazz Age images of flappers and decadent partying images of celebrities like Zelda and F. Scott Fitzgerald (who coined the term "Jazz Age"), there was a growing nostalgia for the Old West. This was possibly fueled by a 1920s census determining for the first time that more Americans now lived in cities. This is best symbolized by Zane Grey's (1872–1939) novel *The Vanishing American* (1925), which was serialized during 1922 in the country's most popular magazine, *Ladies Home Journal*. The book's Native American hero was loosely patterned on Jim Thorpe, who won gold medals in the 1912 Olympic pentathlon and decathlon, before going on to play professional football and Major League Baseball. (The Associated Press later voted him the "greatest athlete" of the first half of the 20th century.)

Moreover, Grey's best-selling Western novels, starting with 1912's *Riders of the Purple Sage*, had a profound impact upon both the genre and Hollywood. William Fox brought the rights to *Riders* in 1916, and for a time Grey formed his own movie production company. By doing this he had more control over the scores of Westerns made from his non-stop production of best-selling horse operas. All this further fueled an American film industry which credited *The Great Train Robbery* (1903) as its first narrative movie—playing upon vaudeville circuits in which Keaton and family were appearing. (The film also produced one of film's earliest stars, Broncho Billy Anderson.)

Along related Western lines, the popular presidency of Theodore Roosevelt (1901–1909) was famous for the high priority he placed upon wilderness conservation, which resulted in establishing the United States Forest Service, and was coupled with the creation of five national parks and 100-plus national forests. The catalyst for this was Roosevelt's sickly childhood, which was reversed by a profound part of his youth being spent in the West. The later hearty, overly virile persona he created was anchored to a "cowboy" identity. This was forever augmented by his creation and inclusion in the Western constituency of "Rough Rider" cavalry members during 1898's Spanish-American War.

The well-liked president also further cemented himself to the West in another unusual and indirect manner. Roosevelt had long been displeased with the less than artistic state of American coins. A movement to correct this situation was instituted during his administration, eventually resulting in creating the Buffalo or Indian Head Nickel, minted from 1913 to 1938. The coin was graced with an image of a Native American on one side, and the buffalo, then recently threatened by extinction, on the reverse.

Interestingly, one can easily boomerang this brief overview of a Western resurgence back to a Keaton parody of the genre. All that is necessary is connecting a few of the historical dots already noted. Writer Owen Wister (1860–1938), a Harvard classmate of Roosevelt and the "father" of Western fiction, wrote the groundbreaking 1902 novel *The Virginian*. It is generally considered the first cowboy novel and is dedicated to Roosevelt. Fascinated by the same Western backdrop of Indians and buffalos he shared with his political friend, the book was Zane Grey's pivotal template for the dozens of cowboy and Indian novels he would write. Plus, for Western aficionados, *The Virginian* contains the genre's still most iconic line. After being put in a threatening position, the title character says, "When you call me that, *smile!*"[4]

What better signature Western sequence could there be for a spoof than to assign a variation of that line to a personality comedian who did not smile, à la Keaton's "Great Stone Face"? (To be appraised shortly.) Moreover, Western parodies were clearly something the comedian had shown a knack for in his short subjects. Among period critics, only *LIFE*'s repeatedly astute Robert E. Sherwood makes a brief reference to Keaton's 1922 spoof *The Paleface*. Yet, what goes unnoted is that when coupled with the comedian's biting 1922 *Frozen North* parody, which borders upon extreme satire of iconic Western figure William S. Hart, these short subjects were among Keaton's darkest burlesques. Indeed, he even changes "teams" in *Paleface*. That is, under his leadership, using the moniker "Little Chief Paleface," he successfully leads the Indians against several cowboy crooks attempting to steal the tribe's oil-rich land.

Tough Cowboy Keaton in *The Frozen North*—who knew the subway went that far?

In *The Frozen North*, with an assist from the wronged Fatty Arbuckle (see Chapter 2), Keaton bludgeons silent film's most realistic cowboy. Moreover, one senses Hart was humor-impaired. He could praise the act but he could not take it. How else does one square Hart's anger over *North* but have him later state in a 1920's *Los Angeles Times* interview: "Quick wit is always a saving quality … [for] the old-time Western gun men."[5] Regardless, in the decade's second half he was usurped by the flashy and often amusing Tom Mix. Here was a cowboy with attention-grabbing stunts on his horse Tony and flamboyant showy Western garb, complete with what seemed to be a 15-gallon hat, instead of the stereotypical ten-gallon variety. To put this dark parody in more contemporary terms, one might compare the pared-down cowboy idolatry given the later Randolph Scott, especially when paired with director Budd Boetticher), to the earlier status of Hart.

Scott is now overshadowed by Western stars like John Wayne and Clint Eastwood. Yet, there is a bareboned cowboy essence to Scott which Wayne and Eastwood cannot touch. It was no accident that in Mel Brooks' Western parody *Blazing Saddles* (1974), he has the black sheriff (Cleavon Little) elicit support from his racist town by simply stating: "You'd do it for Randolph Scott." This is immediately followed by the seated citizens rising, and placing their hands over their hearts as they religiously repeat "Randolph Scott," which is simultaneously echoed by a soundtrack chorus of a worshipful sounding Mormon Tabernacle–like choir. Plus, keep in mind, this occurs after all the celebrated John Ford/Wayne Westerns, and Eastwood's Sergio Leone-directed Spaghetti Westerns.

Third, the point to this is that the Keaton milieu anticipation of existentialism's "I just don't care—what's the point?" mantra seemingly had to be embraced by Keaton the artist at some instinctual level. Chaplin and Harold Lloyd wanted this public to like them. For example, as previously noted, the working title of Chaplin's then provocative 1923 *A Woman of Paris* was even *Public Opinion*. Had the film been a commercial megahit, the Tramp would have been toast, and movie enthusiasts would now be talking about the "Chaplin Touch," instead of that designation of sophisticated subtly being credited to director Ernst Lubitsch, who admitted owing everything to *Paris*. And as to Lloyd, this book has just skimmed the surface on how the comedian's PR machine pandered to the public ad nauseam.

Yes, on a survival level in the expensive medium of film, Keaton wanted to be liked, too. However, the appreciation needed to be on his terms. The comedian's increasing push for authenticity and on-location shooting during the 1920s doomed the later, now much acclaimed *General* (1926), years before its production. What is more, how else does one explain Keaton's propensity to risk public approval with dark comedy gags ranging from his Sacco and Vanzetti–like police-killing bomb gag in *Cops* (1922), to his lacerating of the aforementioned, almost sacred star Hart. However, Keaton's theatre of the absurd topper comes with the parody focus of *Go West*. While the full narrative will be set forth shortly, the crux of the tale is that Keaton's greenhorn cowboy Friendless metaphorically falls in love with the "friendless" cow Brown Eyes.

While no one is suggesting Buster ends up bedding the cow à la Gene Wilder's romancing a sheep in Woody Allen's 1972 *Everything You Always Wanted to Know About Sex (But Were Afraid to Ask)*, or has similar barnyard tastes as the male lead in Edward Albee's *The Goat, or Who Is Sylvia?* (2002, from the multiple Pulitzer Prize and Tony–winning playwright). Yet, when the appreciative *Go West* rancher, whose spread Buster has saved, offers him anything he has, including a beautiful appreciative teenage daughter (Kathleen Myers), the comedian chooses the cow. Moreover, in an inspired misdirection by Keaton, whose work seldom received much pre-release PR (compared to Chaplin and Lloyd), a full one-half year before opening the *Los Angeles Times* ran the article "Keaton Has [Discovered] New Woman for 'Go West.'"[6] Plus, it gets better. The piece makes no mention of Buster's real moo-moo leading lady, and states how Ms. Myers has spent most of her formative years in a convent school. One can just imagine Keaton telling his recent detractors: "So you wanted something different after complaining *Seven Chances* was a mediocre adaptation of an old play, further weighed down by my recycled shtick. Well, how do you like these apples—*new* enough for you?"

Consistent with Keaton's past, this parody also took a harsh look at sagebrush territory, from cowboys ignoring him until the appreciative rancher close, to providing a new twist to the age-old "wink wink" Western innuendo that cowboys seemed to like their horses just a little too much. Even Bob Hope's 1952 *Son of Paleface* more than implied that of Roy Rogers and Trigger (instead of Jane Russell!) back in the dumbing down decade of McCarthyism.[7] Now one might explain Buster's choice away easily by repeating an earlier suggestion in the text, that he is merely a boy/man, with the accent on the former. Yet, by this time in Keaton's career, his fleeting youth is beginning to fray a bit along that explanation. (This is a fate awaiting most comedians, save but a few, like the eternally delightful dirty old man, Groucho Marx.)

Yet, because Keaton so anticipates the impending existentialism of art, I am reminded of a comment by the *New York Times* chief theatre critic Ben Brantley on Albee: "If you left one of his plays feeling good about yourself then it would seem that Mr. Albee hadn't done his job."[8] Yet, how can one apply that to funny Mr. Keaton? Because he makes us think, too. And often his plight makes us consider ours. For example, *Day Dreams* (1922) visualized a basic component of Keaton's oeuvre—life is merely a treadmill. *Our Hospitality* (1923) most pointedly speaks of human hypocrisy and could be called a stepping stone to

Jean Renoir's later *Rules of the Game* (1939). *College*'s (1927) close is best summarized by an older lady in Woody Allen's *Annie Hall* (1977): "Love fades."

A fourth period point, which might also double down as an extension of existentialism is that there is most definitely a George Herriman *Krazy Kat* newspaper comic strip influence upon Keaton's previous picture, *Seven Chances* (see preceding chapter). And peeled to its most basic premise, what is the comic about? Unnatural animal liaisons. That is, the Kat loves Ignate Mouse, who rejects any advances with an endless supply of thrown bricks. Plus, Offisso (police dog) Pupp loves Kat, and attempts to protect Kat. Ever since Gilbert Seldes' 1924 *The Seven Lively Arts* this has been considered the greatest and most cerebral of strips. Yet, like Keaton, it was never fully appreciated in its time. The continued publication of *Krazy Kat* into the 1940s was largely because newspaper magnate William Randolph Hearst—the figure upon which 1941's long-extolled *Citizen Kane* is based—loved the strip.

One could "read" the possible *Krazy Kat* factor several ways. Maybe the comic strip component merely reinforces the Keaton-as-kid element. Though I would never apply another basic Albee premise to explain the Keaton-and-cow coupling—that "civilized settings merely masked primitive instincts"—*Go West* certainly merits a footnote on the way to *The Goat, or Who Is Sylvia?*[9] Moreover, Keaton's film at least flirts with the basic core of Albee's philosophy: "[viewers] should be challenged to confront situations and ideas that lie outside their comfort zones."[10] In fact, it is not unlike later spoofs that did not suggest such interpretations. For instance, in Arthur Penn's Western dark comedy/parody of reaffirmation *Little Big Man* (1930), Chief Dan George's figure casually complains to Dustin Hoffman's

Buster and his heroine, Brown Eyes—paging George Harriman and Edward Albee.

title character that his latest wife copulates with horses. Though the Chief knows it to be true, he respects her denials, and even rechristens her "Doesn't Like Horses."

As an added addendum to 1925 and what was, at least for the period, an abnormal link between man and other creatures, the "Scopes Monkey Trial" took place—contesting the teaching of evolution in any state-funded school. Arguably the trial of the century, it galvanized national attention throughout 1925, and is still a controversial subject. Yet it encouraged biting humor, from newspaper composite pictures of monkey men, to satirical cracks from the 1920s high profile writer/personality H. L. Mencken, such as stating the jury was "hot for Genesis," or the Dayton, Ohio setting was full of "yokels" and "morons." These are cracks atheist Keaton would have enjoyed.

A fifth and final period take possibly contributing to *Go West* was merely stating the obvious—his signature deadpan dislike of sentimentality. The comedian constantly found himself second to Chaplin and Lloyd because of the former comedian's inspired pathos, and the latter's clever mechanical gags forever relating to a sappy happy ending. Lloyd even married his leading lady (Mildred Davis, 1923), a union which further contributed to the hemorrhaging of pap promotional ballyhoo. This included print documentation of everything from frequent trips and anniversaries, to domestic incidents for possible screen use. So, if one were a cynical Keaton, why not fall in love with a cow?

As with *The Three Ages* (1923), Griffith was often a spoofing source. However, instead of using the film master's cinematic framework for a parody punching bag, Keaton spoofed more bitingly—darkly reflecting the quickly declining status of the aging artist in Jazz Age Hollywood. For example, Griffith's 1916 epic *Intolerance* features actress Margery Wilson as Brown Eyes, the name of Keaton's cow. And the comedian's moniker, "Friendless," was a variation on the Miriam Cooper description from the same movie—"The Friendless One." Keaton's aping of *Intolerance*'s lack of names with descriptions further underlines the sentimentality of Griffith even in the previous decade. Of course, it helps if the subject struggled with comedy, despite his epic visions. As film historian Gerald Mast quipped to me at a 1980s conference, "John Ford is essentially Griffith with a sense of humor." Regardless, other specific jabs at Griffith will be noted in the forthcoming overview of *Go West*. However, examples such as these should help squelch questions as to whether Keaton was going for parody or pathos.

The movie begins in Indiana, with one of the opening titles stating: "In a little town in Indiana the social standing of a certain young man had kept him continually on the move." Keaton leaves a shack pulling a bed with his modest possessions piled on top. Stopping to sell everything at the local general store, he receives a whopping $1.65 for everything. Then, when he pauses to retrieve a few articles of clothing from a bureau drawer, and a picture of his mother, the local skinflint charges him the original sales price—save a nickel. And before he can comprehend this example of callousness squared, a flighty airhead girl comes by and takes the last coin. Even Sinclair Lewis could not have ratcheted up a better example of the period's small town *Babbitt* booboisie.... Buster was merely imitating the then current literary "Revolt from the Village" movement.

Yet, one need not stop at this insensitive tightwad for potential satire in the sequence. Given that Keaton had a love-hate relationship with his Hoosier-born father (who has a brief cameo in the film), the setting selected seems hardly happenstance. Yet, a darker inside dig hidden in the sequence might suggest that this *small*-town unfairness was from a filmmaker still infuriated that his best friend, Fatty Arbuckle, continued to be blacklisted by provincial prejudice. Indeed, a few months before *Go West* appeared, *Photoplay* even ran a piece criticizing allegedly open-minded mainstream America as being hypocritical about not giving Arbuckle a "square deal." [Period audiences would have recognized the latter phrase as the name President Theodore Roosevelt gave his earlier administration.][11]

These suggestions are mere provocative hypotheses. Still, Indiana was a more obvious parody-friendly state for 1920 fans of the Western thanks to film scholar Dave Smith's exhaustively researched coffee table-sized study, *Hoosiers in Hollywood*. He chronicles no less than ten Indiana-born prominent Western performers in the silent film era: Buck Jones, Ken Maynard, Allan "Rocky" Lane, Max Terhune, Chubby Johnson, Steve Clark, Kenneth McDonald, Tex Terry, Fred Gamble, and Major Gordon W. "Pawnee Bill" Lillie.[12] Indeed, Buck Jones rivaled Tom Mix and Hart as the most idolized of silent Western stars, with Ken Maynard and Allan "Rocky" Lane not far behind.

There seemed to be a Hoosier-to-Hollywood pipeline of silent film sagebrush heroes. Moreover, dozens of other Indiana-born performers populated the film capital at this time. And while one does not now associate them with the Western, this genre often represented their minor league entry into the movie major leagues. This is best represented by 1930s' favorite screwball comedy heroine Carole Lombard. Known as the "Profane Angel" for her salty language, even though toned down for public consumption, Lombard was comically blunt about her Western beginnings. After appearing in Buck Jones' *Gold and the Girl*, *Hearts and Spurs*, and *Durand of the Badlands* (all 1925, the same year as *Go West*), her mitigated mincing would surface in the period publication *Film Pictorial*: "All I had to do was simper prettily at the hero and scream with terror while he battled with the villain. Never once was I allowed to give my screen love's opponent a good, hearty kick—as I would have done in similar [real] circumstances!"[13] And after further movie movement up the Western ladder in Tom Mix's *Dick Turpin* (also 1925), if there was any geographical question about the state's boots-and-saddles assembly-line tradition to La La Land, Lombard's more well-known moniker, "The Hoosier Tornado," was a quick reminder. Thus, for a period audience, when Keaton's *Go West* begins in Indiana, Western fans no doubt were already affectionately elbowing fellow viewers about the appropriateness of the location, however comically incongruous it might seem.

Later even the once-reluctant "Hoosier Tornado" fully embraced the state's Western gift to cinema. She used it as a metaphor for how to handle life's difficulties. Consequently, in another period publication, *Liberty* magazine columnist/friend Adela Rogers St. Johns put Lombard's philosophy thus: "When you see trouble coming that's too big for you to handle, move fast and keep on moving and save all you can."[14]

This could be called Buster's motto for *Go West*, too. His odyssey eventually takes him coast to coast. Yet, after almost being crushed in a human stampede in New York City (rushing pedestrians), he lingers longest in the West, where he meets Brown Eyes. Plus, as yet another reminder from the gender-squared *Krazy Kat* strip first noted in the previous chapter, cowboy-land was also the backdrop for that confused character. And of course, Buster finally arrives in the West by his favorite means of transportation—an extensive series of train-hopping. Yet, his sudden exit is strictly accidental—the beer barrel he has chosen to call home, and several others randomly fall from his iron horse boxcar and unceremoniously but comically deliver him into the desert amidst its shattered remnants.

With this contemporary Western set in the Prohibition 1920s, having Buster briefly find sanctuary in a railway car of empty beer barrels gives one parody pause. Drinking was illegal in the United States from 1920 to 1933—a "Progressive" era failure, or as my grandfather later explained the "experiment" to me: "A political program that raised the toxic immunity of America 87.3% in 14 years." Yet, shortly before Keaton started *Go West*, a *New York Times* front page story had appeared: "[President Calvin] Coolidge To Press Dry Law To Limit, [Indiana Senator James E.] Watson Declares."[15] Moreover, the day before a high profile dumping of 10,000 barrels of confiscated beer had been dumped in New York harbor. Possibly this helped plant a beer barrel joke in hard drinking Buster's mind. Regardless, empty beer barrels in the saloon-happy West was a joke unto itself, whether the era was "wet" or "dry." One might even call it an absurdist gag, or political commentary on period hypocrisy, in the same category as the comedian's bomb gag in *Cops*. Moreover, *any* Prohibition era boxcar full of empty beer barrels ironically begs a gag line which would later be the title of the last "A" picture in which Keaton would be top billed—*What, No Beer?* (1933). And fittingly, a pivotal sequence in that picture would also involve runaway beer barrels borrowing from the close of Keaton's *Seven Chances* (1927).

Eventually *Go West* finds Buster wandering into a ranch setting in which he is more tolerated than hired for an undermanned outfit. He only bonds with another "friendless one"—the cow Brown Eyes. While Keaton characters seem not entirely of this world, Brown Eyes gets her outsider status more naturally; she is a dairy cow among a herd of longhorn beef cattle. Normally, this would save her from the slaughterhouse but she is also milk barren, not that Keaton has a clue about milking. In fact, his lack of dairy farming skill, mixed with ranching incompetence—an inability to catch and saddle a horse, walk in chaps, or rope a cow—make them perfect range outsiders. Yet, Buster being Buster, he wins the oddity contest by still sticking with his pork pie hat, despite the Western garb, and carrying a gun so small he needs a string to fish it out of his holster.

Since a close period examination of *Go West* continually favors parody over pathos, what undeniably cements the duo of Keaton and cow, is when he removes a stone from her hoof—a self-evident fable spoof of Androcles and the lion. The tale dates from ancient Greece and later turns up both in *Aesop's Fables* and George Bernard Shaw's 1912 play *Androcles and the Lion*. At its most basic, Androcles is a runaway Roman slave who takes shelter in the cave of a wounded lion. The slave removes a large thorn from said lion's paw, and the beast later saves Androcles when he attempts to re-enter civilization. That is, the slave is captured and sentenced by the emperor to be devoured by wild beasts. However, one of the creatures turns out to be the lion, who protects Androcles. Following the rescue, the twosome *forever* become inseparable. Consequently, after Keaton's act of kindness to Brown Eyes, she protects the oblivious pork pie hat-wearing cowboy from a charging longhorn bull. And as with Androcles and the lion, this Western duo also become inseparable—to the point of Brown Eyes even sitting next to Keaton in the back seat of a Model-T Ford at the film's conclusion. Granted, the rancher's attractive daughter is in the car's front seat, but as they say in real estate: "location, location, location."

Keaton has come a long way from his 1923 *Three Ages* parody. Though yes, this film spoofed Griffith's multi-period *Intolerance* (1916), the comedian also needed several time periods in which to create enough jokes to parody a feature-length film. By the time of *Go West* he had parody's compounding phenomenon well in hand.[16] That is, although parody has a focus genre or auteur under comic attack, it frequently is peppered with eclectic references to other structures or texts, such as Androcles and the lion. Fittingly, Keaton has been inspired by the most inherently American (incomparably familiar) genre—the Western.

As previously noted, the 1920s were especially taken with horse operas, with many of Hollywood's "cowboys" literally having once been cowboys. Indeed, Wyatt Earp (1848–1929) actually lived long enough to later be a technical advisor on some silent Westerns. In fact, the Earps have probably always come out as the good guys in the many cinematic renditions of the controversial "Gunfight at the O. K. Corral" because Wyatt helped establish the template. Regardless, the 1920s produced such wonderful Western detail even in the seemingly most unlikely of places, such as *Ladies Home Journal*. During the 1920s it showcased many Western-themed authors besides Zane Grey. Moreover, the color illustrations for these stories were a stunning anticipation of Monument Valley backdrops of John Ford films like *The Searchers* (1956).

Still, the West is arguably America's defining genre, whatever the age, and Keaton was the first of a long line of major comedians to make a feature-length parody of the West. Other notable examples *followed*: Laurel & Hardy's *Way Out West* (1937), W. C. Fields and Mae West's *My Little Chickadee* (1940), the Marx Brothers' *Go West* (1940, on which Keaton worked), Abbott & Costello's *The Wistful Widow of Wagon Gap* (1947), Bob Hope's multiple examples including *Paleface* (1948), and *Son of Paleface* (1952), Martin & Lewis' *Pardners* (1956), Mel Brooks' *Blazing Saddles* (1974), 1986's Steve Martin/Chevy Chase/Martin Short *¡Three Amigos!*, and the Jackie Chan/Owen Wilson *Shanghai Noon* (2000).

Of all these, however, Keaton's cow-loving rendition of the West is easily the most absurd. In fact, this particular film anticipates existentialistic novelist Harry Mathews (1930–2017), because each artist embraced the experimentalist tradition of Kafka, Beckett and Joyce ... "[abiding] by rules of writing ... [which fellow absurdist Georges Perec described as coming] 'from another planet.'"[17] The term experimentalist is pivotal here, because, like dark comedy, it bravely clutches at the unknowable. Yet, Keaton and Mathews seem closer because their stories seem to start with a foot in reality and then fold back into an ambiguity that seems to have "a definitive answer but it all falls apart."[18]

For example, Mathews' first novel, 1962's *Conversations*, has parallels with Keaton's *Seven Chances*. A wealthy individual dies and a task must be performed to inherit a fortune. Yes, Buster did not want to do the adaptation of *Seven Chances*—but the goal of finding a bride is the conventional viable beginning of a tale, just as *Conversations* starts with a seemingly simple task of breaking a code to become rich. But in the latter half of Keaton's film, he manages to make the picture absurdly his own. In a like manner, *Conversations* later becomes this side of obtuse ... although in the tradition of human nature, one wants to think the answer is close. Granted, Buster seems to achieve his *Seven Chances* task, but the film's prolonged beginning chronicling his inability to propose does not bode well for the eventual success of a money-driven marriage. Along similar lines, when Buster ultimately rides off into *Go West*'s Model T sunset seated next to his cow, does the viewer actually feel comfortable with the ending? After all, this is the same comedian 1920's *Moving Picture World* described as fitting and selling "a fancy pair of shoes to a beautiful horse" in *The Blacksmith*, just like she was the stereotypical pretty girl next door.[19] Keaton fan and humorist Robert Benchley, a fellow *LIFE* columnist friend of Robert E. Sherwood, so often such an insightful Buster film critic and once nearly a story contributor to the comedian, seems to have mischievously played with *Go West*'s sexual innuendo. In Benchley's 1927 *LIFE* comic essay "The Passing of the Cow," which appeared at a time when *Go West* would still have been playing in the smaller markets of pre-saturation booking Hollywood, he wrote, in part: "Prior to 1847 it was thought that all these animals [cows] were horses. You can imagine the surprise of the man who first discovered otherwise.... Just what is to be done about ... ["The Passing of the Cow"] is a problem. Some suggest moving lots of cows ... from the East.... The alternative seems to be to bring the cowboys on to where the cows are but that wouldn't work out, because—oh, because it *wouldn't*, that's all. And so it comes

6. Go West *(November 23, 1925)* 111

about that romance dies and Civilization charges ahead. But some of us are wondering, 'Is it all worth it?'"[20]

Benchley's remarks further suggest that Keaton's *Go West* was spoofing all the way. Plus, it also implies that a provocative Buster was saying, "I just don't care," in a pre-existentialistic manner, "whether the world keeps up ... because life is absurd anyway." Keaton films could double as a paraphrasing of novelist Graham Greene's world view: "Life is not black and white but black and gray."[21] Indeed, Greene once described a short story character as if he had Keaton's otherwise blank persona in mind: "His eyes were observant, sad, and curious, like those of a mad corpse in some great catastrophe."[22] And though Greene's twisted Catholicism is often part of his work, whereas atheist Keaton had no time for religion (especially that of the Catholic Talmadges), the novelist was perfectly comfortable in writing the darkly comic international film noir classic *The Third Man* (1949). Even Green referred to himself as a "dubious Catholic." In fact, a key component of existentialism—ambiguity—is why Greene shared another trait with Keaton: love of train travel. For the novelist, it represented the imperceptible merging of countries nondiscriminately divided by what Jean Renoir called "rules of the game." The Keaton explanation is usually his vaudeville youth. Yet, the comedian's rationale might metaphorically be linked to Greene's justification by likening train travel to how film joins often dissimilar pieces of time into one frequently absurd but continuous tale, à la 1924's *Sherlock, Jr.*

Naturally, a train is also central to *Go West* (as in most Keaton films), with cattle being shipped to a Los Angeles market. Yet, Buster will look out for Brown Eyes several times before departure. For example, he saves her from branding by shaving a small section of her hide and then drawing on the ranch logo. Later he also takes some large mounted elk antlers with multiple points (tines/sharp points) from the bunk house and attaches them to the cow's head. Buster does not want her to be at a disadvantage among the longhorn cattle. He also milks the gag along the three-part comic

The Gold Rush (1925), **Chaplin's greatest film.**

"topping" nature of an old gag. First, just the sight of a slightly undersized cow with these fierce-looking, battle-ready antlers fastened to her head is funny. Second, if any of the longhorn cattle were once threatening, now *they* are afraid. Third, when the ranch owner spots Brown Eyes outfitted for primal war, he acts even more surprised than his cattle. Once again parody, actually compound parody, wins out over any question of pathos. If anything, this cow could take on the army and double as the world's largest hat rack.

Then, just before the day of the shipping, filmmaker Keaton blatantly creates a spoofingly comic *anti-pathos* scene. That is, earlier that year Chaplin, the king of pathos, had released *The Gold Rush* (1925) with a comparable scene which, not surprisingly, successfully nailed its poignant goal. And this was not just any Chaplin film. Throughout the silent era every Tramp film had been treated as if it had been FedExed from God, yet this was both his greatest picture, and the one for which he later repeatedly said he wanted to be remembered.

What was the sequence? The Tramp had joined the 1890s Klondike Gold Rush. Upon entering his first saloon he is immediately smitten with a bar hostess (Georgia Hale) across the room. She seems to acknowledge the Tramp with an affectionate wave and rushes towards him. Chaplin's "Little Fellow" is euphoric, only to be devastated when she bolts past him—embracing someone nearby. There is universal pathos here. Who has not had something like this happen? An important or attractive or just plain friendly figure at an otherwise lonely gathering suddenly shows warm signs of recognition and comes your way. Then, when it suddenly turns into an error, one is humiliated, made to feel even more lonely, especially if one has instinctively returned some amiable response to said person.

Now whether Keaton was purposely parodying Chaplin's scene or not, when a comparable sequence appears later in *Go West*, the period viewer would have known what to expect. If s/he was a student of humor they would have seen *The Gold Rush*—by far the top grossing comedy of the silent era. However, if s/he had somehow missed it, remember that Keaton's *Go West* character is called "Friendless." Buster even ups the possible mortification factor. That is, with the Tramp one does have a saloon full of miners to soften the emotional blow. However, the Keaton scene is potentially more haunting. The rancher's daughter has a sliver in her hand and motions to Buster, or the one and only cowboy nearby, that she needs help. She then darts over. Of course, the viewer is pre-conditioned to have her select the drover. However, she goes right to Buster. Besides Keaton the filmmaker scoring another point for *Go West* being a parody rather than pathos (with Chaplin joining Griffith as another possible target), Buster has demonstrated one of the oldest comedy theories—surprise.

Interestingly, while the situation seems to parrot the earlier Androcles myth, only now substituting a splinter from a hand versus a stone taken from the Brown Eyes' hoof, Keaton again underlines parody over pathos. That is, the first time around Keaton had immediately buried the pebble, as if to say, "Bad rock!" The sliver spoofing is even more overt. In order to remove said sliver, he produces a huge switchblade-sized pocketknife, again eliciting surprise both because it is much too large for the task, and because the knife so dwarfs the size of his lost-in-the-holster tiny pistol. However, Keaton does manage to perform the task without cutting off the girl's hand.

Shortly after this "surgery" Buster performs his greatest act of parody, the insertion of the aforementioned variation upon Owen Wister's iconic Western line: "When you call me that, smile!" The catalyst for using it comes after Buster has attempted every way to keep Brown Eyes off the train to market, from pulling his little midget gun to trying to buy her. Since Keaton as a gunslinger is a joke, and he does not have enough money to purchase the cow, he comically tries to raise money by getting into a poker game.

Just as Keaton's cowboy (so called) is less than capable with riding, roping, and revolvers, he shows little skill with poker. But he is desperate enough that he calls one of the two drovers with whom he is playing for cheating. The response in a title is the nearly exact Wister line: "When you say that—SMILE." Knowing he does not have a chance against this real cowboy, Buster must comply. Not only is it possibly the best genre to comedian spoof ever executed in film, it succeeds on three levels. First, it is a burlesque of Wister and his groundbreaking Western novel, which period audiences would have recalled, though it slips by the majority of my college students.

Second, as if written with a future "Great Stone Face" in mind, it is one of cinema's most definitive examples of self-parody. Third, however, the manner in which Keaton produces said smile is arguably a cruel spoof of a famous Lillian Gish scene from Griffith's *Broken Blossoms* (1919). As noted previously in the text, this is another *Go West* body blow burlesque of Griffith. Gish's Lillian Burrows is the title character Broken Blossoms—the abused daughter of Donald Crisp's Battling Burrows (who had worked briefly on Keaton's *The Navigator*, before being let go). After one of Lillian's beatings, her father forces her to smile, and this seemingly impossible task is accomplished using a finger on either side of her mouth to push her lips into a sad semblance of a smile. This is also how Keaton accomplishes his equally sorrowful smile.

Again period audiences would have been aware of the tie-in, since *Blossoms*, produced on the cusp of the Jazz Age, is one of sentimental Griffith's last significant films. Yet, most viewers today would miss the connections, unless they were true Griffith aficionados. However, one can push Keaton's dark parody of this film further by briefly rehashing the slender narrative of what was originally fully titled *Broken Blossoms or The Yellow Man and the Girl*. Richard Barthelomess plays Cheng Huan, who is attempting to spread the peace of Buddha to the London slums. His idealistic goal is fading until he meets Lillian and attempts to bring joy and compassion into her tragic existence. Though given the times this can only be a platonic relationship, it also has the hauntingly sad feel of a "what if" romance.

However, after an extremely grim assault by her father, Lillian can only find safety and care in Cheng's small apartment. Later, when the drunken Burrows learns her whereabouts, and Cheng is momentarily gone, the father comes and drags her home. Ultimately, he pummels Broken Blossom to death. Not knowing this outcome, Cheng races to rescue her. After Cheng discovers the worst, Burrows attacks him with a hatchet and Cheng shoots the father to death, then takes his own life. Thus, there are five possible additional hard parody moments Keaton is drawing upon. First, the original spoof of making Buster break his signature persona norm does not stop there. Gish's character was in such a sorry state that she was also being bullied into doing something outside the norm. Second, *Blossoms* also showcased two "friendless" creatures in a harsh setting.

Third, Cheng, like Keaton, repeatedly tried to assist Lillian from what literally became a "slaughterhouse" situation. Fourth, the story dictated that the gentle Cheng take actions, like Keaton drawing a gun; these were unnatural to both characters. Five, any kind of accepted union then was not possible for Lillian and Cheng, just as the Buster-Brown Eyes continues to be outside the pale. Keaton pulls no punches in extrapolating broad burlesque from Griffith.

Regardless, when it is time for the steers and Brown Eyes to head off to market, Buster is in the boxcar with them. But the trip to Los Angeles will be far from uneventful, because a rival rancher is out to stop the action until cattle prices are better. Though this would help Keaton's cause, he remains loyal to his boss while still holding hope for Brown Eyes. Meanwhile, the owner of the herd and his daughter hear about the attempted cattle train ambush and rush to Los Angeles by car.

When Buster and the train reach Los Angeles' slaughterhouse area, he experiences what the French would call "arriving like a flower," intimating he is ready to be plucked, or more to the point, Brown Eyes is in danger. Yet, a more fitting theatre of the absurd take on the situation comes from comedian Irwin Corey, whom critic Kenneth Tynan called "Chaplin's clown with a college education."[23] Corey's signature saying superbly fits this quandary: "If we don't change directions soon, we'll end up where we're going." Regardless, Keaton immediately thinks of rescue by chaos. He begins to open the cattle cars and turn the longhorn's loose on downtown Los Angeles.

Though there is no proverbial "bull in a china shop," one gets the picture, as some of the cattle investigate everything from a barbershop to a Turkish bath. Once Keaton has found and safely parked Brown Eyes, he again strives to help his boss by attempting to herd the cattle toward the stockyards. This is no easy task, with what appears to be longhorn window-shopping. But eventually he produces a modest stampede. Unfortunately, it is neither as hilarious as the stampeding brides of *Seven Chances*, nor concluded as creatively, when the brides and Buster play dodge ball with the rockslide.

Keaton's play to direct the moving cattle is to enter a nearby costume shop and rent a *red* devil's costume. With this living matador cape as an added incentive Buster is able to funnel the longhorns into the city's stockyards. Plus, since the cattle are chasing him, it also allows the comedian to exhibit what he does best, which is to run. And as Hollywood's most entertaining track star, this man with no reverse gear is the best thing in *Go West*'s near-finale.

Ultimately, he is successful. For both stopping the ambush and getting the cattle to market, a grateful rancher tells Buster, via a title card: "My home and anything I have is yours for the asking." Moreover, his pretty and equally sympathetic daughter is just behind him. Now, in a variation upon the earlier anti-pathos choice made by said daughter, with regard to choosing Buster to remove the sliver, the comedian seems to return the favor by way of another title card reading: "I want her." However, this is another anti-pathos *gottcha* which cheats slightly. Because just out of audience eyesight is Keaton's real choice—Brown Eyes.

Father and daughter laugh nervously as if Buster is kidding. However, the film ends with the *foursome* driving off together, with Brown Eyes joining Keaton in the back seat. Many modern critics and/or historians, who will be addressed shortly, seem to leave the parody or pathos choice up in the air. And this is their right, à la D. H. Lawrence's "Trust the tale, not the teller." Be that as it may, given the mega-accumulation of parody examples cited, from Western generic (Keaton being unable to rope or ride), to dark Griffith spoofs with the same rhythms as combat, it does not seem hard to pick a lane—it was dark comedy parody.[24]

So what was the period response to *Go West?* Going back to the chapter's opening, it generally matched Keaton's inability to roll a cigarette Western-style. The theatre-oriented *Harrison's Reports* guide said, "Pretty good but Mr. Keaton has made many comedies better than this one. There are some novel comedy situations introduced, but they soon wear out from constant using."[25] *Photoplay* complained: "It's rather a sad state of affairs when our old friend Buster Keaton can't put over the laughs. He prances around with that frozen look on his face trying to be funny and with the aid of a big cow does his best with an improbable story. The gags are not what they should be and they don't come fast enough."[26] Though this review and most of the ones to follow nervously often found something positive to say, *Motion Picture Classic* still had to grumble: "'Go West,' Buster Keaton's new comedy, was another disappointment to me. This story of Buster's adventures on a cattle range ... should have had more possibilities than 'Go West' reveals.... Even President Coolidge [whom period critics kidded "appeared to have been weaned on a dill pickle," and thus should be predisposed to a laugh] will agree with me ... that this is far, far inferior to the Keaton classic, 'The Navigator.'"[27] *Screenland* groused: "The trouble with 'Go West' isn't that it is not funny but that it isn't funny enough. Buster wrote the story himself, and he suffered the fate of all authors who get so wrapped up in their creative efforts that they lose their sense of values. If he had boiled down his own story to a couple of reels [the period short subject] and added to it a few reels of somebody else's gags, he would have had a more satisfying comedy."[28] The *New York World* protested, "[Buster] chooses to laugh at cowboys, or rather to make you laugh at his conception of a cowboy. You laugh but not inordinately."[29] Syndicated critic/columnist Louella O. Parsons observed in the *New York American*: "'Go West' is one of those comedies that has a different mission. By that I mean you are supposed to laugh and failing to do this there is not much left. The plot is obscure. The burden of the picture rests on the shoulders of the unassuming Mr. Keaton, who gives us ample reasons for imitating him [and his 'frozen face']. 'The Navigator' is infinitely superior.... In fact, any recent Keaton ... has much more to recommend it...."[30] *Variety* added to Keaton's period woes by positing: "This latest comedy has Buster Keaton slipping over a series of comedy stunts that cause but mild laughter ... treading on the toes of the Western stars.... Tom Mix has 'Tony,' Bill Hart his 'Pinto,' so along comes Buster with his 'Brown Eyes.' [But] the laughs are few and far between ... too much of it is shot in the distance and the audience does not get a chance to watch ... whatever laughs there might have been.... The Capitol audience that jammed the house Sunday missed them if there."[31]

Modern takes, however, on *Go West* being a period failure are still misleading. First, there were some good reviews from prestigious sources, such as the *New York Times*, which noted: "Although Buster Keaton's new film ... is somewhat lackadaisical in the introductory sequences, when the fun does start popping it is rich and uproarious, with countless novel comedy twists."[32] The *Los Angeles Times*, without actually labeling *Go West* "an art house film," attempted to praise the fact that Keaton's dark parody was taking comedy in a new direction.[33] But it did not yet have the vocabulary with which to adequately describe it: Though struggling for a future phrase, like "reaffirmation parody," the review was still titled: "GREAT COMEDY: Buster Keaton Triumphs in Go West."[34]

Keaton's most insightful period champion, *LIFE*'s Robert E. Sherwood, also struggled to articulate the dark comedy realm to which Keaton had gone in *Go West*. Yet, Sherwood intuitively recognized the comedian had done something special: "Buster Keaton plays it with his usual deadpan, and with occasional sidesteps into the realms of ridiculousness. In these moments he is terribly funny, but for the major part of the picture he is inexpressively sad.... Towards the end ... Buster loses control.... But 'Go West' is a good picture—best, I think, that Keaton has done since 'Our Hospitality.'"[35] Keaton's 180-degree twists from "usual deadpan," to "ridiculousness," to "inexpressively sad," and so on, are reminiscent of what I encountered in doing books on Chaplin and dark comedy, especially pertaining to his *The Great Dictator* 1940.[36] For example, *New York Times* Bosley Crowther suggested in an otherwise positive review of Chaplin's film that for many people, "the subject of it [Hitler] is much too grim for jesting."[37] Along similar lines, John Masher's generally positive

New Yorker review opens with a telling overview of the then shell-shocked (over dark comedy) viewing public: "There's a general feeling ... prevalent around town that *The Great Dictator* is a very curious affair indeed, something distinctly odd, and certainly unique. People aren't sure that they like it, or anyhow they aren't very eloquent about why they do, or ... why they don't."[38] Masher goes on to say a great many laudatory things about the movie, such as calling "the [globe] dance of the dictator at play with the world ... just about as delightful a bit as Charlie Chaplin has ever given us anywhere."[39] Still, Masher's opening time capsule take on the uneasy state of dark comedy in 1940 remains his most telling contribution to the film's literature.

Now, go back fifteen more years and substitute Keaton dating a cow for Hitler, and one gets a sense of what pioneering film critics were wrestling with on *Go West*. It was not until *Dr. Strangelove or: How I Learned to Stop Worrying and Love the Bomb* (1964) finally dragged dark comedy to center stage that *some* people found it acceptable.[40] Of course, when any example of the genre becomes acceptable it is no longer dark comedy. "Offensive or shocking" is mandatory. For example, what follows is a Kurt Vonnegut observation from over a decade ago. By now most of its provocation has gone, though hopefully a few may still find it discourteous: "I have some good news for you and some bad news. The bad news is that the Martians have landed in New York City and are staying in the Waldorf Astoria. The good news is that they only eat homeless men, woman, and children of all colors, and they pee gasoline."[41]

Regardless, beyond a 1920s attempt to grasp Keaton coupling dark comedy to parody, deciphering difficulty of the same phenomenon in future films will never completely go away—no matter the comedian. Black humor recalibrates all things provocative as comedy. And as one age morphs into another, there is constant flux. Plus, another dark comedy component and/or its merging with another genre (such as parody or satire) raises free speech to absurdity as art—a right not granted groundbreakers like Lenny Bruce (1924–1966). Consequently or not, some period *Go West* critics were actually operating under this umbrella, too. For instance, *The New Yorker* review opens so far overboard in what might be mistakenly labeled as pathos that it qualifies as its own form of dark comedy lite parody: "BUSTER KEATON had better have a care. For a good half of 'Go West' (Capitol) he made us weep—not furtive drips of glycerin but copious deluges of real salt drops. The ninety-seven tons of water that recently fell on London was a mere creek compared to our Niagara."[42]

This was not meant to be taken seriously as pathos praise for Keaton but rather, like *Go West*, over-the-top spoofing of pathos. One never reads about a film from Chaplin, potentate of pathos, along these lines. This is the kind of thing which describes *missing* the Chaplin touch and slip sliding into mawkishness. It is underlined later when *The New Yorker* critic acknowledges basically enjoying *Go West*, notwithstanding for him, its strange parody. Moreover, in a comedy critique, references to tears are more likely to occur when the comedian *unsuccessfully* attempts to produce pathos. This is best demonstrated in a 1927 *New York Sun* review of Langdon's poor post–Capra picture, *Three's a Crowd*: "the funnyman's cherished 'tears behind the laugh,' has been exploited at the expense of the laugh. The tears are many. The jokes are few. Even the [signature] birdlike gestures and mobile face of the star could not make them [laughs] adequate in number."[43]

Beyond these reasons, there was another rationale to qualify the modern era's blanket statement that *Go West* was a 1920s critical failure. Reviewers were either not reluctant, as noted earlier, to still find something redeeming in the film, or there was at least an acknowledgment of a cult-like following for Keaton. To illustrate, even *Screenplay*'s harsh review conceded that, "while he won't gain new friends by this one, his old fans will stick by him and keep a hopeful eye open for his next."[44] His dark comedy of the absurd was simply ahead of its time, more fitting for existentialistic today than Lloyd's *be happy* 1920s. Indeed, one might even couple Keaton with the darkly comic, anti-establishment cultish success of the Depression's underrated W. C. Fields.[45]

As a brief addendum to the preceding reference to Lloyd, Edmund Wilson brings a biting late 1925 *New Republic* slant to the preceding discussion. He grants that the pathos success of Chaplin's *The Gold Rush* could have influenced both *Go West* and Lloyd's *The Freshmen* (all 1925). If so, however, Wilson found them failing.[46] He only seems to have considered the point because "Lloyd has never been a very good actor ... but Keaton is an able pantomimist ... [capable of] a certain sympathy."[47]

Regardless, Keaton period literature for *Go West* also mapped out invaluable additional insights on the comedian. First, it further underlined that during the 1920s *The Navigator* remained the benchmark for Keaton's work. This would not be changed by the period's later less than enthusiastic reception for *The General* (1926, see Chapter 8), which is so highly praised today. Plus, there still remained a lingering fondness for Keaton's *Our Hospitality* (1923) throughout the 1920s. Second, like his existentialistic films, Keaton seemed to increasingly embrace that perspective in his work, until *The General* debacle. To illustrate, after the disappointing reception of *Seven Chances*, he decides to do an expensive on-location dark comedy parody with a cow for his heroine. In contrast, after Chaplin's dispiritedness over the tepid commercial reception to *A Woman of Paris* (1923), by 1928 he had not only returned to the Tramp, his *Circus* was seen as an inspired return to an earlier, broader comic era. To illustrate, among the film's innumerable rhapsodizing reviews and articles was this 1928 statement from a *Los Angeles Times* article: "'The Circus' will probably rate as one of the biggest popular successes that Chaplin has produced in years. It is in the nature of a return to his earlier style."[48]

Third, modern historians do not know what to do with *Go West*. It is considered a beloved oddity or a provocative oddity. Texts frequently neglect it given its fascinating yet poor period reception, or underline its apparent break with much of the Keaton cynical mode—read, "pathos." *Yet*, since Buster is all about *dark parody and absurdity*, why would he not take it to a really *waiting-for-existentialism* extreme? Moreover, if your persona never smiles anyway, would it not really be compelling to at least once push that tendency into some prairie dust—especially with literature's most famous cowboy being threatened to smile. If these seem like fighting words, the next chapter is about boxing. Thus, attempt to follow Keaton's dark comedy parody signal and tune out the other noise.

7

Battling Butler (August 30, 1926)

"I'd like to marry that pretty little mountain girl."—Alfred Butler (Buster Keaton) to his valet (Snitz Edwards)

This film title observation occurs fairly early in *Battling Butler*, a movie in which Buster Keaton returns to a variation of *The Navigator*'s (1924) pampered boy/man Rollo Treadway, who eventually plays at being a professional fighter. The opening quote has been chosen for three reasons. First, the comedian was returning to his popular mainstream characterization after the release of his last picture—the dark parody absurdity *Go West* (1925). This existentialism-anticipating picture was far from a critical darling, but it still had a then hard to describe allure for Keaton's sometimes cultish following. A pocket review from *Photoplay*'s May 1926 issue might best capture the odd film's original reception: "Hardly a comedy because hardly a laugh. Yet, the picture is very interesting."[1] This Rollo safety valve figure had first been "essayed" by Keaton as the title character of *The Saphead* (1920), a mediocre movie in which the comedian had only acted, yet he had run away with the reviews.

Second, Buster and his valet Snitz (1868–1937) are a minimalist delightful team of sorts, which could be ranked with such later pleasurable rich/servant duos as *My Man Godfrey*'s (1936) Carole Lombard and William Powell, or *Arthur*'s (1981) Dudley Moore and, ironically, valet *Sir* John Gielgud. Among the many delights of the Buster-Snitz twosome is the frequent repetition of the comedian telling his valet some entitled variation of "Arrange it" whenever the story presents a time-consuming task.

Snitz had appeared earlier with Buster in *Seven Chances* (1925) as the lawyer who presents the narrative catalyst will, and he would surface yet again as Dean Edwards (recycling his surname) in Keaton's *College* (1927). However, *Battling Butler* provides Snitz with more screen time, and a chance to greatly enhance the humor of the picture in a part closely tied to Keaton. Moreover, the character actor represents a variation of what sometimes unfortunately occurs in an auteur study. That is, as years pass, supporting elements are eliminated by the weight of time, and the focus artist too often receives all the attention. Such is the case here.

Snitz is normally mentioned in modern accounts of Keaton films but seemingly only because of his humorously homely face, or because he was shorter than small Keaton (ah, ego). For example, in Rudi Blesh's much later Keaton biography, he notes both the size factor and a comic description of Snitz: "an unforgettable face, quizzical, bird-eyed, and wizened."[2] The end. Yet, Snitz did not get there accidentally. In the 1920s he was a popular high-profile character actor in major productions. For example, he had appeared in the

Ernst Lubitsch-directed Mary Pickford film *Rosita* (1923), with *Variety* observing, "Snitz Edwards as a bloodthirsty little jailor is a scream."[3]

The following year Edwards was second-billed to Douglas Fairbanks in the swashbuckler's epic sensation *The Thief of Bagdad* (1924). *Variety* said his ties to Fairbanks as an "associate in the [story's] evil days is one of the outstanding figures [in the picture]."[4] Edwards' filmography might have been larger, but he was also a popular stage performer on Broadway and the West Coast. For instance, before production started on *Battling Butler*, the *Los Angeles Times* stated in a 1926 article titled "Snitz Edwards to Appear at the Potboilers [Art Theatre]": "Snitz Edwards, eminent stage and screen actor, will play the character role in Alan Brooks' one-act play, 'No Women Should Do It' ... Edwards will be remembered as the humorous companion of Douglas Fairbanks in 'The Thief of Bagdad' and also for many other distinctive characters on the screen."[5]

Third, the Keaton reference to wanting to marry the "mountain girl" (Sally O'Neil) is significant for several reasons. One could just call it a family in-joke, since his sister-in-law Constance Talmadge's first major part was the "mountain girl" in D. W. Griffith's *Intolerance* (1916). Also, it could be Keaton once again (see previous chapter) harshly spoofing Griffith's overly conspicuous sentimentality by not even giving his love interest a proper name. And though without Snitz's acting resume, O'Neil had had her breakout performance the preceding year in *Sally, Irene and Mary* (1925), a chronicle of three chorus girls—costarring future stars Constance Bennett and Joan Crawford. Fittingly for *Battling Butler*, O'Neil's Mary was the good girl who settles down. In addition, like Snitz, O'Neil was comfortable on stage, too. In a later large *Los Angeles Times* (November 23, 1928) fawning photo, she was praised: "Girl with a Sparkle Rules Stage."

For me, however, O'Neil's leading lady was that rare Keaton heroine with whom a real romantic connection is made. Of course, one might say that was not difficult to do, since his last show of passion was for *Go West*'s cow, Brown Eyes. Plus, another more serious negative would be that, as in *The Navigator*, his decision to marry simply comes out of nowhere. Indeed, the *Butler* choice is all the more sudden since Buster has just met her, whereas his *Navigator* leading actress (Kathryn McGuire) had at least been his screen neighbor—implying some sort of shared background, however minor.

Still, just as the film's closing fight is memorable for being realistic, versus yet another comic film fisticuffs, earlier there had been a tender parting of the two which felt poignantly genuine. It occurs just after a surprise wedding Buster had not seen coming. That is, to impress O'Neil's giant father and brother he was not a weakling, he pretended to be Battling Butler, a challenger to the lightweight champion. Assuming the champion would win, the Butler story would just fade away and Keaton and the girl could get back to their romance. Leaving the country with Snitz as a cover for the alleged fight, the real Butler pulls an upset. Thus, honorable Buster returns to confess, assuming there is no way to continue the masquerade, expecting the girl to drop him. However, since the mountain girl's community has not seen the fight, he is feted as a champion.

Instead of losing the girl by confessing a lie, the subterfuge continues with the father having organized a wedding and a banquet for the new couple. But wanting his story by association to continue, this patriarch immediately declares Keaton must go into training for his next fight. The comedian then gives Snitz yet another funny "Arrange it" command, via a title. Not surprisingly, the new bride wants to go with Keaton and his comic sidekick, who had hatched the whole fraud when the girl's Neanderthal family had not incorrectly first seen Butler as less than manly. Consequently, in order to continue the duplicity, this boy/man creates an uproarious whopper to keep her home. A title announces: "I want you to know me as I am—not the brutal blood-thirsty beast that I am when fighting." Then comes the 180-degree mood change. They kiss good-bye but she follows him outside for yet another peck. And before the flatbacked trunkless period car can pull away, this new bride has gone to the vehicle's rear window for a restrained yet spontaneous lips to the glass final farewell. It is hardly the sort of bona fide show of emotion one expects of the usually self-centered demanding Talmadge-like Keaton heroine. There is also an added ardent reaction to the scene, because he appears to like her as much as "Brown Eyes," and fears it is a real farewell, because it no longer seems possible to sustain his false identity.

Be that as it may, one now needs to flesh out the complete narrative of what had recently been a hit Broadway *musical*. Yes, Keaton was primed to make an even bigger hit *silent* comedy from a play that as recently as an October 1923 *New York Herald* ad promised "*BATTLING BUTLER*: A Musical Knockout."[6] A special change is made, however, to the story to play to Keaton's boy/man persona. Plus, this was a play Keaton personally selected, unlike the earlier *Seven Chances*, which his brother-in-law boss Joseph Schenck had purchased for the less-than-pleased comedian. Some modern Keaton texts suggest otherwise, but several late 1925 *Los Angeles Times* articles make it clear this was Buster's choice. There was even a sense of mystery in the early coverage. For example, on October 25 it was reported: "Buster Keaton plans to make his next photoscreen entirely different from any comedy he has ever brought to the screen. Although the frozen-faced farceur will retain his pancake chapeau [hat, which actually proves to be false].... The picture itself is scheduled as a revelation."[7] The term "revelation" also speaks to the aforementioned added realism Buster brings to both his relationship with the heroine and to the comedian's closing fight.

With Keaton still playing this next project close to the vest, another *Times* piece from October 16 stated, "One of the comedian's objectives when he went East was to procure ... a new laugh-provoker, and he is reported to have found the type of story he sought."[8] (Though not noted, the article says "one" of the reasons for the eastern trip was also to enable the baseball-loving Keaton to take in the annual "fall classic" World Series.) Yet, it is not until a December 16 *Los Angeles Times* essay that the comedian is willing to reveal what the project will be, underlining that it was entirely a Keaton-driven project: "The deal for the screen rights to 'Battling Butler' was opened in September but the manager [Lou Anger] recruited the new staff and completed plans to make the picture before confirming the purchase."[9] Of course, Keaton's short-lived secrecy about *Battling Butler* was hardly new to Hollywood. Chaplin frequently would forbid his players from even discussing a current project. Plus, his working film titles were often just whatever the chronological number that feature happened to be in his filmography. However, with regard to Keaton and the term "feature," it seems curious and/or prophetic that the previously quoted *Times* piece was entitled "Keaton's Next Is Prize-Fight Comedy Feature."[10] By this time in the 1920s all Keaton's comedies were features; the headline seems redundant. Granted, comedy features ran shorter during this period, usually around an hour. For example, *Seven Chances* is 57 minutes long, and even though *Sherlock, Jr.* (1924) clocks in at just 45 minutes, it is also granted feature status. These observations are merely noted because *Battling Butler* runs over 80 minutes, Keaton's longest film to date. Moreover, it was obvious from his preproduction comments and the previously highlighted serious scenes that this picture was a turning point in his evolution as an artist. This is also suggested in the period reviews, which will be addressed shortly. In addition, it hardly seems coincidence that his most sober-minded feature, *The General* (1926), follows *Battling Butler*.

Be that as it may, *Butler* begins as one would expect a Saphead/Rollo-inspired film would. A father disgusted with a do-nothing boy/man son suggests his offspring visit the country. By title his father states, in part: "go out and rough it. Maybe it will make a man out of you if you have to take care of yourself for a while." However, one must pause briefly to note a key change before continuing. In the original play the central character is a Thurberesque husband using such trips as a getaway. In an October 1923 *New York Evening Telegraph* review of the hit stage production, Charles Ruggles' wealthy central character is described as being so "dominated by his masterful wife that he grows so extremely weary of his spouse and his quiet New Hampshire home ... that he [periodically] poses before his wife and the merry villagers as 'Battling Butler' ... [and escapes to some vague country] training camp, where he makes things hum [parties]."[11] The film story is more realistic and better fits Buster's youthful screen alter ego, which will soon become part of a series of problems, as a troubled personal life contributes to the comedian prematurely aging.

Regardless, Buster's version quickly becomes a compound joke. He takes his man servant Snitz, with the audience getting both the first example of the comedian's valet mantra "Arrange it," and then seeing them leave, in a Rolls Royce and an attached trailer. The latter vehicle will essentially be shown to contain a tent large enough to reproduce his elegant bedroom suite, not to mention a fashionable dining room table, all the essential delicacies, and the means for Snitz to prepare them. Moreover, this back –to-nature expedition also includes daily visits by the paperboy and ice man (for a 1920s version of a refrigerator). Even with his go-to servant, the audience quickly realizes Butler also has no talent for hunting (though a zoo-sized assortment of wildlife is showcased around him). Plus, his abilities as a fisherman are worse—topped off by shooting a hole in his rowboat and sinking.

Set against this Davy Crockett backdrop, however, Buster doubles down on his amusing incompetence by the comic incongruity of his various lavishly ostentatious hunting and fishing outfits, not to mention a gentleman's posh bedroom attire. The most amusing outfit, however, is his firearm-toting garb, which could double for actor Basil Rathbone's signature Sherlock Holmes costume in the future "B" film series. One half expects to see the London fog roll in at any moment, or hear Big Ben in the distance. Still, Buster is most handsome in the assorted clothing, which further adds to the humor, since it looks as if he has wandered away from some rustic photo shoot. In fact, historian/theorist Gerald Mast would later write there is a suggestion of a male fashion show."[12] Regardless, though attired like the hunting aristocrats of Jean Renoir's later *Rules of the Game* (1939), this in one outing in which the animals could safely have settled down for a picnic.

Keaton's appearance as "Mr. Outdoorsman" was a more subtle variation on his earlier spoofs of "How to" books and magazines which had become so popular during a period when, for the first time, many Americans had more free time. Indeed, later in *Butler* Keaton will be getting romantic hints from a newspaper column called *Advice to the Lovesick* by the comically yet fittingly named author Beatrice Faircatch. Regardless, while magazines like *Field & Stream* (1895) and *Outdoor Life* (1898) had been around for some time, their circulation, and that of magazines like them, increased during this era. In fact, the same year *Butler* appeared, the journal *Western Hunter Magazine* (1926) first materialized. Again, while absurdity was central to his oeuvre, it need not be the broad genius of his surrealistically assembled house from 1920s *One Week*. The more subdued parody of his incongruously fashionable garb worked, too. As Laura Collins-Hughes has written, "The primary job of interpreting the classics—absolutely primary job—is to discover the immediate significance of the work in ... [its] time."[13] And Keaton was dovetailing his parody into the preposterous promises of increased Jazz Age consumerism. In point of fact, even that wonderfully strange *One Week* kit house which Buster assembled incorrectly, because the box numbers were scrambled, was a sign of the times. For example, the Sears catalog of the late 1910s and early 1920s offered ready-to-be-assembled kit homes.

A provocative footnote to an often key Keaton component of playing upon popular commercial trends was a February 1923 *New York Daily News* declaration denouncing the "growth of commercialism in the movies," by several film stars.[14] This early declaration against what a later age would call "product placement" is not without interest in and of itself. However, it is most striking with regard to non-signer Keaton by some who added their names—comedy competitors Chaplin and Lloyd, and both of Buster's sisters-in-law, Norma and Constance Talmadge. Though consistent with the originality of Chaplin, it seems rather hypocritical of Lloyd, who often played upon current trends, and the aforementioned fashion-setting fads of Buster's relatives. (Here was one more source of conflict with his sisters-in-law.)

Regardless, along those topical lines, a key difference between Lloyd and Keaton is that both comedians often played upon these promises of progress ... but Lloyd ultimately embraced the lie and succeeded, while poor "Zero" Keaton failed. For instance, if *Butler* had waited long enough for Keaton to bag something, despite an abundance of animals (via a nature montage befitting Disney), it would have made your cable guy seem punctual. Moreover, Buster further tops the absurdity in all this show by forever remaining in polite society mode, even after sinking his boat. In fact, it briefly seemed as if the artist was returning to the ratcheted up surrealism of his early short subjects. That is, after he sinks his boat, mountain girl rows by and Keaton politely tips his hat, though only his head and hat are above water.

There is even surrealism in what begins as a *traditional romantic sequence*, a phrase seldom attributed to a Keaton film. The couple have an informal lunch with the most formal of culinary regalia set against a lush forest backdrop. Though all thanks go to ever-present Snitz, Keaton and the girl are quite oblivious as they talk the day away. Yet, a series of dissolves cleverly and comically mark the passage of time—the legs of the fancy card table are gradually sinking into the soft soil. By twilight the wood surface could be doubling for a picnic blanket as the duo are now lying on the ground facing each other and still chatting with no sense of time. A special connection has been made, though it would seem that neither had been schooled in the phenomenon. I found Keaton's sincerity here striking. As commented upon earlier, the comedian's persona is essentially based upon a childhood universe. No one has better expressed this tendency than James Baldwin's movie-related book *The Devil Finds Work*: "A child is far too self-centered to relate to any dilemma which does not, somehow, relate to him—to his own evolving dilemma. A child escapes into what he would like his situation to be."[15] Ultimately, at twilight, of course, one soon returns to comic normal when Keaton then walks her home, only to become disoriented, and she must then walk him back.

This is definitely the young lady for Buster, and naturally he turns to the aforementioned *Advice to the Lovesick* for assistance. Now prior to this sequence, a self-help text for Keaton characters represented a joke onto itself. The implication was either the aid did not help, or as in *Sherlock, Jr.*, his detective primer nearly cost him the girl. However, in *Butler* he eclipses all other spoofing put-downs of these items. His man/child works hard studying this dubious guide for confessing his adoration, even playing both parts. *Lovesick* suggests an exchange of dialogue hoary with age even for 1926, with the possible dialogue-starting scenario:

7. Battling Butler *(August 30, 1926)*

A *Battling Butler* lobby card depicting two Keatons, a photograph of a young man and a cartoon Buster as a boy boxer. Who will it be?

> BOY: Do you think you could learn to love me?
> GIRL: What—what do you mean?
> BOY: I'm crazy about you.
> GIRL: This is so sudden....

But when Buster starts the litany, he gets no further than its opening before the mountain girl blows the "how to" model out of the water. A second title starts:

> BUSTER: Do you think you could learn to love me?
> GIRL: I have.

Keaton's oh-so-expressive eyes seem to say, "Tricked again by alleged logic." He tears up the column and kisses her.

This is the point in the film when Buster's man Friday, Snitz, hatches the plan that his boss is a famous boxer with the same name training in their woods. Because the valet realizes the girl's Neanderthal-like father and brother—two creatures who only recently seem to have learned how to walk erect, are less than impressed with Keaton's manliness. However, the father-son duo buy into the chicanery, assisted by a "Battling Butler" boxing article in the newspaper of the comedian's wilderness-delivering paperboy.

Consequently, Buster and Snitz then leave for the actual location of the champion's training camp. This will help preserve Keaton's cover, since his correspondence with the mountain girl will have the same address. On the drive Keaton and his valet happen to pick up the flirtatious wife of the real champion boxer (Francis McDonald). Out for a walk, she has broken a heel off a shoe. Keaton and Snitz drop her off at the hotel in which they will also be staying.

The jealous champion sees the trio together and gets the wrong idea. This is further suggested when Buster later goes to watch the boxer train. (At that time such camps were open to the public for PR purposes.) Seeing the champion's wife, Keaton innocently asks in title: "How's your heel?" But she laughs, thinking the comedian has made a witty pun about her husband. They leave together but when Buster sees the mountain girl in the distance, he heads back to the gym. His new love having arrived, he pretends to work out, with the champion having left to do some "road work" running.

The following day both women happen to meet and just as Buster is about to have his smokescreen blown, the ever-reliable Snitz comes to the rescue. He quickly explains the situation to McDonald's nearby champion and begs for help. Surprisingly, the boxer is more than gracious and plays along. But on his way out he tells Buster that the comedian will be the one fighting the champion's challenger—"The Alabama Murderer." The comment is then fleshed out in the following title, when the champion tells his manager: "If he wants to be Battling Butler let him fight the Alabama Murderer, and he'll never flirt with anybody's wife again." It is quickly followed by a follow-up title comment by the champion to the manager: "I'm through—get him [Buster] in shape the best you can."

This then establishes the perfect reason for an extended comic sequence in which boy/man Keaton attempts to become a boxer. This is a scenario in which a high percentage of major comedians have at sometimes played at being a boxer. The gold standard belongs to Chaplin's brilliantly choreographed fight in *City Lights* (1931), which inventively makes excellent use of the referee, too. Of the many possible runners-up, Jerry Lewis' tour de force in *Sailor Beware* (1931), arguably his funniest solo routine, would be an excellent second.

In contrast, Keaton's situation is slightly different since it keys upon the learning process more than on an actual fight, not unlike similar sequences with Harold Lloyd early in *The Milky Way* (1936), and somewhat replicated by Danny Kaye's *The Kid From Brooklyn* (1946) remake.[16] Of course, both these films, as well as Keaton's *Battling Butler*, will ultimately result in a big fight sequence. Yet, the best and most sustained comic boxing bits occur in the learning scenes.

With Keaton's character being a pampered boy/man, once his sparring partner starts to hit him he runs away, not unlike Lewis' novice in *Sailor Beware*. He also hides behind his manager, a comic defense maneuver Chaplin used in *City Lights*—only his inadvertent protector is the referee. Yet, the funniest Keaton sequence is when our fearful "Zero" figure runs and jumps into his manager's arms, much, as was noted earlier, Johnny Carson later did with his sidekick Ed McMahon.

Naturally, as with seemingly all clowns doing a boxing sketch, Keaton also had problems with the ropes around the ring. After nearly being strangled on one of his first efforts to navigate this obstacle, he borrows a safer technique from his favorite sport—baseball. That is, Buster takes to just sliding under the ropes, an unconventional technique which is funnier each time. These Keaton boxing turns, and several others, are randomly funny but without the single tight sketch quality of the aforementioned Chaplin and Lewis routines. However, Keaton had at least one topper to all previous comic examples. His little boy/man easily seemed the most terrified. Buster was in the loopy big-eyed realm of a vampire surprised by a cross.

Because of this, it makes the picture's concluding realistic fight all the more significant. However, the metamorphosis finale merits setting up. The champion had lied to Buster. If the proverb is true that "revenge is a dish best served cold," how much more satisfying it would be to provide two helpings. The champion had always planned to take on the challenger, which he successfully does. As noted, his payback had two entrees. First, the champion had put Keaton through both the psychological horror and the physical pain of preparing to fight a challenger named "The Alabama Murderer." Second, after destroying said boxer, he planned to privately do the same to Buster, away from the arena's crowd. Innocent Keaton walked straight into phase two. Going up to this possessive husband, he ironically said, via a title: "Thanks for saving me." However, here is where the bullying champion's revenge really kicks in. The attentive viewer has already noted that he has given his coquettish wife an off-screen black eye. He now plans to annihilate Buster for allegedly flirting with her.

At this point O'Neil's mountain girl still does not know Buster is impersonating the professional boxer with the same name. Strategist Snitz had locked her in a closet during the title fight (continuing to maintain Keaton's secret), while ordering an ambulance for his boss—given Keaton's complete lack of boxing skills. Sadly, the waiting hospital vehicle still could be necessary given the way the champion begins to rain punches down on the comedian ... only now it has ceased to be a comedy. Unlike any of the previously noted funnymen boxing sequences, none had ever turned deadly serious. Only when Buster's mountain girl wife appears in the room does Keaton somehow transform himself into a boxer bar none. He suddenly so dominates the champion that the once antihero has to be pulled off his antagonist.

One would have thought Buster had received some artificial stimulant, such as when Chaplin's Tramp accidently sits on a heroin needle in *Easy Street* (1917), and suddenly is able to protect himself from a villain. But Keaton just could not bear to be shamed in front of his bride. Plus, there is authenticity in his fighting, since it is primal punching without any style other than survival. One could contrast it with his successful yet contrived athletic conclusion to *College*, when he somehow flawlessly utilizes a litany of track skills to save the girl—all of which he had failed at miserably earlier in the film. Even the strikingly different conclusions to *Battling Butler* and *College* seem to bear this out. The former has a comically happy finale, as he and his wife joyfully walk down a New York street (the arena was meant to have been Madison Square Garden), with him still in his boxing trunks but sporting a top hat. *College* closes with the aforementioned series of depressing dissolves that end on two tombstones. (As a postscript, his *College* girl was also the more typical nagging Keaton heroine who wanted to change him; however, when his Butler figure finally confesses by title card to the mountain girl, "I'm not a fighter," she sincerely replies, "I'm glad.")

The film opened in late August 1926. Earlier in this text it was noted that Keaton, like contemporary print satirist Will Cuppy, often had a distracting event occur around the time his movies premiered. Ironically, it happened again with *Battling Butler*. The famed original "Latin Lover," Rudolph Valentino, died unexpectedly on August 23, producing filmland's first death extravaganza. His New York demise, after surgery on a perforated liver, was coast-to-coast front page news, such as the *New York Sun*'s large print caption: "DEATH ENDS VALENTINO'S CAREER AT 31."[17] Shock and possible scandal also swirled around Valentino's death, given both his youth and the fact that one of his most critical and commercial hits, *Son of the Sheik* (1926), a sequel to 1921's *The Shiek*, had just opened the preceding month. Over 100,000 people turned out for his Manhattan public viewing, complete with riots and alleged suicides. His *first* funeral was even christened "The Day Hollywood Wept," with fellow swashbuckling hero, Douglas Fairbanks, Sr., as one of the pallbearers.

Moreover, like some celluloid Lincoln, his coffin's cross country train trip produced large crowds at every stop. Once in Hollywood, there would be a second, even more star-studded, memorial circus. However, nothing quite topped European drama queen Pola

Negri fainting twice at the first ceremony—with her claiming to have been secretly engaged to Valentino. Of course, period accounts suggested it was a secret she had kept from Valentino, too. Negri was Hollywood's serial fiancée, with a 1923 *New York Tribune* article documenting how she could even *briefly* browbeat Chaplin into an engagement: "Charlie blushed, swallowed hard and affirmed the marriage compact [engagement] in answer to a little shake and Pola's question. 'Eez sat not so Charlie?' Charlie gulped. A bridegroom's blush swept up to his grey temples. 'Yes' was his sole rejoinder."[18]

Regardless, did Valentino's death hurt Keaton's picture? *Battling Butler*'s high box office returns would suggest otherwise. But besides crediting Keaton's excellent film, for once his movie's opening paralleled another news event which would have undoubtedly helped to fuel his turnstile numbers. The night that Valentino died, iconic heavyweight champion Jack Dempsey fought challenger Gene Tunney before over 120,000 fans at Philadelphia's Sesquicentennial Municipal Stadium. This produced the first two million dollar–plus gate in boxing history, equal to over $24 million today.

Dempsey was one of the five legendary athletes of the 1920s, joining baseball's Babe Ruth, college football's Red Grange, golf's Bobby Jones, and tennis' Bill Tilden. In 1950 the Associated Press picked Dempsey as the greatest fighter of the first half of the 20th century. For most Americans today, boxing has all but dropped off the radar. But in the 1920s baseball's position as the national game was seriously rivaled by boxing. Thus, the day after the papers were filled with coverage of Valentino's death, the upset of Dempsey was an even bigger story across the nation, with the *New York Times* running a three-tiered front page headline on the fight. Moreover, in the *months* leading up to the match scores of newspaper articles fanned the interest, not to mention film footage of the fight.

Plus, keep in mind that while 1920s baseball had a World Series, it was limited to the United States. This clashed with the international nature of heavyweight boxing. Dempsey held the title from 1919 to 1926 and toured the globe. For example, a 1922 *New York American* article chronicled that the champion was being booked for exhibitions in "England, France, Germany, Norway and probably Ireland."[19] Moreover, Dempsey even impacted the arts—what is considered America's greatest sports painting in history documented his 1923 fight with Argentina's Luis Ángel Firpo, before 80,000 fans in New York's Polo Grounds. The 1924 painting, by celebrated "Lyrical Leftist" George Bellows (1882–1925), is simply entitled *Dempsey and Firpo*. And while the extraordinary work chronicles a short brutal fight won by the American, it paradoxically showcases the amazing moment when a punch from Firpo actually sent Dempsey out of the ring.

Consequently, one could argue that Keaton's boxing picture had had a two-to-three month barely subliminal promotion going on via the build-up to the Dempsey-Tunney fight. Moreover, though baseball then carried that "national game" moniker, with no Major League teams west of the Mississippi until the late 1950s, boxing was essentially of equal status in California during Hollywood's glory years. Moreover, Tom McCarey, the father of later multiple Oscar-winning director Lee McCarey, was *the* West Coast boxing promoter of the early twentieth century, with his fights drawing a who's who of cinema celebrities. Indeed, the bouts often even influenced the film capital's movies. For example, Chaplin utilized an unlikely but true fighting incident from the older McCarey's promoting career to conclude the boxing sequence in *City Lights*—a bout in which the boxers connect simultaneously and both go down.[20] Indeed, Chaplin even discovered the film's leading lady (Virginia Cherrill) at another fight promoted by Leo's father. Plus, the aforementioned Lloyd boxing picture, *The Milky Way*, was directed by the younger McCarey.

7. Battling Butler *(August 30, 1926)*

Though the text has well-documented Keaton's love of baseball and boxing, *Battling Butler* merits briefly pulling up a chair one more time to a 1926 *Motion Picture Classic* article which appeared shortly before the release of his boxing picture. Entitled "They Told Buster to Stick to It," it addressed the comedian's autograph book from his vaudeville days as part of "The Three Keatons."[21] It records that his earliest and most supportive heroes were revered figures from the world of boxing. Young Buster was befriended and encouraged by pioneering fighting legends John L. Sullivan, the first heavyweight champion of gloved boxing (1882–1892), "Gentleman Jim" Corbett, who defeated Sullivan and held the title until 1897, and 1890s' near heavyweight champion Tom Sharkey. Their comments to Keaton are noted earlier in the text but a partial Sharkey axiom to the boy comedian might best capture Keaton's future films when the boxer likens life to a dreamlike state.[22] Consequently, the timing of the article underlines the noteworthiness of both boxing, and this particular picture, to Keaton. Plus, Buster took a solo *Butler* directing credit—usually a sign of an added personal commitment.

Moreover, boxing's significance in *Butler* is demonstrated in another way, too. While Buster "Parody" Keaton spoofs elements of the sport during the training sequences, the only fight in which Keaton is involved—the brutal finale—is deadly serious, and was not even in the original Broadway play. Plus, as noted when compared to *College*, there are no pugilistic style points here but rather the raw violence of Dempsey, or Sullivan—who was also the last "Bare-knuckled Heavyweight Champion," too.

Much later, Keaton would often call *Butler* his favorite film, a designation he would frequently also confer upon *The Navigator* and *The General* (1927). *Butler's* eminence, however, has generally been lost upon modern critics. For example, Leonard Maltin calls it "one of Buster's weaker silent features."[23] David Robinson even goes so far as to classify it as "possibly the least attractive of all Keaton features."[24] Gerald Mast mistakenly pawned it off, as many latter-day historians have, as yet another example of a formulaic narrative thrust upon Keaton.[25] Generally speaking, its contemporary rating might best be labeled "so-so," though Martin Scorsese has always been impressed with the realistic manner in which Keaton staged the official ring fights.[26]

This was hardly how the 1920s saw the film. In fact, pour on a heavy dose of irony, because other than an occasional vote for *The Navigator*, *Butler* is often credited with being Keaton's top grossing silent picture, with reviews to match. Indeed, in collecting more period critiques (15) for *Butler* than any other picture in the study, I found that the Keaton film had, in the baseball vernacular of the comedian, the best batting average—1.000, 15 for 15. Plus, the movie's huge critical and commercial success essentially gave him carte blanch power to shoot a follow-up picture, *The General*, which would be his most expensive large-scale opus. Paradoxically, it proved to be both an epic critical and commercial failure. Ironically, now *The General* is generally seen as a masterpiece.

To adequately consider the incongruities of *Butler*'s initial reception and its current reputation, one might best borrow a line from *Washington Post* columnist Richard Cohen— "[It would necessitate being] trailed by an asterisk or two."[27] Consequently, various perspectives merit exploring. However, before getting into the heavy lifting, I would posit that the 1920s viewpoint is a better reading of the film than the contemporary verdict. Moreover, I would propose that *Butler*'s neglected significance goes much further than being a megahit which made *The General*'s production possible. But first *Butler*'s period reviews warrant further scrutinization to better explain the aforementioned disparity.

First, one could play what might be called the "Lloyd card," in which a work is repre-

A most serious Keaton in *The General*—*Butler's* success encouraged the comedian to take his parody to an even darker place.

sentationally popular for a given era but without the artistic ballast to sustain serious later study. The *Los Angeles Times*, without noting the Dempsey fight, could be said to have some period characteristics along these lines, given its punning description of *Butler* as a "comedy with a big punch," as well as suggesting it was more geared for a male audience.[28] Yet, the overall tone of the piece carries it past such a limited "reading": "Buster Keaton has a winner this time [following *Go West*]. 'Battling Butler' is probably his highest-powered comedy since 'The Navigator.' It is comedy with a big punch at the finish: it draws a rippling series of laughs ... and there are whoops of mirth fairly frequently.... It may not be quite as popular with the feminine portion of the audience ... as the masculine but it may be nominated as enjoyable in both cases."[29] The crucial point to note is its link to *The Navigator*, a picture which will be argued in the following chapter as superseding *The General* as Keaton's greatest picture.

Second, without a direct reference to Keaton's earlier more absurdist short subjects, the *New Yorker* critique ties its praise to *Butler's* enduring sense of incongruity: "Keaton, as is his want, makes his appeal direct ... to your sense of the ridiculous. And that he does successfully."[30] Moreover, this sophisticated magazine's exuberant praise also segues nicely into part of the foundation for my third point, as well as matching the satirical publication's tradition of wit: "Good comedies are so rare and bad ones are so terrible and so frequent that the advent of such a frolicsome bit as 'Battling Butler' ... gives this department an urge to herald the happening with the grandeur of a tabloid announcement of a new murder. It has a smooth and workman like trend that never lets you down."[31] Though without the *New Yorker* critic's drollness, *Cinema Art*'s review also doubles down on Keaton's gift for "ridiculous situations, incongruous costumes, and such…. He is just absurd."[32]

Third, *Butler* is a major pivot picture for Buster. In the early 1920s both Keaton and Chaplin trusted in their audiences to grow with their changing perspectives. Yet, *A Woman of Paris*' (1923) modest commercial returns spooked Chaplin and he returned to the Tramp. However, Keaton continued to believe, even after his provocative cow-as-heroine in *Go West*. Call Keaton more stubborn, but in his unconventional Western there is a foreshadowing of existentialism baked into his child-like persona. Indeed, there is a line in Edward Albee's much later Tony Award-winning play *The Goat or Who Is Sylvia?*, the twisted farce about a child/man having an affair with the title character that is reminiscent of Buster's screen alter ego in *Go West*: "There are times we don't know what the fuck's going on—to us, *with* us, *about* us—and that's most of the time. I'm talking about us so-called adolescents."[33] Some *Battling Butler* reviews caught Keaton tweaking his persona in just the opposite direction, such as *Variety* observing Keaton in an atypical stance—highlighting the tender parting between his poor little rich boy, Alfred Butler, and O'Neil's mountain girl: "At least one new wrinkle is a 'good-bye' scene between him and the girl is bound to be copped [copied] by the other boys supervising camera action. It drew comment from the laity [religious] members present at the Capitol. [Theatre] which is fair enough."[34]

When Keaton fights to preserve his dignity before a new bride he is also tweaking his normal little boy persona of not really caring about the unconventional picture's nominal heroine, unless it is something like a cow or a steam engine. If one were in Lloyd-land, winning the girl as such would be business as usual. But again, it is *not* so for Keaton. Instinctual or not, the comedian was now in his early thirties. And despite still having a youthful appearance, it makes more sense for this boy/man to make a man over boy experiment, especially with his boxing attire showing off a well-toned body.

However, if one wanted to attach a Kafkaesque slant to this seemingly conventional close, one merely needs to remember that the writer, like contemporary artist Keaton, tended to combine jarringly conflicting dichotomies in his work, such as dreams versus reality, unemployment versus work, and the child vs. adulthood.[35] Thus, as a boy, Buster's character would not have fought, but here adulthood can only be embraced by violence. As noted, even prior to the finale, one has the *adult* champion beating his offscreen wife for flirting. Plus, during the champion's bout we see fight fans either emulating the violence in the ring, or being able to casually eat during the brutality. And the absurd topper to this graduation to manhood via violence is that it did not make any difference to an O'Neil girl raised in a savage setting. To rehash, when Keaton says he is not a fighter, she replies, "I'm glad." The close anticipates Robert Wise's 1949 boxing picture *The Set-Up*, in which the wife just loves her husband and hates this *grown-up* sport, whose participants are *continually* "just one punch away" from glory.[36]

Playing further upon the lost childhood motif is filmmaker David Cronenberg (director of such pictures as the 1986 remake of *The Fly* and 2005's *History of Violence*), who penned a fascinating introduction to Susan Bernofsky's 2014 translation of Kafka's *The Metamorphosis* (1913). Buster's Butler suddenly transforming into "Battling Butler" mode/man is in the same neighborhood of Cronenberg's wonderfully universal opening: "I wake up one morning to discover that I was a seventy-year-old man. Is this different from what happens to Gregor Samsa in *The Metamorphosis*? He wakes up to find that he's become a near-human-sized beetle.... Our reactions, mine and Gregor's, are very similar. We are confused and bemused, and think that it's a momentary delusion that will soon dissipate."[37] The lightening change from boy to man, whether of a physical or psychological nature, is most movingly articulated by *Finding Neverland*'s (2004) Johnny Depp, when a boy realizes the seriousness of his mother's illness and stands up to his bullying grandmother: "The boy is gone. In the last 30 seconds ... you became grown-up."

Be that as it may, Keaton and Kafka have so much in common regarding these twisted dichotomies. One is supposed to escape a nightmare by waking up, but just the opposite is usually true of the duo. For example, one morning Kafka comes to as a beetle, while a snoozing Keaton is a famous detective (*Sherlock, Jr.*, 1923) who awakens as an antihero projectionist. There are also similar conflicting dichotomies for the two Ks regarding employment. *The Metamorphosis'* Gregor works at a thankless job to help his family but when he can go on no longer he seemingly wills himself into being a beetle, à la a metaphorical suicide, which becomes real when he stops eating. Only then does the reader discover Gregor's family actually had money in reserve. In Keaton's *Cops* (1922), his girlfriend demands he get a job, and by a series of miscues he wills himself into a position as one of the story's enemies—a cop. However, he is still rejected by the girl and gives himself over to suicide by cop via a beating by the police squad. Moreover, just before this occurs one discovers no unwanted job was necessary.... Keaton's wannabe girl is the wealthy daughter of a city official.

Fourth, *Battling Butler*'s current status is also in line for an upgrade based on several reviews anticipating, by decades, journalist, writer, critic, editor, and actor George Plimpton's (1927–2003) ricocheting about in a real world Walter Mitty only daydreamed about. (That is, in James Thurber's short story "The Secret Life of Walter Mitty," the antihero who escapes a controlling wife through manly adventuresome daydreams—anthologized in Thurber's darkly titled *My World and Welcome to It* [1942].[38]) Plimpton later embraced this dark comedy when he played against professional athletes for antihero writing material, chronicled in books like *Out of My League* (baseball, 1961) and *Paper Lion* (football, 1966, and a popular 1968 film). If one asked the down-to-earth Plimpton what these misadventures were like, he tended to paraphrase Ernest Hemingway's dust jacket blurb for the baseball text: "It is the dark side of the moon Walter Mitty."[39]

Granted, Buster did not assume *Battling Butler*'s identification for glory, but falls into it over a misunderstanding in which he shares the boxer's last name. However, there is still an element of the Mitty/Plimpton connection going on. Fittingly, of the period critics to make a similar connection, the most insightful comes from the already much praised *LIFE* reviewer, Robert E. Sherwood.[40] His critique compares the film's scenario to the 1922 film *The Hottentot*, in which an antihero is so often mistaken for a famous jockey he eventually begins to assume some of the perks ... until a day of reckoning on the back of a dangerous horse. Plus, Sherwood thought so much of Keaton's film and how it anticipated a later comic twist that no less a literary giant than Hemingway would describe it as the aforementioned Mitty "dark side." Moreover, the 1920s critic would later designate *Battling Butler* as one of the pivotal films of 1926.[41]

A fifth reason for *Battling Butler* to be given a critical rehabilitation is to liken it to Keaton's greatest hits. That is, frequently when a director is tweaking his persona and/or making a career shift, he or she makes the change more palatable by maintaining some of what Bob Fosse would liken to giving his audience the old misdirection "razzle-dazzle." This is best demonstrated by Chaplin's *Modern Times* (1935) and *The Great Dictator* (1940). *City Lights* (1931) was to have been his last Tramp film. But social issues (the Depression and World War II) pulled him back with both *Times* and the *Dictator*. Messages were made, but proven material was also retained to help sell it. Both of these latter pictures apply this ploy—especially *Times*. But *Dictator*, the much more provocative of the two, leans most upon what Chaplin considered his key talisman—the Tramp. Thus, while the "Dictator" gets all the attention, more than a semblance of the Tramp remains with the Jewish barber.

Consequently, while *Battling Butler* has Keaton embarking upon a more serious dramatic direction to his work, he also insightfully pads it with many of his given auteur components, from parody to absurdity—"housed" in the Sap character. Appropriately, an audience appreciation of this tactic, without many or most of them fully understanding what was soon coming with *The General*, responded in kind. Thus, *Battling Butler* received arguably the best silent comedy reviews of his life. And this can begin with *not one* but *two* different *New York Times* pieces—a publication modern historians are always quick to say was not favorable to Keaton? What they should say is that the later Mordaunt Hall reviews suddenly cooled on Keaton. Regardless, one of the two *Times* pieces on *Butler* simply resorts to reporting on the audience around the critic: "[Keaton] is so successful that his antics elicited both applause and laughter of no mean volume."[42] In less than a week, the *Times* felt the need to rephrase their description of the people's response under the title "Phlegmatic Mr. Keaton Is a Stylist as Jester": "Mr. Keaton [has] the opportunity of eliciting both laughter and applause from the spectator."[43]

New York Daily News critic Irene Thirer quantified such praise with the wit of the aforementioned *New Yorker* critic: "You're pretty much of an icicle yourself if you don't get at least a dozen chuckles out of that frozen faced Keaton chap's latest in fanfare at the Capitol [Theatre]. Blustering Buster has done a rip-roaring cinema treatment of 'Battling Buster,' erstwhile of the speaking and singing stage."[44] However, *Screenland*'s topper review to this ballyhoo was just the sort of thing to give credence to Buster's belief that his audience was up to the task of understanding and appreciating the comedian's ongoing growth as a serious comedy artist: "Keaton always gives you some good, fairly intelligent reason for howling, too. Not once does he insult you by requesting your mirth at some time-worn trick. He knows there is more than one joke, or at least more than one way of telling that one."[45]

And then came *The General*.

8

The General (December 22, 1926)
Groundbreaking Dark Comedy but Keaton's Greatest Film?

> "Mr. Keaton appears to have gone to a great deal of trouble and expense in making 'The General,' and there is a quaint air of quiet thoughtfulness about it which seems to reflect very accurately the attitude and the personality of the comedian himself."
> —*New York Evening Post*, 1926[1]

This is one chapter which needs to be teed up, since similar to the provocative new revelations offered for 1925's *Sherlock, Jr.* (see Chapter 3), this text takes an iconoclastic position on what is often considered Keaton's masterpiece. However, one hastens to add, this book questions neither the greatness of *The General* (1926), nor its significance in the evolution of Keaton as an artist. Indeed, the chapter provides both a neglected factor for that greatness, and a key reason for its initial critical and commercial failure. But all in good time.

Never has a quote, such as the one which opens this text, been more truthful about its subject, nor more prophetic about how a comedian's film is about to be received. Because right after the "quiet thoughtfulness" comes "The humor is seldom obvious and never boisterous."[2] This is neither a good opening for what becomes a Keaton pan, nor for a personality comedy in general. This is *one* genre in which shtick squashes story. In other picture categories the viewer is willing to allow some time to transpire in order to set up a narrative. But personality comedy needs to be funny quickly, because the fan is *not* there to view some New Age plot device. S/he is there to see a favorite funny person replicate a specialty, be it Chaplin's metamorphic mime, or Abbot & Castello performing more verbal slapstick, à la "Who's on First?"

This need not happen with the speed of Kramer entering a room on *Seinfeld*, a bit borrowed from Ed Norton's entrances on *The Honeymooners*. Yet, it best happen quickly. Indeed, throughout Keaton's career his *movie mantra* was some variation of this 1922 *New York Telegraph* quote: "Keaton said that his scenarios were on postal cards"—a single post card, a single picture.[3] He had fleshed this out even earlier in 1920's *Picture-Play Magazine*: "My pictures are made without script or written directions of any kind. We simply figure out enough story to build sets around, then we pull our gags and 'quick stuff' in the set as we happen on the ideas. After we feel that we've shot enough to make about six pictures, we assemble it, rip out whatever is left of the 'story'—and make one picture of what's left."[4] In an even earlier 1920 article, from the *Los Angeles Times*, this philosophy is credited to the comedian's film mentor: "[Keaton] says he's following Fatty Arbuckle's method, getting a plot first, then builds the picture, leaving all the plot out."[5] The approach seemed to be showing immediate results, since the piece was titled "Buster Bursts Into Stardom."

Keaton and Arbuckle only differed on audience mentality. Buster later noted in his memoir that when they met in 1917 Fatty told him, "You must never forget that the average mentality of our movie audience is twelve years."[6] As this text has suggested, especially with each succeeding chapter, Keaton gave audiences increasingly more credit for growing right along with a developing artist. Indeed, in a 1926 *Ladies Home Journal* interview (a valuable period publication on film), Keaton went as far as to say: "We have educated audiences, and they have gone beyond and demanded more of us.... With this increased importance has come a different type of comedy; space is now needed to work out logically and adequately a good idea or source."[7]

However, one could argue that Keaton was whistling in the dark, since *The General* was already proving a critical and commercial failure. In fact, Chaplin had been in a similar denial for months after his faith in a mature audience let him down following the commercial failure of 1923's *A Woman of Paris*. (For example, see the February 1924 *Los Angeles Herald* article whose title echoes the comedian's ongoing belief in *Paris*' box office potential, "Famous Comedian Sees Own Picture for Fourth Time."[8])

Regardless, there is a certain "walking it back" ring to the demands of a mature audience, when Keaton later discusses, in the same *Ladies Home Journal* article, the making of 1924's *The Navigator*—the picture for which I will subsequently make a case for being *the* Keaton picture. Be that as it may, Keaton observes at length that besides the chance acquisition of an ocean liner for *The Navigator*: "It had always occurred to me that there was a good deal of comedy to be found under the sea, and I ordered a regulation diver's suit that weighed two hundred and twenty pounds. The only variation was that more glass was put into the front of the helmet.... [My] face, even though it is not a smiling one, must be seen in comedy. That was the beginning of *The Navigator*. The story was built up from that diver's suit."[9] A postcard-sized script indeed. Fatty Arbuckle might have still been standing behind him. Naturally, this is not to suggest that viewers cannot grow. Yet, as Chaplin learned with *A Woman of Paris,* a filmmaker originally in Keaton's camp about ever more progressive patrons, many mainstream audiences cannot keep up with the snowballing talents of a Keaton or a Chaplin. Moreover, to paraphrase a popular old Hollywood axiom about the film industry: "No one ever lost any money on overestimating the public's intelligence." Indeed, even Winston Churchill was once quoted as saying the best argument against democracy is a five-minute conversation with an average voter.[10]

Such questioning of the masses brings one back to Arbuckle's original advice to Keaton. And since most historians do not so much study the past as haunt it, there is a 1919 *Picture and Picturegoer* article by the rotund comedian that reads as almost prophetic about the initial failure of his protégé's *The General*.[11] Since the chapter has not yet put forth its film overview, let me note four key points about Keaton's picture that Arbuckle's essay anticipates. The first already has been lightly touched upon. Fatty notes how other genres have a template which guarantees a certain modicum of success, versus comedians essentially having to reinvent the wheel each time.

Second, Keaton had become increasing more introspectively serious, culminating with *Battling Butler*'s non-comic real fight finale. As noted by last chapter's chronicling of critics and box office, everyone seemed onboard with Keaton's evolving darker persona. *The General* pushed the black humor card further but suddenly his audience did *not* follow him, and some were even offended. Seven years earlier Arbuckle had written, "The public's sense of humor changes continually. Thus, the expense of producing movies."[12] And dark comedy's detrimental effect upon the reception of *The General* will be elaborated upon shortly.

Third, as briefly noted periodically in the text, the title character of *The General* is a train—which was even more important than Keaton's girlfriend. For authenticity's sake, moreover, the comedian had spent a great deal of money finding the same gauge of train tracks still in use during the Civil War setting of his film. Plus, the near finale of the film would feature the most expensive sight gag thus far in film history—a locomotive would pratfall into a river as the burning bridge supporting it would collapse. Yet, it produced more of an action adventure spectacular effect than something funny—not unlike Steven Spielberg's gargantuan out-of-control ferris wheel in *1941* (1979). The bigger-is-funnier school of thought has a poor batting average.

Amazingly, just prior to Arbuckle writing his *Picture and Picturegoer* article, the comedian had been working on a film in "which two Ford cars were completely demolished in a wreck with a weighty locomotive, whose owner had received a handsome cheque."[13] Fatty had labeled it a "first rate joke," but when the footage was projected for a group of studio co-workers, it had not produced a "giggle." Eventually, something salvageable was made of the sequence, but another comparably big expensive gag was simply scrapped.

Fourth, Keaton's *The General* had gone way over budget, as the comedian went to the nth degree in both the picture's epic proportions (such as the falling train gag), as well reproducing everything possible which could double for a Civil War era artifact. Indeed, a reproduced period tricycle-like bike Buster used to briefly chase his stolen train now rests in Washington, D.C.'s Smithsonian Institution. Consequently, Arbuckle's final message, which was interwoven through the piece, was how easy it was to go over budget for the ephemeral laugh.

Moreover, there is also a noteworthy irony connected to the locomotive's epic near-concluding crash in Buster's opus. Some might have argued Buster was merely emulating mentor Arbuckle in not sparing money in search of a laugh. In fact, in Keaton's later memoir he even says, "Money somehow has never seemed important to me."[14] Yet, Buster was breaking a rule he had learned in 1922's *Blacksmith*. The comedian had even evoked this directly to his staff when they considered sinking the ocean liner to conclude *The Navigator*: "He reminded them of the Rolls Royce he had beaten up in *The Blacksmith*.... The scene, considered surefire [funny], had met a cold, hostile silence. 'You guys remember *that* dud? If we sink a beautiful ocean liner, they'll hiss ... you can't do it in comedy.... Those same people who wish *they* had a Rolls would be wishing they could inherit a liner like I had, or even just take a trip on one.'"[15] Furthermore, one could double down on this very valid point by considering the character as well as the audience. Keaton's well-known fascination with trains went well beyond *The General*, including the inspired *Our Hospitality* (1923) locomotive seemingly from Willy Wonkaland. Thus, a viewer's hurt for Keaton's favorite oversized prop being destroyed would certainly further eclipse any viewer's wish to own and/or ride upon a locomotive.

One might best compare it to the conclusion of the later groundbreaking screwball comedy *Bringing Up Baby* (1938).[16] Here is a genre in which a rigid male, or one threatened with such a lifestyle, is freed from his fate by a free-spirited woman. In this movie Cary Grant's stiff professor is symbolized by the dead brontosaurus skeleton he is reconstructing. Katharine Hepburn plays the uninvited rescuer with her equally symbolic lovely, lively pet leopard. The finale has her accidently collapsing the professor's brontosaurus skeleton, thus ending the last vestiges of his academic rigidity. No single scene better metaphorically captures the freeing spirit of the genre. However, as with *The General*, *Bringing Up Baby* was initially a critical and commercial failure which is now considered a classic ... yet the crashing conclusions of both can still make one wince.

Regardless, a brief synopsis of *The General* must begin with the conclusion of *Battling Butler*. The commercial hit received critical kudos for an ending which favored realistic adventure over comedy. Thus, Clyde Bruckman and Keaton adapted a true Civil War action story from William Pittenger's 1893 memoir *The Great Locomotive Chase*—also known as "Andrews' Raid." Pittenger was part of an 1862 Union Army guerrilla-style railroad raid into Georgia. (The veteran's involvement would later result in his being an early recipient of the Medal of Honor.) However, he was a *Northern* soldier, while Keaton's version told the tale from the Confederate perspective, with the train-loving comedian as a Southern civilian locomotive engineer. Pittenger's book had been republished in 1916, hoping to draw upon the renewal of interest generated by all the 1915 ceremonies and parodies marking the conflict's 50th anniversary. And of course, the famous/infamous *Birth of a Nation* was released in 1915, too. Keaton was a student of that film. But more importantly, according to a March 1927 *Los Angeles Times* article, "[Keaton] is a walking encyclopedia on Civil War lore."[17]

Interestingly, while the stolen train's name eventually becomes the film moniker, *The General*, a March 1926 *Variety* article gave that honor to Keaton's character. The initial

A *General* lobby card which suggests deadly serious things—a parody ahead of its time.

working title was *The Engine Driver*.¹⁸ The switch helped play up the oddity that Buster's character, Johnnie Gray, loved his train more than his girlfriend, Annabel Lee (Marion Mack). Using Annabel Lee as a screen name is ironic on four levels. First, it is also the name of the celebrated last completed poem of Edgar Allen Poe, a writer Keaton admired. The verse chronicles a young man haunted by his lover's death. Thus, the first paradox is that tragic love is seldom comic material, even if the comedian had decided to embrace more serious material. Of course, it slowly becomes more appropriate as the movie dovetails into being a dark comedy.

Second, the tragic love which inspired the poem (a woman whose identify Poe scholars still debate), only manages to make it more ironic when tied to the nuts and bolts of Keaton's locomotive. Third, the way the comedian treats the girl throughout the picture hardly suggests a love that will linger past the movie's conclusion, let alone death. In fact, at one point she so frustrates "Buster" (a name that better describes his feelings towards her) that he starts to *strangle* Annabel. Fourth, she does survive in the movie but as with so many Keaton heroines, one sees a relationship which will eventually mirror the negative dissolves of his *College* (1927).

As a footnote to the attention given Annabel Lee, authors do not randomly assign names to key characters. Indeed, another telling example of this in *The General* is Keaton's character being named Johnnie Gray. During the Civil War, Union soldiers called their Confederate counterparts "Graybacks," given the color of their uniforms. Consequently, when Annabel and her family see Keaton's character as disloyal to the South it is an automatic dig at their intelligence given a name metaphorically linked to the cause—a point validated later in the movie when Annabel does some very stupid things to "help" Buster.

Yet, countless movies use and abuse character names to ironic and/or insightful points. A choice example occurs in the dark comedy/noir classic *Chinatown* (1974).¹⁹ John Huston's evil but ever so courtly villain is named Noah Cross. His surname is most distant from the goodness associated with Christianity's cross. More directly comic is that a man named Noah is attempting to gain control of Los Angeles' water rights. Cross also provides another telling example of character insights via names. Huston constantly mispronounces the last name of Jack Nicholson's private eye, J. J. Gittes, even when it is brought to his attention. What is the reason? Cross is so powerful and disrespectful that he just does not care.

Be that as it may, when Buster's Johnnie Gray stops the *General* in Annabel's Georgia hometown, he goes for a visit. While there, the Civil War breaks out and Buster is pressured to enlist, following the examples of Annabel's father and brother. Neither one of them is particularly fond of him—anti-family duos like this are something of a Keaton film given. Regardless, both men are accepted by the recruiters, while Buster is turned down. He is more important to the Confederacy as a train engineer, when the recruiters learn his occupation.

Unfortunately, no one tells Keaton. Thus, he comically attempts to join twice more. First, he gets back in the enlistment line, and while partially obscuring his face, he gives his occupation as bartender. But he is recognized and again denied. This would imply Buster has at least intuitively recognized that one's occupation has something to do with being accepted. Yet the recruiters neither volunteer any information about this importance as an engineer, nor does he ask.

Period critics were sometimes bothered by such Keaton fluctuations between being smart and dumb in *The General*, which will be addressed later in the text. However, one such example, which occurs near the picture's conclusion provides a sense of the problem—a February 1927 *New York Times* review states, "This man [Keaton], who has difficulty in crossing a road, is supposed to be crafty enough to outwit the Northern General."[20] Be that as it may, the catalyst for Buster's second attempt to enlist follows him comparing his physique with two other recent enlistees. The first towers over him, but the second is, if anything, smaller than the modest-sized Keaton. Thus, this time little Johnnie Gray avoids the line and slickly steals an enlistment slip okay while another would-be soldier is distracted. Alas, Buster is caught yet again and tossed out of the recruiting office. He responds, via a title with reserved anger: "If you lose this war don't blame me."

Before continuing with this pocket plotline, it bears noting that previous pictures, such as the transitional *Battling Butler*, still often began with the early prototype "Sap" boy/man character, and had him experience a modest learning curve. In contrast, *The General* immediately embarks with him as seemingly a very capable figure. In the early minutes of the film examples would range from his professional demeanor as a locomotive engineer arriving in town, to how he comically rids himself of two young boy groupies.

In the latter case, the youngsters shadow his every move, including the walk to Annabel's home. The boys even enter the house with him, but he immediately sizes up the situation and concocts a gentle way of losing them. While Buster has taken his hat off and sat down upon entering the dwelling, he now calmly gets up, places his non-pork pie hat back on his head and opens the door as if to leave. The boys anticipate his exit and go through the open door. Keaton then simply closes the door and returns to a seated, hatless position in hopes of some privacy with Annabel. However, even this does not last long. Her brother rushes in and tell their father about the pending war. What immediately follows are the comedian's aforementioned failed attempts to enlist. Annabel thus thinks him a coward, despite his explanation. She responds: "Please don't lie [about attempting to enlist]. I don't want you to speak to me again until you are in uniform." It has the tone of many previous Keaton heroines, such as the job-demanding girlfriend who opens 1922's *Cops*.

One of *The General*'s signature scenes comes at the end of the film's first act. The story is about to jump ahead one year to the eve of "Andrews' Raid," which essentially composes the rest of the movie. However, this pivotal sequence preceding act two keys upon Keaton attempting to process Annabel's rejection. A bewildered Buster sits down on the exterior drive shaft of his beloved locomotive. The comedian's ability to deep-six reality into a netherworld then kicks in, years before James Thurber's Walter Mitty. And arguably this is Buster's best example of the phenomenon. Consequently, he remains in this deep dreamlike state for several moments after the drive shaft begins to rise and fall with its oblivious passenger. The often insightful but always provocatively dramatic critic/historian David Thomson states: "I would swap all of *Modern Time* for that glorious moment in *The General* when Buster's meditation fails to notice the growing motion of the engine's drive shaft on which he is sitting."[21] Paradoxically, one might better argue the Tramp being swallowed by *Modern Times*' machine as more quintessential for contemporary society with each passing year. Regardless, this Keaton sequence certainly ranks as a pivotal scene in the comedian's oeuvre.

However, the key for not granting this shaft scene *The General*'s number one sequence would be later dark comedy depictions of death, which contributed greatly to why the film was a 1927 critical and commercial failure. That being said, another perspective on Keaton's up and down drive shaft ride—which has surprisingly not been commented upon—related to the comedian's other worldly connection to all things mechanical. His "Zero" persona has already been described as a "clockwork orange" figure—part man, part machine. Given that perspective, and the fact that this locomotive is his first love, the scene has always suggested to me that the iron horse is giving its troubled engineer a rocking chair-like moment of comfort during a troubled time.

Nevertheless, as previously noted, act two begins with a year having passed since Buster and Mack's Annabel have spoken, but ironically, she must now travel north on his train to visit her wounded father. Simultaneously, Andrews' Union Raiders, who had traveled south through neutral Kentucky dressed as civilians, are now posed to steal Buster's beloved *General*. The locomotive is delivering needed Confederate supplies, and once the passenger cars are secretly uncoupled, the Raiders will take the supply train north while disrupting telegraph lines along the way. Unfortunately, Annabel had gone to the baggage car just as the operation began, and the Union men are forced to take her along as a prisoner.

Buster is washing to eat when suddenly his train is "liberated." Immediately, the soapy-handed antihero leads a running group after the *General*. With what a future generation might describe as his Speedy Gonzales cartoon-like speed, a basic component of his persona (second only to his "Great Stone Face"), he loses his flatfooted posse and continues alone. Luckily, he can shift to third gear when a sidecar turns up on a railroad siding. Unfortunately, the Raiders have disrupted the tracks, which soon results in a comic Keaton crash into a nearby river. Yet, as if Buster is giving the viewer a period transportation showcase, à la the *Battling Buster* clothing display, he now steals that zany looking "boneshaker" bicycle, with an authenticity as legitimate as *Our Hospitality*'s odd train. The "boneshaker" soon lives up to its Civil War era name, and Buster has another spectacular wreck all on his own.

However, he finally reaches a train station in Chattanooga, with a nearby detachment of Confederate troops. What follows is another smart-to-dumb action by our antihero. He has responsibly followed the train, and professionally, explained the situation to the local commander. Plus, he has taken charge of a local locomotive, the *Texas*, which enables a Confederate company of soldiers to board a flatbed car behind him. Thus, Buster's behavior would have impressed the action adventure hero of your choice. But then he seems to have been hit with the proverbial stupid stick and speeds away with his new locomotive ... without coupling the flatbed of soldiers to the *Texas*. Compounding this major error, he again goes into another deep-six mode and does not note his missing mini-Confederate Army until it is too late.

However, as luck would have it, he still manages to discover some added firepower when he spots a flatbed-mounted artillery piece on another railroad siding. He soon attaches it to the *Texas*, with plans to use it immediately. And in one of the film's most sustained comic sequences, he first prepares to shoot a cannon toward the stolen train. But he uses too little gunpowder and when the lit fuse goes off, Keaton's "Zero" nickname might have been literally applied—since the cannonball travels only as far as the locomotive cab to which he has returned—which might have "erased" him.

Consequently, he tries again and goes for broke—using his artillery piece plunger to stuff a whole can of powder down the barrel before loading another ball. But after lighting a second fuse, in his haste to get back to the cab, his foot becomes entangled in the coupling for the flatbed holding the cannon. Worse yet, the connecting link involves a tongue-like paw which one might liken to the handle on a child's wagon. When Keaton's Johnny Gray finally becomes disengaged, the linking tongue has jarred the artillery piece's flatbed—dropping the barrel's level so that it is pointed directly at him. Director Keaton has embellished a similar comic quandary he had created with a small signal cannon in *The Navigator*. However, Buster's quickness provides humorous safety. In morph speed he climbs over the

8. The General (December 22, 1926)

coal tender and then manages to maneuver along the precarious side of the *Texas*, hopefully to find safety on the low-riding cow catcher at the front of the train. Used to deflect rail obstacles, it is the safest spot short of jumping.

However, Keaton's character now catches a triple break. The tracks are approaching a curve and when the artillery piece fires, the cannonball goes off to the side, completely missing Keaton and his engine. Moreover, because of the added gunpowder, that curve in the tracks, and the lowered trajectory of this mounted field gun, Keaton nearly scores a direct hit on the stolen train he is chasing. Andrews' Raiders are impressively frightened, and they begin a series of defensive ploys, including scattering railroad ties on the tracks to slow or derail Keaton's new locomotive. Conveniently, with Buster already on the cow catcher, at one point he displays entertainingly athletic prowess by lifting up one heavy wood tie and somehow projecting it at such an angle as to flip another track-blocking tie off the rails.

The Raiders also decouple a boxcar to stop Keaton and the *Texas*. He stops and gets it pushed off onto a side rail, but through an unusual twist it manages to again get in front of him. This produces a wonderful uniquely Keaton double-take, limited to his oh-so-expressive eyes. Regardless, the chase continues and Buster goes into his "Zero"—squared distraction state—only focused upon the chase. While he is busy stoking his engine's fire, his Confederate Army is retreating in the background. But as if wearing blinders, he presses on, and soon is equally unconscious of a Northern Army advancing in that beautifully used expanse of background space.

Not that long after the theatrical run of *The General*, Keaton fan and fellow antiheroic artist Robert Benchley wrote the perfect comic essay to describe this particular talent for missing history. Indeed, even its title is punningly appropriate for Keaton's Johnny Gray: "Johnny-on-the-Spot."[22] Later anthologized in the inspiringly nonsensically titled *From Bed to Worse or Comforting Thoughts About the Bison*, Benchley describes antiheros like himself and Keaton thus: "If you want to get a good perspective on history in the making, just skim through a collection of newsphotographs which have been

Robert Benchley (circa mid–1920s) was a pivotal period humorist and critic whose admiration for Keaton was anchored in comedy parallels.

snapped at those very moments when cataclysmic events were taking place throughout the world. In almost every picture you can discover one guy ... who is looking in exactly the opposite direction from the excitement, totally oblivious to the fact that the world is shaking beneath his feet. That would be me."[23] Who knows, maybe Keaton helped inspire the piece. Benchley, a great admirer of *Our Hospitality*, made his first trip to Hollywood the same year *The General* appeared. And with several common friends, and a goal to mingle with the film community's elite, it would seem highly unlikely that these two hard-drinking, antiheroic-orientated artists would not have met.[24]

Nevertheless, Andrews' Raiders eventually realize they are being chased by a one-man army, and Buster must ditch the *Texas* and head for safety in a nearby forest, or as a tongue-twisting screen title summarizes: "In the enemy's country—hopelessly lost, helplessly cold and horribly hungry." And then, as if Keaton were seeding a classic scene for Mel Brooks' 1974 *Young Frankenstein*, one is reminded of the dialogue between Gene Wilder's title character, and his hunchbacked assistant Igor (pop-eyed Marty Feldman) as they dig up a coffin for body parts:

WILDER: What a filthy job!
FELDMAN: Could be worse.
WILDER: How?
FELDMAN: Could be raining.

It then promptly begins to pour, which also quickly became Johnny Gray's added comic travail, too, almost fifty years before.

However, Keaton's wannabe Confederate is not totally without some dumb luck. He happens onto the house in which the Union officers are plotting their counterattack on the Southern forces. Moreover, the hungry engineer is also favored by being drawn to a table with food, which becomes his hiding place when Union soldiers enter the room, and he slips under the tablecloth. As the Northern officers discuss their secret plan Buster is able to hear every word ... well, almost every word—one soldier strikes the table to emphasize a point, and the comedian's ear, which is metaphorically glued to the underbelly of that precise point of table, assumes a direct hit.

Besides seeing stars, poor Buster is also burned by a careless Union soldier's cigar as it sears through the tablecloth. Yet, this allows clever filmmaker Keaton to turn the burnt hole into an iris shot, enabling accidental spy Johnny Gray to better proceed with what one could legitimately call his *undercover* work. Indeed, through said iris he spots Annabel, who continues to be a prisoner of Andrews' Raiders. In a low-key rescue, this plot-driven reaffirmation parody/dark comedy has Buster and the girl escaping into the rainy night. However, neither the weather nor the enemy is their most immediate threat—director Keaton includes bear traps around which his couple must navigate for added black humor.

However, the duo survives this worst case scenario evening with Annabel demonstrating the following morning both her obliviousness to their man-hunting surroundings and her man himself. That is, she immediately gushes a mistaken romantic observation, seldom a promising omen in a Keaton picture, via a title: "It was so brave of you to risk your life, coming into the enemy's country, just to save me." Naturally, she has it topsy-turvy; it had always been about rescuing Buster's first love, his locomotive the *General*. But now being in his smart mode, Keaton does not correct her, and wisely observes, again with a title: "We've got to get back to our lines somehow and warn them of this coming attack."

Still wearing the Union uniform that facilitated Annabel's rescue the proceeding night, he realizes he can mingle with the Northern soldiers loading a nearby supply train, if he has something to toss into the rail car being loaded with the supplies. Now, while Annabel no doubt discerns this as a part of Buster's ongoing rescue, the comedian merely sees her as a prop to retake his locomotive—actually saving his first love in order to warn the Confederate Army. Thus, she is briskly put into a burlap sack and unceremoniously dumped into the supply car. Before being tossed, however, he has instructed Annabel to decouple a car behind the locomotive to aid their escape. Once this is done, though, she is plunked onto the growing supply pile, like a large lumpy sock, just before a large box is dropped on her. To Buster's "romantic" credit, he does cover his eyes. Yet, since his blank visage eyes are the only thing which could pass for a semblance of soul, by covering them, Buster's budding existentialism suggests he can live with Annabel being squashed like a cartoon Kafka bug.

Yet, in a miracle of miracles, Annabel survives without being flattened, and the twosome eventually bolt for freedom, with Keaton at the controls of the *General*. Of course, as suggested earlier, while being chased, her attempts to assist him in providing fuel for the wood–burning locomotive do little to bolster any Buster affection in his less-than-intimate persona. Thus, Annabel might better be rechristened Exasperation, from stoking the fire with a wood chip, to discarding an ideal piece of wood because it is flawed by having a knot. Yet, her pièce de résistance is accidently starting a fire early on the bridge Buster hopes to burn down—thus saving them from their Union pursuers, and helping to halt a Northern Army's advance.

Because of Annabel, however, he finds himself on the wrong (Union) side of the fire, and in a swashbuckling attempt to jump the flames he succeeds ... but falls through the bridge's railroad tie spacing and lands in the river below. Yet, at this point the duo have essentially escaped and the focus returns to Buster. He delivers his valuable spy-related information to the local Confederate commander, and then, as suggested in that earlier period review, he again flip-flops from hero to buffoon. For example, the rush of Confederate mounted troops reduces him to a stop-start child trying to cross a rush-hour interstate, and he keeps falling down as he tries to run with a loosely belted saber at his waist. He is as vulnerable as the children caught in the road during the botched *dramatic* Western robbery that opens 1969's *The Wild Bunch*, with its murderous montage.

Examining the movie's final rousing minutes, with an antiheroic Keaton attempting to play soldier, constitutes a good start on why *The General* was labeled a 1920s failure. First, as noted earlier, the burning bridge allows a real locomotive to take an unforgettable free fall into a stream—but it is not funny. Besides going against Keaton's rule of *not* destroying desirable sought-after objects—it is a train! Buster loved trains! The whole catalyst for the film was to retrieve his beloved title "character"—the *General*. So beyond any viewer remorse over destroying a train, the Keaton fan cannot help but have remorse for their antihero. And while this was not *the* locomotive to take the swan dive, it is difficult to separate the two. Indeed, validating a Keaton film is almost to ask: "Does it include a train? In all of cinema, only Alfred Hitchcock also approaches this train obsession.

Second, the crashing locomotive worked as a sensational *dramatic* device. *The General* was a "reaffirmation parody" of action films played so close to the genre being spoofed that period audiences generally missed the joke.[25] And this amazing near-finale locomotive crash was a microcosm of what seemed more like a 1920s action film occasionally using some underplayed comedy. Thus, the audience approval he received for the serious conclusion of his preceding *Battling Butler* was not up to the more somber tone being played throughout this follow-up film.

Third, *The General* is a groundbreaking dark comedy, yet the public was not yet ready for the degree of realism Keaton brought to the genre near his picture's close. Though still not a mainstream film genre, in special cases audiences could mix war and comedy—such as Chaplin's 1918 film *Shoulder Arms*.[26] Advised not to make it, especially during the closing days of World War I, Chaplin's film went on to be a huge critical and commercial hit with critics and public alike. This also included most men in uniform. In fact, Chaplin's 1922 book, *My Trip Abroad*, shares, in part, the following remarkable letter: "One young soldier sent me four medals he had gotten during the big war. He said that he was sending them because I had never been properly recognized. His part was so small and mine so big ... that he wanted me to have his *Croix de Guerre* [awarded for gallantry and courage, and] his regimental and other medals."[27]

In the final battle of Keaton's picture, he walks back and forth like a child near an artillery unit—not quite certain on how to "play" war. Three times viewers see a Union sniper shoot and kill one of the Confederate gunnery crew members. A clownish Keaton acts befuddled and decides pulling out his sword would look militia-like. Moreover, it has already been established that Buster's saber tends to separate from its hilt when handled with an enthusiastic flourish. Well, the flourish returns and once again the saber does not. However, this time director Keaton cuts to a now dead Union sniper with the comic's blade in his back. Though such violence is common by today's dark comedy standards, these on-screen *General* deaths still register something of a shock, given Jazz Age comedy film norms. And if one counts the lifelike dummy at the controls of the downed locomotive, Keaton tallies up five on-screen killings in just a few minutes. In contrast, there were none in *Shoulder Arms*, and the same thing applied to Chaplin's later even more controversial dark comedy, *The Great Dictator* (1940). Keaton's near-finale realistic passings were the ones which undoubtedly most bothered contemporary critics, and will be addressed shortly. Indeed, this factor is ironically bolstered even more by the fact that Chaplin had reissued *Shoulder Arms* the same time *The General* was in theatres, with the former film garnering more kudos—best demonstrated by the title of a March 1927 *Los Angeles Times* article: "Reshowing of Chaplin Comedy Scores Success."[28]

Fourth, playing the dark comedy card with more discernment, the genre cannot hold any subject as out of bounds. Usually this is obvious, yet occasionally on artist is blindsided. Such was the case with Keaton when he tackled the Civil War, especially *The General*'s closing moments. One might ask, what about the popular 1926 Civil War comedy *Hands Up*, done the previous year by popular period comedian Raymond Griffith? First, it was neither a dark comedy nor really a Civil War tale. Both points are central to getting a better handle on how one then had to tread lightly on anything cosmetically related to the conflict.

Hands Up essentially circumvents the Civil War by dealing fictitiously (versus Keaton's real tale) with the war. The story involves President Lincoln sending an army officer to some Western gold mine so rich it will be able to fund the Union's Civil War expenses. Naturally, this attracts the attention of the Confederacy. After that, the film essentially becomes a Western. For example, 1926's positive *New York Times* critique describes a signature comedy scene: "Mr. Griffith, as a Confederate spy, shakes dice with a redskin in full regalia and wins everything the Indian has ... the way in which the man of copper hue is initiated into the mysteries of shooting craps is in itself delightful, especially when the Indian grasps how fortunate is a player who throws a seven or an eleven."[29] Moreover, even though this is a pure personality comedy, with not a black humor cloud in the sky, and basically dovetails into another genre, note how *Variety*'s affirmative period review describes *Hands Up* tiptoeing around anything which might be even misconstrued as disrespectable to the Civil War: "A clever touch in casting was ... placing George Billings in the role of the president, the character he achieved fame in in 'Abraham Lincoln' and the scenes in which he appears *are shot with all seriousness* [italics mine]."[30]

So what about *The General*'s negative period reviews? Not all keyed upon its treatment of the Civil War, but if not mentioned, it was frequently a subtextual presence. Of course, from "word one" there was nothing subtextual about *Photoplay*'s wordsmithing pan: "They're kidding everything now and any time you may expect to see U.S. Grant and Robert E. Lee break into a Charleston. Not that they do in "The General" but Buster Keaton spoofs the Civil War most uncivilly in his new comedy."[31] The *Los Angeles Times*' March 12, 1927, review is captured in its title: "Comedy Is Lost In War Incidents."[32] However, a more telling *General*-related *Los Angeles Times* article appeared the following day. Called a "Locomotive with a Soul," it might better have been dubbed "In Defense of a Historical Epic."[33] The brunt of the essay is a four-part build-up to a quasi–Keaton apology.

First, "Locomotive with a Soul" establishes Keaton as a "walking encyclopedia" on the war, code for how much he respects it.[34] Second, this knowledge and passion about a real event inspired the comedian to make an almost educational tribute to the hostilities. Third, no expense was spared to make this happen. For example, $50,000 alone was spent on the collapsing bridge/locomotive crash—which would equal $500,000 today. Fourth, one could almost say it is not a comedy: "Gags play but little part in the picture. In fact, Buster says it is too hard to find new gags nowadays. 'The General' is best described as a melodramatic comedy [a period attempt to describe dark comedy?], and the laughs are based upon thrills…. One thing that Keaton has discovered is that while the great war might have had its humorous interludes, nothing even faintly amusing happened during the Civil War that is in the minds of some people. An Ohio censor became quite wrathful at 'an attempt to make light of history.'"[35] After these four attempts to explain how *The General*'s production was made in good faith, the article closes with by and large a self-deprecating Keaton apology: "But he does not make light of history, the star said. He himself is a humorous character but there is not attempt to burlesque the actual historic occurrence."[36]

This humiliating acknowledgment by Keaton of offending many fans is not noted in modern examinations of *The General*. Instead, the focus is the more obvious irony of a now celebrated film being a critical and commercial failure when it was released, such as the Marx Brothers' later *Duck Soup* (1933). Yes, that *The General* going over budget greatly contributed to crippling his independence is often noted. Yet, this neglected personalized public humbling is a foreshadowing of Keaton's approaching decline which cannot be overemphasized. It must now be counted as another *major*, yet overlooked, factor in how he was essentially forced and/or manipulated into having his next picture be *College* (1927, see the following chapter), followed by *Steamboat Bill, Jr.* (1928, see Chapter 10), in which it was felt necessary he have a *co-star*—Ernest Torrence. The significance of the latter factor is also missing from modern Keaton criticism—but it was given a great deal of period print attention. And this too will be further fleshed out later in the text.

Regardless, this forgotten bombshell of an article could be compared to the later more well-known 1942 *New York Times* defense director Ernest Lubitsch made for his then also controversial dark comedy, *To Be or Not to Be*.[37] Once again, a now much-praised picture was initially met with critical and commercial disappointment. Except in this case, as the article title suggests. "Mr. Lubitsch Takes the Floor for Rebuttal," there was no apology involved—despite the parallel of two dark comedies on war being punished for being ahead of their time.³⁸ Moreover, for audiences still struggling with this genre, *The General* and *To Be* had something else in common—critics and audiences also grappling with what would now be called "compound genres." Indeed, Keaton was just previously quoted as calling *The General* a "melodramatic comedy." Fascinatingly, almost fifteen years later to the day, *New York Sun* critic Eileen Creelman had faulted Lubitsch's *To Be* for attempting to merge melodrama and comedy.³⁹ Even in Lubitsch's "Rebuttal" he comes close to this "melodramatic comedy" phrase when he states his film could be called "a tragic farce or a farcical tragedy—I do not care."⁴⁰

Unfortunately, many audiences still had problems with such genre juxtapositioning. Yet, unlike a pioneering Keaton, Lubitsch pushed back. He recognized that a pivotal element of what is now called dark comedy was this on-the-edge quality—life never limits itself to one emotion. Lubitsch was also aware that a still unrecognized genre had emerged which did not limit itself to one emotion: "I have tried to break away from the traditional.... I was tired of two established ... recipes: drama with comedy relief ... [and vice versa]. I had made up my mind to make a picture with no attempt to relieve anybody from anything."⁴¹ Lubitsch's last comments here are especially significant—"no attempt to relieve anybody from anything" is essentially a definition of black humor. More recently, in the text *Genre-Busting Dark Comedy of the 1970s*, I further scrutinized how black humor's compound nature has become more complex.⁴² That is, dark comedy plays with misdirection subversive tactics by even breaking the templates of the genres combined.

Be that as it may, in returning to additional period reviews of *The General*, Keaton's film was savaged in an assortment of other ways, too. For instance, *Variety* was the bluntest. It called the film a "flop"—"far from funny ... [without] a single bit in the picture that brings a real howl."⁴³ As Keaton once used his 1921 *Playhouse* to satirize filmmakers who wore too many creative hats, the *New York American* applied the same criticism to *The General*: "It seems that as well as appearing in it as its star, Buster wrote and directed this story: And perhaps that is the answer to what is wrong with this picture ... [of] seven reels with only a mildly amusing story."⁴⁴ Strangely enough, after a column of negatives, the *American* closed by suggesting Keaton cultists might still enjoy it. The *New York Sun* took much the same perspective, implying Keaton tried to do too much and succumbed to every comedian's weakness—attempting to play a quasi-serious "'Hamlet' Complex."⁴⁵ Yet, the newspaper also suggested some Keaton "special admirers" might find him funny.⁴⁶

This Keaton still for *The General* showcases him as more leading man handsome than comic, which was where his reaffirmation parody was taking him.

As with the *New York Sun*, a second *New York Times* piece felt Keaton "appears to have bitten off more than he can chew."[47] But paradoxically, the *Times* review then neglected any cultish Keaton fear and simply sounded cultish itself: "He is more the acrobat than the clown, and his vehicle might be described as a mixture of cast iron and jelly."[48] *Picture-Play Magazine*'s review returned to the Civil War as a negative but not as something in bad taste. The reviewer's problem was simply that the subject's "underlying solemnity in the proceedings ... puts rather a crimp on the farcical treatment."[49] However, the magazine's later capsule review, long before saturation booking, was harsher! "Not at all worthy of Buster Keaton. [A] long dull comedy."[50]

The *Harrison's Report* 1927 overview was less harsh (maybe two stars out of four in today's ratings), yet missed any serious goals for which Keaton's *The General* aspired: "Most of the laughs are caused by the "boobish' acts of the hero."[51] Most surprising, however, was how *Life*'s insightful Keaton champion, Robert E. Sherwood, responded to *The General*. While he too found fault with Keaton's attempt to enter the "epic" class, he was both very disturbed with the film's dark comedy, and the most protracted critic in his reprimand: "it is difficult to derive laughter from the sight of men being killed in battle. Many of his gags at the end of the picture [related to the Union sniper] are in such gruesomely bad taste that the sympathetic spectator is inclined to look the other way."[52] This would have been a *devastating* review to Keaton, since Sherwood previously had been the period critic who best grasped Keaton's "Zero" persona. Moreover, Buster admired his *Life* writing skills, later observing in his memoir: "One could tell ... from the perceptive and amusing reviews he wrote that he had a true comic mind."[53] Indeed, as noted earlier, the two had once almost collaborated on a short subject, when Sherwood had taken a Hollywood vacation.

Before, however, moving on *The General*'s amazing reversal of merit, in which the American Film Institute (AFI) now ranks it as the "18th greatest" movie (of all genres) in Hollywood history, Sherwood's biting comments on dark comedy bring to mind some Lubitsch-like insights from another major filmmaker—Alfred Hitchcock. In François Truffaut's groundbreaking book-length interview of "the master of suspense," there is a pertinent comment related to Buster's initial dilemma with *The General*.[54] Hitchcock, a Keaton fan (maybe it started with their joint obsession with trains), also saw most of his movies as dark comedies. And in discussing two of his underrated films with Truffaut, Hitchcock stated: "I feel that both *I Confess* and *The Wrong Man* suffer from a lack of humor. The only question then is whether one should always have a sense of humor in dealing with a serious subject ... it's the most difficult thing in the world to control that so as to get just the right dosage. It's only after the picture's done that one can judge that properly ... [and] if the basic idea is not acceptable to the public, it compromises the picture."[55]

Well, in cinema's modern era suddenly *The General*'s dark comedy "dosage" was just right, and a masterpiece was declared. Credit for correcting this error starts with James Agee's game-changing essay, "Comedy's Greatest Era," which was discussed early in the text. Yet, if one were to choose a second critic/historian who has most contributed to that ongoing reversal, a solid candidate would be Gerald Mast, particularly his *A Short History of the Movies*. Originally published in the early 1970s, it has gone through numerous revisions by Bruce F. Kawin, after the untimely death of Mast.[56] It was and continues to be *the* "history of the movies," though the term "short" is becoming a more questionable word.

Within the text is a brief but memorable comparison of the two giants of silent comedy, by way of Chaplin's *The Gold Rush* (1925) and Keaton's *The General*.[57] The stark contrasts of the two artists are played out by juxtaposing these tour de force works. Generally this works wonderfully. For example, the litany of deviations includes Chaplin aiming for the heart while Keaton is cerebrally directed; the Tramp's world is intimate and interior, while Keaton's "canvas" is the great outdoors and everything massive that goes with it, from locomotives and ocean liners, to floods and cyclones. These alternative worlds necessitate a more demonstrative comedy for the "Little Fellow," versus a full-body athleticism for Keaton's "Zero" persona—to the point of a speedy body in the distance, or if necessary, a "Great Stone Face," when the action draws closer.

Before continuing, it should be stated that the loving detail given the contrasts further augments the uniqueness of both films. However, while the examination of *The Gold Rush* easily qualifies it as representative of the Chaplin Tramp oeuvre, the comments made about *The General* provide a knowledgeable running commentary on this extraordinary film— but at times the attributes imply this is typical Keaton. For instance, much is made of Buster's various ways of misusing his heroine as comic prop, which is effectively true of *The General* but is hardly typical of his filmography. Granted, Chaplin idolized heroines and Keaton had little use for his leading ladies. *But* his "Zero" was the one usually badly or unfairly treated by women. To illustrate, earlier in the text a *New Yorker* review stated how atypically Keaton treated *The General*'s Marion Mack: "a *new* [italics mine] treatment of the lady ... [which] may not be an inspiring light for American womanhood to be placed in but it is certainly a novel one."[58]

Also, the comparison accents Chaplin's standard episodic nature and contrasts it with *The General*'s tight narrative—which is hardly typical of Buster "Random" Keaton. Indeed, arguably Keaton's supreme film is the ever so haphazard *Navigator*, which might better have been labeled *Everything That Can Happen on an Empty Ocean Liner Adrift, and Don't Forget About the Cannibals*. Moreover, *The Navigator* has no ending, so it is back to the ancient Greeks and hello deus ex machina. That is, just as Buster and a girl who eventually turns up on the ship are about to be supper for the local branch of people-eaters, a submarine (?) surfaces under them and they can live to do something *unplanned* the next day. Indeed, as previously noted, personality comedy is the one genre in which narrative is *not* paramount—one sees the film for a favorite clown's shtick, not a plotline.[59]

The Mast text comparison also discusses how Buster succeeds in *The General* despite his antiheroic nature. And while this is true, as it is for most personality comedians, Keaton merits a special asterisk for two reasons, if his complete filmography is examined. First, Buster's batting average for happy endings is lower than most clowns, be it *One Week*'s (1920) destruction of a formerly boxed pre-fab house, or simply the closing destruction of Buster himself in *Cops* (1922, complete with a tombstone). Second, even Keaton happy endings are either negated directly, such as the depressing dissolves of *College*, or are so cheery as to be decoded as dark comedy satire. Buster did not get the nickname "Zero" for nothing.

One must also note how the otherwise brilliant back and forth of Mast's comparison of *The General* and *The Gold Rush* leaves no room for Keaton's often inspired absurdity, such as drawing a hook on the wall in order to hang his hat in 1920's *High Sign*, or his *Sherlock, Jr.* (1924) ability to walk into a film within a film. Even Leonard Maltin's four-star pocket review of *The General* describes it as "not as fanciful as other Keaton films but beautifully done."[60]

None of this is meant to take away from the extraordinary accomplishment of *The General*. Indeed, one should also praise it for pushing its reaffirmation parody to the point of being a pioneering dark comedy. The goal of these last Mast-related comments was merely to say this is not always what one would call a typical Keaton film, though one can certainly see how his evolution as an artist was pushing him in this direction. Thus, I find myself in the iconoclastic position of arguing against today's still seeming coronation of *The General* as *the* Keaton picture, when a much stronger case can be made for *The Navigator* or *Sherlock, Jr*. Put another way, maybe *The General* was his greatest film ... but not the greatest *Keaton* film.

As a final addendum to the chapter, my central incredulity in exploring *General* period literature neither was the dark comedy component, nor the need to reconfigure Keaton's constellation of significant films. Past research forays had prepared me for these things. My greatest bewilderment was the lingering Civil War sensibility that so unfairly maligned the movie. I had never thought that seriously past John Kennedy Toole's basic dark comedy premise in his Pulitzer Prize winning novel *A Confederacy of Dunces* (1980)—that the South essentially felt the Civil War had ended in a tie.[61] However, in further scrutiny for this text a history professor friend and colleague, Andy Warner, brought to my attention Burke Davis' book *Our Incredible Civil War* (1960).[62]

Davis' text shared a semblance of the ongoing bitterness Keaton would have had to endure. The book accounts a Gettysburg reunion of aging Blue and Gray veterans many years after the war's conclusion. At some point the elderly Confederates got into shaky ranks and began walking across the field where Major General George Pickett had led his Southern soldiers' charge: "The watching ancients in the blue could not long remain bystanders, and the feeble ranks moved up the slope toward the spot ... on Cemetery Ridge [at which they were stopped], there were Yankee yells: 'Come on, boys! By God they never made it then—and they'll not do it now.' Upon which the old boys of the Grand Army of the Republic ... [ran] into position along the ridge and when the Confederate veterans hobbled up, to have sprung upon them tooth and nail, the whole mass tangled in a fierce scrap until officials managed to part them."[63] And there were still many veterans alive when Keaton made his movie. Maybe things would have gone better for *The General*, if the South had had Pickett's dark sense of humor. Years after the war, when asked why the charge had failed, he said, "I've always thought the Yankees had something to do with it."

Regardless, in the final analysis, it should just be enough to credit *The General* with author Philipp Meyers' thoughts on the nature of art: "[It] should move you before you understand why. It should feel as if you're in the presence of something holy—that you've come across some ancient code that explains the human race. In the end, that is what art really does; it connects your mind and soul with the mind and soul of humanity at large. You ... [experience it] and you realize: Hey, I'm not alone."[64] *The General* does all of that and more. Still, one has a creative dilemma. The overly upbeat ending plays, as noted earlier, to dark comedy's message of "one cannot take this seriously"—a mindset in which Keaton was at home. However, this writer feels *The General* would have been a greater *Keaton* picture, if he had tacked on an unexpected tombstone conclusion à la *College*, after winning an underserving heroine, following the hollow military win for the *wrong* side. The filmmaker would have anticipated a pivotal passage in a text from another central period artist, Ernest Hemingway. In the novelist's *A Farewell to Arms* (1929) he wrote: "I was always embarrassed by the words sacred, glorious, and sacrifice and the expression in vain ... proclamations that were slapped up by billposters ... the things that were glorious had no glory and the sacrifices were like the stockyards at Chicago if nothing was done with the meat except to bury it."[65]

9

College (September 10, 1927)
Punishment by Way of Harold Lloyd Land

> Buster Keaton, the sad-faced comic, is the latest screen star to go rah-rah. in "College," at the Mark Strand, he brings the [rowing] crew to victory for dear old Clayton.
> —*New York Evening News*,1927[1]

Sometimes it is not immediately beneficial to scrutinize an artist's next project without a full autopsy on what creatively preceded it. This has never been more necessary than now, with Keaton's personalized opus having laid an egg. Plus, as the chapter subtitle suggests, the critical and projected commercial failure of *The General* (1927) convinced his brother-in-law boss Joseph Schenck to put the actor is a more commercial property not to Keaton's liking. Among the cinema army of comedians already having taken this route was high-profile Harold Lloyd and his definitive *The Freshman* (1925). As previously suggested, period critics could see no wrong in Lloyd's work; thus, why revisit it? And if the reviewers did not suggest they were constantly feeling redundant in repeating Lloyd's praise, there were also positive guarantees. For instance, the *New York Daily News*' first critique line for *The Freshman* read: "Your money refunded if you don't laugh"—and this from a picture that had opened almost exactly *two years* to the day before *College*.[2] Indeed, one of *College*'s period ads would play upon Lloyd's title, and unfortunately mix it with a sexist reference: "Funnier than a freshman—Friskier than a Blonde Coed."[3] Plus, among the recommended street music to be used with Keaton's *College* was "Frenchie," which had also been put forward for Lloyd's *Freshman*.

What is more, even nonprofessional actors had also made university-related hit films. For instance, the iconic 1920s football star Red Grange's *One Minute to Play* (1926) had premiered to excellent reviews nearly one year to the day prior to *College*, with the *Los Angeles Times*' autumn praise:

> Whatever fate may have in store for the future of Red Grange as a film actor, it is certain that America's gridiron idol has written a good lively page into current chronicles with his first picture ... he really acts his role amazingly well ... he shows so much promise that further pictures made by him will doubtless elicit interest.[4]

The film and Grange's performance were no doubt assisted by the direction of Sam Wood. Though now remembered as an MGM journeyman director, he was a competent craftsman in a variety of genres, including populist sports-related films, such as his later critical and commercial hits *The Pride of the Yankees* (1942, with Gary Cooper playing the legendary

Lou Gehrig), and *The Stratton Story* (1949, with Jimmy Stewart as Monty Stratton, the baseball player who returned to action after losing a leg).

Consequently, Keaton had to wonder if he was reluctantly returning to a *safe* sports genre, or one which had been *overworked*. Also, there are several other period questions which merit second-guessing, following the failure of his belabored and beloved epic *The General*. First, Buster was not a good businessman, but going over budget on *The General* was not the only thing which hurt its profit-loss sheet. This was his first film released through United Artists, a studio whose box office returns were always compromised by not having vast theatre chains, á la MGM or Paramount. Thus, while there is little doubt Keaton's extra push for expensive authenticity guaranteed a monetary loss, he would not have taken such a financial bath had MGM been the distributor, as it was on *Battling Butler* (1926). Schenck should have protected Keaton.

Second, as suggested in the previous chapter, the 1926 Hollywood buzz about comedies needing to take on more serious ballast should have boded well for *The General*. Indeed, even his sister-in-law Norma Talmadge had profited from an increased acting balance in *Kiki* (1926), despite sister Constance being considered the more comic performer. Yet, scanning the 1926 *Los Angeles Times*, one finds articles like "Norma Talmadge Hailed As Chaplin Counterpart By Clarence L. Brown, Director."[5] Brown, already a top Hollywood filmmaker and a Keaton acquaintance who would go on to a long and distinguished career with Hollywood's Cadillac studio (MGM), observed:

> At heart [both Chaplin and Talmadge] are Peter Pans. And yet, if they please to do so, both can plunge on audience into tears—the same as they can set them a-tingle with merriment. "Kiki," for instance, is not all comedy—there are many bits of pathos.[6]

As an addendum to the Peter Pan/Chaplin comment, this would not have been taken as a flippant Jazz Age remark. In Chaplin's 1922 popular travel book *My Trip Abroad*, the comedian shares that upon meeting James Barrie, *Peter Pan*'s author, "[He] tells me that he is looking for someone to play Peter Pan and says he wants me to play it. He bowls me over completely."[7]

Third, the catalyst for Keaton making *The General* is always credited to Clyde Bruckman (who co-directed the film) lending the comedian the book from which the picture was adapted, *The Great Locomotive Chase* (see previous chapter).[8] Add to this Keaton's fascination with both trains and the Civil War and one has more than enough reason for Buster making the picture. However, I have always wondered why Keaton broke his rule about not destroying coveted objects in a comedy when *The General* did just that with a collapsing bridge and a free-falling locomotive. Ultimately, I chalked it up to Keaton merely following period encouragement to add drama to one's comedy.

However, in closely scrutinizing the 1920's *Los Angeles Times*, there is a tantalizing possible puzzle piece to the aforementioned question. Plus, it makes for another feasible "Why didn't it work for me?" query that might have been hypothetically pinballing around in Keaton's mind after *The General*'s failure. In some circles, this is known as pondering a "person's 'Rosebud,'" an early and/or revealing memory.[9] Regardless, in early 1924, less than two months after the release of Buster's first train-related feature, *Our Hospitality* (1923), the aforementioned Clarence Brown directed one of Hollywood's first celebrated action adventure crashes. A January 1924 *Los Angeles Time* article, "Perfectly Good Train Is Wrecked: Spectacular Finale for 'Signal Tower' filmed at Universal," chronicles in detail the staging of a stunt Keaton would undoubtedly have been following, given the previously noted Buster ties, not to mention filmland itself flocking to the extravaganza.[10] This detailed article, flawed only by a title which should have started with "Two Perfectly Good Trains Are Wrecked...," stated, in part:

> There was a personally conducted train wreck ... yesterday, and while the destruction was great there were no casualties. Clarence L. Brown, who is directing super-jewels [film], conducted the wreck in connection with the completion of "The Signal Tower," which has railroad life as its background.... Brown, who has a university degree of engineering, superintended the construction of tracks, trestles and the like, and when all had been prepared the two trains were set in motion, the engineers jumped and the cameras recorded details of a real collision. It cost ... $10,000 or more for this fleeting but exciting incident of "The Signal Tower."[11]

Of course, besides knowing the director had an engineering degree, which Keaton frequently mentioned would have been his first academic choice had he had a chance at a formal education, one cannot help "Rosebudding" whether Keaton thought: "How had the *Signal Tower* worked when his "trumpet" (*The General*) garnered only a pennywhistle.

Thankfully for Keaton, however, any lingering embarrassment over *The General*'s failure, as Keaton began production on *College*, was lost in Charlie Chaplin's messy and prolonged divorce case from second wife Lita Grey. One might best chronicle a brief summary of the lengthy case from the daily newspaper telegrams of America's favorite print humorist, quasi–Beverly Hills mayor, and sometimes filmmaker Will Rogers. In a January 1927 telegram, even before *The General*'s February release, Rogers wrote:

> In the mayor's much regretted absence ... I hereby and hereon do this day appoint as Lieutenant Mayor Charles Spencer Chaplin, who is temporarily out of a wife, and can therefor devote all his humor to the office.[12]

Keaton's Hollywood humiliation of a print apology for offending many moviegoers over *The General* using the Civil War as comedy subject matter was at least relatively brief.[13] However, Chaplin had to weather nearly a year of comic barbs. The proceedings were still going on in late summer, with Rogers continuing to mine material:

> Good joke on me. I left Hollywood to keep from being named in the Chaplin trial and now they go and don't name anybody. Not a name was mentioned but Charlie's bank. Charlie is not what I would call a devoted husband but he certainly is worth marrying.[14]

Things had not settled down for Chaplin until over a month after the August 1927 release of *College*, with Rogers breaking bread with the creator of the Tramp:

> Just been over visiting Charlie Chaplin at his studio.... I wanted to see how a man acted that had just been separated from a million [the actual amount was $670,000 the largest settlement then in American history]. That would be the supreme test of a comedian. He is funnier than ever.... If the next wife settles for a cent less than two and a half million, she is a chump.[15]

Regardless, there was a redeeming two-part bonus for the athletic Keaton being subjected to *College*. First, there was the plus of both getting to play various sports *on-camera* (versus Keaton's downtime habit of playing baseball for fun and/or to recharge his creative batteries if gag ideas were not coming). Second, it allowed the comedian to interact with many name athletes, since most college comedies came down to winning the big game, which was usually football, like Lloyd's game-winning touchdown *Freshman* finale. For that very reason, Keaton keys on other sports in *College*, though when he unpacks at school one spots some shoulder pads and various "how to" sports manuals, including one on football. Consequently, maybe Buster was initially keeping his options open. So what sports does Keaton end up playing, and who were some of the famous athletes showcased? The focus athletic events were baseball, track, and rowing. The first sport was coached by former Major League star Sam Crawford, who was later elected to the Baseball Hall of Fame. At the time of the *College* production Crawford was the head coach of the University of Southern California baseball team, where some of the film was shot.

The highlight reel of famous athletes, however, occurred in the track and field sequences. It included "Bud" Houser, who won gold medals in both the shot put and discus at the 1924 Amsterdam summer Olympics, and fellow teammate Lee Barnes, gold medalist in the pole vault. These games were later made even more famous by the Oscar-winning Best Picture *Chariots of Fire* (1981). *College* also featured 100-yard-dash co-world record holder Charley Borah, who won Olympic gold the following summer in Paris (1928, in the 4 × 100 relay), with Houser taking another gold medal in the discus). Barnes would also gain the unique distinction of allegedly being the only man to ever double for Buster in a silent movie—pole vaulting into a second floor dorm room near the picture's conclusion.

The use of the athletes not only made the *College* shoot more tolerable for Keaton, it also provided great publicity for the film, such as the August 1927 *Los Angeles Times* article, "Athletes Take Part in New Keaton Film."[16] Keep in mind the Jazz Age was when college sports became big business via the accessibility made possible by the automobile. Plus, that new household staple—radio, helped fuel the interest all the more. But only movie newsreels and films like Keaton's *College* allowed most of the public to actually see their sports heroes in action. Consequently, this was a definite draw for Buster's picture. Moreover, if articles did not highlight the athletes, other pieces underlined the extremes to which *College* went to be funny *and authentic*. For example, another *Los Angeles Times* article reported:

> Buster Keaton is at it again [accuracy]! This time one phase of his forthcoming comedy is concerned with rowing and therefore ... several crack oarsmen are being recruited for the race scenes. Three racing shells, one of which was used by the University of Washington crew when it won the championship in the East, are now in the possession of the Keaton studios. Ben Wallis, who coached the University of California oarsman the year they defeated Stanford and the University of Washington, has been engaged to handle the crews.... Mr. Keaton and his company will soon leave for Balboa, where the race scenes will be filmed before a big crowd.[17]

Of course, the irony involved in Keaton comically struggling with these various sports is that the comedian was very athletic, and worked out regularly at a gym he maintained at the studio, not unlike his swashbuckling contemporary, Douglas Fairbanks, Sr. And he was forever playing baseball. Consequently, while this was periodically documented throughout the decade, there is still a certain paradox in the subtitle of yet another *Los Angeles Times* period article on the film: "Comedian Turns Athlete in 'College.'"[18] Indeed, if there is any minor flaw or inconsistency in the sports scenes, it occurs when one sees him in his tracksuit. He has a small but well-built body, and as my sports-minded father would say, "he walks like an athlete." For a comparison, think of Chaplin in his brilliantly choreographed *City Lights* (1931) boxing sequence. Chaplin in shorts reveals not a toned muscle in sight.

Who knows? While certainly not like the generally non–PR Keaton, especially one known as "The Great Stone Face," Buster incurred an injury while *College* was still in broad release which might modestly have helped its box office. That is, he had a baseball wound perfectly in keeping with his *College* alter ego. Widely reported, the *New York Times* period piece entitled "Keaton's Nose Is Broken" shared:

The accident occurred while an in-door baseball team composed of moving picture people was playing a local team. Keaton, catcher for the "movie" team, removed his mask in the eighth inning. A few minutes later a fast ball crashed into his nose.[19]

Keaton inadvertently took one for the team.... I mean the movie.

So what was the story catalyst for all this *College* athleticism? Fittingly, for a Keaton comedy, he was doing it for a girl. As much as the comedian did not want to make the movie, the demands of his heroine were frequently the impetus for his film, whether it was his *Cops* (1922) girlfriend's ultimatum he make good in business, or *The General's* leading lady stipulating he had no future with her until he was in a uniform. However, in *College* Keaton has brought on the conflict himself. As the most gifted student at his high school (a personal irony for a filmmaker who had no formal education), his graduation speech is on the "curse of athletics" (another private paradox for the comedian). His talk quickly empties the school auditorium with a rant that also displays his complete ignorance of organized sports, including the following title: "What Have Ty Ruth [sic] or Babe Dempsey [sic] Done for Science?"

By the speech's conclusion only his loyal mother remains. One should add that the mass exodus was further hastened by the ongoingly comic ridiculousness of his appearance undercutting any scholarly dignity he might have projected. That is, he and his mother had walked to the ceremony in a thunderstorm with no help from a discombobulated umbrella.

After Keaton's high school graduation, his views on education become as wet as the weather, as he ponders *College* athletics, with screen mother Florence Turner.

Arriving soaked, by the time of his talk his drying clothes had begun to shrink, accompanied by flying buttons and the pièce de resistance of male embarrassment—split pants. Even the Gettysburg Address might not have saved him. Regardless, his speech on the quasi-criminalization of sports guaranteed a total audience withdrawal. It also reconfigured the meaning of an earlier observation made by the girl he hoped to date: "...you're all wet." Of course, after that comment his leading lady Mary (Anne Cornwall) makes it clear via a title: "When you change your mind about athletics, then I'll change my mind about you."

One should add that the shrinking clothes gag also brings to mind Lloyd's *Freshman*. Only in his case the routine involved a big dance in which Harold's suit had only been basted together and started to come apart while he was "cutting the rug," to use the vernacular of the day. However, the beauty of Keaton's earlier diatribe against all sports, meant that *College* could spend more time comically displaying his athletic incompetence—in order to impress the girl—instead of becoming mired in all the underclassman woes explored by Lloyd's *Freshman*.

However, since his mother cannot afford to pay for college, Buster must find a job. And his brief sequence as a soda jerk is an ideal set-up for his soon-to-come athletic incompetence, because the regular fellow behind the counter is an ice cream virtuoso. For example, Buster makes a comic travesty of himself as he attempts to replicate this fellow's talent for tossing ice cream dips in the air, or dramatically pours the contents of shake from one container to another. Still, Keaton might have soldiered through but then his wannabe girlfriend comes in with their former high school sports star ... who took seven years to graduate, and an embarrassed Buster pretends to be a customer and loses the job.

Unfortunately, what follows is one of those scenes that scores highly on the cringe meter. Buster in blackface finds work in an African American-only soda fountain. As noted before, humor of this order was common for most comedians of the period, except for Chaplin. It was ingrained in America's long minstrel/vaudeville tradition, with major white screen stars commonly appearing in blackface into the 1940s and beyond. What makes this second soda shop scene more problematic, however, is its prolonged nature, with Keaton replicating ethnic stereotypes, such as a shuffling walk. There is even the unfortunate inclusion of a coconut, which is only noted because Keaton grabs it and runs like a halfback upon becoming discovered—thus suggesting again that a later football sequence might have been planned and/or cut.

Again, one must put all this in a period time frame. However, Keaton was definitely more likely to go there than any of the other major silent comedians. Moreover, it is just in such marked contrast to Chaplin, his only artistic silent comedy rival. Even beyond their films, it is obvious in Chaplin's *My Trip Abroad* that he is aware of the first burgeoning of the decade's groundbreaking "Harlem Renaissances," in which African American culture exploded upon the scene, including music, dance, and literature. Thus, during his trip to Europe, Chaplin made a New York meeting happen with Claude McKay, a poet he admired who also was an early pioneering force in the movement.[20] They discussed McKay's work and Chaplin later even reproduced McKay's "The Tropics of New York" in the text.[21]

In another section of Chaplin's text he also expresses admiration for poet Carl Sandburg, with no dot-dot-dot connection to black America.[22] However, what would have been an obvious link to period audiences, and is sadly neglected today, is that the future two-time Pulitzer Prize-winning Sandburg (for poetry and his multiple volume Lincoln biography), was a political activist on the mistreatment of post–World War I blacks. In 1919 there had been 25 race riots across the country, fueled by segregated slums, racial hatred from unskilled laborers resentful of blacks competing for jobs in the war economy, and most ironically—the experiences of returning black veterans who had fought for:

> ... the war's avowedly democratic aims ... [beginning] to demand the rights long denied them ... yet white supremacists were determined to keep the Negroes in their place.... Turning to terrorism, lynch mobs in the South made victims of more than seventy Negroes in 1919, ten of them veterans in uniforms.[23]

Sandburg had written an acclaimed series of articles on the Chicago race riots from the black perspective, which was later published in book form as the *Chicago Race Riots: July 1919*.[24] I only belabor this Chaplin/Sandburg perspective in order to document the fact that while using blacks for comic effect might have been the 1920s norm, there were enlightened artists, too.

Be that as it may, sandwiched between attempts at employment, Buster tries out for the college baseball team and interacts with the aforementioned future Hall of Famer Sam Crawford. And it is likely the comedian had even seen Crawford play. Though the diamond star had retired from the Major Leagues in 1917, he continued to play in the highly respected Pacific Coast League (triple A level). Putting up big numbers for the Los Angeles Angles from 1918–1921, he helped them win two league championships.

Of course, in *College* the comedian is the worst player Crawford would ever have seen. Cataloging his errors could fill pages, but what follows are some of his best worst moments. Told to play third base for the second team, Buster arrives at his position decked out in a catchers' full protective regalia. Yet taking off the protective gear is no help and the position soon lives up to its "hot spot" nickname as a batter immediately hits one through his legs. Next, a player successfully steals a base on him—with the catcher's throw being high and hard enough to both knock off Buster's glove and hurt his hand. Suddenly I am remembering a favorite line from *The Princess Bride* (1987): "Get used to disappointment."

At bat Keaton is even worse, meaning he has ratcheted-up the humor. Observing a slugger swinging several bats at once to warm up, he attempts the feat and gives himself a minor concussion when all of that "lumber" hits him in the back of the head. Still groggy when he goes up to bat, the right-handed Keaton finds himself facing the pitcher with home plate *behind* him. And he continues to stand on the left side at home. Next, the normally almost energy emitting Buster, like a dog straining at a leash, freezes at the plate and is hit by a pitch.

Still, he is on base. Sadly, the next better hits a high easy-to-catch pop-up, known then as "a can of corn," from when a crackerbarrel grocer would hook a requested food item from an elevated shelf. Unfortunately, Buster had not studied his "how to" book on baseball and takes off running. In doing so he passes two runners ahead of him and then makes a comically quirky slide into home—adding up to three outs on one play. Naturally, Crawford kicks him off the team. Returning to *The Princess Bride*, had it been out, Crawford would no doubt have been tempted to use another of its classic lines: "Inconceivable!"

The next sport Buster Keaton tries is track and field, which arguably offers even more ways for the athletically gifted Keaton to play the fool. Though there is much to choose from, my favorite occurs first. Buster and the viewers are gifted with watching rare footage of the reigning Olympic shot-put champion, "Bud" Houser, showcase his power with a massive launch or two. When he leaves the throwing circle, Buster comes over to see what he can do ... but it is a short session because it takes *both* of his hands just to lift the shot.

All the time one watches the sporting events, with the exception of a sprinting Buster being passed by some casually running kids who happen to be near the track, the viewer needs to keep in mind that it takes a great athlete to pretend to be so incompetent. For example, his inability to control his swinging hammer throw is a hoot, but his travails with the high jump in an extended sequence rivals his inability to pick up the shot. Between various crashes into the bar, and a flawed theory that if he just keeps backing up further and further from the bar in order to run faster to clear it, he scores comic point after comic point. (During this persevering period Mary's affection for him starts to return.)

Regardless, his attempt at throwing the discus goes awry and knocks off the hat of the visiting dean—Buster's frequent reliable sidekick, Snitz Edwards. Later the dean becomes an understanding mentor when Buster's sports activities bring his grades down. It seems that Snitz was once in a similar ultimatum situation with another young lady ... and that is why the dean is still a bachelor! Regardless, before closing *College*'s track and field chapter, one should note Buster's effort to throw the javelin. Prior to his attempt, another athlete in the extreme distance approaches what will one day be known as "deep focus" as the remote throw lands in the foreground placemat of the camera. In contrast, when Buster heaves a seemingly mighty throw in a medium shot, there is a short pause, and then the javelin comes down near another camera placement mere feet away ... aping that aforementioned baseball pop-up. Buster has failed in yet another sport.

Appropriately, however, these activities have taken place on the exterior large canvas of a stadium, versus the intimate interior world of a Chaplin picture. Also, while the Keaton coliseum sequence begins with many athletes, he continues alone well past practice time and the empty area appropriately fits his "Zero" persona—with nothing being more lonely than an empty man-made setting designed for thousands. It anticipates his future skillful miming of baseball basics in *The Camerman*'s (1928) empty Yankee Stadium.

Next, Dean Snitz pulls some strings to get Keaton the coxswain position on the college rowing team. His duties involve both steering the racing shell, as well as keeping the oarsmen in time with his megaphone. This does not sit well with the coach, and he arranges to have Buster be given a Mickey Finn (a knockout drink) by the team's regular coxswain (an unbilled Charlie Hall, soon to be a Laurel & Hardy regular). Naturally, this backfires and Keaton will lead the oarsmen. While this is occurring, heroine Mary's quasi-boyfriend jock has locked himself in her dorm room. Having been expelled, his plan is that with both of them discovered there, she will also be expelled and pressured to marry him.

Regardless, it is now time for the race, which begins with an in-joke. The racing shell is called the *Damfino*—the name of Keaton's ship in *The Boat* (1921), which eventually sank, despite the comedian sending out more than one SOS. But when he contacted the Coast Guard and they asked who it was, he responded in Morse Code: "d-a-m-i-n-o." Assuming it was a "damn if I know" prank, his message is disregarded. (This way around censorship anticipates W. C. Fields' later sound era veiled curse "Godfrey Daniels" for "God damn.") Nevertheless, *Damfino*'s plight was prophetic, since Buster jumped into the so-named racing shell and immediately sank it, too.

Taking no chances, the new crew boat is named *Old Iron Bottom*. The race gets off to a shaky start, including Buster capsizing the boat and later pulling off the rudder. However, Keaton straps it to his tush, and sitting at the extreme end of the racing shell, with his combination rudder/heinie in the water he leads them to victory—with a picture of Mary superimposed inside his megaphone. Appropriately, just after the win, the still kidnapped girl manages to call him for help when he reaches the locker room.

Now, miraculously, all the physical skills he had previously struggled with come together, and his running, jumping, and even pole vaulting skills (thanks to Lee Barnes) allow him to rescue Mary in her second story dormitory room. Once there, his newfound sports skills also help him subdue the jock deadbeat holding her there by switching to adapt cutting-edge diamond talents. Any metaphorical "early inning" baseball handicaps dissipate into an accurate throwing arm which pins down Mary's keeper by hitting him dead-on with whatever is available to throw. Moreover, he is now also able to return any incoming "pitched" objects with the finesse of two someones he once called "Ty Ruth."

He has now rescued the girl; they soon marry and the Harold Lloyd position of the movie ends. Indeed, something along these happy lines closed out essentially all of these period comic college subgenre films ... except for Buster's *College*. In fact, as noted earlier, in the film's final seconds he manages to sabotage the preceding minutes of what anticipates Norman Rockwell America. Through a series of dissolves the couple's remaining years are reduced to a hard-pressed middle age, angry senior years, and then matching tombstones. Keaton has thus managed to take a middling college picture and completely redefined it with a nihilistic ending. In terms of Keaton's "Zero" character in a theory of the absurd world, the viewer is lulled into a rope-a-dope close which is actually a more typical Keaton picture than the ballyhooed *General*. This includes *College*'s episodic nature and no false happy-ever-after ending. What is more, this has never been fully appreciated by American critics, then or now.

The reputation that the *New York Times* was generally critical to Keaton stems from this period and its earlier review of *The General*. Prior to this the prestigious publication was usually more than kind to his work. However, *Times* critic Mordaunt Hall easily had the harshest period take on *College*, from line one of his review: "There is such a thing as a character, even in a farce, being so outrageously stupid that he seems more to be sympathized with then laughed at."[25] Ironically, another *College* jab by Hall could actually be used as a Keaton defense, since most of the foolishly funny things Buster attempts are sports he has never played: "Everything he does is so silly that one can't possibly look upon him as a bookworm."[26] Yet, as a multiple high school letterman, I frequently saw intelligent friends struggle badly when they first attempted a sports tryout. And Keaton's character was a student athlete beginning at the *major college* level.

The more typical *College* review was that while it was sometimes funny, this school subgenre had recently been overdone. For example, the *New York Sun* would be the perfect model: "...it follows the formula of [Lloyd's] 'The Freshman' and its subsequent imitations ... but manages to be, off and on, quite funny."[27] The *New York American* strikes up a similar tone but without noting the Lloyd pattern: "[Keaton] manages to make the most of the movie material supplied him, and as the gags aren't, in many cases, too original, his clever pantomime sees him through."[28] The *New York Evening News*' less than enthusiastic "rah-rah" notice opened the text, while *The New Yorker* could be no more passionate than, " 'College' is fair but it is far from being his best."[29]

Paradoxically, The *Los Angeles Times* complained: "... in spite of the fact that much of the action transpires on a local campus ... "College" is not in the least collegiate in the proper sense of the word—no, not even in the wildest flights of imagination."[30] The *Times* even underlined the picture's lack of university cross-section with its review title: " 'College' Needy of Education."[31] This was no doubt a result of *College* largely focusing on Keaton failing at multiple sports. Regardless, while the critic had not liked *The General* either, he managed to remember the one thing about it he liked to further knock Keaton's campus comedy: " 'The General' at least had some thrills but 'College' is not particularly exciting."[32]

The all-important *Variety* review was not much better:

> Buster Keaton's odd twists of indirect humor never get a chance to function, so determined have the scenario writer and director been to get on a series of gags which would be fool-proof. Instead of leaving the laughs to come from this genuinely funny comedian's pantomime....[33]

But unlike the *New York Times*, at least *Variety* goes on to say the material is not up to one of the silent pantheon greats, with Chaplin and Lloyd.[34] *Photoplay*, however, was simply disappointed. Indeed, their pocket review pan took on an expected criticism, with a title which underscored Keaton's inability to get assured laughs by playing up a sure thing racial stereotype—the black soda fountain scene, never mind the inappropriateness of the sequence: "Black But Not Blue: Our Comedians [Even] Struggle in the Dark for Laughs."[35] Another *Photoplay* pocket critique two months later had improved to only: "Not overwhelmingly funny."[36]

A rare American across-the-boards positive review came from *Harrison's Reports:*

> An excellent entertainment. It is, in fact, a better comedy than any of those that Mr. Keaton has produced in the last three years [such as 1926's controversial Civil War saga, *The General*, or falling for a cow in *Go West*, 1925]. There are laughs all the way through.[37]

While not necessarily disingenuous, this was a publication geared towards theatre owners, whose bottom line was playing it safe and making a profit. *College* comedies were a proven commodity. And while no longer a cutting edge subgenre, Keaton's name on it seemed a safer bet than messing with the sacred Civil War, or getting arty with a cow named "Brown Eyes."

While it would now seem as if both period reviewers and a contemporary critic see *College* as second-tier Keaton, one must qualify the interpretations. In 1920s Europe surrealists like Luis Buñuel were celebrating the film and Keaton as a:

> ... great specialist against all sentimental infection.... Buster never tries to make us cry.... In cinema we always prefer the monochord expression of a Keaton ... the expression is as modest as that of a bottle.... But the bottle and the face of Buster have their viewpoints in infinity. Superfilms [epics] serve to give lessons to technicians; those of Keaton [as defined by the modest *College*] to give lessons to reality itself, with or without the techniques of reality.[38]

Buñuel sees the world's horror in mankind's mundane day-to-day life masking of an unknowable infinity. This is the everyman tragedy that never merits history's chronicling yet includes *everyone*. Indeed, the point is even more effectively driven home by being depicted in this common overworked college subgenre. Fittingly, the only American critic to seemingly understand this period vantage point is the frequent Keaton champion, *Life*'s Robert Sherwood. He deemed *College* a "...crazy comedy ... ridiculous enough to be extremely funny."[39] Sherwood wrote in the same vein as his previously cited 1922 observation on Keaton's inherent dark comedy base: "life ... is a foolishly inconsequential affair."[40] And these were not just random comments assigned to Buster. In a 1925 piece sans Keaton and written by Sherwood's close *LIFE* friend, Robert Benchley, the humorist even coins the earlier noted phrase associated with dark comedy decades before Kurt Vonnegut used it as the mantra of hopeless resignation in his seminal novel of the genre, *Slaughterhouse-Five*, "And so it goes."[41]

Paradoxically, *College*'s game-changing existentially bleak close was only noted by one of over 12 period critics, *Los Angeles Times*' panning Marquis Busby.[42] Yet, its big picture significance for Keaton's overall oeuvre went right over Busby's head—treating it as a mere clever idea in a picture he did not like. Moreover, Busby misses again when he counts as a negative a theatre of the absurd anticipating basic which elevated the European period significance of *College*, describing Keaton's actions to be "so frightfully absurd."[43]

Ironically, another way in which *College* foresees noirish existentialism plays upon a negative component of the philosophy which goes beyond the broad absurdity of life. As previously noted, the *Photoplay* review notes in passing the overdone stereotype *College* humor based upon race, when Buster assumes blackface to work in a "colored" only soda shop. To better understand the link, remember that the French intelligentsia were the first to recognize the new 1940s genre "film noir"—a combination of the American literary movement "Tough Guy Fiction," which encompassed a darker fatalistic world view, and the anti–Sherlock Holmes know-it-all detective, and a city at night visual style reminiscent of German Expression.

This awareness was fueled by the hundreds of American films formerly barred by the Nazi occupation of Europe between 1940–1945, which flooded the continent immediately after World War II. Containing early examples of noir, more immediate examples were also included in the deluge, arguably best represented by *The Big Sleep* (1946). This simultaneous cinema spate had critics and/or fans experiencing what is now referred to as "binge watching—viewing many episodes of something similar over a short period of time. When this occurs it better allows an audience to see specific patterns and/or themes.

It was during this time that Boris Vian's 1946 French noir novel *I Shall Spit on Your Grave* appeared. Years later, black American writer and activist James Baldwin, long expatriated to France, wrote the racially funneled novella-length memoir *The Devil Finds Work*, noting that Vian's novel looks:

> … at the black American problem…. [And] the curious, and, on the whole, rather obvious doctrine of l'estentialisme flourished, and the word négritude, though it was beginning to be muttered, had yet to be heard…. *I Shall Spit on Your Grave*, and Vian himself … rather terrified wonder about [racist] Americans … [and it was] part of this noir ferment….[44]

One might better posit the genre's use of bigotry in the neo-noir *Chinatown* (1974). Part of the reason the movie's "Chinatown" area is a mystery is not mystery at all. For the same reason courtly villain Noah Cross (John Huston) never attempts to pronounce private eye J. J. Gittes' (Jack Nicholson) name correctly throughout the picture, Los Angeles shows neither respect, nor even interest, in the Chinese. This ethnic group is an invisible lesser race who merely launder clothing, such as the movies' comic slurs involving spitting in the wash, working in multitude of domestic servant positions, and serving as the butt of jokes. Indeed, Jake's mocking of their broken English has him missing a key plot point early in the movie. While waiting for what initially appears to be the genre's femme fatale, Mrs. Mulwray (Faye Dunaway), Gittes spots a shiny object in her backyard saltwater tidal pool. Before her sudden appearance prevents him from fishing it out, Jake engages in a brief, condescending exchange with her tidal pool-cleaning Chinese gardener, whose accent makes him seem to say, "Bad for glass [grass]," a nonsense phrase Nicholson's haunty character flippantly parrots back without thinking. Only later, during another visit to the same location, when the gardener further fleshes out his original statement: "Saltwater bad for glass," does Jake begin to connect the dots: The drowned Hollis had saltwater in his lungs, despite being removed from a freshwater reservoir.[45] And racist Jake, the nominal good guy anti-hero, is still part, on a lesser level, of the ugly noir world.

Award-winning poet/critic Ellen Bryant Voigt is even harsher on Jake:

He doesn't hurt Evelyn [and ultimately cause her death] by "trying to help," as he claims happened before in Chinatown: What does harm is his insistent, arrogant need to know, to simplify, to name, to solve. He cannot in fact tolerate truth, with its nuances and reversals, its contradictions and multiplicity.[46]

Personally, this seems too harsh. It is mankind's nature to be driven to explain the unexplainable. This is the same reason humanity conjured up art and mythology and religion ... such things can provide comfort where comfort is needed. Moreover, in this theatre of the absurd world, most people would be hard pressed to get up that proverbial hill without a metaphorical crutch. As some brave comic once said, "My ultimate philosophy is simply, 'cling to the wreckage.'" Yet, throw one's walking stick aside and listen to a paraphrasing of Mark Twain on how to simply tell a so called story and how it still bumps into the preposterousness that rules the planet, as well as underlining yet again that personality comedy is character driven: "... string incongruities together in a wandering and sometimes purposeless way, and seem innocently unaware that the absurdities, are the basis of American art."[47]

In *College* Buster, like most people, is just trying to get by. Yet, he must change so much for the heroine how could there be any hope for a happy future? Yet, even his only mentor, dear old Dean Snitz, encourages him, because he himself had not given into the rules of the game and compromised for a sweetheart ... and now was alone and lonely. Thus, either way was "Get used to disappointment." Consequently, Pulitzer Prize-winning writer Charles Simic's thoughts on *Cops*, a film so much like *College*, sums up a great deal about the comedian:

> Let's see if we can make our fate laugh, is his hope. Comedy at such a high level says more about the predicament of the ordinary individual in the world than tragedy does. If you seek true seriousness and you suspect that it is inseparable from laughter, then Buster Keaton ought to be your favorite philosopher.[48]

Yet, Simic provides an ever more introspective impression of the comedian in a casual aside: "Whatever he attempts ... comes to nothing, because he cannot outrun his destiny."[49]

In the final analysis, *College*, at least in America, remains second shelf Keaton, both when released, and today. Europe's greater appreciation of the picture, both then and now, has not significantly elevated the film in the United States. Yet, the picture ending negative dissolves, after the most conventional of episodic sequences (a period negative), reinvents the film, like the spinning totem close to Christopher Nolan's *Inception* (2010). With this brief *College* twist, Keaton has made the movie truer to his oeuvre than *The General*. The latter movie, *however*, is extraordinary because of its pioneering dark comedy, *not* because of overstated claims that it is *the* Buster template.

Moreover, since *College* follows this much celebrated *General*—whose status was greatly assisted by attaining public domain status just as Keaton was being rediscovered, it remains unlikely the former film will ever make much headway against *The General*'s stockpiled hosannas. Plus, *College*'s substantial sequence with Keaton in blackface will increasingly encourage other Buster films to receive preferential screening. Consequently, and paradoxically, *College* was underrated in the 1920s, and remains so today—but for largely different reasons.

As an added postscript, a true *Buster* picture is not about soft landings, which speaks more to *College* over *The General*'s happy close. New Age author Robert Pirsig might have called *College* a culture-bearer, from his Swedish mother's native term—"Kulturbarer." For Pirsig:

A culture-bearing book [or any artistic work] is not necessarily great. It does not change the culture already underway. "Uncle Tom's Cabin," an indictment of slavery published before the Civil War, was a culture-bearing book.[50]

There is some of this phenomenon in *The General*'s groundbreaking dark comedy. Yet, *College*'s existentialistic close is much more about "a change already under way." In contrast, *The General*'s Civil War happy ending, which combines storybook romance and a victory for the Confederacy—becomes less and less of a "soft landing" with each passing year.

This questioning close of *College* had Keaton continuing to push beyond the American literary movement of the late 1910s and of the 1920s known as "The Revolt from the Village." Initially seen as a spotlight on small-town hypocrisy and emptiness it "was in actuality an overall attack on middle-class American civilization."[51] The backlash was precipitated by Edgar Lee Master's *Spoon River Anthology* (1915), "though it required five years for the influence of that book to pass thoroughly over from poetry to prose."[52] And one should add film, too; because the movement was born just as Keaton was entering cinema. However, the pioneering filmmaker's theatre of the absurd mindset encompassed all of humanity—which had generated Buñuel's praise for *College*.

10

Steamboat Bill, Jr. (June 2, 1928)

> "Steamboat Bill, Jr." is "light" entertainment—about eight million candle power and as many laughs. I like it better than the "Navigator."
> —Charlie Chaplin, *Los Angeles Times* ad, June 5, 1928[1]

Steamboat Bill, Jr. (1928) was Buster Keaton's last independent production. Released through the smaller United Artists, as were his previous two pictures, the studio seemed to modestly ratchet up the publicity before he moved under the thumb of MGM. Thus, besides the plug from United Artists co-founder Chaplin, perhaps a more telling recommendation came from another of the studio's co-founders, Douglas Fairbanks: "Congratulations, Buster Keaton-congratulations Ernest Torrence—congratulations United Artists Theatre. 'Steamboat Bill, Jr.' will make your audiences scream with hilarity."[2]

The second endorsement is accented because of the attention given Ernest Torrence (1878–1933). The most glaring omission in modern *Steamboat Bill, Jr.* analysis is the lack of attention paid this major Hollywood player's involvement in the production. Indeed, no one even mentions that this was the only actor ever given co-starring status in one of Keaton's independently-produced silent features. Yet, period publications are peppered with both this Keaton connection and his career in general. For example, a 1926 *Los Angeles Times* article helps put his early film work in perspective: "Although Ernest Torrence's powerful screen personality was first discovered in 'Tol'able David' [1921], the Richard Barthelmess picture directed by Henry King, it was in 'The Covered Wagon' [1923], that never-to-be-forgotten Western epic made by James Cruze, that this player's name became famous wherever motion pictures are shown. Today he is one of the most popular actors in pictures."[3] Shortly after this piece appeared, and fresh from a trip to his native Scotland after deciding to become a freelance artist, a detailed *Los Angeles Times* essay on Torrence, opening with a quote from the actor, communicated in part: "It is going to be rather a tremendous experience to play in Cecil B. Demille's 'King of Kings' [1927].' Ernest Torrence stands 6 feet 4 inches, in his stockings, and has a charming intellect unusual in husky giants. He has a dainty little English wife, a delightful son … and an enviable home in Hollywood that escapes looking like a luxurious furniture store."[4] Yet, comments from the well-liked actor were always in demand on a myriad of subjects, such as the former classically trained stage actor and singer discussing make-up. Thus, a 1924 *Los Angeles Evening Herald* piece shared: "Ernest Torrence, whose film career though short has been exceptionally brilliant, says that the art of make-up has advanced a thousand fold since the advent of motion pictures. 'The camera,' says Torrence [17 years Keaton's senior], 'reveals inferior make-up more readily than the naked eye. Players have thus learned a great deal about make-up which the stage could never teach them.'"[5] Dying early in the sound era at only 55 undoubtedly hurt Torrence's legacy, but the *New York Times'* lengthy 1933 obituary certainly celebrated his multi-talented career, stating, in part: "One of the most beloved ... actors on the screen.... He was a successful concert and operatic singer long before Hollywood claimed him, but he is best remembered for his portrayal of the homicidal maniac in the first version of 'Tol'able David,' which still is considered by many critics to be the finest silent picture ever produced."[6] The broadness of Torrence's appeal was also demonstrated in heartland newspapers, which often managed to combine a dig at the industry's questionable big city morals while still celebrating the man. To illustrate, the *Indianapolis News* reported: "Funeral services were held ... today for Ernest Torrence, whose last motion picture had just opened two miles downtown in the garish hurly-burly of midtown Broadway ... known to millions of theatregoers, [Torrence] died Monday after an operation."[7] Be this as it may, what was the catalyst for casting him in Keaton's *Steamboat Bill, Jr.*? On the surface, filmland was caught off guard. A 1927 *Los Angeles Times* piece opined:

> About the most startling news that drifted in from Hollywood yesterday was the announcement from the Buster Keaton studio that Ernest Torrence had been engaged to appear with the frozen-faced star in "Steamboat Bill" [sic]. Signing of Torrence is a radical departure for both the comedian and the actor usually identified with villainous portrayals.... "Playing opposite Buster Keaton will be one of the most interesting ventures of my screen career," said Torrence yesterday. "I have long cherished a desire to portray a straight comedy role which would be vastly different from the screen villains in which I have indulged."[8]

Shortly thereafter, another period piece zeroed in on Torrence's astonishment: "The actor returned from a trip to Europe ... to find himself given equal billing with Buster Keaton in 'Steamboat Bill, Jr.' 'It was a great surprise. That's the fascination of this business,' he said. 'You never know.'"[9]

Now that the surprise casting was firmly established, what about the why? One might posit three explanations. First, given Keaton's recent decline in popularity, the pragmatist would say the comedian was merely propping up his popularity by *co-starring* for the first time. It is a legitimate hypothesis, and regardless of its merits, it scored points with many critics. For example, the *Los Angeles Times'* very positive review observed: "It is a generous gesture—Keaton sharing of honors with Torrence.... Stars don't usually do that sort of thing—at least as regards putting a co-worker's name alongside their own above the title of a production."[10] The *Times* also gave Keaton kudos for making the decision himself—"[The comedian's] recognition in this fashion of the capacity of Torrence as an actor is all to his credit."[11]

Second, Keaton's soothsayer Jazz Age critic, *LIFE*'s Robert E. Sherwood, implied a second viable reason. Without mentioning Torrence by name, his positive critique underlined that "lately, Keaton has been going in more and more for dramatic art (as in 'Go West'), and has developed into an extraordinarily good actor."[12] Consequently, it would thus make perfect sense to team him with a significant dramatic actor to better assist the comedian in this ongoing transition.

Third, however, if one accepts the period position that Keaton was responsible for adding Torrence—creating a comic duo would also be equally logical. And the duo are funny together. Plus, at this point in Keaton's career his thoughts on comedy were harkening back to his earliest days in vaudeville, and by extension, his initial film teaming with Fatty Arbuckle—which liberally borrowed from Buster's tried and true funny stage material. Thus, in a 1928 Keaton interview, "What Makes Laughter, Asks Comic," Keaton was most informative when going back to basics: "In vaudeville we come closer to it. We make

10. Steamboat Bill, Jr. (June 2, 1928)   163

The unique period teaming of Ernest Torrence and Keaton—Bill's views of his screen son begin to change as Junior attempts to spring him from jail.

laughter and we hold onto it.... I am standing here doing something funny enough to tickle the crowd out front. I don't walk over here and do something else. I stay where I am and wring my gag dry, and then I hear the laughter begin to taper off. Bingo! I break there; that's all there is to it."[13] Now granted, when something is filmed one cannot tweak it for each new audience, beyond early sneak previews. Yet with Torrence, Keaton is returning to film comedy at its primal level. First, there is the contrast in size—the rangy Torrence was a foot taller than Keaton, and outweighed him by a hundred pounds. This was the comic size difference which went back to the nickelodeon days of John Bunny and Flora Finch. Second, by casting Torrence against his villainous type, by playing a father looking forward to seeing a namesake son (Keaton), once again had an ongoingly guaranteed laugh. Third, this was further milked visually by contrasting the *manly* John Wayne-sized Torrence with the foppishly attired/acting Keaton.

    Buster has come from Boston to meet his Mississippi riverboat father, captain of the dilapidated *Stonewall Jackson*. Torrence and his unseen screen wife had what was then known as a "Victorian divorce"—living separately but never annulling the marriage. However, she had felt Junior should meet his father after his college graduation. However, unlike the macho student athletes of Keaton's *College* (1927), Buster's character is effeminate to the point of matching America's 1920s flamboyant caricature for gays. To illustrate, he arrives with a pencil-thin mustache and wearing a beret—sadly, period Middle America "code" for homosexuality, and any prejudicial harm which might accompany it. Indeed, the closeted gay painter Grand Wood, of later *American Gothic* (1930) fame, was returning home to Iowa from a Parisian art trip at approximately the same time *Steamboat Bill, Jr.* opened. In R. Tripp Evans' definitive and ever so sensitive biography of Wood, his description of the naïve painter's "coded" appearance could have doubled for Junior's.[14] With added irony, just as Torrence then has Buster lose the hat and hair, and get fitted with overalls, art was copying life. Because Wood did *exactly* the same thing after arriving home. Indeed, Wood immediately made wearing *manly* overalls his safety veneer "uniform" for years. Thus, while the painter's cartoonishly dream-like depictions of Iowa rolling hill landscapes, with ice cream cone-shaped trees, are charming, often his portraits—such as the *Daughters of Revolution* (1932), or his signature *American Gothic*—now reveal an added level of narrow-mindedness since his closeted sexuality has emerged.

Thus, just as Keaton had a propensity to overuse black racial stereotypes for comic effect, such as in the extended sequence in *College* (see previous chapter), the comedian also extends the sequence's gay suggestion in *Steamboat*, with additional hackneyed 1920s homosexual symbols. For example, Torrence is to pick up his carnation-wearing son at the train depot. But between his father expecting a large strapping young man, and the little antiheroic Keaton getting off on the wrong platform, the two do not immediately connect. Ironically, yet fittingly for Keaton, this does provide time for silent comedy's most typical one-shot racially-driven gag. Torrence does see a sizable husky fellow from behind, but when accosted, however, the man turns out to be black.

Regardless, the point of these observations is simply to state that Keaton's character is not just shown as a weak mama's boy but rather specific period "cues" for gayness were applied that a modern audience would probably not be aware of. Be that as it may, the father and son continue to wander about the depot puzzled about what went wrong. During this period, Keaton comes upon an unattended baby carriage. Thoughtfully wanting to entertain the unhappy child, Junior begins to prance about playing the ukulele with which he had disembarked. Only then does his father notice his son; yet his angle of vision obscures the baby carriage, and he thinks Junior is just frolicking about as an end in itself.

Again, one has to place this scene in the context of the times. Even Chaplin briefly acts flirtatious toward a boxer in *City Lights*' (1931) locker room scene, when his adversary in a "fixed" bout is forced to leave, and the ring novice Tramp is about to meet a burly pugilist unaware of any "set-up." Thus, Chaplin's ever so fleeting "playfulness" is an act of desperation. In contrast, the whole comic Keaton opening is based upon gay period "cues." Even later in *Steamboat*, Keaton fleetingly returns to the subject when he will not allow his father to see him partially disrobe when preparing for bed.

Be that as it may, *Steamboat* is the final film in Keaton's Southern trilogy, after *Our Hospitality* (1923) and *The General* (1927). It is now considered the weakest of the trio, with Leonard Maltin providing the best modern capsulation! "Not one of Keaton's best silent but there are great moments and a classic eye-popping cyclone finale."[15] Before getting to the highlight reel material, a brief overview of the episodic film is merited. The original idea for the film is often credited to Charlie Chaplin's sometime collaborator, Charles Reisner, who directed the picture with an uncredited Keaton. Moreover, Carl Harbaugh's name is on the screenplay. Still, the film plays so much like yet another back of a Keaton postcard that one is hard pressed, for two reasons, to not just pencil in his name for story.

First, the tale so closely follows other Keaton pictures one is reminded of an axiom attributed to various filmmakers: "All good director essentially remakes the same film over and over." (Though meant as a compliment, it almost sounds like something anti-auteur critic Pauline Kael might have written.) Regardless, what follows are many Keaton components which he has creatively reworked and/or rewoven into *Steamboat* and which Buster aficionados would recognize. For example, Keaton and leading lady Marion Bryon are oblivious to the fact that their budding romance is set against a backdrop of extreme hatred between their fathers. This point, extended to families in general, goes all the way back to Buster's variation on the feuding Hatfield-McCoy foundation of *Our Hospitality*.

Of course, as one moves to another Buster given, it must be stated that the fathers of most Keaton heroines seem to abhor his "Zero" character. The situation also accents factor two—the tradition of Southern sense of hospitality anchored in honor and/or class—which so heightened the murderous irony of *Our Hospitality*. Thus, one does not just detest an individual in Keaton's South; a warped sense of ethics and entitlement could lead to lethal consequences. The wealthy father (aptly named King) of Keaton's almost girlfriend wants to destroy and replace the poverty-stricken steamboat business of Torrence's character with his own. Consequently, at one point he tells Buster's father, via a title: "If I find him [Keaton] on the [*King*] boat again, I'll personally wring his neck."

Another Keaton given found in *Steamboat* goes all the way back to when the comedian was an actor for hire in 1920's *Saphead*: "Zero" also tends to be a great disappointment to his own cinema fathers. Though providing an excellent mainspring for what follows in *Batting Butler* (1926, see Chapter 7), *Steamboat* is the topper. In fact, at one point Torrence's best friend offers him a gun with which to shoot Junior, observing via a title card, "No jury would convict you."

An additional *Steamboat* given involving a core Keaton element is an in-joke about his signature pork pie hat. The comedian's recent period films and/or chronicles of pampered rich kids had had that hat MIA for some time. Thus, when Torrence takes his son to the local haberdashery for a new hat, father and son develop a comic rhythm which provides an extended period of laughs. Buster (and sometimes Torrence) picks out a hat which invariably looks goofy—at which time Dad had no problem with just pitching said hat somewhere off-camera. (No wonder future President Harry S. Truman went broke as a haberdasher during this same time period.) Well, the only hat Torrence neither gets a chance to see or toss is a pork pie number. Keaton quickly reacts to it like it would be an inconceivable choice and flings it faster than an NFL quarterback about to be sacked.

Intriguingly, despite today's interest in *Steamboat* centering around various sequences involving the cyclone close, the hat scene proved of equal interest to many period critics, including the *Los Angeles Times* reviewer: "One of the most adroit things that Keaton has done in the picture is a gag of trying on hats of all shapes and sizes.... This is a great parody on that disillusioning experience that one may go through endeavoring to select suitable headgear, discovering the while how foolish he can look in certain fantastic top pieces."[16] The enjoyment and attention given to this sequence might surprise contemporary readers. But the answer is quickly captured in the title of a children's book by a Keaton contemporary, William Steig (1907–2003). This long life saw a pivotal change, for him, in the fashion world, providing him with the title of his last book, *When Everybody Wore a Hat* (2003).

As an addendum, he and Keaton could probably have been friends. Both had a dark sense, of humor, with the younger Steig illustrating a number of satirical classics, like Will Cuppy's *How to Become Extinct* (1941). Moreover, like Keaton, Steig's questioning view of people and the world around them seconds Buster's qualms about humanity. In a Steig letter to Cuppy, which could have served as one of Keaton's postcard-length Theatre of the

Absurd-like scenarios, the then illustrator wrote: "My idea is to take all [various villain types] & stick them in the state of Rode Island, give them the equivalent of their wealth in consumer goods—4,000 bicycles, 9,000 tennis rackets, 80 bales of condoms, 8,000,000 cans of pimentos ... put a high wall around the place and let them fight it out."[17] But the second reason for this Steig-related detour, besides its pertinence to the Keaton hat sequence, is a description of the illustrator/author by his widow that eventually describes both Buster's character in *Steamboat* and Keaton the artist: "[Steig] hated pretension. He tended to dress as though he had gone into a closet and invited clothes to fall upon him ... everybody looked foolish [in his work]. That's how serious clowns see the world.... He walked with his head bent into the wind [Keaton attempts this trick with the *Steamboat* cyclone] that he knew would come."[18] Sometimes the kindred spirits of artists otherwise not normally linked merit connecting.

Steamboat also embraces the given of the Keaton persona as a child mapped out early in the text. This is most "tenderly" demonstrated (not a common term to be applied to a Keaton film) by how father Torrence drags and/or holds Junior by the hand as they move from one location to another. The great disparity in their size further accents that parent-child connection. Plus, as much as Torrence is initially disappointed in his foppish son, he tries to love this boy/man figure. Plus, piggybacking on the Keaton-as-child component, is that the *Steamboat* heroine and any relationship they might have seems completely arbitrary. Romance for little boys is strictly a back burner concept, and certainly not something to be taken seriously. The rare exception in Keaton's filmography is that *Battling Butler* bond with the "mountain girl."

Just as Buster's *Three Ages* (1923) spoofed D. W. Griffith's multi-era *Intolerance* (1916), the comedian had frequently also employed the older filmmaker's use of the last minute rescue. Once again this device is front and center in *Steamboat*, as Junior saves his father from drowning. Torrence had been jailed for, among many things, his confrontations with the all-powerful rival King. And when the cyclone hits late in the picture, the jailhouse ends up in the raging Mississippi. Finding his father trapped inside his cell, with the water rapidly rising, Buster is dramatically able to free him by piloting the old Stonewall Jackson directly into his lockup and retrieving Torrence from the demolished prison.

Of course, the non–Griffith and pure Keaton dimension to these adventures, besides the humor, is that Buster has somehow changed from inept child figure to a swashbucklingly comic Douglas Fairbanks at the crucial time. Every genre utilizes some degree of what is called "suspension of disbelief." For example, just as one accepts a character bursting into song during a traditional pre–Bob Fosse musical, no one questions the aerodynamics of a fantasy witch staying on that flying broom. The same principle applies to all those amazing Keaton transformations. One just accepts it as part of the personality comedian blueprint. However, as Keaton's films started becoming more dramatic, some critics began to struggle with the metamorphosis (see Chapter 8 on *The General*).

A final Keaton given on display in *Steamboat*, but much more prevalent during his short subjects and early features, was a sometimes sense of the surreal. For instance, at one point during the cyclone sequence, Buster attempts to hang onto a tree trunk. But the wind soon uproots his sanctuary and he goes flying about courtesy of an off-camera crane. The picture also contains his inspiringly comical attempts to walk against the cyclone (off-camera Liberty plane-driven wind machines).

Yet, the surreal occurs in the most modest of *Steamboat* moments, too. At one point Keaton wants to move from the *Stonewall Jackson* to the *King*. Yet, the distance between the ships cannot be jumped, so he connects them with a plank. However, thinking he is about to be discovered, he lies down on the makeshift bridge. As this is happening, his father's friend tosses a cat out on the deck. The animal is soon nestled up on the *Stonewall Jackson* and on the plank. However, as this is occurring, the *King* begins to drift away, leaving that end of the plank in mid-air. While there is no way the cat's weight could actually counterbalance Buster's, the piece of wood defies gravity. One ponders where the giggle is going to go next. For example, maybe I have underestimated the cat's weight, and like the lasagna-eating Garfield of the comic strips and movies, once the cat moves, down goes Buster. However, the still sleeping cat stays put, the plank continues its magic, and when the coast is clear, Keaton's Junior stands up. Unaware the *King* has drifted, he immediately walks/drops into the Mississippi.

The preceding *Steamboat* examples have melded to become the first obvious reason why this was Keaton's episodic storyline, despite not receiving script credit. The second rationale is even more basic; the film plays upon the mythic stories attributed to baby Buster actually being picked up by a cyclone and living to film about it. Much period literature played upon this point, as it had at the start of his career, even as production changes delayed the film's release. Thus, Buster's real father retold this tall tale-like story yet again in the May 1927 *Photoplay* as—what else?—"The Cyclone Baby."[19]

Plus, contemporary urban life does not fully grasp what I will call "Middle America's Cyclone Folktale Phenomenon." I spent mid–20th century summers on the farm of my maternal grandparents, contemporaries of Buster Keaton. Naturally, this meant I also spent lots of time with their friends and older relatives, since parents who could not care for themselves usually lived with their grown children. Well, every family seemed to have a cyclone story, including mine.

Our tale was first told to me by my great grandma, Alice A. McIntyre (1876–1969). When her oldest son Wallace (my grandpa McIntyre, 1901–1975) was about eight or nine, a "big wind" came up. With everyone gathering to head for the storm cellar, her one-year-old son Earl could not be found. My young grandpa finally located him on the side porch, playing by an open door. Just as Wallace pulled Earl into the house a cyclone blew away the entire attached porch. Through the years, well into my teens, I used to quiz my grandfather about our twister tale, and he always corroborated his mother's story. My grandfather was a hard-working Irishman who could "reframe" any task into something fun. But I never detected any "wink wink" quality to his retellings.

Being privy to so many such tales at a young age had me once almost thinking *The Wizard of Oz* (1939) was a documentary. Obviously, many if not most of these tales were hyperbole. But that is not the point. A period baseball story might better explain the subject. In the 1932 World Series the New York Yankee's Babe Ruth supposedly called a home run against the Chicago Cubs. There are viable arguments both for and against the feat, with even Ruth giving conflicting stories. *But* most baseball fans want to believe it. In the end it does not make any difference; to consider it possible makes it mythic. Now, anything "Ruthian" is bigger than life. Thus, I would posit that Buster's cyclone film had a period attraction now lost on modern urban audiences.

Plus, other elements of Keaton's fabled storybook-like childhood were also trotted out again, such as how a tumble as a tot had Harry Houdini nicknaming the child "Buster." Moreover, the old tales were not only recycled but rather given new perspectives. For example, a July 22, 1928, *Los Angeles Times* interview focused upon how being nicknamed Buster had made all the difference: "If my parents had christened me Algernon or Geoffrey or something like that I don't know what would have happened. As a matter of fact, I was named Joseph Francis Keaton, after my father, who bore the same name. But I became Buster at the age of six months, and I believe my name has helped me in bringing what screen success has come my way."[20] The interview was aptly titled "Keaton Says Success and Name Linked."[21] Given that *Steamboat* is Keaton's last independently-produced feature, this return to Cyclone Buster's beginnings give the picture a bookend quality to his silent features. While he would manage to have enough control on his first MGM film—*The Cameraman* (1928)—to nearly match the quality of the earlier movies, *Steamboat* serves as a satisfying close to Keaton the independent artist.

Ironically, *Steamboat*'s natural disaster finale was actually to have been a flood, but his brother-in-law boss Joe Schenck blocked the plan at the 11th hour for fears that Keaton could not get laughs with something which annually resulted in the loss of life. Much later a frustrated Keaton recalled his response:

"That's funny, since it seems to me that Chaplin during World War One made a picture called *Shoulder Arms*, which was the biggest money-maker he'd made at that time. You can't get a bigger disaster than that, and yet he made his biggest laughing picture out of it." He [Schenck] said, "Oh, that's different." I don't know why it was different. I asked if it was all right to make it a cyclone, and he agreed that it was better. Now, he didn't know it but there are four times more people killed in the United States by hurricanes and cyclones than by floods. But it was all right as long as he didn't find out, and so I went ahead with my technical men and did the cyclone.[22]

Paradoxically, given the premise that this cyclone was occurring on the Mississippi, the picture seems like both a cyclone *and* a flood picture. Indeed, period articles keyed more on the challenges of it being a water production. The September 1927 *Photoplay* reported: "how Buster Keaton is building a river town along the Sacramento [which is doubling for the Mississippi] for his new comedy, 'Steamboat Bill.'"[23] The production team spent two months on location. And a June 1928 *Los Angeles Times* article detailed the challenges: "The frozen-faced star and his co-starring ... [Ernest Torrence] are fond of swimming as a rule but received a decided overdose of it during the making of ... [*Steamboat Bill, Jr.*], for they were forced to do it with their clothes on—a great discomfort which was made worse by the fact that ... [it] was filmed during the winter-time and the water wasn't any too warm."[24] The comedy duo was often forced to fall off the steamboat decks five times a day, which naturally necessitated a revolving door between changing clothes and another dunk in the river. However, Torrence was partially prepared by growing up in Scotland, with its breathtaking cold oceanfront. Paradoxically, however, "their duckings did not end there, for when the company returned to Hollywood for final scenes, a huge tank was constructed at the Keaton studio and the daily immersions continued for some time."[25] At least the water was warmer.

Of course, *Steamboat* is made most memorable by the signature shot of Keaton's career. It involves a two-ton building's front crashing down on top of the comedian. His survival is based upon strategically placing a window on the second floor which, for maximum comedy, will be measured so that his body will only have a few inches clearance. His crew was against it but Keaton overruled them. The weight of the storefront was necessary so that the fall was true, especially considering the wind machines. And even with all the numbers calculated correctly, if Keaton does not make his exact mark on the ground, he would die in the pursuit of comedy.

With this type of potentially deadly calibration, why would anyone take such a chance? Granted, Keaton had been embracing comic threats all his life. Yet, his third wife, Eleanor

Norris Keaton, who essentially rescued the comedian from himself during the 1940s, always claimed her husband was willing to take the gamble because he had already surmised that signing with MGM was "The Worse Mistake of My Life"—a chapter title in his later memoir.[26] Others have pooh-poohed Eleanor's comments, given Buster's whole dangerous, "anything for a laugh" perspective on comedy. Yet, she was still most convincing on the subject when I discussed it with her at one of the annual celebrations of Buster during the early 1990s at Pique, Kansas (Keaton's birthplace).[27] Provocatively, it was an action perfectly in keeping with the existentialists who later embraced him.

Ironically, in the many reviews sifted through for the text, only *Variety*, which favorably called the picture "a pip of comedy," noted the risky falling storefront gag.[28] The hat sketch garnered more period attention! *Variety* also flirts with noting another way in which *Steamboat* brought Keaton's career full circle from vaudeville: "He [Buster] also has the same funny stuff when he is blown into the ruins of the town's theatre."[29] But the publication fails to note Buster has stumbled into a trick disappearing box for a magic act, which conjurors up memories of the "Three Keatons" ties with Houdini.

The *Los Angeles Times* was also very positive about the picture: "There is no end of a hullaballoo when a tornado breaks loose in this comedy production in which Buster Keaton and Ernest Torrence share stellar honors."[30] Interestingly, even when the *New York Times'* Mordaunt Hall goes so vitriolic on the film that one feels like Keaton has slighted him in something beyond the picture, Hall's review and most others invariably shower Keaton's co-star with kudos. Thus, Hall notes: "Ernest Torrence succeeds in demonstrating his talent in spite of the lethargy of this film."[31]

Harrison's Reports theatre owner's guide gave *Steamboat* a decidedly mixed review. It begins by describing patrons around the reviewer going into "hysterical laughter," yet moves on to this confusing verdict: "The satisfaction this picture will give will ... depend on whether the theatre is full or empty when it is shown. If it is full, they will like it well; if it is empty they may go away dissatisfied."[32] In contrast, the August 1928 *Motion Picture Classic* actually liked Keaton's mix of adventure and comedy, something some period critics had struggled with since *The General*: "the piece is *up to something every* minute…. It's one of the best Keaton has ever shown."[33] Buster's patron saint among critics, *LIFE*'s Robert Sherwood, also was pleased with *Steamboat*. Fittingly, for someone so often on Keaton's wave length, Sherwood also suggested Keaton had, to a degree, come full circle, by returning to some of the "ingenious contrivances" of his early short subjects.[34]

New York Evening Journal critic Rose Pelswick really liked *Steamboat*, yet felt "much of the credit goes to Ernest Torrence, who is a gorgeous comedian."[35] Again, this "Torrence factor" is something that is seldom if ever addressed in modern Keaton criticism. The *New York Sun* generally panned the picture. Though slightly reminiscent of the *Evening Journal*'s review, the *Sun* was especially fond of the Torrence-driving "merry moment" when Dad was attempting to pick out a hat for Junior.[36] Other publications which provided minimal entertainment coverage were often less than kind. For example, *Time* magazine stated: "Buster Keaton is a thimble-witted college boy. His father (Ernest Torrence) tries to make him a skipper on a muddy river. They reach a climax in a cyclone. Distinctly not funny."[37]

Regardless, before summing up the reaction to *Steamboat* past and present, some non-critique period pieces merit noting. First, Keaton was perfectly correct in calling Schenck on how a flood and/or other acts of nature would not impact a comedy. For example, just two years earlier, a June 1926 *Los Angeles Times* article noted how the "miniature funmaker" comedian George Harris had successfully made a film about "one of the world's greatest calamities, 'The Johnstown Flood.'"[38] Second, Schenck's push back on this subject was just one example of his being out of touch with the film industry. For example, the title of an August 1928 *New York Times* article, a *year* after *The Jazz Singer* (1927), speaks volumes: "'TALKIES' JUST FAD, SAYS JOSEPH SCHENCK: Producer Thinks They Will Lose Popularity."[39]

Third, earlier in the text a tongue-in-cheek reference was made about the release dates of some Keaton pictures being compromised by competing events, just as print satirist Will Cuppy believed there was a comparable conspiracy against his publication dates. Obviously, there was neither a "Hate Keaton" movement, nor a "Hate Cuppy" group, as the latter curmudgeon labeled his imaginary antagonists. Yet, simultaneous to the release of Keaton's middling *Steamboat*, another negative timing incident did occur. A June 1928 *Los Angeles Times* article impressively titled, "Harold Lloyd Picture Sets New Records," still did not help Keaton's film: "The greatest number of persons that have ever seen one picture in New York City in a single week were entertained … by Harold Lloyd's 'Speedy,' reports Mark Luescher [director of the special promotion bureau for Keith-Albee Theatres]. 'It is estimated that 1,310,000 persons attended the Keith-Albee and Proctor Theatres where this comedy film was added to the K. A. vaudeville bills the past week.'"[40] Let one just say that business timing did not always run Keaton's way. Moreover, *Speedy* was not without an apparent influence on Keaton's next picture, *The Cameraman* (1928), the first under his compromised MGM banner. Buster's film apes *Speedy*'s New York location, as well as inviting publicity for being partially shot in Gotham City. Plus, while used differently, each movie has a brief but significant subplot involving Yankee Stadium.

Be that as it may, how does one compare the period response to *Steamboat* versus today's perspective. Ironically, when one gets past the auteur slant that everything by a certain filmmaker is golden, this picture receives above average marks from both eras— *but* for different reasons. First, part of the period failure attached to *Steamboat* was simply going over budget. There were delays ranging from Buster breaking his nose playing baseball, to an expensive reworking of the finale. Plus, Keaton spared no expense in building a town to be destroyed. Yet, unlike Chaplin and Lloyd, Keaton was more of a period cult comedian. If Keaton could keep his costs under $400,000 there was usually a profit. But grosses were still normally under a million dollars—a small margin of error Chaplin and Lloyd never had to worry about.

Worse yet, the *Steamboat* delays caused negative period comments about the picture's quality. For example, a May 1928 *Variety* defense noted these rumors: "It was held back for several months, getting itself concerned in several wild [negative] rumors, all of which were a million miles from facts … it had nothing to do with quality … lovers of comedy and picture house regulars will like this latest Keaton film."[41] Added to this was Keaton just being away from the screen longer than normal. He even missed his traditional fall release, which was partially fueled by his beloved trips East to see the World Series—which would hopefully include his revered Yankees. Less screen time for a Chaplin meant a new film was an event. For a cultish Keaton it was not a plus. Consequently, all things considered, *Steamboat* was relatively well received.

The plus differences from then, however, are items underappreciated today, especially Keaton's entertaining teaming with Torrence—which remains a mystery on why it is still neglected. Plus, the ephemeral nature of comedy makes the period hat routine not as comically relevant to the haberdasher-challenged 21st century. Moreover, while *Steamboat* is most celebrated today for all things cyclone, especially the falling storefront, most period audiences enjoyed them, too. But the bits were not new to Jazz Age audiences, including the death-defying saved-by-the-grace-of-God second story window. Yes, the routines were more elaborate, but Keaton had done variations of them in his celebrated short subjects, which, as noted, some period critics, such as *LIFE*'s Robert E. Sherwood, had included in their reviews.[42] This was all part of *Steamboat*'s coming full circle feel.

Indeed, as noted earlier in the text, Keaton himself had implied as much when he moved from shorts to features. That is, he felt anything was possible, however surreal, when included in a two-reeler—but audiences needed more of a foundation when the film became longer. Yes, he walked into a 1924 *Sherlock, Jr.* screen—but even that "feature" was well under an hour. Indeed, in rereading Mordaunt Hall's *New York Times* pan of *Steamboat*, part of his agitation seems centered in such old school recycling: "[It] appears to rely chiefly on water and [cyclone] smashing scenery to create fun. It seems longer than it really is, and the end strikes one as being brought about through sheer fatigue."[43] And this was from a critic who had once championed Keaton's features, and would again eventually do so. Also, keep in mind, that a December 1928 *LIFE* Best Films of the Year listing had *Steamboat* finishing just outside this honored circle of *all* genres, at a pre–TV time when Hollywood cranked out hundreds more movies.[44] Other now much honored films joining *Steamboat* in *LIFE*'s near second tier included Josef von Sternberg's *The Last Command* (1928, for which Emil Jannings won the Motion Picture Academy's first Best Actor award, coupled with his work in *The Way of All Flesh*); Victor Seastrom's beyond poignant *The Wind* (1928, in arguably Lillian Gish's greatest role), and King Vidor's wonderful spoof of Hollywood, *Show People* (1928, with a rare chance for Marion Davies to show her gift for comedy). Today the lists might just as well be one. Consequently, *Steamboat* hardly went missing in 1928 comic and/or artistic appreciation.

Maybe, however, the biggest difference between recognizing *Steamboat* in 1928 and today can be skimmed from a short dialogue exchange in the neglected dark comedy *Nurse Betty* (2000). Multifaceted hitman Morgan Freeman is tracking Renée Zellweger's title character even as he is falling in love with her. In trying to better understand Betty, he asks one of her waitress co-workers if Zellweger's runaway figure "wanted more out of life." He receives the reply, "Betty doesn't want more out of life, she just wants something out of it."

In 1928 dark comedy, Theatre of the Absurd, existentialism, and the angst-ridden philosophy of your choice were all warming up in the wings. However, most people were still just looking for a laugh, and in many ways, that remains the case. Indeed, the much honored *Nurse Betty* is still a relatively obscure movie. Yet, a few more individuals today are aware that even that modest "something out of life" is missing—there is your Keaton fan. The modern world, though not in overwhelming numbers, better appreciates his "Zero" character. Paradoxically, however, despite the greater recognition, he still remains more of a cult figure. After all, few people really want to think about the nearby abyss around which Keaton insists upon dancing. In some ways, maybe it still is 1928.

11

The Cameraman (September 15, 1928)
A Visit to Yankee Stadium

> Apparently some attempt has been made to inject more romance into the yarn then customary in Buster Keaton films.... [He] is a problem on love interest. In the present case his cow-like adoration of the heroine ... is used to build up sympathy as a counterirritant to his abysmal stupidity in most respects.
>
> —*Variety* review, 1928[1]

This is the seminal quote in *any* period *Cameraman* review. This first Buster Keaton picture under the MGM banner was a critical and commercial hit. Indeed, the opening of the above critique is the perfect succinct overview: "Good laugh picture with Buster Keaton."[2] Yet, even though this would be the only MGM picture in which the comedian allegedly managed to maintain *much* of the control he previously had as an independent filmmaker, maybe history has overstated that claim? That is, Keaton's character incongruously plays into what will be MGM's M.O. during the 1930s and 1940s—homogenizing cultish comedians. To illustrate, in sharp contrast to Keaton's norm, heroine Marceline Day does everything but crank the newsreel camera for Buster's *Cameraman*. Indeed, she *does* show him how to crank the camera, provides more freelance advice then a desperate agent, and even risks her job to give Keaton *the* tip of tips ... and they did not even know each other. She reduces an unconventional comedian, be he darkly comic and/or surrealistically odd, to a conventional mainstream figure. In the forthcoming decades, MGM would *not* be a good studio for comedians for precisely that reason. As *the* dream factory, with "more stars than there are in the heavens," it exercised tighter control over its performers than any other Hollywood studio, *never* a good situation for improvisation-oriented, left of center funny folks. A smothering MGM would definitely be the leading cause of Keaton's early 1930s multi-faceted career crash. But it would be a real paradox if Keaton contributed to the emasculating of his own persona. Because homogenizing and/or minimalizing of comedian's screen time would soon become the studio norm.

One might argue what about that often explosively funny MGM Marx Brothers picture *A Night at the Opera* (1935)? Yes, it is funny and it revived their careers, but what a cost—to broaden their popularity they split their screen time with a sappy love story, an attempt is made to add pathos to both Groucho and Harpo by having them bullied, and the team even supports the opera! Are these the same iconoclastic Groucho-led, take no prisoners

Marxes (minus Zeppo) who both satirized love and threw fruit at Margaret Dumont when she attempted just a bit of opera to close Paramount's *Duck Soup* (1933)?[3] This is a picture which the 2007 American Film Institute (AFI) selected as one of the "100 Greatest American Films of All Time," *25 places* above *A Night at the Opera*.[4] Moreover, in the 1940s MGM so victimized Red Skelton's movie potential, even with the behind-the-scenes mentoring of a Keaton by then fallen to gag man, that the younger comedian bolted to TV as soon as he could.[5]

In his own way, Keaton was as surrealistically other worldly as the Marxes—which is what made them cultishly great. Yet, MGM's specialty was to tone down as many of these quirks as possible in order to make them more palatable for a mainstream audience. The studio also often compartmentalized these clowns into what could be called a variety show format—something for everyone, at a time when audience demographics were broader. Other studios had their own variations of the same theme. But MGM was the most relentless in their control—killing more comedy than vaudeville's Cherry Sisters (a team so bad that patrons actually brought fruit with them to pelt the "act"). Plus, add to this MGM's serious perspective that too much straight comedy was more than audiences could handle, necessitating those amorous subplots. This "too much comedy" philosophy was not exclusively MGM's but the studio was most adamant about enforcing it.

For a much less comedy controlling period studio, Paramount was the place to be. Indeed, for a time, the celebrated director of sophisticated comedies, Ernest Lubitsch, was even head of studio production. This was where the Marx Brothers, W. C. Fields, and Mae West made their best pictures. This laid back approach to personality comedy continued with Hope & Crosby's 1940s "Road Pictures," and Martin & Lewis' antics in the 1950s. In contrast, Keaton was straightjacketed at MGM—which became most obvious when Hollywood went exclusively to sound. But even Keaton's final silent MGM feature, *Spite Marriage* (1929, see the next chapter), is seriously flawed.

The second telling negative to be pulled from the opening *Variety* quote, beyond suddenly making Keaton a romantic sap, is *Variety*'s description of his "abysmal stupidity." Again, Buster would seem to have had a hand in the travesty, too. Yet, regardless of whomever was responsible for this Keaton tweaking, it is hard to contest the entertainment world's Bible stamping the changes as a success. Plus, being Keaton's first MGM picture, the studio would never have had more incentive to embrace the verdict of *the* Hollywood publication. Not surprisingly, Buster's forthcoming MGM pictures would progressively showcase him as dumber—a real paradox if he encouraged it.

One could concede that since *Saphead*, the comedian was sometimes suggested as being either less than bright, and/or was criticized for suddenly flip-flopping between dumb and perceptive in the same picture—especially in *The General* (1926, see Chapter 8). However, the counter argument from this text has been that "Buster" (a childhood-like name) was not ignorant but rather boyishly naïve—an adolescent self-centeredly interested in pseudo mechanical toys of a larger nature, such as ocean liners and trains, or in playing baseball (examined later in the chapter). This boyhood focus could explain his bursts of clever insight, and his pre-puberty disinterest in girls ... beyond Hollywood's obligatory girlfriend component in the personality comedy genre.

In the past, Keaton's leading ladies were generally insignificant. The comedian's own memoir described his simple "penny postcard" scenario thus: "There were usually but three principals—the villain, myself, and the girl, and she was never important."[6] Consequently, if Buster was suddenly totally dependent upon the *Cameraman* heroine, not to mention being atypically instantly smitten to the point of stereotypical gawkiness, he had been reduced to a routine movie sweetheart. If Keaton was responsible, he was playing into MGM's hands.

Previously, if Keaton's screen alter ego made a snap decision about a heroine, as in *The Navigator* (1924), or *Battling Butler* (1926), it had actually embellished his surreal persona. It was an emotionless act which one neither saw coming, nor was there any follow-up sentiment. He might just as well have been ordering a sandwich, or giving some seemingly equal menial task to his endearing *Battling Butler* valet (the winningly offbeat Snitz Edwards). Indeed, in *The Navigator*, when his proposal is refused, Buster not only lives up to the "frozen-faced" nickname, he decides to go on a solo honeymoon anyway. Now, that is talking pre-puberty.

In contrast, soon after seeing *The Cameraman* girl, his eyes provide a heart-rendering expression more suitable to the pathos of Chaplin's Tramp. In fact, this shot, with most of Keaton's face obscured by his camera (practically as if his signature "Great Stone Face" might be cracking), is so memorable—however atypical of Keaton—that for years Turner Classic Movies (TCM) has movingly used it as part of a promotional montage of early screen stars for any programming which addresses silent cinema.

Regardless, if Keaton himself contributed to both of these *Variety*-reported components which tweak his persona, since this was his only starring MGM feature on which he had some control, it would be just one of several *Cameraman* ironies. Another paradox is that despite the film being a critical and commercial hit—with this stated sizeable input from Keaton, the comedian still essentially lost whatever control he had been able to exercise. Is that not the opposite "reading" the studio should have taken away from those results? Maybe MGM was attempting to act surreal themselves?

Third, the studio was so pleased with this homogenized hit, even if it bastardized so many Keaton basics, it became their official comedy training picture for years: "In 1953, when a friend of Buster Keaton asked to see it [*The Cameraman*] projected, he was told.... 'The present print is worn out.... It's been our training picture. Ever since 1928 we've made each new comedian study it. From [Jimmy] Durante to Abbott & Costello, from Mickey Rooney to Red Skelton and the Marx Brothers.'"[7]

A fourth oddity is that despite eventually bequeathing this special honor upon the film, the studio still constantly refused to consider the advice of the artist seemingly most responsible for their comedy template.

What I write about the fifth irony belongs in a broader context of what I bring in research and analytical skills, such as they are, of my maturity. How does MGM producer Irving Thalberg (1899–1936), the man most responsible for both clipping Keaton's wings after *The Cameraman*, as well as later emasculating the Marxes in *A Night at the Opera*, get to keep his "boy genius" moniker—not to mention having an award given in his honor annually at the Oscars? While Keaton was fascinated by sound pictures, it is now clear that if he had followed Chaplin's limited response to talkies, à la sounds effects, or *City Lights'* (1931) gibberish speeches, the Great Stone Face's quality career could have been lengthened. (Plus his deep voice further sabotaged Buster's youthful persona.) Yet Thalberg, a full month after Keaton's last silent film, gave a highlighted 1929 *Los Angeles Times* interview in which he boldly stated: "Of course, not all pictures should be talkies. It is ridiculous to thrust dialogue into certain subjects that are better done in pantomime. Certain productions which have great variety of movement [such as Buster in full flight from 1925's army of brides in *Seven Chances*] and pictorial appeal are definitely for the silent form."[8]

11. The Cameraman *(September 15, 1928)* 175

If I may be indulged with one further irony to come, how is it that the MGM Marx Brothers and MGM Red Skelton paid little comedy attention to Keaton's later tips even when it had direct ties to *The Cameraman*, such as Skelton's 1950 remake, *Watch the Birdie*?[9] One can couple this situation with another enigma. When Keaton helped add uncredited humor to Clark Gable's action adventure picture, *Too Hot to Handle* (1938, about another newsreel cameraman), Keaton called him "one of the best-liked ... easiest to work with stars in Hollywood."[10] The brilliant comic bit Keaton created, causing a toy plane to cast an ominous overhead shadow, only to be comically diffused by a boy falling out of a nearby tree, was not a recycled *Cameraman* gag. However, the dramatic Chinatown Tong War shootout Keaton had filmed for his film immediately brings to mind a similar sequence in *Too Hot*. There is a neglected connection between the two films which merits attention in a future project. Be that as it may, Keaton's MGM influences, credited or not, hardly stopped with comedy. Who knows, maybe even Buster's lingering fame for doing his own stunts had inspired the appreciative Gable. That is, at one point in shooting *Too Hot*: "Gable became a real-life national hero when an on-the-set fire went out of control and firemen prepared to rescue [co-star Myrna] Loy, who was an aviatrix [woman pilot] trapped in a burning plane. [Gable yelled:] 'Keep the cameras rolling, damn it! I'll get her out myself.'"[11]

Beyond these paradoxes is Keaton's choice of subjects for the film. He already seemed to be thinking like a company man, which gives added credibility to his making of the aforementioned persona changes. That is, he wanted to make a newsreel picture and felt

Buster has some serious preparation for the Tong War shootout.

he had a better chance both because it could provide PR for MGM's own news operation, which would also generate media attention in the William Randolph Hearst (Orson Welles' model for *Citizen Kane*'s 1941 title character) media empire. Hearst had a great deal of MGM stock, because his underrated actress mistress (Marion Davies) had her MGM production unit.

So what was "company man" controversial about the choice of subjects? As noted earlier, Keaton had been upset about having to do 1927's *College* (see Chapter 9), because there was a glut of campus pictures on the market. Yet, 1928 was awash with newsreel pictures. In fact, though *The Cameraman* would be a hit, most of its critical pans made note of the already crowded field. One such period knock came from the *New York American*:

Clark Gable, with behind-the-scenes assistance from Keaton, in *Too Hot to Handle*.

"The story of the newsreel photographer's experiences and adventures seems to be enjoying a vogue just now ... at any rate, 'The Cameraman' drags himself and his little black box through several reels without anything particularly funny happening to relieve the monotony.... Mr. Keaton seems to have missed it on this one."[12] The *New York Daily News*' critique had the same retread negative start. Given that fact, the *News* felt Keaton's film "loses lots of its flavor. It's a two star movie, with four stars as maximum."[13] Luckily, most of *The Cameraman* reviews were closer to *Photoplay*'s October 1928 response: "Buster Keaton clicks again, and we don't mean perhaps. He's a reformed tintype [street photographer] this time, trying to break into the newsreel service all because his heart aches for the office stenographer. He takes his famous poker face through fire, water and jail for the type-writing lady."[14]

Yet, keep in mind, while this was just one of many 1928 positive *Cameraman* reviews, it was aware of Keaton's persona being somewhat different. In this case it was lovey-dovey behavior towards the heroine being atypical for the Great Stone Face. This is a pivotal observation to underline. While today Keaton is more revered, contemporary critics and historians just wallow in the fact that he somehow got one more significant picture made, despite MGM grabbing at his control. Though ironically, as this chapter has suggested, Buster may have been party to his own demise.

Regardless, to better set the 1928 scene, however, what was a taste of the competition like? Keaton's film was most hurt by an earlier popular hit from the well-liked comedienne Bebe Daniels' Paramount picture *Hot News*. *Variety* opined: "A lively little story of the news reel, with enough action and quite some comedy, both in situations and titles, makes this a good picture for Bebe Daniels and a better than average Paramount."[15] The *New York Times'* critique of *Hot News* might have even given a hint as to why Keaton's heroine's importance was so bulked up: "Miss Daniels carries on the doctrine that women are equal to men in all things—even to being a newsreel photographer."[16]

Another newsreel which beat Keaton's picture to the screen was Fox's *The News Parade*. More of a programmer, without a star, *Variety* said: "Its chief contribution is that Fox has modestly refrained from plugging its own news service and [M. S.] Boylan has titled [the film] so as to boost the newsreel in general."[17] (Unlike this Fox picture, Keaton's *Cameraman*, as he anticipated, *so* plugged MGM's newsreel service the film might have doubled as a documentary on MGM product placement.) Keaton's character was constantly in and out of the studio's news department, which was peppered with studio-related signs, not to mention their pivotal assignment desk heroine.

Hot News, *The News Parade*, and a series of other newsreel-related stories came out in the first half of 1928. Yet, even after *The Cameraman*'s autumn release, the fascination for these pictures continued, culminating with the now celebrated Diziga Vertov Russian experimental documentary *Man with a Movie Camera* (1929). It was not fully appreciated at the time, with its mix of film techniques, such as double exposures, jump cuts, slow motion, and other formalistic tactics—a modus operandi in which the filmmaker puts his self-conscious signature on the movie. This is, of course, in direct contrast to Hollywood's longstanding more realistic style of "invisible editing." The American filmmaker attempted to assemble his footage in such a matter that the viewer would become so immersed in the story that the audience forgets he or she is watching a movie.

Paradoxically, Keaton, the once surrealistic filmmaker, which was one of the reasons he could never have the period success of a Harold Lloyd, manages to include a sequence in his largely mainstream MGM *Cameraman* which would not be out of place in Vertov's picture. The setting is the competing newsreel filmmakers' screening room—what will the boss select? The raw footage of Keaton's first attempt to be a cameraman is shown. Buster's character has made a litany of rookie mistakes and is hooted out of the place. Yet, the short sequence is fascinatingly surreal, especially in its double exposure of a battleship at sea somehow simultaneously jump cutting itself up 5th Avenue among traditional speeded up traffic.

Earlier Buster's idiotic lovesick puppy disappointingly seems to be pandering to a safe, noncontroversial MGM à la Babbit, America. Then here, Buster briefly jerks the viewer back to the absurdity that lurks beneath the surface in Keaton-land. Maybe not so viscerally shocking as his tombstone conclusions to *Cops* (1922) or *College*, it still provides "absurdity joy" in a picture one worried would go without. In now rehashing the basic postcard tale, one must start with the one prolonged example of unadulterated Keaton—a signature sequence which can stand with any other Buster scene as definitive of his "Zero" character world.

Once again there is irony; this consummate Keaton scene of otherworldliness actually involves America's national pastime, as well as the Yankee fan comedian's obsessive hobby. His title character *Cameraman* has gone to Yankee Stadium for some freelance footage.[18] Naturally, the team is out of town. Just as an empty ocean liner seems to swallow him up in arguably his greatest film, *The Navigator*, he finds himself alone in the cavernous "House That Ruth Built." What occurs next by this refugee from an Edward Hopper painting is yet another example of Keaton's peculiar under glass world—like a boy, he decides to play an imaginary game of "shadow ball."

Keaton goes to the mound, shakes off the catcher's sign, and then nods "yes" to the next pitch call. However, he initially holds the runners on first and third and even throws to third. Once the comedian gets the ball back, he looks at another phantom runner on second while motioning his right fielder over. Finally, he delivers the ball and it is a hot grounder to him. He fields it and starts a second-to-first double play. The opponent on third is caught in a rundown attempting to score. Keaton takes a high throw from the third baseman and manages to tag the runner at the plate. Keaton is out of the inning and acknowledges imaginary applause.

The "game" continues as Keaton comes to bat. He dirties his hands for a better grip and steps into the box. Buster takes some practice swings, digs in, and suddenly hits the ground—the pitcher has tried, to use period language, to "stick it in his ear." Angry over the knockdown he takes a few steps towards the mound and words are exchanged. Keaton shakes it off, nods to the umpire that he is ready, and digs in again. This time he hammers the horsehide. Tearing around first base, he momentarily slows at second but the ball gets by the left fielder. He sprints to third and is given the green light to go home. Buster scores with an unyielding headfirst slide. Casually brushing himself off, he again accedes to the appreciative phantom fans—until a groundkeeper appears and Keaton's childhood mind game is over.

Unable to interact in social settings, Keaton's robotic "clockwork orange" figure survives best in the most lonely of settings—venues meant for myriad of people, such as an empty ship, train, or stadium. Indeed, period Yankee Stadium was the best of these examples—a 24-acre site capable of seating over 50,000 people. As novelist and playwright Samuel Beckett's Vladimir observes in the absurdist play *Waiting for Godot* (1953), "This [waiting] is becoming really insignificant [but] it'd pass the time." Fittingly, as previously noted, Keaton's "Zero" character later plans the puzzling central role of O in Beckett's only movie, a short subject entitled *Film* (1965).

The shorter picture could be a description of Keaton's solo sojourn to Yankee Stadium—a camera following a peculiar outsider. Regardless, since existentialism essentially is about killing time until life's ninth inning, watching the exploits of the diamond works for me. Moreover, maybe Keaton anticipated linking Beckett to baseball. After all, as Yankee Yogi Berra later warned, "The future ain't what it used to be."

The dazzling baseball nuances Keaton brought to this lengthy central scene point to the picture's central flaw—trying to link his masterful Mr. Baseball and normally asexual adolescent to that moonstruck idiot, who could not even exit the heroine's office without always breaking the glass in her workplace door. Okay, the Three Stooges later made an art of breaking plate-glass door windows, starting with their one and only Oscar-nominated Best Short Subject—*Men in Black* (1934). However, with all due respect to that comedy team, no one would ever confuse Keaton's silent film artistry with the later Stooges. Again, while only a handful of period intellectuals, such as *LIFE*'s Robert E. Sherwood, fully grasped the extent of Keaton's gift (and even Sherwood struggled with the dark comedy of *The General*), contemporary commentators finally celebrate Buster's art, yet little to nothing is said about artistic disconnects.

Moreover, while this seminal *Cameraman* sequence is not missing from contemporary appreciations of the film, make note of the fact that it was *the* single most keyed upon scene noted by *period* reviewers. Not surprisingly, the most passionately in-depth, seemingly modern critique of the sequence's significance is Sherwood's. Plus given his future illustrious career as a playwright, the review is also artfully graced with humor even if his subject is a precursor to the Theatre of the Absurd:

> In one scene in "The Cameraman," Buster Keaton ... wants to make good in the newsreel game [and] goes to Yankee Stadium to get some views of Babe Ruth in action. He finds that the Yankees aren't playing.... The huge stadium is absolutely deserted. So Buster furtively steps out to the pitcher's box and delivers a series of imaginary pitches at which an imaginary batter (probably the Babe himself) swings futilely. Then, having retired the side, Buster steps up to the plate himself and after an imaginary argument with the umpire, hits an imaginary home run, and acknowledges gracefully the thundering cheers of the imaginary spectators. The scene is beautiful and true and infinitely touching. It is typical of Buster Keaton at his best.[19]

One must pause to put this Keaton baseball sequence in period perspective. While today the sport remains the "national game" for many, a sizable group would now place the National Football League (NFL) first. Along these lines, though I am decidedly to the left of political columnist George Will, I am very much in his pro-baseball camp when this sometimes "diamond" historian recites his famous axiom, "Football combines the two worst features of modern American life—it's violence punctuated by a committee meeting." But to put baseball in 1920s period terms, *The Cameraman* had an importance lost on modern viewers.[20] When Ken Burns opened the fifth installment of his award-winning epic documentary *Baseball* (1994) with then-New York governor Mario Cuomo, the statesmen underlined the assimilation significance of the game in Keaton's time. For the new kid on the block and/or the child of immigrants, playing baseball was a passport to becoming American. Then Cuomo movingly makes the baseball to democracy connection: "You need all nine people [players] to work ... giving yourself up for the good of the whole [team].... I love the idea of the bunt, the sacrifice ... that's *Jeremiah*. The Bible tried to do that and didn't teach you. Baseball did."[21]

And no one symbolized America's Jazz Age excess and fun more than Keaton's Yankee friend Babe Ruth. The same year Buster made *The Cameraman*, New York played the St. Louis Cardinals in a World Series Keaton attended, as was his autumn habit. It was a contest in which Ruth also showed his moxie and good-naturedness on the road, too. As an outfielder, the star had been so targeted by thrown pop bottles that his position was littered with glass—that was the sort of passion the game then produced. Regardless, the man whose period nickname was "The Sultan of Swat," showed the proverbial "grace under pressure" *without* his bat. In a game Keaton was probably at, since he followed the "Series" road trips, too, Will Rogers, a comedian Buster greatly admired, described a scene the Great Stone Face might have used in a movie: "[Ruth] just kidded with 'em [the crowd], and tossed the bottles aside, and then in the very last of the ninth [with the Cardinals threatening] ... a long high foul was hit, and ... he leaped from bottle to bottle ... [as more rained down] and that gave him a little higher lift, so all he was able to do was make a sensational one-handed catch.... He is the only athlete that ever rose to the heights with nothing but a foundation of Coca Cola under him."[22]

One also embellishes the Ruth and/or baseball link for further period color connection to *The Cameraman*. For example, of the dozen-plus period rhapsodizing appraisals of Keaton's baseball pantomime in "The House That Ruth Built," the *New York Sun*'s critic, Irene Thirer, somehow missed the significance of why it was more appropriate for Keaton's persona to be alone: "If Babe Ruth were in evidence or the rest of the Yankees there'd have been lots more interest to the scene."[23] Thirer was undoubtedly a greater fan of Harold

Keaton and his simian co-star with director Edward Sedgwick, Jr., on *The Cameraman* set.

Lloyd's *Speedy* (1928), which opened five months earlier than *The Cameraman*, and showcased Ruth in a small but effective supportive role, as well as including documentary footage of him homering at Yankee Stadium.

While Keaton's film is superior, these sorts of period details often get buried under the mountainous accumulation of time, such as the aggregate of fictionalized newsreel films which had opened prior to *The Cameraman*. Indeed, for the cynic, there are other "play it safe" threads in *The Cameraman* that, in their accumulation, further suggest MGM's play-it-for-profit policy, with artistic considerations to the rear. This meant go mainstream, and/or use already successful popular story cogs. Today's history always suggests this was studio driven. Buster literature harps on how he somehow managed one more time to create a Keaton classic, *despite* MGM. However, as with the comedian's Hearst PR proposal, period detail suggests that he had already sipped some of the MGM "Kool-Aid." For example, here are three additional instances which fly counter to Buster world. All are interlocked near *The Cameraman*'s conclusion. They begin with a cute little monkey awkwardly inserted into the narrative.

This Keaton simian sidekick had initially seemed more pest than positive to the comedian's wannabe newsreel aspirations. Yet, the monkey is a major asset in Buster getting some great footage of the Tong War, including the little creature actually helping to milk the action along by even manning one of the machine guns! Second, and more importantly, the monkey shoots the footage—initially thought to be missing—of Keaton rescuing the heroine from almost drowning.

Keaton and creature had been at the tony Westport Yacht Club regatta to film some footage of a race. The leading lady and her quasi-boyfriend (an actual real photographer) are there recklessly speeding in his motorboat when it capsizes. Naturally, he abandons her, since viewers have already seen him bullying Buster at the newsreel office. Buster comes to the rescue from the beach and only briefly leaves the saved yet unconscious woman to get smelling salts with which to revive her. Sadly, the cowardly cad comes back and takes the credit in the comedian's absence. When Buster returns they are gone and he collapses to his knees in a pathos-dripping scene reminiscent of Chaplin's solo close to *The Circus* (1928), which had opened nine months before *The Cameraman*. One has arguably just witnessed MGM's first emasculating of a major comedy persona.

First, in what world is Buster ever artfully posed in calamitous tragedy over love? In the majority of Keaton's filmography to this point, not to mention a personal life in which his wife had withheld sex after the birth of their second child, the comedian's philosophy in this area is closer to the title of Charles Bukowski's collected poems, *Love Is a Dog from Hell*.[24] If that seems comically overstated, one might better use another truly Keatonesque line from Bukowski's novel, *Factotum*, "A woman is a full-time job. You have to choose your profession."[25] Large mechanical objects, like trains, ships, and even the surreal house way back in 1920's *One Week*, have invariably placed first in Buster's films. Moreover, the only believably passionate *Cameraman* sequence was his joyful little boy game of "shadow ball" in the empty cavernous Yankee Stadium.

This is not random conjecture, Bukowski's definitive biographer, Barry Miles, has made a similar if broader connection of linking the writer's persona to a Keaton-like loner image of an American archetype, from silent cinema's "little man ... [to] the alienated individual of Sam Fuller's movies ... the disenfranchised ... the [purely] dysfunctional."[26] Regardless, as a punning transition to the second contradiction *The Cameraman* makes to the true Keaton world, one could quote the subtitle to my novelized memoir of the comedian (Red Skelton) Buster most attempted to mentor—*A Man, His Movies, and Sometimes His Monkeys*.[27]

Second, Keaton's little monkey has not been forgotten. Since the simian greatly assisted in filming the Chinatown Tong War scoop, and then cranked the footage of the comedian saving the drowning heroine, Buster gets both his coveted job and the girl. The ending, though consistent with the mainstream theme of the picture, then returns Keaton to idiot mode. *The Cameraman* inserts real newsreel footage of the previous year's (1927) ticker tape parade for Charles Lindbergh's solo trans-Atlantic flight and Buster mistakenly thinks it is for him. Yet, the best Buster material for modern audiences does not end with happiness. It is supposed to be tombstones or absurdity, such as the deus ex machina close to *The Navigator* (1924). And while he might be a "Zero," he is a "Zero" aware of the fact. Yes, *The Cameraman* was a hit, but *The Navigator* was actually a greater period success.

Third, *The Cameraman* borrows yet again from another film. Early that year (1928), Chaplin had released the aforementioned *Circus*—his funniest feature. However, it is often neglected because it falls between his two more multi-faceted masterpieces, *The Gold Rush* (1925), and *City Lights* (1931). Be that as it may, at the close of *The Circus*, Chaplin is losing his self-respect by losing the girl. Thus, he attempts something brave—subbing for the missing tightrope walker. Yet, initially he has a safety harness. But about the time the Tramp realizes he has lost his security belt and wire line, some escaped monkeys (it is a circus, after all) become affectionate but uninvited partners in the high wire act. But like Buster's brave rescue of the drowning girl, Chaplin's character has only attempted this suicide substitution in order to win the heroine.

The Tramp's monkeys, though putting him at risk, also help his career, like Buster's solo simian. That is, in *The Circus*, the audience just thinks the fury "assistants" are an excitingly inventive addition to the act. And in all honesty, their arrival is the comic highlight of the high wire act, as the simians do everything from pulling down his pants, to one's wayward tail actually finding its way into the struggling Tramp's mouth.

Consequently, in their own diverse ways, the monkeys help make successes of both comedians, as well as help them get the girls—though the Tramp thinks it best the couple go their separate ways. Regardless, period reviews make important note of these miniature supporting players. For example, the *New York Times*' review of *The Circus* states: "Finally, the [safety] rope brakes and the Tramp, not knowing of the accident, goes on just the same, and then his task is made all the more [comically] hazardous by his being attacked by three monkeys."[28] Consequently, it is difficult to not make a period connection when later 1928's *Picture-Play* magazine saved its greatest praise for Buster's little *Cameraman* helper: "the 'acting' of a nameless monkey approaches the stellar realm."[29] Also, the 1928 *Harrison's Reports*' positive critique more broadly stated recycled material: "The comedy situations in this picture are old stuff and silly but they make the spectators laugh just the same."[30]

All this is not to denigrate the continuous entertainment level of The *Cameraman*. However, it is important to state that it comes at a cost—the homogenizing of Keaton's edgy persona, regardless of how much he willingly went along with it, or not. Thus, it is a funny film, just not always a funny *Keaton* film, not to mention the comedian's normal hostility to recycling variation upon the same theme. Buster's greatness makes the bits live on, but period scrutiny often destroys the aura of originality with which today's critic and historians often anoint them.

Regardless, one has to agree that Keaton's signing with MGM had released the PR ballyhoo boys. So much mundane material began to appear that one was reminded of the aforementioned glut of "who cares" items with which Harold Lloyd had always kept his name in the newspapers. A recycling of a period vaudeville joke applies nicely to the petty press items Lloyd's studio was constantly hemorrhaging: "He would go to the opening of an envelope." Thus, what follows is a May 1928 *Variety* article fittingly titled "Buster Keaton's Bicycle"—which is a classic example of mainstream Mr. Average tripe in order to repackage Keaton. And it even appeared just shortly after the comedian's last independent film *Steamboat Bill, Jr.* (1928) opened—well before *The Cameraman* premiered: "To keep in condition befitting an athlete, Buster rides to and from his work at the Metro-Goldwyn-Mayer studios on a bicycle, a distance of four miles one way. In addition to this, Buster has equipped a bungalow near the studio with gymnasium paraphernalia, where he makes use of it between scenes."[31]

Sadly, unlike Lloyd, this is just the sort of thing Keaton hated. Sometimes the MGM material went beyond embarrassing to humiliating. Buster prided himself on doing all his own stunts, and sometimes even doubling for other people in the same film. His basic axiom on the subject was always a variation of, "stuntmen don't get laughs." But MGM was taking no chances on their new star getting hurt and holding up costly production. It has always been claimed that prior to MGM his only double was for the pole vaulting sequence which nearly closes *College* (see Chapter 9). Yet, in early 1929 a rather curious article appeared in the *Los Angeles Times* sports section. Keaton was in the midst of his first MGM contract and his double is revealed to be sometimes major league clutch hitter, Ernie Orsatti. Both the article and its title played upon the pun that Orsatti also had a knack for hitting baseball doubles: "Ernie Orsatti: He Doubles For Buster Keaton in the Movies—But He Can Sock a Mean Double for Himself, as Well."[32]

So what was odd about the article? It was 1929 and a given that MGM required a Keaton double. Plus, at face value, MGM even seemed to score plus points, because the studio apparently let Buster choose. Because Orsatti was a longtime friend whose baseball career had been both assisted and supported by the diamond-loving comedian. The peculiar part of the essay, however, is that it implies Orsatti had done some doubling for Keaton during Buster's *independent* features. Now, no one is implying that Keaton had aped Harold Lloyd's lie about doing all the skyscraping work in *Safety Last* (1928), only to have it revealed decades later as false.

However, unlike Lloyd, whether credited or not, Keaton had a hand in so much of his personally run productions, especially the directing, that it is quite possible Keaton also had some uncredited minor doubling done for him prior to MGM. And what gives this particular piece more credence is that the article is in the newspaper's sports section, *not* entertainment. More importantly, Orsatti is *the* featured player, not Keaton. Consequently, while this does not negate it being an MGM "plant," it lessens the chances, since the studio was not exactly in the business of promoting utility baseball players. However, it takes away from the fact that Keaton basically did the vast majority of all his stunts, unlike a Lloyd.

Regardless, besides MGM enhancing Keaton's presence in the public media, the studio's impressive *Metro-Goldwyn-Mayer Picture Newspaper* was hardly shy about plugging its new star. While disseminated in various ways, including period press kits, some articles were just cut and pasted into mainstream publications. A typical article from the studio newspaper, simply dated 1928, was entitled "Keaton's Bungalow Really Star's Gymnasium": "One of the strangest spots in motion pictures is the 'Keaton Bungalow.' This is a little green bungalow, just outside the Metro-Goldwyn-Mayer Studio.... A complete gymnasium, a kitchen where a cook prepared his training menu, and a place in front to play baseball were among the details. Keaton ... always goes into rigid athletic training for a role."[33] Keaton was neither a good business man, à la being pressured into signing with MGM, nor was he good at confrontation. However, a modest example of independence is indirectly noted in the previous article excerpt. That is, for a time he refused to have his production home bungalow officially on the MGM lot.

Despite all that was good about *The Cameraman*, reading between the lines, it marks the beginning of Keaton's artistic decline. And the professional and personal plummet, going hand-in-hand, would occur relatively quickly. As drama critic Ashton Stevens once said so hauntingly of John Barrymore, "Nobody can run downhill as fast as a thoroughbred."[34] Moreover, as the final following chapter and Epilogue note, while there would still be moments of isolated brilliance to come, Keaton, like W. C. Fields and Barrymore, would essentially be his "own executioner."[35] Yet, paradoxically for Keaton, maybe that was somehow appropriate for an artist whose work so exuded existentialism and dark comedy in all its absurd forms.

12

Spite Marriage (April 22, 1929)
Somewhat Saved by Silence

> The sound film "The Great Power" [1929] proved to be so hard on ... [Capitol Theatre] ears that it was taken off after ... [two days and] succeeded by ... "Spite Marriage," which was such a relief after "The Great Power" that it received more laughs than it was entitled to.
> —*New York Times*, 1929[1]

Paradoxically, the above quote was both typical and atypical for period *Spite Marriage* critiques. That is, it was more the odd coin resting on its edge. Because, while it was rare to find reviews that did not make reference to Keaton's film rescuing a theatre stuck with an early primitive "talkie," the majority of the *Spite Marriage* appraisals were very favorable and/or almost nostalgic for the loss of an art form (silent film) which had reached a truly unique apogee. Lillian Gish, whose career stretched well into the sound era, was later fond of saying, "It would have made more sense if silent films had actually followed sound pictures."[2] Regardless, that sense of silent film wistfulness, à la *Spite Marriage*, occurs in the March 1929 *New York Sun* critique: "for although the film was not much above general average, it elicited applause several times. Indeed it was refreshing to look at pantomime once more, after the many inefficient novelties that the talking films have already put forth, and part of this applause, I am certain, came from the pleasantness of a return to silence."[3] The *Sun*'s review title was even more succinct on its verdict: "The New Photoplay: 'Spite Marriage' with Mr. Keaton, Quickly Displaces 'The Great Power,' a Talkie."[4]

Ironically, the same *New York Times* critic, Mordaunt Hall, whose chapter opening qualifier on Keaton receiving "more laughs than he was entitled to," had said this in a later thought piece on the film. Yet Hall, normally not in Keaton's critical corner, had pitched a silence-preferred review in his *Spite Marriage* critique a week earlier: "Words can hardly tell of the relief it was to look at Mr. Keaton's imaginative but silly silent antics in his latest farce, 'Spite Marriage.' The theatre that had been filled with pain and gloom was aroused to a state of high glee, and whether.... Keaton endeavored to help a girl who had imbibed more champagne than was good for her, or he bailed out the engine room ... yacht ... there were waves of laughter from top to bottom of the house."[5] Once again his short review title said it all: "The Screen: Silence Wins."[6]

Recently, a text has appeared which, while having nothing to do with Keaton, carries a title that encapsules the complexity with which to address *Spite Marriage*: *Down The Up Staircase*.[7] That is, under MGM Keaton was in decline with *Spite Marriage*. Yet, because it was still a silent film, Keaton was able to manage some wiggle room in his visual artistry.

Plus, he was able to successfully argue for what would be his final signature routine—a bit he would replicate in later lesser movies, in live theatre here and abroad, and on TV for the rest of his career. The sketch was the second most commented upon item in *Spite Marriage* reviews, after the film's rescue of *Capitol Theatre* from a bad talkie.

So what is the enduring comic turn? Keaton has fallen for a leading lady (Dorothy Sebastian), who is a major theatrical star within the film named Trilby Drew, à la spoofing the famous real Drew/Barrymore stage family. Extending the parody further, she is in love with her leading man, Lionel Benmore (Edward Earle), which conjures up images of real matinee idol John Barrymore. But when he drops her for a blonde, Sebastian spitefully marries Keaton's nattily attired, seemingly wealthy Stage Door Johnny—thus the title. That night Keaton and Sebastian go to a nightclub and she gets properly sauced. The *Los Angeles Times* reported: "[Keaton,] ... reverently attentive, is faced with the problem of getting [her limp body] out of the café [Prohibition is still in effect] and home [mixing a cross between wrestling and a fireman's carry]. Finally, he does. This has been all very funny but the ensuing scene in the hotel [room] where they have parked their belongings [and he must get her ready for bed] had yesterday's matinee audience almost rolling on the floor in shouts of laughter."[8] Since this was a coast away from the *Capitol*, and well after the film's premiere, there was no theatre rescue mentioned. But the *Los Angeles Times* critic felt compelled to add: "advocates of the talkies ... can praise ... [them] to the skies and enjoy them but just for a glimpse of the days gone by, it would be well if they went to see Mister Buster Keaton in good old old-fashioned pantomime comedy. The title is 'Spite Marriage.'"[9]

Still, the faulty sound of early talkies would not be enough to stop them from eventually taking over. But these last hurrahs for pictures like *Spite Marriage* are now all but forgotten. Yet, Chaplin was able to buck the change to sound by essentially not changing at all for over a decade. And even then, *The Great Dictator* (1940) showcased Chaplin in dual roles, with a talkative title character and a little Tramp-like Jewish barber who minimized his speaking. Keaton might have done the same, had he not relinquished his control to MGM. Yet, as was noted on *The Cameraman* (1928, see previous chapter), and even with the silent *Spite Marriage*—without yet being married to a *word-driven* MGM script, Keaton could still occasionally manage to apply his "penny postcard" story (improvisations) and gift the picture with his athletic-driven comedy of movement.

Granted, one could readily see MGM's further clipping of Keaton's comedy wings from *The Cameraman* to *Spite Marriage*. For instance, the studio made him even more of a romantic sap in this picture, with Buster going to Sebastian's play 35 consecutive nights because he is so moonstruck. Buster Keaton? MGM has not only made this previously asexual boy/man a romantic, but Keaton's heroine humiliates him by merely marrying him out of spite. At least in *The Cameraman* one might have semi-qualified the schmaltz because the girl honestly seemed to be looking out for Buster's wannabe cameraman.

This brings one to MGM's next negating of Keaton's persona. The character who had capably operated trains and an ocean liner, or had been born into wealth, was reduced in *Spite Marriage* to being a lowly pants presser. The fancy clothes he wore to Sebastian's performances, or when he party crashed tony events, were actually borrowed from his day dry cleaning job. Indeed, the morning after the inspired sketch in which he somehow puts his bombed bride to bed is followed by debasing comments on Keaton's character from her theatrical entourage, via a title: "—don't' you realize? If the papers find out you married a cheap little pants presser your career is ruined."

Ironically, as MGM would use *The Cameraman* as an official studio training film for comedy, Keaton became an unofficial template for how to homogenize future provocative and/or cultish comedians even beyond what was noted in the previous chapter. For example, after MGM humbled Buster's *Spite Marriage* position, the studio made him an unknowingly dumb talent manager in his abysmal first sound feature, *Free and Easy* (1930).

Expanding upon MGM similar downgrading of Marx Brothers in the previous chapter—flash forward to comedian-friendly Paramount having Groucho playing *Duck Soup's* (1933) outrageous Freedonian Prime Minister Rufus T. Firefly, who declares war as a whim with neighboring country Sylvania. This makes for a brilliant comic paranoid link anticipating Sterling Hayden's mad as a hatter General Jack Ripper in the world ending *Dr. Strangelove or: How I Learned to Stop Worrying and Love the Bomb* (1964).

Earlier Paramount's Groucho had played a not dissimilar part from Rufus as the unhinged college president of *Horse Feathers'* (1932) Huxley College. And like Keaton being diminished to an ignored *Free and Easy* talent agent in his first talkie, Groucho is also minimized to being a third-rate talent agent in the Marxes' first MGM film, 1935's *A Night at the Opera*.[10] This is quite a comedown from the mustached Marx's dictatorial powers as Huxley's leader. For instance, this demented academic president had immediately announced his nihilistic public policy via the song "[Whatever It Is] I'm Against It." This might also have doubled as his curmudgeon mantra throughout the superior iconoclastic Paramount Pictures.

Regardless, maybe the best way to encapsulate how much MGM had already altered Keaton's persona, even in the silent era, is an excerpt from a still positive 1929 *Photoplay* critique of *Spite Marriage*: "It is as Chaplinesque as anything Buster Keaton has ever done...."[11] *Yet*, the very reason Keaton has now reached near contemporary parity status with Chaplin, as the text has frequently emphasized, is that Buster's absurd world is at odds with that of the 1920s Tramp—more cerebral than sentimental, more cynically contemporary than Victorian optimistic ... ultimately more *Waiting for Godot* than *David Copperfield*.

Despite MGM's travesty of dumbing down for dollars, or trading culture for cash in the overplotted *Spite Marriage* (another MGM liability), enough of the still silent Keaton persona remains to almost qualify the film as underrated. This is more compromisingly obvious when *Spite Marriage* is compared to Buster's next picture—his first sound feature, the embarrassing *Free and Easy*. And it only becomes more mortifyingly incontestable with the handful of starring sound MGM features which followed before he was fired in 1933.

So what are these *Spite Marriage* Buster basics which still make it worth watching? First, one has to return to the aforementioned sketch of Keaton getting his inebriated wife to bed. Even though the picture loses points for making Keaton gooey with love for the thus far unsympathetic Dorothy Sebastian character, it is no easy task to move the dead weight of his plastered wife. Plus, keep in mind, this does not just involve exiting the nightclub and getting her back to their hotel room—a flight of steps is also thrown in to increase the comic degree of difficulty. (Any Olympic judges of comedy would have at least given him a nine plus score.)

Most importantly, however, though Buster might love her, this task necessitates manhandling Sebastian in such a manner the viewer is hardly reminded of hearts and flowers. Thus, she is mauled in a manner on par with Marian Mack's travails in *The General* (1926, see Chapter 8). Moreover, despite any plot point about fondness, what one *sees* is the comedian's normally less than simpatico relationship with women. Plus, there are several added comic perks involved. Since Sebastian has yet to treat the comedian nicely, the audience enjoys her inadvertently rough treatment more than they would in a neutral setting.

12. Spite Marriage *(April 22, 1929)*

Another advantage to the sequence is that it is a silent movie. The reviewer is one step removed from reality. This means one's enjoyment of pure slapstick is not dissipated by any possible sympathy that might occur if Keaton were either overly verbal in his concern for her well-being, or Sebastian was equally auditory in any painful manner, such as moaning. This "one step from reality" comedy was a lesson Harold Lloyd learned on his first talkie, *Welcome Danger* (1929). Returning to his signature component of thrill comedy, à la *Safety Last* (1923), the former film was a commercial hit. But it was because people were curious to hear him speak. Thrill comedy proved not as laugh provoking if the individual involved expressed verbal fear and/or if the sounds of a dangerous setting ratcheted up the reality.

Yet another factor aiding the popularity of Keaton getting the blotto person to bed sequence was Sebastian's talent for playing a human sack of potatoes. One might think nothing could be easier than essentially playing dead. But it must be a finely coordinated and choreographed effort between the two people. And period critics recognized her contribution, with *Variety* stating, "Miss Sebastian distinguished herself in the night club souse scene and the return-to-the-hotel aftermath."[12] *LIFE*'s (post–Robert E. Sherwood) critic was so taken by her comedy contribution that he was inspired to add comedy to his review—but warned that a few tony types might be offended by the sketch: "Sebastian ... does some surprisingly clever comedy ... [in] an intoxicated act in a nightclub which will be greeted by most folks with hearty chuckles, and condemned as rough-house by the very refined.... Sebastian has played in pictures that gave her more chances to display artistic qualities, but she has never appeared in one that gave her more exercise."[13]

A blotto bride (Dorothy Sebastian) helps save the picture, and a sketch which becomes a future part of Keaton's comic repertoire.

Importantly, with regard to good tastes, *Harrison's Reports* (which doubled as a theatre owner's guide) also enjoyed the scene and gave it a pass, except for children: "Her husband has a hard time trying to get her back to the hotel and to bed. (There are other funny scenes; they are handled delicately.) Although they are harmless, they are nevertheless, unsuitable for children."[14] This would, of course, be a drastic change from today, in which the sketch would be G-rated. Indeed as previously noted, Keaton would continue to play the routine for the rest of his days, with his final partner being the last of Keaton's three wives—Eleanor Norris Keaton (who also later rescued the comedian from his alcoholism.) As an addendum to Sebastian's collaboration with Buster, exactly 60 years after *Spite Marriage*, Terry Kiser's title character in the dark comedy *Weekend at Bernie's* (1989) is reminiscent of all the nuances Sebastian brought to her part. Except in Kiser's care, instead of being dead drunk, his figure is actually dead. Though not in a league with Keaton's picture, the later film was popular enough to spawn a sequel, *Weekend at Bernie's II* (1993), with Kiser reprising his role.

Spite Marriage also launched a more modest but very funny "hat tipping" routine which is repeated several times in the film, including serving as the movie's conclusion. It simply involved a person tipping his top hat to someone just as that hatted person is attempting to shake hands. This causes hat person number one to stop his tipping and try to shake hands. But now hat person two has stopped his tipping and attempts to shake hands. This sketch can be milked ad infinitum, with never a hand being touched. Keaton would use it in later films. And there are also many comic variations of the routine, including one involving bowing in arguably Woody Allen's funniest film, *Love and Death* (1975). Interestingly, Allen's sequence goes to silence, with only comic sound effects, when presented. (*Spite Marriage* did have sound effects, too but these were not crucial to the hat routine.)

Ironically, while MGM's over plotting of *Spite Marriage* did not improve the film (it actually feels like a short double feature), it did provide Keaton with his last sustained sequences of athletic comedy brilliance in an "A" feature, other than a brief running scene in the otherwise dreadful *Parlor, Bedroom and Bath* (1932). Plus, since this tacked-on material involves murderous smugglers, Buster gets to show off to his cinema fans all his established nautical skills. Thus, it allows the comedian one last prolonged MGM sequence in which to demonstrate he is not an idiot. What is more, between this shipboard comedy in motion skills, and a brief intensely realistic fight, which briefly brings back memories of the *Battling Butler* conclusion (1926, see Chapter 7), Keaton is legitimately allowed to both save the day and win the loving respect of the leading lady. A late screen title/newspaper headline summarizes the about-face for Buster:

> Missing Yacht
> Sighted off Harbor
> Trilby Drew Saved
> In Sea Mystery

This ultimate winning of the girl is not remotely close to *Spite Marriage*'s preliminary romantic blather. For example, earlier there is a not-to-be-believed potentially diabetic coma producing sequence in which poor Buster buys Sebastian a toy stuffed dog with a tear under one eye. And he attempts to bring it to her attention by getting on his knees in an adjoining room and then playfully making it sort of prance into her presence through a doorway. In contrast, the final connection between Sebastian's character and Keaton's *Spite Marriage* screen alter ego is essentially part of the personality comedian genre formula expected of any clown personality, whether he is so inclined or not. After all, Buster could not put tombstones at the end of all his pictures, especially after the move to MGM.

To set the analysis meter on pause a moment, Keaton's plight at MGM is reminiscent of the then contemporary author, Sherwood Anderson, best known for his 1919 novel *Winesburg, Ohio*, who had the same questioning dark world view as Keaton. Critic Malcolm

12. Spite Marriage *(April 22, 1929)*

Cowley later described a working method for Anderson that is comparable to Keaton's "postcard" brief improvisation, which essentially doomed the comedian when the wordy MGM's sound scripts became studio policy: "[Anderson] never even wrote a book in the strict sense of the word. A book should have a structure and a development, whereas for Anderson there was chiefly the flash of lightening [improvisation] that revealed a life without changing it."[15] For Keaton, even with an MGM governor placed upon his creative artistry, continued silence allowed him to get by with two above average comedies, *The Cameraman* and *Spite Marriage*. However, once sound placed him in complete lockdown mode, what followed was tragic. Loss of artistic control fueled his alcoholic tendencies and any attempts to maintain his discrete open marriage to Natalie Talmadge were abandoned. Moreover, his relationship with the extended Talmadge family, forever shaky at best, also deteriorated.

Three additional factors ate away at Keaton's comedy-directed life. First, with the MGM machine behind him, while dumbing down his persona, and eventually even teaming him with second banana Jimmy Durante—who was quickly becoming showcased as *the* important comic of the duo—the films were grossing more money than Keaton's silent classics, with even positive reviews documenting artistic decline? Second, while Keaton was always fascinated by new technology, such as talkies, his gravely *adult* voice did not mesh with his silent comedy boy/man persona. Moreover, age (he turned 35 in 1930), accented by his alcoholically self-destructive lifestyle made his silent boyish alter ego appearance increasingly difficult to maintain.

Even if one momentarily disregarded his inevitable "Dorian Gray" problem, the *London Times* review of his second sound feature, *Doughboys* (1930, titled *Forward March* in England), directly addressed points one and two:

> [Keaton] is of that small company of film comedians whose audience is ready to laugh before the entertainment begins.... But the knockabout comedy that tickles us so often seems to have been imposed on Mr. Keaton by thoughtful adjutants and not emerge, as before, from the heart of the man. It is this fault, and the comedian's unbecoming voice, which frequently make the fun ring false ... where an actor raises high expectations and easy applauses by his earlier victories, he risks both in as great a measure by any deflection from them ... when an audience will laugh at anything, there must certainly be moments when it is laughing at nothing.[16]

Despite an increasing public interest in sound films, there still remained a strong rearguard movement throughout 1929 that documented the ongoing popularity of silent films, such as *Spite Marriage*. One such chronicling was a *Los Angeles Times* article from September 1929 entitled, "SILENTS WITHSTAND ONSLAUGHT."[17] This essay, without noting Keaton by name, perceptively explored an added complexity beyond just tossing in sound: "the stressing of personality as it was known in silent films is becoming rather a lost art. The trick of building up the player with a voice personality will have to be developed. In that connection, some of the screen players would be a good deal better off if they were still making silent pictures, rather than attempting the new field."[18] Nothing better describes what happened to Keaton when he went down that "talkie" road. Plus, in lockstep agreement with the "voice personality" comment is a corroborating comment less than two weeks later in a *Los Angeles Times* review of Will Rogers' first sound film, *They Had to See Paris* (1929): "he scored definitely as a personality of the screen-voice medium."[19] A supplementary observation in the critique also validates an earlier observation in this chapter about sound defusing Lloyd's thrill comedy, "Rogers has the inescapable quality of being real."[20]

The third disturbing element of the sound era for Keaton, once MGM's rigidity became clear, might best be likened to the hoary expression "pouring salt in a wound." At the beginning of the talkie revolution, before dubbing an actor's voice became the norm, performers were forced to remake parts, or all of their movies for foreign speaking markets. Thus English speaking actors would read the phonetically spelled comparable foreign dialogue off "idiot cards" just beyond camera range. Though all major studios eventually went this route, Universal seems to have led the way. An August 1929 *Los Angeles Times* article entitled "Films Made in Many Tongues" stated: "Pioneering another enterprise, as it has done before, Universal is going ahead and making talking pictures in foreign languages, it became known yesterday."[21]

So what would that mean to Keaton? First, the one bitter element that still lingered in his 1960 memoir was being talked into giving up his artistic license by signing with MGM.[22] In an otherwise most even-tempered autobiography, given his many travails, he devotes a whole chapter to: "The Worst Mistake of My Life."[23] Consequently, Keaton was grossly unhappy that he was handcuffed by what the *London Times* called "adjutants" who had "imposed" their will upon the comedian. Yet, the greatest shackling of his art was the aforementioned dumbing down of his persona, or as the *New York Times* correctly articulated: "[In *Dough Boys* his] character is too crackbrained even for low comedy and the result is that Mr. Keaton's hardy attempts to create laughter often misfire."[24]

Second, Keaton had to stomach this humiliation not once or twice but three or four times, as these travesties were reshot for multiple markets—focusing upon France, Germany, and Spain. Moreover, even if all versions had been done in English, the repetition factor would have undoubtedly diminished quality—then factor in they were phonically reading unknown words off idiot cards! Point two ultimately dovetails into factor three—the sheer absurdity of this increasingly dollar-driven industry. Keaton had fallen from literally risking death for daffiness (and possibly just not caring, given the direction his career was headed), to statically reading foreign gibberish. Any historian would see the sheer absurdity his real artistic life had become. Indeed, Buster had become like those city dignitaries Chaplin would later mock at the opening of *City Lights* (1931), where gobbledygook speeches jeer both general officialdom, and specifically early sound film.

The irony is that it still did not need to be like this. Even as late as Buster's last starring feature film for MGM, *What, No Beer?* (1933), there are bits Keaton and/or the studio included which are teasing enticements from his earlier silent pictures. Yet, each routine is not allowed to be milked to comic fruition. For example, Keaton's character needs men for the *Beer* brewery he owns with co-star Jimmy Durante. But when Keaton goes to the unemployment office (well into the Depression) looking for workers, a stampede of wannabe wage earners chase after him. One immediately anticipates the mob of almost brides pursing him in *Seven Chances* (1925). However, the movie quickly moves on after a brief laugh.

Another *Beer* example tease comes from a woman Buster attempts to assist after she pretends to faint. The comedian's effort to carry her to a safe location is an instant link to the *Spite Marriage* sketch in which his drunkenly comatose wife must somehow be lugged from a nightclub to their hotel room. Again, nothing but a quick laugh is allowed before the narrative moves on. However, the most disappointing "what if?" returns the viewer anew to *Seven Chances*, and the inspired rock slide sequence. *Beer* has a most promising scene in which Buster must dodge beer barrels coming down a hill. But the comic danger is immediately transferred to other passing people, and yet one more promising revisionist riff is lost.

Ironically, the perfect metaphor for Keaton's unsuccessful teaming with Durante occurs

12. Spite Marriage (April 22, 1929)

early in *Beer*—the duo are briefly handcuffed together. Verbal comic saturation sound and silence had worked for Paramount with Groucho and Harpo Marx, but such was not to be the case with MGM's Keaton and Durante. And while the latter duo's pictures increasingly favored Durante, the comedian's definitive biographer, Jhan Robbins, chronicled in *Inka Dinka Doo: The Life of Jimmy Durante*, that his subject was also less than happy with MGM's treatment.[25] Though Robbins underestimates the period popularity of the Keaton and Durante watered down comedies, he briefly chronicles the latter comedian's attempt to help Buster's fading career.

Thankfully, however, that is for someone else's sad saga. Instead this revisionist text has closely combed 1920s Keaton period literature from his silent feature heyday—hopefully providing some major bombshell discoveries, further fleshing out comic details of the films, documenting odd period quirks, proposing a reappraisal that *The General* was not the greatest truly *Keaton* film, suggesting period literature saw Keaton more along cult comedian status, and chronicling how even his most perceptive period critics had an almost total blind spot concerning his reaffirmation parody dark comedy style. These factors and more are quantified in the following Epilogue. Plus, a Keaton-Chaplin comparison of their 1920s work showcases how Keaton is more timely with each passing year.

Epilogue
Period Material Provides a Modern View

> Today Charlot [Chaplin] is hymned by the literati ... the beautiful and the damning.... The critics have decided that the abominable movies have produced something worth while in this harlequin of the mustaches and baggy trousers.[1]
> —*Picture-Play Magazine*, March 1923

What Has Been Learned?

This text has been an attempt to explore how Jazz Age critics and their public saw a comedian, Buster Keaton, who has now come to reach near parity status with behemoth Charlie Chaplin, as the two pantheon comedians of the silent era. This has involved examining a great deal of period literature between 1923 and 1929—when Keaton moved to silent features. While epilogues by their very nature necessitate some degree of repetition, every effort has been made to both add new items, and view pivotal facts through a prism which, if not making them new again, will at least enhance insights provided by grouping them together. (In such cases, one is encouraged to return to individual chapters of each film). Secondly, a modern juxtapositioning of Keaton and Chaplin is provided to demonstrate the radically different mindsets each now has to offer.

Keaton's mentor in the late 1910s was Fatty Arbuckle, with whom he made over a dozen short subjects between 1917 and 1919, besides squeezing in some military service. However, in 1920 Buster was chosen to play the title role in the feature *The Saphead*. In a *Los Angeles Times* interview that year he complained: "[I] Don't know why they chose me for the part, only I've got a blank pan.... Winchell Smith watches me all the time. He's the author and he's afraid I'll ... try to get funny."[2] Contemporary Keaton literature does not give enough importance to the picture. This was not the case in 1920. For example, the previous interview was entitled "Buster Bursts Into Stardom."[3] While the movie was mediocre at best, Keaton stole the picture with the most understated comedy, and suddenly he had his own short subject studio, as Arbuckle moved on to features. Regardless, *The Saphead* introduced an alternative world to Buster's pork pie hat character—a wealthy, pampered boy/man dressed to the nines. While Keaton complained at the time about the fine clothes, he periodically returned to this character and the wardrobes in his later features—realizing he both looked good in the attire and the character was ripe for parody. For instance, his screen alter ego is reading the book *How to Win the Modern Girl*, one of many self-help texts he would spoof in the future. Modern studies generally neglect how the period's new affluence played directly to his ex-vaudevillian parody strength. Plus, Buster's wannabe girlfriend's father also hated him—usually a given in his later features, too.

Regardless, while talented, his gestation period was without the amazing speed of Chaplin or the Beatles. Indeed, his first personal feature was not until 1923's *The Three Ages*, versus Chaplin's instant 1920 classic, *The Kid*. Moreover, Keaton was so nervous it would not succeed, that he constructed it as a parody of D. W. Griffith's epic 1916 *Intolerance* through the ages—meaning the comedian could split it into three short subjects if it did not work.

This play fooled no period critics. And while it was successful enough to remain a feature, and allow Keaton to continue in this longer format, it was not as widely reviewed as some of his short subjects. In fact, modern criticism misses that fact, and also the sometime period suggestion that he best remain in short subjects. Several other *Three Ages* basics are also often missing from many modern examinations of the film. These additional templates include Griffith's 1912 *Man's Genesis*, and Winsor McCay's 1914 animated *Gertie the Dinosaur*—both in conjunction with *Three Ages*' cave man segment.

Plus, Keaton's Roman episode in *Three Ages* was heavily focused on chariot humor. Yet, it is often neglected today that Lew Wallace's *Ben Hur: A Tale of the Christ*, arguably the best-selling novel of the 19th century, had enthralled theatre goers from Broadway to the sticks, during the first two decades of the 20th century. And the adaptation's money sequence involved *chariots* and live running horses on theatre treadmills. Plus, there had even been a 1907 short subject *Ben Hur* which keyed upon the chariots. Besides being a universally popular roadshow engagement, it also played throughout vaudeville while young Buster was performing in "The Three Keatons." (There were also other period cinematic epics from which Buster undoubtedly borrowed.)

An even greater blind spot for contemporary critiquing of *Three Ages*, which usually gets short shrift anyway, was the period print attention devoted to Keaton casting budding star Wallace Beery as his nemesis throughout the ages. Like the comedian playing parody with high profile targets, Beery was yet more insurance for making this first feature foray work. Moreover, just as spoofing was being established as Keaton's favorite go-to comedy genre to mix with his personality comedian core, having a strong supporting player was now a potential given, too. Keep in mind that the popular emaciated character actor Snitz Edwards would have pivotal parts in three of Buster's future features, and almost stole the show, for Jazz Age audiences, in *Battling Buster* (1926). In addition, major dramatic star Ernest Torrence was co-billed with Keaton on *Steamboat Bill, Jr.* (1928), when the comedian's box office was declining. And Beery, Edwards, and Torrence never received less than favorable notices in period reviews, but they receive little attention today.

Moreover, modern criticism misses Keaton's more-cult-than-mainstream status in the 1920s. And once again, despite *Three Ages*' uneven quality, this first feature provides a signature example of how Buster could never commercially compete with the era's boy next door, Harold Lloyd. In *Three Ages*' modern segment, Buster finds himself in an important college football game—this being the decade when the sport became big business—and the ball is kicked to him. However, when he sees an army of enemy opponents' ready to squish him, he flips the ball to some other poor schmuck, who is quickly reduced to road kill. Is winning one for the old black and gold (or the color scheme of your choice) really that important? Yet, two years later Lloyd takes a similar kick in 1925's *The Freshman* and scores the winning touchdown. Those two scenes are all one needs to know about these characters.

Finally, current criticism pays little attention to how *Three Ages* might have failed by merely casting an amateur prize-winner as Keaton's leading lady, Margaret Leahy. The comedian's brother-in-law boss, Joseph Schenck, had arranged for a PR British beauty pageant winner to star in his wife's (Norma Talmadge) next film. Hailed with every comeliness compliment possible, à la "England's most lovely lady," it was soon obvious Ms. Leahy was an acting cipher. Neither wanting to jeopardize his spouse's new picture, nor become entangled in a lawsuit, if Ms. Leahy did not appear in something, Schenck suddenly decided she had an amazing gift for comedy and was foisted on Keaton's first feature.

Schenck's only excuse to Buster was that the comedian has always downplayed the importance of his leading ladies. Keaton was soon corrected; the woman was also humor deprived. This necessitated the re-shooting of many *Three Ages* sequences. Moreover, period film critics now had a double whammy field day with the actress—kidding her alleged beauty and lack of comedy/acting talent. Thus, contemporary criticism usually just gives the film modest attention without sharing how many Jazz Age reviewers sometimes had the picture flirting with "amateur hour." Moreover, these abridged facts have been recycled to show how *Three Ages* established yet another precedent—Schenck, who would later talk Buster into giving up his independence to MGM, would periodically sideswipe Keaton's career throughout the 1920s—unlike today's focus on the final blow.

In Keaton's second feature, *Our Hospitality* (1923), again the supporting cast is pivotal but in a different way. Three Keaton generations appear in the picture—the star's father Joe (as an engineer), and Buster's baby son Joseph (as a newborn Keaton). The comedian's wife Natalie also plays his leading lady. Much favorable press was garnered from this boon, which is generally minimized in passing by current studies—thus missing a bigger point. Hollywood was still recovering from scandals largely brought about by the miscarriage of justice against Fatty Arbuckle. Thus, as important as the dense Keaton *family* casting was for the picture, it was a major asset for the industry. (Ironically, Keaton would later lend the wonderfully wacky-looking—but historically accurate "Rocket" train—to Arbuckle to use in the short subject *The Iron Mule*, 1925.)

Our Hospitality would establish two important precedents for Keaton's Jazz Age career. It would be the first and only commercially successful picture of his Southern trilogy, which would also be his most successful application of a more advanced form of spoofing—reaffirmation parody. This genre is frequently heavily dosed with dark comedy, and was not fully embraced by the general public for decades, which is why it failed in *The General*. At its most basic, it plays so closely to the genre and/or specific film being burlesqued that viewers do not always realize it is a parody. A more modern example would be the original *Scream* trilogy (1996, 1997, 2000), which doubles as both horror and darkly comic spoofing examinations of the genre's basic conventions.

I am not aware of any current criticism which has applied reaffirmation parody to either *Our Hospitality*, or *The General*. So why did it work in the 1920s for the former film but not the latter? After all, both movies are based upon true deadly stories—the Hatfield-McCoy feud, which was a product of the Civil War, and the Civil War itself. First, by the time of Keaton's *Our Hospitality*, the feud had long assumed a status of preposterousness which people, especially in West Virginia and Kentucky, wanted to put behind them. Plus, when combined with a sort of hillbilly *Romeo and Juliet* element, with Keaton ratcheting up the ludicrousness of a Southern hospitality code in which guests were only safe in the home base—sort of a potentially lethal "kick the can" game. In addition, while this film still flirted with dark comedy each time Buster attempted to leave the house, the stupidity of the feud is finally acknowledged and ended when Buster and real life wife Natalie manage to marry before anything deadly can occur.

Moreover, besides the absurdity of the basic premise, much time is taken up with Buster's innocent journey from New York to a surprise battleground South on the most delightfully goofy-looking reproduction of the groundbreaking "Rocket" steam engine. Yet, another often missing modern critical examination of *Our Hospitality* is the establishment of another future detrimental pattern. For example, Buster added a historical exactness which drove up the budget, and of which period audiences would often not even be aware—such as using an antiquated 100-year-old railroad gauge track. No one is suggesting the comedian was on the verge of becoming a comic Eric von Stroheim (1885–1957), whose acclaimed 42-reel *Greed* (1924) would have run nearly eight hours if shown as completed. (Eventually butchered down to 132 minutes by the company soon to ironically become Keaton nemesis, MGM, Stroheim's *Greed* was the beginning catalyst for his directing career to end.)

In contrast, the added historical expense Keaton brought to *Our Hospitality* did not keep it from being a critical and commercial hit. Yet, the comedian's newfound fascination for authenticity would later greatly push *The General* over budget, contributing to its commercial failure. Since Keaton was more of a cult figure than mainstream Lloyd (again, still hardly admitted today) he had little wiggle room for a financial success if the film did not stay within his allocated expenses. Moreover, in becoming bolder with letting his historical-minded budget balloon, he also pushed his reaffirmation parody tendencies even further. Thus, many period *General* audiences saw it as more of an action adventure saga than a comedy. Still, contemporary historians are often too harsh on Jazz Age audiences under-appreciating *The General*. The film still had its champions, because cult fans expect something nontraditional from their favorites.

However, Keaton did not anticipate two major 1920s negatives applied to *The General*. First, while he had used dark comedy throughout his career, he had never taken it to the extremes present here. Moreover, *The General* employed *on-screen* death for humor. In addition, with Buster's wayward saber, and his burning of the railroad trestle which seemed to take a locomotive engineer to his death, the comedian *himself* was directly responsible for using loss of life for laughter. Not even Keaton's extraordinary 1920s critical champion, *Life*'s Robert E. Sherwood, could condone this. Consequently, by pushing reaffirmation parody past 1920s extremes, he had produced a watershed dark comedy way ahead of its time.

The second negative Keaton did not anticipate with *The General*'s release was the multifaceted sacredness with which so much of the nation still held the Civil War. With 600,000 plus casualties, it was the country's deadliest war, with all fatalities being directly or indirectly administered by other Americans. The old Latin proverb, that "still waters run deep," could never be applied to the Civil War, because the waters had hardly stilled, and the "deep" still remains bottomless. In dark comedy, nothing is sacred. But for many during the 1920s, the Civil War was off-limits. Why, even as I write these words (July 2017), the removal of Confederate statues is controversial, some state legislatures work hard to disenfranchise black Americans, and in the South, it is still not uncommon to hear the conflict called "the War of the Rebellion," even "The War of Northern Aggression."

Consequently, Keaton took his dark comedy into a buzz saw. And once again, this aspect of *The General*'s failure is not addressed in contemporary criticism. Yet, the backlash was *so strong* that Keaton had to apologize for his film and belittle his status as a mere comedian—where is that factor in contemporary criticism? Moreover, there is a certain irony in this, because of all the major silent comedians of the Jazz Age, Buster was the one most likely to use racial stereotypes for humor. Yes, as a historian one must attempt the impossible and put all things disagreeable in the confines of "that was then." Naturally, this is something briefly addressed in modern Keaton criticism. But "briefly" is usually the optimal word to use.

Period criticism of such racial material shows just how common it was by reviewers complaining that such jokes suffer because the material has been done too much. Yet, contemporary historians should at least note extremes, such as Keaton's blackface sequence in *College* (1927) actually making that a difficult film to watch and teach in college, despite its most memorable of endings. And *The Navigator*, which I would leapfrog over *The General* as the greatest *Keaton* film, is marred by the cannibal sequences. Indeed, at one point, when the heroine is surrounded by the natives, it is difficult to not visualize certain scenes from *Birth of a Nation* (1915).

Regardless, returning to the Epilogue's chronological look at Keaton period criticism of his silent features, versus today's perspective, his next feature offers the text's two most substantial bombshells. The film in question is 1924's *Sherlock, Jr.* And if any Buster film is to usurp the number one status normally attributed to *The General* besides *The Navigator*, this is the one. Much has been written about Keaton's dreaming projectionist entering the screen, and then the movie within the movie. However, pre–Jazz Age reporting suggests that America's first international screen clown, John Bunny, was both the inspiration for the trick and the manner in which it was accomplished. No one else has linked it to the pioneering older comedian's triumphant touring stage show, *Bunny in Funnyland* (1914–1915); yet period Bunny print material described parallels.

Without taking anything away from Keaton's inspired movie, this seems a most logical catalyst, given the older comedian's then amazing popularity. Moreover, "The Three Keatons" were touring in vaudeville at the same time. Secondly, both of Keaton's sisters-in-law started their screen careers at Bunny's Brooklyn-based home studio, Vitagraph. Indeed, Norma Talmadge appeared in several Bunny short subjects, and their mother's egoistical memoir/family biography with the epic title *The Talmadge Sisters: Norma, Constance, Natalie: An Intimate Story of the World's Most Famous Screen Family by Their Mother* (1924), had their clan close friends of Bunny.

The second *Sherlock, Jr.*, revelation, which goes beyond the logical Bunny-Keaton entering of the screen link, is the January 28, 1924, *Los Angeles Times* article, "Hick-Town Censors—Look Out!" This has *Sherlock, Jr.* originally being an entirely *different picture*, as well as filling in some questions on both the picture's delayed release, and the never fully explained degree of Arbuckle involvement. Moreover, an attack on the small town prejudice against the innocent Fatty would have been a tempting payback grounded in Keaton's loyalty to his friend. This period article remains this book's most *provocative find*.

After *Sherlock, Jr.*, which runs a mere 45 minutes—more suggestion there was another drastically edited-down picture and/or a fast forward do-over falling back on his former short subject fantasy forte—is my pick as the comedian's greatest film—*The Navigator*. A case could be made for it being the most inventive compendium of everything one needs to know about Keaton's other worldliness. It starts with the pampered boy/man of the *Sap*. And then plops him down in a definitive Buster setting—a huge deserted space meant to be occupied by a multitude—an empty ocean liner. Even when it turns out there is someone else on board (the heroine), it still has the solitary nature of an Edward Hopper painting—alone unto himself. This is best exemplified in signature Hopper works, like the *Nighthawks*

(1942), or the *Automat*'s (1927) single individual. Indeed, the latter painting especially is representative of 1920s Keaton. A Hopper persona under glass at first seems "'realistic' but that shifts to a troubled inner life ... tinged with a profound sense of cosmic loneliness and anxiety."[4] Moreover, there is a sense of Keaton's often dream-like state. As the painter observed: "One reproduces only that which is striking, that is to say, the necessary. Thus one's recollections and inventions are liberated from the tyranny which nature exerts."[5] Plus, like Keaton's *Navigator*, the *Automat* woman is in a place which should be bustling with people, not to mention the New York sidewalk behind her. Indeed, she casts no reflection in that plate glass window. Is this a dream image?

Regardless, Keaton's loner nature as child has never been played out more effectively than in *The Navigator*. Little boys are running dynamos. Notwithstanding the army of wannabe brides chasing him in *Seven Chances*, Buster's racing around the multiple *Navigator* decks is his most charmingly realistic example of what little boys do. Keaton literature from all periods rightfully speaks of his athleticism, but rarely if ever is it attached to simply being a boy. This energetic lad factor is also the most logical attachment to all the chances he takes—both here and in most of his films. Little boys do not think about danger; they just go for it. It does not make them/Buster dumb, a label increasingly attached to his persona over time—it is being young and naïve. Why, "taking a dare" is boyhood business as usual. It is a wonder any of us survived.

Another period painting, Edward Hopper's *Automat* (1925), with ties to Keaton's world (Hopper Estate/Des Moines Art Museum).

Keaton's *Navigator* as boy splices nicely to his turning the huge galley into a Rube Goldberg series of toy gadgets. Play time then doubles down when he puts on the spaceman-like deep sea diving outfit. It is a combination of little boy adventure and Halloween. Playing as a child was always more fun with a costume, especially when one could multitask in it. For example, down in the deep he gets to play his own Theatre of the Absurd version of a swashbuckling Douglas Fairbanks—using a swordfish to dual another swordfish in an outfit seemingly from another world. My biggest disappointment of Keaton literature old and new was this *boyhood* blind spot ... even with *Buster* for a name.

The Navigator also offers a wealth of Keaton existential situations, starting with being set adrift in an absurd world in an equally absurd setting, on an empty ocean liner. He seems to be straddling parallel universes, neither of which makes much sense, whether it is deciding to go on a honeymoon without a bride, or then having that same person randomly turn up. And when land is discovered, alleged safety presumed, only to discover one's perceived rescuers would rather eat you. Little boys love to play various forms of "war." Now Buster is confronted with a most surreal version of war. That is, if man is gifted with any blessing, it is having been removed from the food chain. Well, not here. Finally, in the most cockamamie of closes—absurdity squared—just as all seems lost, a submarine surfaces and saves them, only to immediately go into an irrational *spin*, which is a fitting term for the engaging visit to Keaton-land—something period critics and audiences intuitively understood more than many contemporary viewers.

Given this apogee of creativity, it is no wonder Keaton was soon again upset by Schenck. Buster's alleged business mentor let him down again by buying the rights to adapt *Seven Chances* (1925) *without* even consulting the comedian. The rockslide conclusion, literally an 11th hour addition after a disappointing sneak preview, has helped elevate the film to a higher contemporary status than it merits. While receiving respectable period reviews, Jazz Age critics seemed to recognize and acknowledge it was a more second half picture than today's Keaton aficionados. It is, however, a textbook exercise on how an auteur can tweak his way into making an inappropriate property appear to resemble something in his wheelhouse.

What current criticism has also missed are the many period events reported on which now enhance *Seven Chances*' humor. While this is a key catalyst for the text, besides major discoveries connected to such films as *Sherlock, Jr.* and *The General*—*Seven Chances* seemly lost an inordinate number of engagingly documented details to time. These Jazz Age articles, from art copying life in what occurred when a cattle call request was announced for potential screen brides, to the many levels of humor connected to Buster's screen alter ego accidently proposing to not just any female impersonator (revisit Chapter 5). Moreover, the film's captivating time exposure opening also has direct ties to yet another forgotten 1920s Keaton article about a similar long range film project Buster had begun about recording his two sons growth through the years.

Regardless, whether consciously or not, *Seven Chances* was followed by both a payback at Schenck, and Keaton, as Alfred Hitchcock would later do, creating an extra production challenge just to make things interesting. The picture was *Go West* (1925), and it involved training a Jersey cow as his *love interest*! The Schenck retaliation was a Keaton concept in both being an original story (no surprise play to adapt), and being another acute example of reaffirmation parody dark comedy. Period and current criticism on the film is all over the map on the movie's merits and/or meaning. But again, there is *no* contemporary assessment of it being a seemingly obvious extreme example of his increasingly dark use of parody, despite Beckett's appreciation of a unique showcase of loneliness.

Keaton conclusion better encapsulates his nihilistic worldview as he dissolves his way to the cemetery. It is a tour de force finale equal to the walloping turnaround surprise that later followed Muhammad Ali's 1974 rope-a-dope "Rumble in the Jungle" defeat of George Foreman. Ironically, *College*'s often comically mundane material which precedes it enhances the existentialistic conclusion of Keaton's "Zero" character. This was the Buster that his period critic/interpreter Robert Sherwood had already credited with having an insight to life as being "a foolishly inconsequential affair."[7] No other American critic, past or present, has better encased the essence of the Keaton screen character.

That being said, a handful of European period critics, especially Luis Buñuel, also understood the uniqueness of the film, summarized marvelously from a lengthy quote in Chapter 9: "[Keaton is] a great specialist against all sentimental infection."[8] Even today, *College* is more appreciated in Europe than in the United States. And how paradoxical, that the best Rosetta Stone understanding and articulation of what the comedian is about still comes from two period critics. Moreover, there is the further paradox that the close makes such a big noise in a film which often seems mediocre and at times disturbing related to racial stereotypes. Such is the nature of art.

Keaton's final independent production, if one gets by the often problematic producer Schenck, is also the last film in his Southern trilogy—*Steamboat Bill, Jr.* By this time in their collaboration, Keaton and Schenck had seemingly evolved into a little two-step tradition. Again, while hardly played up by current historians, it went something like this: whenever the comedian would go into a provocative and potentially less profitable direction, such as *The General*, he would get slapped with a safer box office property, like *College*. When that picture did marginally okay at the turnstiles, Keaton was unleashed somewhat, to do a more personalized project. Such was the case after *College*.

As with *The General*, *Steamboat Bill, Jr.* would go over budget and not turn a profit. However, in this case, Schenck merits more of the blame because he decided during the production that a cyclone conclusion would be less likely to alienate a potential audience then the planned flood conclusion. This necessitated, among other things, the expense of bringing in large wind machines—large liberty motor airplane engines, as well as constructing a hinged hospital building which would appear to be blown away—exposing patient Keaton to all matter of wind currents.

The joke of the change, as Keaton later confessed and as is repeated ad nauseam by modern historians, was that each year more American lives are lost by twisters than floods. However, what has always amazed me, is that contemporary critics never seem to notice that it is still equal parts a flood film. Indeed upon first seeing the picture as a child, I was more disturbed by Keaton's screen father (Ernest Torrence) nearly being drowned by his dislodged jail, in which he was locked into a cell, entering a rampaging river.

Regardless, the cyclone factor allowed Keaton and the PR people to resurrect the comedian's hyperbolic twister beginnings, as well as inspire a much more dangerous gag in which a storefront falls upon the comedian and only the minute clearance of a second story window saves his life. This, for some, a career defining stunt, is emblematic of what *Steamboat Bill, Jr.,* and Buster's final two silent pictures, *The Cameraman* (1928) and *Spite Marriage* (1929), are reduced to—tour de force sequences in films in which his antisentimental, existentialistic screen persona is comprised.

Consequently, quintessential Keaton in *The Cameraman* is the Yankee Stadium sequence; *Spite Marriage*'s wrestling match to get a deadweight drunk from bar to bed is what makes that film worth watching. Given that each is still silent, there are additional

Keaton plusses, despite the piped-in sentimentality by new boss MGM, which manage to remain. Yet, it is largely downhill after *Steamboat Bill, Jr.* One might even lobby for starting the decline with *College*, except for Buster's seminal persona-defining exit. Yet, *College*'s multitude of limp life-defining issues—a potential partner dictating one's life, making any athletic team, marrying someone with whom one has little in common and/or possibly marriage itself, are what give *College*'s close such a nihilistic kick.

All in all, going back to period texts has been even more valuable than I could have imagined. First, it enabled me to better balance yesterday's and today's analysis of the major silent comedians—reconfiguring James Agee's still important but rather calcified essay "Comedy's Greatest Era." (1949). Thus, Chaplin remains number one, but the degree to which he was deified during the 1920s was surprising, though writing *Chaplin's War Trilogy: An Evolving Lens in Three Dark Comedies, 1918–1947* (2014) had somewhat prepared me for this perspective. Though Lloyd has clearly been perceived as tertiary to Chaplin and Keaton for years, Jazz Age criticism of his work amazingly showcased how much he was both part of, and contributed to H. L. Mencken's christened America's "booboisie." Moreover, while 1920s literature never put him close to Chaplin, it was eye-opening to see how critics of the period felt his comedies, however thin, were so dependably funny it was almost redundant to keep reviewing them.

Harry Langdon's star has fallen for some time but it was instructive to see what a short period, even then, that he had both been considered among the rarefied air of *the* trio, as well as not having a handle on his own persona. Indeed, Agee should never have included him with Chaplin, Keaton, and Lloyd. A better fourth choice would have been Laurel & Hardy—especially since comedy shorts carried much more weight during that decade than current criticism has ever suggested. Finally, it was engrossing, though certainly to be expected, that given Keaton's march towards an increasingly dark comedy parody of reaffirmation, he was then seen as a somewhat cultish figure. Thus, even when taking amazing chances, such as in *Go West* (1925), he still had a loyal following.

It was also astonishing to find a critic, *LIFE*'s Robert Sherwood, who, despite struggling with *The General*'s dark comedy, could so appreciate the comedian in essentially today's Theatre of the Absurd terms. Indeed there were other period reviewers who intrinsically sensed Keaton's postmodernism, yet did not quite have the words and/or big picture mindset to better celebrate his work—yet they kept coming back to this figure nicknamed "Zero." Thus, I was more than impressed with many of these pioneering film reviewers, just a few years removed from nickelodeon days. And Sherwood more than deserves to be mentioned in the same breath as Agee, and the often neglected Otis Ferguson.

Keaton's "Zero" vs. Chaplin's Tramp in a Contemporary Look at Their 1920s Work

So what were the decade's extreme differences between the Keaton and Chaplin antiheroes that allowed the former fringe figure to now come roaring back to rival the cinema's greatest auteur, regardless of eras? Simple: Keaton's cultish figure of absurdity now seems more current. In fact, one can still call him cultish because society and art now seem more fragmented than ever before. Keaton's M. O. in the 1920's suggested life was chaos ending in nothingness. Emotion was a dangerous infection which lessened one's chance of survival, let alone hope. The Great Stone Face is a protective mask. The ongoing Keaton joke was the indecipherableness of life itself, and the meaningless games we play killing time until it kills us. Cultishness is the new norm, with institutions, such as organized religion fanning false hope—franchises which promise perverse layaway plans. Pay now and just trust us. Yet, more people are rejecting this omission of logic ... making atheist Keaton increasingly timely. Enough sermonizing, to clasp Keaton is to know dark comedy.

In contrast, Chaplin's 1920s Tramp is a poignant exercise in humanism—trying to make sense of life's emotional and intellectual experiences. The key human action is sacrifice, even when that means letting go of love because it is the right thing to do, such as the close of 1928's *The Circus*. Even pain is seen as resilience and a down payment on a ticket to that ephemeral future of false promises. The Chaplin 1920s plan plays into that age-old comfort zone axiom "Art is where you get it right," as a Woody Allen character later suggests at the end of *Annie Hall* (1977). Yet, even this is a hopeful lie, because as the same movie also states, "Love fades"—something so quickly and devastatingly chronicled at the close of Keaton's *College*. As previously noted, Keaton, like Kafka, suggests "the meaning of life is death."

Chaplin's Jazz Age would look back to a past with emotional hope, in which a goofy "little fellow" could find love and wealth in the 1890s Yukon of *The Gold Rush* (1925). Chaplin moved even further into the past for his Dickensian *The Kid* (1920), which pairs the Tramp with an abandoned child born out of wedlock, dropped into childhood poverty, only to eventually be reunited with a now loving and wealthy mother, with his Tramp caretaker even welcomed into this shiny new world—brilliantly conceived and orchestrated by Chaplin, but the films are fantasies which were not even true in Dickens' day. Keaton's recognition and illustration of worldly absurdity is today—it rings true, though hardly comforting. Yet, there is an honesty in not leaning upon metaphorical crutches and bravely facing the abyss. That is why cherished comics are always cast to play the beloved duo endlessly *Waiting on Godot*/god. One must be distracted from the nothingness to come.

To further underline this perspective, Chaplin's comedy becomes increasingly darker after the 1920s, culminating in his last masterpiece—*Monsieur Verdoux* (1947). This exercise in black humor is based upon a real Bluebeard, marrying and murdering rich widows for survival. Society seems out to destroy the individual. Why not turn the tables? Dark comedy now pervades most genres, and infiltrates most thoughts, from Yogi Berra once observing, "Even if the world were perfect, it wouldn't be," to an older Chaplin being fond of saying, "In the end, everything is a gag."

If religions or other institutions do not propagate lying comfort, we distract ourselves with a growing number of comforts, such as cell phones or electronic finger toys. Keep in mind that the government managed people through pleasure in Aldous Huxley's *Brave New World* (1932), whereas George Orwell's anti-utopian novel *1984* fell back on control, in part, through pain.[9] Then pivot again, with Orwell making us aware of herding the public through language. For example, in time we would become used to calling civilian deaths during wars merely "collateral damage," or soldiers dying not by accident but by "friendly fire." Yet, he was merely reporting a new normal. The same year *1984* was completed (1948, the title reversing that date's last two digits), American history provided a perfect example of this "hide and seek" use of language, which Orwell called "Newspeak"; the United States' Department of War rechristening itself the Defense Department.

All this, of course, says nothing of our drug dodge ball with the unpleasant. For example, as suggested by writer Ron Padgett, there was a time if you asked someone what they were on, Earth would be a solid answer. Today, for most people, the same question elicits a pharmaceutical panacea.[10] Regardless, just as Stanley Kubrick's 1972 adaptation of Anthony Burgess' near future dystopian novel *A Clockwork Orange* ends with its again disturbing title character announcing he is back, it is safe to say Keaton's once cultish absurd world is back ... but now as the mainstream dark comedy norm.

It seems hardly coincidental that the same decade Keaton finally came to center stage (1960s), so did both the genre of dark comedy, and questioning the relevancy of whether a deity existed. A 1966 *Time* magazine cover even asked, "Is God Dead?"[11] Keaton's silent feature films were merely foreseeing a future, with other contemporaries, ranging from Kafka to F. Scott Fitzgerald, and later joined by artists like Camus and Beckett, of a much more secularized world ... without a clue. And though it took a post–Holocaust world nearly two more decades to nudge it along, this is why Keaton is so of today. The comedian was fond of saying, "I don't feel qualified to talk about my work." Yet it is all there in the enigma of his Great Stone Face.

Filmography

Buster Keaton was a total auteur, capable of writing, directing, and starring in films. However, he was very modest and generous in crediting other filmmakers' assistance. In fact, he so abhorred those people who took all the credit that he satirized that very subject in his short subject *The Playhouse* (1921). Thus, even when not credited in the categories of directing and writing, he should be given an uncredited acknowledgment. However, keep in mind that until he went to MGM for his final two silent features, 1928's *The Cameraman* and 1929's *Spite Marriage*, the term "screenplay" was often no more than an outline from which to improvise. Plus, though the aforementioned MGM pictures were technically scripted, their silent nature still allowed Keaton a great deal of influence, with regard to "writing" and directing. Finally, release dates can vary slightly from text to text based upon a variety of categories, including special event openings, the then prestigious New York City premiere, and the picture's general release. The dates used here come from celebrated film historian David Robinson's pioneering 1969 text *Buster Keaton*.

July 25, 1923—*The Three Ages*

(Metro Pictures Corporations, 63 minutes). Director: Buster Keaton and Eddie Cline. Screenplay: Clyde Bruckman, Joseph Mitchell, and Jean Havez. Stars: Keaton (Boy), Margaret Leahy (Girl), Walace Beery (Rival), Joe Roberts (Girl's Father), Lillian Lawrence (Girls' Mother).

November 20, 1923—*Our Hospitality*

(Metro Pictures Corporation, 74 minutes). Director: Buster Keaton and Jack Blystone. Screenplay: Clyde Bruckman, Joseph Mitchell, and Jean Havez. Stars: Buster Keaton (Willie McKay), Joe Roberts (Joseph Canfield), Natalie Talmadge Keaton (Virginia, His Daughter), Joe Keaton (Engineer), Joseph Keaton (Willie as a Baby), Craig Wad (Virginia's Brother Lee Canfield), Ralph Bushman (Virginia's Brother Clayton Canfield).

April 4, 1924—*Sherlock, Jr.*

(Metro Pictures Corporations, 45 minutes). Director: Buster Keaton. Screenplay: Clyde Bruckman, Jean Havez, and Joseph Mitchell; Stars: Buster Keaton (Sherlock, Jr.), Kathryn McGuire (The Girl), Joe Keaton (The Girl's Father), Ward Crane (The Rival), Erwin Connelly (The Butler).

October 14, 1924—*The Navigator*

(Metro-Goldwyn Pictures Corporation, 59 minutes). Director: Buster Keaton and Donald Crisp. Screenplay: Clyde Bruckman, Jean Havez, and Joseph Mitchell. Stars: Buster Keaton (Rollo Treadway), Kathryn McGuire (The Girl), Frederick Vroom (The Girl's Father), Noble Johnson (Cannibal Chief).

April 22, 1925—*Seven Chances*

(Metro-Goldwyn Pictures Corporation, 56 minutes). Director: Buster Keaton. Screenplay: Clyde Bruckman, Jean Havez, and Joseph Mitchell, based loosely upon the Roi Cooper Megrue play. Stars: Buster Keaton (Jimme Shannon), Ray Barnes (His Partner), Snitz Edwards (The Lawyer), Ruth Dwyer (Mary Jones, the Girl).

November 23, 1925 — *Go West*

(Metro-Goldwyn Pictures Corporation, 81 minutes). Director/Screenplay: Buster Keaton, assisted by Lex Neal. Stars: Buster Keaton, (Friendless), Brown Eyes (The Cow as Herself), Howard Truesdale (Ranch Owner), Kathleen Myers (His Daughter).

August 30, 1926 — *Battling Butler*

(Metro-Goldwyn-Mayer Corporation, 71 minutes). Director: Buster Keaton. Screenplay: Ballard MacDonald, Paul Gerard Smith, Albert Boasbery, Lex Neal, and Charles Smith; loosely based on the musical comedy play by Stanley Brightman, Austin Melford, Philip Brabham, Walker L. Rosemont, and Douglas Furber. Stars: Buster Keaton (Alfred Butler), Snitz Edwards (Valet), Sally O'Neil (Mountain Girl), Walter James (Her Father), Bud Fine (Her Brother), Francis McDonald (Alfred "Battling" Butler), Mary O'Brien (His Wife).

December 22, 1926 — *The General*

(United Artists Corporation, 75 minutes). Director/Screenplay: Buster Keaton and Clyde Bruckman, adapted from William Pittenger's 1893 memoir *The Great Locomotive Chase* (an early version appeared in 1863). Film adaptation assistance by Al Boasburg and Charles Smith. Stars: Buster Keaton (Johnnie Gray), Marion Mack (Annabelle Lee, the Girl), Charles Smith (Her Father), Frank Barnes (Annabelle's Brother), Glen Cavender (Captain Anderson, Union Leader of the Raid) Joe Keaton (One of the Union Generals).

September 10, 1927 — *College*

(United Artists, 65 minutes). Director: James W. Horne. Screenplay: Carl Harbough and Bryan Foy. Cast: Buster Keaton (Ronald), Florence Turner (Ronald's Mother), Snitz Edwards (Dean Edwards), Ann Cornwall (Mary Haines, the Girl), Harold Goodwin (Jeff Brown, the Rival), and a number of world class athletes in cameos, from future Hall of Fame Baseball player Sam Crawford (Baseball Coach), to Olympic Gold Medalist Lee Barnes (Keaton's pole vault double near the film's close).

June 2, 1928 — *Steamboat Bill, Jr.*

(United Artists, 71 minutes). Director: Charles F. "Chuck" Reisner. Screenplay: Carl Harbaugh Stars: Buster Keaton (Willie), Ernest Torrence (Steamboat Bill), Tom Lewis, (Bill's Best Friend), Tom McGuire (King, Bill's River Rival), Marion Byron (King's Daughter, the Girl), Joe Keaton (Barber).

September 15, 1928 — *The Cameraman*

(MGM, 69 minutes). Director: Edward Sedgwick. Story: Clyde Bruckman, Lew Lipton, and Buster Keaton. Screenplay: Richard Schayer. Stars: Buster Keaton (Luke Shannon), Marceline Day (Sally the Secretary), Harold Goodwin (The Rival), Harry Gibbon (Cop).

April 22, 1929 — *Spite Marriage*

(MGM, 75 minutes). Director: Edward Sedgwick. Screenplay: Lew Lipton and Ernest S. Pagano. Continuity: Richard Schayer. Stars: Buster Keaton (Elmer Edgemont), Dorothy Sebastian (Trilby Drew), Edward Earle (Lionel Benmore, The One-Sided Rival).

Chapter Notes

Prologue

1. James Agee, "Comedy's Greatest Era," *Life*, September 3, 1949.
2. Harold Lloyd (with Wesley W. Stout), *An American Comedy* (1928; rpt. New York: Dover, 1971).
3. See Frank Capra's *Frank Capra: The Name Above the Title* (New York: Macmillian, 1977). In conversations and correspondence with the author, particularly a letter dated December 10, 1979, Capra confessed that Langdon's persona was based upon his *perception* of Jaroslav Hăsek's simpleton literary character The Good Soldier Švejk, the title character of an already famous unfinished 1923 Czech novel, not yet translated into English. (In Capra's memoir he implies he has read the book.)
4. Bob Hope and Bob Thomas, *The Road to Hollywood* (Garden City, NY: Doubleday, 1977), 12.
5. Mason Wiley and Damien Bona, *Inside Oscar* (1986; rpt. New York: Ballantine, 1993), 932.
6. Fred Klein and Ronald Dean Nolen, *The Film Encyclopedia* (New York: HarperResource, 2001), 732.
7. Robert E. Sherwood, "Life of the Silent Drama: 'The Chaser,'" *Life*, April 26, 1928, 19.
8. Louis E. Bisch, M.D., Ph.D., "What Makes You Laugh?" *Photoplay*, June 1928, 34.
9. Malcolm H. Oettinger, "Low Comedy as High Art," *Picture-Play*, March 1923, 59.
10. Adele Rogers St. Johns, "Can a Genius Be a Husband?" *Photoplay*, January 1927, 116.
11. "His Play [Film] Rends [Removes] Veil of Comedy," *Los Angeles Times*, October 21, 1923, Part 3:28.
12. Ruth Waterbury, "Why Women Like Sophisticated Men," *Photoplay*, May 1926, 32.
13. Robert E. Sherwood, "The Silent Drama: 'The Circus,'" *Life*, February 2, 1928, 26.
14. "'Grandma's Boy' to Show at Miller's [Theatre]," *Los Angeles Times*, April 6, 1923, Part 2:7.
15. Edwin Schallart, "Harold on Rampage," *Los Angeles Times*, October 1923, Part 2:11.
16. "Hilarious Troubles of a 'Freshie' at the Colony," *New York Sun*, September 21, 1925, 22.
17. Robert E. Sherwood, "The Silent Drama: 'Speedy,'" *Life*, May 10, 1928, 30.
18. "Swelled Head Not Funny," *Los Angeles Times*, April 8, 1923, Part 3:27.
19. *Ibid.*
20. "Harold Lloyd Offers $500.00 in Prizes for Your Letters: He Want to Know Which of His Films You Liked Best," *Screenland*, December 1924, 38–39.
21. Harold Lloyd, "Don't Be Discouraged!" *Picture-Play*, December 1925, 19, 105.
22. *Ibid.*
23. "Harold Lloyd's Latest at Brooklyn Strand," *Brooklyn Eagle*, August 29, 1926, Part E:3.
24. A. L. Wooldridge, "Yes Men Need Not Apply," *Picture-Play*, September 1926, 24.
25. *The Kid Brother*, *Time*, February 7, 1927, 44.
26. *Ibid.*
27. "Harold Lloyd Does Marathon to Studio," *Los Angeles Times*, August 18, 1923, Part 2:7.
28. "New Disease Hits Harold Lloyd Fans," *Los Angeles Times*, June 7, 1923, Part 2:11.
29. "Laugh Bill Still Showing at Rialto," *Los Angeles Time*, December 11, 1923, Part 2:18.
30. Joe Keaton, "The Cyclone Baby," *Photoplay*, May 1927, 124.
31. Buster Keaton, "Why I Never Smile," *Ladies Home Journal*, June 1926, 20, 173–174.
32. *Ibid.*, 174.
33. Buster Keaton (with Charles Samuels), *My Wonderful World of Slapstick* (Garden City, NY: Doubleday, 1960).
34. F. W., "Melancholy Monarchs of Mirth," *Picture Show*, November 25, 1922, 20.
35. Albert Camus, *The Plague* (1948; rpt. New York: Vintage, 1975), 271.
36. James Knowlson, *Damned to Fame: The Life of Samuel Beckett* (New York: Simon & Schuster, 1996).
37. As an obsessive comedy scholar I have long been aware of the curious possible link between *The Lovable Cheat* and *Waiting for Godot*. However, I would be remiss for not mentioning a superb Alan W. Friedman article on the subject: "Samuel Beckett Meets Buster Keaton: Godeau, *Film*, and New York," *Texas Studies in Literature and Language*, Spring 2009, 41–46.
38. Knowlson, *Damned to Fame*, 71.
39. Keaton, *Ladies Home Journal*, 174.
40. Albert Camus, *The Stranger* (1946; rpt. New York: Vintage, 1989).
41. Linda Ben-Zvi, *Samuel Beckett* (Boston: Twayne, 1986), 199.

42. Alison Smith, "The Screen in Review: 'Pay Day,'" *Picture Play*, June 1922, 57.
43. "The Shadow Stage: 'The Circus,'" *Photoplay*, January 1928, 45.
44. Richard Griffith, "Introductory Note," in Harold Lloyd and Wesley W. Stout's *An American Comedy*, v.
45. See the author's *Parody as Film Genre: "Never Give a Saga an Even Break"* (Westport, CT: Greenwood Press, 1999).
46. O. C., "The Current Cinema: 'Battling Butler,'" *The New Yorker*, August 28, 1926, 36.
47. Robert E. Sherwood, "The Silent Drama: 'Young Mr. Keaton,'" *Life*, November 16, 1922.

Chapter 1

1. Albert Camus (trans. Philip Thody), *Notebooks: 1935–1942* (1962; rpt. Chicago: Ivan R. Dee, 2010), 199.
2. See the author's *Genre-Busting Dark Comedies of the 1970s: Twelve American Films* (Jefferson, NC: McFarland, 2016).
3. See the author's extensive writing on Chaplin, especially his award-winning study, *Chaplin's War Trilogy: An Evolving Lens in Three Dark Comedies, 1918–1947* (Jefferson, NC: McFarland, 2014).
4. Charlie Chaplin, *Charlie Chaplin's Own Story* (Indianapolis: Bobbs-Merrill, 1916).
5. Charles Chaplin, *My Autobiography* (1964; rpt. New York: Pocket Books, 1966), 350.
6. Harold Lloyd (with Wesley W. Stout), *An American Comedy* (1928; rpt. New York: Dover, 1971), 3, 5.
7. "Harold Lloyd Football Costume from the 'Freshmen' [1925] Free to the Fan Who Writes the Best Harold Lloyd Letter," *Screenland*, February 1926, 37.
8. *Ibid.*
9. Laurence Reid, "The Celluloid Critic," *Motion Picture Classic*, December 1924, 49.
10. "Sinclair Lewis Hornet's Nest," *Literary Digest*, May 29, 1926, 27.
11. Scott Eyman, *Ernst Lubitsch: Laughter in Paradise* (New York: Simon & Schuster, 1993), 293; also see the author's *Forties Film Funnymen: The Decade's Great Comedians at Work in the Shadow of War* (Jefferson, NC: McFarland, 2010).
12. Jack Benny and daughter Joan Benny, *Sunday Night at Seven: The Jack Benny Story* (New York: Warner Books, 1990), 150.
13. Edwin Schallert, "The Comedian's Hour of Triumph," in *The Pre-View: A Weekly Film Magazine* insert in the *Los Angeles Times*, November 24, 1924, 2.
14. "Lloyd Staff in Team Work," *Los Angeles Times*, November 2, 1924, Part 3:26.
15. Lisle Foote, *Buster Keaton's Crew* (Jefferson, NC: McFarland, 2014).
16. David Thomson, "Harold Lloyd," in *The New Biographical Dictionary of Film* (New York: Alfred A. Knopf, 2003), 525.
17. "Lloyd's New Gag Man," *Los Angeles Times*, April 4, 1925, Part 1:7.
18. Agnes Smith, "The Screen in Review: 'The Kid,'" *Picture-Play*, October 1921, 62.
19. "Lloyd's Clean Film Wins," *Los Angeles Times*, December 14, 1924, Part 3:24.
20. *Ibid.*
21. Charlie Chaplin files, Lincoln Center's New York Public Library of the Performing Arts.
22. *Ibid.*
23. Joyce Milton, *Tramp: The Life of Charlie Chaplin* (New York: HarperCollins, 1996), 202.
24. Charlie Chaplin, *My Trip Abroad* (New York: Harper and Brothers, 1922), 8.
25. Ruth Waterbury, "Why Women Like Sophisticated Men," *Photoplay*, May 1926, 32; and "Real Art of Chaplin Revealed," *Los Angeles Times*, January 27, 1924, Part 3:19.
26. See the author's frequent Chaplin-focused writing, bookended by *Charlie Chaplin: A Bio-Bibliography* (Westport, CT: Greenwood Press, 1983), and *Chaplin's War Trilogy: An Evolving Lens in Three Dark Comedies, 1918- 1947* (Jefferson, NC: McFarland, 2014).
27. Will Rogers, "We Save Money, Egypt Loses It" (December 14, 1924, syndicated weekly newspaper article), in *Will Rogers Weekly Articles*, vol. 1, *The Harding/Coolidge Years: 1922–1925*, ed. James M. Smallwood (Stillwater: Oklahoma State University Press, 1980), 333–334.
28. Buster Keaton (with Charles Samuels), *My Wonderful World of Slapstick* (Garden City, NY: Doubleday, 1960), 31.
29. Joe Keaton, "The Cyclone Baby," *Photoplay*, May 1927, 98, 125.
30. "He Likes Pictures Better Than Stage," *Los Angeles Times*, April 19, 1923, Part 2:9.
31. Luis Buñuel, "Buster Keaton's 'College,'" in Francisco Aranda's *Luis Buñuel: A Critical Biography*, trans. and ed. David Robinson (1975; rpt. New York: Da Capo Press, 1976), 273; Also see the author's *Steve McQueen: The Great Escape* (Indianapolis: Indiana Historical Society Press, 2009).
32. Harry Brand, "They Told Buster to Stick to It," *Motion Picture Classic*, June 1926, 80.
33. *Ibid.*
34. *Ibid.*
35. Robert E. Sherwood, "The Movies: 'The Cameraman,'" *Life*, October 5, 1928, 28.
36. "Buster Keaton," in *The Blue Book of the Screen* (Hollywood: Blue Book of the Screen, 1923), 133.
37. Grace Kingsley, "Buster Keaton's Tumbling to Success," *Picture Show*, August 5, 1922, 21.
38. Edward McPherson, *Buster Keaton: Tempest in a Flat Hat* (2004; rpt. New York: New Market Press, 2005), 3.
39. William Lindsay Gresham, *Houdini: The Man Who Walked Through Walls* (New York: Henry Holt, 1959); Milbourne Christopher, *Houdini: The Untold Story* (New York: Thomas Y. Crowell, 1969); Edward C. Meyer, M.D., *Houdini: A Mind in Chains* (New York: E. P. Dutton, 1976); Kenneth Silverman, *Hou-*

dini: *The Career of Ehrich Weiss* (New York: HarperCollins, 1996).
40. Christopher, *Houdini: The Untold Story*, 30.
41. Buster Keaton, "Why I Never Smile," *Ladies Home Journal*, June 1926, 20.
42. Conversations with Buster Keaton's third wife and widow, Eleanor Norris Keaton, at one of Pique, Kansas,' annual Buster Keaton festivals in the 1990s. I was both giving a talk on Chaplin and Keaton, while researching a book on Red Skelton, whom Keaton had mentored at MGM in the 1940s and early 1950s.
43. Joe Keaton, "The Cyclone Baby," 125.
44. Mark Twain, *The Adventure of Huckleberry Finn* (1884; rpt. New York: Barnes & Noble Classics, 2003). 3.
45. Adela Rogers St. Johns, "Interviewing Joseph Talmadge Keaton," *Photoplay*, October 1922, 51, 93.
46. "Buster Would Write Book on 'How to Smile,'" *Los Angeles Times*, May 11, 1923, Part 2:9.
47. Ibid.
48. See the author's *American Dark Comedy: Beyond Satire* (Westport, CT: Greenwood Press, 1996).
49. See the author's *Chaplin's War Trilogy: An Evolving Lens in Three Dark Comedies, 1918–1947*.
50. See the author's *Red Skelton: The Mask Behind the Mask* (Indianapolis: Indiana Historical Society Press, 2008).
51. "Buster Keaton," in *The Blue Book of the Screen*, 133.
52. Jason Stanley, "My Parents' Mixed Message on the Holocaust," *New York Times*, August 21, 2016, Sunday Review section: 9.
53. See the author's *W. C. Fields: A Bio-Bibliography* (Westport, CT: Greenwood Press, 1984); and *Groucho & W. C. Fields: Huckster Comedians* (Jackson: University Press of Mississippi, 1994).
54. Keaton, "Why I Never Smile," 173.
55. Robert E. Sherwood, "Silent Drama: Young Mr. Keaton," *Life*, November 16, 1922, 24.
56. Marion Meade, *Buster Keaton: Cut to the Chase* (1995 rpt. New York: Da Capo Press, 1997), 295.
57. "Buster Keaton Gets Grins At Symphony," *Los Angeles Times*, April 9, 1923, Part 2:15.
58. "Buster Keaton," *Los Angeles Times*, April 22, 1923, Part 3:27.
59. Ibid.
60. Mack Sennett, "Two Reels Are Enough for Comedy," *Los Angeles Times*, February 22, 1925, Part 3:19–20.
61. Ibid., 19.
62. R. Tripp Evans, *Grant Wood: A Life* (New York: Alfred A. Knopf, 2010).
63. Ibid., 190.
64. See the author's *American Dark Comedy: Beyond Satire* (Westport, CT: Greenwood Press, 1996); and his *Harold and Maude* chapter in *Genre-Busting Dark Comedies of the 1970s: Twelve American Films*, 68–85.
65. "'The General'—United Artists," *Photoplay*, March 1927, 52.
66. O.C., "The Current Cinema: 'Battling Butler,'" *The New Yorker*, August 28, 1926, 36.
67. "'The Blacksmith' Review," *Moving Picture World*, December 16, 1922, 672.
68. "'Electric House' Is Worth Laughing At,' *Los Angeles Times*, October 22, 1923, Part 2:9.
69. "'The High Sign' [Review]," *New York Times*, March 20, 1922, 10.
70. Margaret L. Talmadge, *The Talmadge Sisters: Norma, Constance, Natalie: An Intimate Story of the World's Most Famous Screen Family, by Their Mother* (Philadelphia: J. B. Lippincott, 1924).
71. Wilis Goldbeck, "Only Three Weeks," *Motion Picture*, October 1921.

Chapter 2

1. Malcolm H. Oettinger, "Low Comedy as High Art," *Picture-Play Magazine*, March 1923.
2. Ibid.
3. Robert E. Sherwood, ed., *The Best Moving Pictures of 1922–1923* (Boston: Small, Maynard, 1923).
4. Robert E. Sherwood, "Short Subjects," in his *The Best Moving Pictures of 1922–1923* (Boston: Small, Maynard, 1923), 121.
5. Fatty Arbuckle, "Nothing to Laugh At," *Picture and Picturegoer*, July 19, 1919, 76.
6. Mack Sennett, "Two Reels Are Enough for Comedy," *Los Angeles Times*, February 22, 1925, Part 3:19–20.
7. "Newest Reviews and Comments: 'The Saphead,'" *Moving Picture World*, February 1926, 1091; Burns Mantle, "The Shadow Stage: 'The Saphead,'" *Photoplay*, May 1921, 53.
8. Robert E. Sherwood, "The Perils of Monotony," *Photoplay*, November, 1925, 70, 123.
9. Ibid., 70.
10. Ibid.
11. Will Cuppy, *How to Be a Hermit* (1929; rpt. New York: Liveright, 1987 (see also the author's *Will Cuppy: American Satirist: A Biography* [Jefferson, NC: McFarland, 2013]); and James Thurber and E. B. White, *Is Sex Necessary?* (1929; rpt. New York: Harper & Row, 1975).
12. See the author's *Parody as Film Genre: "Never Give a Saga an Even Break"* (Westport, CT: Greenwood Press, 1999). Whenever parody genre basics are discussed in this text, this book will be the key source.
13. "The Screen: 'The Mark of Zorro,'" *New York Times*, November 29, 1920, 20.
14. Ibid.
15. "'Mark of Zorro' [Review]," *Variety*, December 3, 1920.
16. H. L. Mencken, "Notes on Journalism," September 19, 1926, *Chicago Daily Tribune*.
17. See the author's *Chaplin's War Trilogy: An Evolving Lens in Three Dark Comedies, 1918–1947* (Jefferson, NC: McFarland, 2014).
18. Edwin Schallert, "Playdom: Title Is Settled," *Los Angeles Times*, July 18, 1923, Part 2:2.
19. "Charlie Chaplin, as a Comedian, Contem-

plates Suicide," *Current Opinion*, February 1922, 209–210.

20. Frank Vreeland, "Chaplin Seeths with Revolutionary Plans," *Los Angeles Times*, October 21, 1923, Part 3:24.

21. Agnes Smith, "The Screen in Review: 'A Woman of Paris,'" *Picture-Play Magazine*, January 1924, 52.

22. Edwin Schallert, "Chaplin Opens New Epoch," *Los Angeles Times*, September 27, 1923, Part 2:9.

23. Helen Klumph, "Highbrows Are for It," *Los Angeles Times*, October 7, 1928, Part 3:33.

24. Robert E. Sherwood, "The Silent Drama: 'A Woman of Paris,'" *Life*, November 29, 1923, 24.

25. Douglas Fairbanks, "Films for the Fifty Million," *Ladies Home Journal*, April 1924, 27.

26. Conversations with Buster Keaton's third wife and widow, Eleanor Norris Keaton, at one of Pique, Kansas' annual Buster Keaton festivals in the 1990s. I was both giving a talk on Chaplin and Keaton, while researching a book on Red Skelton, who Keaton had mentored at MGM in the 1940s and early 1950s.

27. "Buster to Build If He Can Find a Hill," *Los Angeles Times*, May 4, 1924, Part 3:21.

28. Robert E. Sherwood, *Roosevelt and Hopkins: An Intimate Biography* (New York: Harper & Brothers, 1948), 8.

29. Jason Zinoman, "Once Too Raw, a Carlin Special Resurfaces," *New York Times*, September 5, 2016, C-4.

30. "Three-Reeler One of Buster's Best," *Los Angeles Times*, April 16, 1923, Part 2:7; Kenneth Taylor, "And Now the Comedians Seem to Have Succumbed to the Costume Vogue," *Los Angeles Times*, August 5, 1923, Section 4:27.

31. "'Three Ages' High Stepping Burlesque," *Los Angeles Times*, September 10, 1923, Part 2:5.

32. "'Clansman' Revival," *Los Angeles Times*, March 25, 1923, Part 3:3.

33. *Documentary on Three Ages*, a bonus feature on Kino's Blue-Ray edition of *Three Ages*, a film written and directed by John Bengtson, 2010 (10 minutes).

34. Harriette Underhill, "On the Screen: 'Three Ages,'" *New York Tribune*, October 1, 1923, 9.

35. "Brief Reviews of Current Pictures: 'Three Ages,'" *Photoplay*, November 1923, 102.

36. "Public Demand Puts Beery Back in Villain Class," *Los Angeles Times*, June 3, 1923, Part 3:28.

37. *Ibid.*

38. Edwin Schallert, "The Scene Stealers," *Picture-Play*, November 1924, 65.

39. "'Three Ages' High Stepping Burlesque," *Los Angeles Times*, September 10, 1923, Part 2:5.

40. "'Three Ages' [Review]," *Moving Picture World*, September 8, 1923, 155.

41. Robert E. Sherwood, "The Silent Drama: 'Three Ages,'" *Life*, October 25, 1923, 24.

42. *Ibid.*

43. Buster Keaton (with Charles Samuels), *My Wonderful World of Slapstick* (Garden City, NY: Doubleday, 1960), 132.

44. "'Three Ages'—with Buster Keaton, *Harrison's Reports*, September 24, 1923.

45. "'Three Ages' [Review]," *Variety*, October 4, 1923.

46. Bruce Weber quote of critic Brooks Atkinson in "Edward Albee, Trenchant Playwright of Desperate Era," *New York Times*, September 18, 2016, Part 1:23.

47. *Ibid.*

48. Margaret Werner, "How Buster Keaton Got That Way," *Movie Weekly*, November 10, 1923, 12.

49. *Ibid.*

50. Barry Paris, *Louise Brooks* (1989; rpt. New York: Anchor Books Doubleday, 1990), 228.

51. Margaret L. Talmadge, *The Talmadge Sisters: Norma, Constance, Natalie: An Intimate Story of the World's Most Famous Screen Family by Their Mother* (Philadelphia: J. B. Lippincott, 1924), 179–180.

52. Connie Mack telegram, November 15, 1921, in Babe Ruth Scrapbook Volume 1, Part 3:46; Helen Keller telegram, November 14, 1921, in Babe Ruth Scrapbook Volume 1, Part 3:47, Baseball Hall of Fame, Cooperstown, New York.

53. Buster Keaton telegram, November 14, 1921, in Babe Ruth Scrapbook Volume 1, Part 3:61, Baseball Hall of Fame, Cooperstown, New York.

54. "Certainly Mr. Keaton Believes," *Los Angeles Times*, April 15, 1923, Part 3:1.

55. Chicago White Sox telegram, November 14, 1921, in Babe Ruth Scrapbook Volume 1, Part 3:50, Baseball Hall of Fame, Cooperstown, New York.

56. The quote comes from the second source: "Keaton Frolics In Historic Costumes," *Los Angeles Times*, September 6, 1923, Part 2:11.

57. "Buster Keaton Has First Call with Navy Men," *Los Angeles Times*, September 30, 1923, Part 3:33.

58. See the author's *Chaplin's War Trilogy: An Evolving Lens In Three Dark Comedies, 1918–1947*.

59. "'Our Hospitality' [Review]," *Variety*, December 13, 1923.

60. "'Our Hospitality' [Review]," *Screenland*, January 1924.

61. Robert Sherwood, "The Silent Drama: 'Our Hospitality,'" *Life*, January 3, 1924, 24.

62. "'Rocket' Gets Into Comedy," *Los Angeles Times*, September 2, 1923, Part 3:21.

63. *Ibid.*

64. *Ibid.*

65. "'Our Hospitality'—with Buster Keaton," *Harrison's Reports*, November 19, 1923.

66. "'Our Hospitality' [Review]," *Moving Picture World*, November 24, 1923, 405.

67. "'Our Hospitality' [Review]," *Picture-Play Magazine*, December 1923.

68. Alma Whitaker, "Buster Smiles For This Scribe," *Los Angeles Times*, August 29, 1926, Part 3:19.

69. For example, see the *Our Hospitality* ad from the *New York Herald Tribune* December 11, 1923, 12.

70. *Ibid.*

71. Grace Kingsley, "Buster Burlesque," *Los Angeles Times*, December 10, 1923, Part 1:13.

72. *Ibid.*

73. Carl Sandburg, "'Our Hospitality' [Review]," *Chicago Daily News*, March 17, 1924.
74. Carl Sandburg, "'The Three Ages' [Review]," *Chicago Daily News*, November 14, 1923.
75. "On the Screen in City Theatres: Buster Keaton at Rialto," *New York Sun*, December 10, 1923, 21.
76. *Ibid.*
77. Gehring, *Parody as Film Genre: "Never Give a Saga an Even Break."*
78. "'Our Hospitality' [Review]," *New York Times*, December 10, 1923.
79. See the author's *Some Like It Hot* chapter in *Movie Comedians of the 1950s: Defining a New Era of Big Screen Comedy* (Jefferson, NC: McFarland, 2016).
80. Neil Schmitz, *Huck and Alice: Humorous Writing in American Literature* (Minneapolis: University of Minnesota Press, 1983), 9.
81. "'Cops' [Review]," *Moving Picture World*, March 11, 1922. 198.
82. "Keaton's Bill for Expenses Rouses [Lou] Anger," *Los Angeles Times*, November 25, 1923, Part 3:33.
83. *Ibid.*
84. *Ibid.*
85. Jackie Chan (with Jeff Yang), *I Am Jackie Chan: My Life in Action* (New York: Ballantine, 1998), 174.
86. Kingsley, "Buster Burlesque."
87. "At the Rialto: Buster Keaton in 'Our Hospitality,'" *New York World*, December 10, 1923, 9.
88. Jay Leyda, *Kino: A History of the Russian and Soviet Film* (1960; rpt. New York: Allen, 1983), 227.
89. See the author's *"Mr. B" or Comforting Thoughts About the Bison: A Critical Biography of Robert Benchley* (Westport, CT: Greenwood Press, 1992).
90. Robert Benchley, "Drama: A General Readjustment," *Life*, March 5, 1925, 18.

Chapter 3

1. Robert Benchley, "Drama: A General Readjustment," *Life*, March 5, 1925, 18.
2. Robert Benchley, "Fascinating Crimes 1," in *The Early Worm* (New York: Henry Holt, 1927), 21–22; see also the author's *"Mr. B" or Comforting Thoughts About the Bison: A Critical Biography of Robert Benchley* (Westport, CT: Greenwood Press, 1992).
3. Buster Keaton (with Charles Samuels), *My Wonderful World of Slapstick* (Garden City, NY: Doubleday, 1960), 194.
4. Louella O. Parsons, "'Sherlock Holmes, Jr.,' Feature at Rialto," *New York Sun*, May 27, 1924, 11.
5. Anthony Lane, "Seeing Things," *The New Yorker*, October 17, 2016, 108.
6. See the author's *Steve McQueen: "The Great Escape"* (Indianapolis: Indiana Historical Society Press, 2009).
7. Albert Camus, *The Stranger* (1946; rpt. New York: Random House, 1988), 122.
8. Stephen Galloway, "No, Woody Allen Won't Read This Interview," *Hollywood Reporter*, May 13, 2016, 73–74.
9. "Keaton's Comedy Has New Wrinkles," *Los Angeles Times*, April 25, 1924, Part 2:9.
10. "Keaton Finds Real Comedy in Reel Troubles," *Los Angeles Times*, May 4, 1924, Part 3:27.
11. Robert Franklin and Joan Franklin, "Interview with Buster Keaton," in *Buster Keaton Interviews*, ed. Kevin W. Sweeney (Jackson: University Press of Mississippi, 2007), 90.
12. "Death of Mr. John Bunny," *London Times*, April 29, 1915, 5-D.
13. John Palmer, "Mr. Bunny," *London Saturday Review*, April 1914, 466.
14. Henry Wysham Lanier, "The Coquelin of the Movies," *World's Work*, March 1915, 566–577.
15. Ralph Brock Pemberton, "A Man Seen Daily by Millions," *American Magazine*, August 1914, 60.
16. "John Bunny Again," *Indianapolis Star*, January 10, 1915, 12.
17. Vachel Lindsay, *The Art of the Moving Picture* (1915; rpt. New York: Liveright, 1970), 50–51.
18. Wes D. Gehring, Unpublished interview with John Bunny scholar Sam Gill, Los Angeles, California, summer 1975. See Gill's "John Bunny: A Filmography Compiled By Sam Gill," *The Silent Picture*, Summer 1972, 8–15. Gehring has also written "John Bunny: America's First Important Comedian, *Literature/Film Quarterly* 25, no. 2 (1995), 120–124; and "Bunny to Buster: Beyond Just Bookends to Silent Film Comedy," *USA Today Magazine* September 2016, 72–74.
19. Paul Murray Kendall, *The Art of Biography* (1965; rpt. New York: W. W. Norton, 1985), 130.
20. "Lyceum—John Bunny," *Indianapolis Star*, January 15, 1915, 15.
21. "Lyceum—John Bunny, Himself," *Indianapolis Star*, November 10, 1914, 15.
22. "Auditorium—'Funnyland,'" *Chicago Tribune*, October 11, 1914, Part 8:2.
23. David Robinson, *Buster Keaton* (1969; rpt. Bloomington: Indiana University Press, 1970), 105.
24. Gill, "John Bunny: A Filmography Compiled By Sam Gill," 12.
25. Margaret L. Talmadge, *The Talmadge Sisters: Norma, Constance, Natalie: An Intimate Story of the World's Most Famous Screen Family by Their Mother* (Philadelphia: J. B. Lippincott, 1924), 56.
26. *Ibid.*
27. *Ibid.*, 93.
28. Joseph Lelyveld, *His Final Battle: The Last Months of Franklin Roosevelt* (New York: Alfred A. Knopf, 2016), 57.
29. David B. Pearson, "Playing Detective: Possible Solutions to the Production Mysteries of *Sherlock, Jr.*," in *Buster Keaton's Sherlock Jr.*, ed. Andrew Horton (Cambridge: Cambridge University Press, 1997), 140–157.
30. David Yallop, *The Day the Laughter Stopped* (New York: St. Martin's Press, 1976), 278.
31. John Montgomery, *Comedy Films: 1894–1954* (1954; rpt. London: George Allen & Unwin, 1968), 141.

32. "Hick-Town Censors—Look Out! Buster Keaton on War Path with New Comedy, Showing Gang at Work," *Los Angeles Times*, January 28, 1924, Part 2:8.
33. Ibid.
34. Pearson, "Playing Detective: Possible Solutions to the Production Mysteries of Sherlock, Jr.," 146.
35. Marion Meade, *Buster Keaton: Cut to the Chase* (1995; rpt. New York: Da Capo Press, 1997), 147.
36. "'Sherlock, Jr.' [Review]," *Variety*, May 28, 1924.
37. "'Sherlock, Jr.' [Review]," *New York Times*, May 26, 1924, 21.
38. Kenneth Taylor, "Keaton Comic in Latest Picture," *Los Angeles Times*, April 28, 1924, Part 2:9.
39. "'Sherlock, Jr.'—Metro," *Photoplay*, July 1924, 46.
40. Ibid.
41. Louella O. Parsons, "'Sherlock Holmes, Jr.,' Feature Picture at Rialto," *New York American*, May 27, 1924, 11.
42. Ibid.
43. "On the Screens in City Theatres: Buster Keaton Says It with Laughter at Rialto," *New York Sun*, May 28, 1924, 20.
44. Alexander Woollcott, "Preface" in *Beggar on Horseback* (New York: Horace Liveright, 1924), 14.
45. "The New Picture: 'Sherlock Jr.,'" *Time* June 2, 1924, 17
46. "'Sherlock, Jr.'—with Buster Keaton," *Harrison's Reports*, April 21, 1924.
47. Harriette Underhill, "On the Screen," *New York Herald Tribune*, May 27, 1924, 10.
48. "'Sherlock, Jr.'" *Moving Picture World*, May 17, 1924, 319.
49. Robert E. Sherwood, "'Sherlock, Jr.,'" *Life*, June 19, 1924, 28.
50. Cal York, "Studio News Gossip East and by West," *Photoplay*, April 1926, 49.
51. "Flashes: Metro Hums," *Los Angeles Times*, February 28, 1924, Part 2:12.
52. David Yallop, *The Day the Laughter Stopped*.

Chapter 4

1. Adam Gopnik, "Magic in a Web," *New York Times*, November 13, 2016, Book Review section: 24.
2. John Griffith, *Charlotte's Web: A Pig's Salvations* (1980; rpt. New York: Twayne, 1993), 81.
3. Ibid.
4. Rudi Blesh, *Keaton* (1966; rpt. New York: Collier Books, 1966), 255.
5. Budd Schulberg, *The Disenchanted* (New York: Random House, 1950), 212.
6. Mordaunt Hall, "New Vitaphone Features: *New York Times*, February 13, 1927, Part 7:7.
7. Robert Knopf, *The Theatre and Cinema of Buster Keaton* (Princeton: Princeton University Press, 1999), 53.
8. See the author's chapter "Martin & Lewis: Artists and Models," in his *Movie Comedians of the 1950s: Defining a New Era of Big Screen Comedy* (Jefferson, NC: McFarland, 2016).
9. Douglas Fairbanks, *Laugh and Live* (New York: Britton, 1917); Douglas Fairbanks, *Make Life Worth While* (New York: Britton, 1918).
10. See Harry Kreisler's complete interview of Robert Wise in the author's *Robert Wise: Shadowland* (Indianapolis: Indiana Historical Society Press, 2013), 3.
11. See the author's chapter "Hope & Crosby": The *Road to Bali*," in *Movie Comedians of the 1950s: Defining a New Era of Big Screen Comedy*.
12. See the author's *Leo McCarey: From Marx to McCarthy* (Lanham, MD: Scarecrow Press, 2005).
13. "Deluge Buster With All Kinds of Kid Stuff," *Los Angeles Times*, January 3, 1924, Part 2:11.
14. Ibid.
15. Carl Sandburg, "'The Navigator' [Review]," *Chicago Daily News*, November 18, 1924.
16. "Deep Sea Comedy: Buster Keaton Collecting Shipload For Next Comedy," *Los Angeles Times*, May 11, 1924, Part 3:23.
17. Ibid.
18. "Keaton's Ship Was Lure for Whole Family," *Los Angeles Times*, October 26, 1924, Part 3:24.
19. Grace Kingsley, "'Navigator' Great," *Los Angeles Times*, October 6, 1924, Part 1:7.
20. William Grimes, "William Trevor, Who Rendered the Ordinary Extraordinary, Dies at 88," *New York Times*, November 22, 2016, A-27.
21. "Keaton Fills Capital [Theatre] With Laughter," *New York Sun*, October 13, 1924, 18.
22. "'Navigator' Great," Part 1:7.
23. Grace Kingsley, "Which Shall It Be? Syd Chaplin Is Undecided Between Star Offers," *Los Angeles Times*, February 8, 1924, Part 2:11.
24. "Buster Gets Along Without Flappers," *Los Angeles Times*, October 3, 1924, Part 2:9.
25. Ibid.
26. Grace Kingsley, "Flashes: Didn't Ask to See License," *Los Angeles Times*, October 10, 1924, Part 2:9.
27. Marion Meade, *Buster Keaton: Cut to the Chase* (1995; rpt. New York: Da Capo Press, 1997), 151.
28. "Chaplin Shows Art of Pictures Century Hence," *Los Angeles Times*, February 7, 1924, Part 3:11.
29. "The New Picture: *The Navigator*," *Time*, October 20, 1924, 13.
30. "On a Drifting Vessel," *New York Times*, October 13, 1924, 24.
31. Arthur Marx, *Red Skelton* (New York: E. P. Dutton, 1979). In contrast, consult one of the author's three books on the comedian, especially his award-winning *Red Skelton: The Mask Behind the Mask* (Indianapolis: Indiana Historical Society, 2008).
32. "'The Navigator' [Review]," *Variety*, October 15, 1924.
33. Harriette Underhill, "On the Screen: Buster Keaton Is Just Himself in 'The Navigator,'" *New York Herald Tribune*, October 13, 1924, 10.

34. Ibid.
35. Quinn Martin, "At the Capitol: Buster Keaton In 'The Navigator,'" *New York World*, October 13, 1924, 9.
36. "'The Navigator'—with Buster Keaton," *Harrison's Reports*, October 13, 1924.
37. "Keaton Fills Capital [Theatre] with Laughter."
38. "A Confidential Guide to Current Releases: 'The Navigator'—Metro-Goldwyn," *Picture-Play Magazine*, May 1925, 60; "Brief Reviews of Current Pictures: 'The Navigator,'" *Photoplay*, May 1925, 11.
39. "Second Choice [Category]," *Picture-Play Magazine*, May 1925, 60.
40. Louella O. Parsons, "New Films Reviewed: Capitol Showing Buster Keaton Comedy," *New York American*, October 14, 1924, 14.
41. Robert E. Sherwood, "The Silent Drama: 'The Navigator,'" *Life*, November 6, 1924, 26.
42. Ibid.
43. Robert E. Sherwood, "The Silent Drama: Young Mr. Keaton," *Life*, November 16, 1922, 24.
44. Buster Keaton (with Charles Samuels), *My Wonderful World of Slapstick* (Garden City, NY: Doubleday, 1960), 132–134.
45. Ibid., 133.
46. Carl Sandburg, "Limited," in *Chicago Poems* (New York: Henry Holt, 1916).

Chapter 5

1. Helen T. Verongos, "Shirley Hazzard, BS, Writer Who Shared Life's Cruelties," *New York Times*, December 14, 2016, B-14.
2. "Film Star Goes in for New Style," *Los Angeles Times*, February 9, 1926, Part 2:11.
3. "Houdini's Latest Act Is Unique," *Los Angeles Times*, April 22, 1923, Part 3:30.
4. Richard Sandomir, "Rodney Smith, 68, Photographer of Surrealistic Whimsy," *New York Times*, December 17, 2016, A-19.
5. Ibid.
6. Charles Busch, "I Performed in Drag," *New York Times*, December 25, 2016, Arts & Leisure section: 6.
7. Randy Kennedy, "Donald Judd, Unexpected Philosopher," *New York Times*, December 26, 2016, C-6.
8. Daniel Moews, *Keaton: The Silent Features Close Up* (Los Angeles: University of California Press, 1977).
9. "A Movie Without Headlines [Titles]," *Literary Digest*, February 28, 1925, 26.
10. "Youngest Keaton Baby Named Bob," *Los Angeles Times*, March 19, 1924, Part 2:11.
11. "Films Will Tell Story of Keatons," *Los Angeles Times*, October 8, 1924, Part 2:9.
12. See the author's *Genre-Busting Dark Comedies of the 1970s: Twelve American Films* (Jefferson, NC: McFarland, 2016).
13. Michael Tisserand, *Krazy: George Herriman, a Life in Black and White* (New York: HarperCollins, 2016), 272.

14. Ibid., 343.
15. Guy Price, "Guy Price's Gossop [sic] of the Silverscreen," *Los Angeles Evening Herald*, May 19, 1924, B-8.
16. Gerald Mast, *The Comic Mind: Comedy and the Movies* (Indianapolis: Bobbs-Merrill, 1973), 194.
17. "Noted Comic Artist Leads a Strenuous Life," *Los Angeles Evening Herald*, May 12, 1924, B-7.
18. "Comedian Has to Be [an] Athlete," *Los Angeles Times*, June 17, 1923, Part 3:34.
19. See the author's extensive writing on Red Skelton, including his award-winning biography: *Red Skelton: The Mask Behind the Mask* (Indianapolis: Indiana Historical Society, 2008).
20. Grace Kingsley, "Buster Keaton's Tumbling to Success," *Picture Show*, August 5, 1922, 21.
21. "At the Capitol: Buster Keaton In 'Seven Chances,'" *New York World*, March 16, 1925, 13.
22. Ibid.
23. Carl Sandburg, "'Seven Chances' [Review]," *Chicago Daily News*, April 16, 1925, 13.
24. Mordaunt Hall, "A Slump in Fun," *New York Times*, March 17, 1925, 18.
25. Ibid.
26. *Variety*, "'Seven Chances' [Review]," March 18, 1925.
27. Ibid.
28. "'Seven Chances'—with Buster Keaton," *Harrison's Reports*, March 21, 1925.
29. "Seven Chances' [Review]," *Time*, March 23, 1925; Mildred Spain, "Buster Keaton Provides 82 Laughs in Chase for Bride," *New York Daily News*, March 17, 1925.
30. Spain, "Buster Keaton Provides 82 Laughs in Chase for Bride."
31. Robert E. Sherwood, "'Seven Chances' [Review]," *Life*, April 19, 1925, 26.
32. Ibid.
33. George Nelson, "Invisibly Black," *New York Times*, January 15, 2017, Book Review section: 14–15.
34. See the author's *Will Cuppy, American Satirist: A Biography* (Jefferson, NC: McFarland, 2013), 23–24, 25, 58, 75, 103, 122, 126, 150, 155, 163.

Chapter 6

1. "Buster Prefers to Smoke Tailor-Made," *Los Angeles Times*, November 26, 1925, Part 2:11.
2. Rudi Blesh, *Keaton* (1966; rpt. New York: Collier Books, 1971), 260; Larry Edwards, *Buster: A Legend in Laughter* (Bradenton, FL: McGuinn & McGuire, 1995), 71.
3. Daniel Moews, *Keaton: The Silent Features Close Up* (Los Angeles: University of California Press, 1977), 181.
4. Owen Wister, *The Virginian* (1902; rpt. New York: New American Library, 1979), 19.
5. "W. S. Hart Tells of Wit Shown by Wild Bill Hickok," *Los Angeles Times*, October 7, 1928, Part 3:33.
6. "Keaton Has [Discovered] New Leading Woman for 'Go West,'" *Los Angeles Times*, May 30, 1925, Part 2:7.

7. See the author's *Movie Comedian of the 1950s: Defining a New Era of Big Screen Comedy* (Jefferson, NC: McFarland, 2016).
8. Ben Brantley, "A Playwright Intent on Naming, and Goading, the Beast Within," *New York Times*, September 19, 2016, C-2.
9. *Ibid.*
10. Bruce Weber, "Edward Albee, Trenchant Playwright of a Desperate Era, Dies at 88," *New York Times*, September 18, 2016, Part 1:23.
11. James R. Quirk, "Speaking of Pictures," *Photoplay*, August 20, 2015.
12. Dave Smith, *Hoosiers in Hollywood* (Indianapolis: Indiana Historical Society, 2006).
13. Frederick Russell, "The Life Story of Carole Lombard," *Film Pictorial*, July 4, 1936, Part 2:17; also see the author's *Carole Lombard: The Hoosier Tornado* (Indianapolis: Indiana Historical Society Press, 2003).
14. Adela Rogers St. Johns, "A Gallant Lady … Carole Lombard," *Liberty*: Part 2, March 7, 1942, 25.
15. "Coolidge to Press Dry Law to Limit, Watson Declares," *New York Times*, May 20, 1925, 1, 12.
16. See the author's *Parody as Film Genre: "Never Give a Saga an Even Break"* (Westport, CT: Greenwood Press, 1999).
17. Sam Roberts, "Harry Mathews Dies at 86; Writer Who Experimented," *New York Times*, February 3, 2017, A-22.
18. *Ibid.*
19. "'The Blacksmith [Review],'" *Moving Picture World*, December 16, 1922, 672.
20. Robert Benchley, "The Passing of the Cow," *Life*, July 14, 1927, 9.
21. "Seeing Green," by Charles Drazin (1949), bonus material on 1949's *The Third Man*, DVD (New York: Criterion Collection, 2007).
22. *Ibid.* (Any other Graham Green quotes are drawn from this documentary.)
23. Ron Wertheimer, "Irwin Corey, Comedian, Dies at 102; Posed as World's 'Foremost Authority,'" *New York Times*, February 8, 2017, B-11.
24. Neil Genzlinger, "With Good Timing, a Look Back at Comedy," *New York Times*, February 9, 2017, C-4.
25. "'Go West'—with Buster Keaton," *Harrison's Reports*, November 1, 1925, 174.
26. "The Shadow Stage: 'Go West,'" *Photoplay*, January 1926, 49.
27. Frederick James Smith, "The New Screen Plays in Review: 'Go West,'" *Motion Picture Classic*, January 1926, 81.
28. "'Go West' [Review]," *Screenland*, January 1926, 42.
29. "At the Capitol: Buster Keaton in 'Go West,'" *New York World*, October 26, 1925, 11.
30. Louella O. Parsons, "'Go West,' Keaton Comedy at Capitol," *New York American*, October 26, 1925, 8.
31. "'Go West' review," *Variety*, October 28, 1928.
32. "Mr. Keaton's Cow," *New York Times*, October 26, 1925, 25.
33. Grace Kingsley, "Great Comedy: Buster Keaton Triumphs in 'Go West,'" *Los Angeles Times*, November 23, 1925, Part 2:9.
34. *Ibid.*
35. Robert E. Sherwood, "The Silent Drama: 'Go West,'" *Life*, November 19, 1925, 26.
36. See especially the author's *Chaplin's War Trilogy: An Evolving Lens in Three Dark Comedies, 1918–1947* (Jefferson, NC: McFarland, 2014); and *Genre-Busting Dark Comedies of the 1970s: Twelve American Films* (Jefferson, NC: McFarland, 2016).
37. Bosley Crowther, "In 'The Great Dictator' Charlie Chaplin Reveals Again the Greatness in Himself," *New York Times*, October 20, 1940.
38. John Masher, "The Current Cinema: Charlie's Hitler," *The New Yorker*, October 26, 1940, 78.
39. *Ibid.*
40. See the author's *American Dark Comedy: Beyond Satire* (Westport, CT: Greenwood Press, 1996).
41. Kurt Vonnegut, *A Man Without a Country* (New York: Seven Stories Press, 2005), 115.
42. "Motion Pictures: 'Go West,'" *The New Yorker*, October 31, 1925, 19.
43. "The New Photoplay: Harry Langdon Tries a Tragic-Comedy," *New York Sun*, October 3, 1927, 17.
44. "'Go West' [Review]," *Screenland*.
45. See the author's extensive writing on W. C. Fields, especially, *Groucho & W. C. Fields: Huckster Comedians* (Jackson: University Press of Mississippi, 1994).
46. Edmund Wilson, "Some Recent Films," *New Republic*, December 16, 1925, 109.
47. *Ibid.*
48. Edwin Schallert, "Pathos Mood In Prospect," *Los Angeles Times*, March 25, 1928, Part 3:12.

Chapter 7

1. "'Go West'—Metro-Goldwyn," *Photoplay*, May 1926, 12.
2. Rudi Blesh, *Keaton* (1966; rpt. New York: Collier Books, 1971), 266.
3. "'Rosita' [Review]," *Variety*, September 6, 1923.
4. 'Thief of Bagdad' [Review]," *Variety*, March 26, 1924.
5. "Snitz Edwards to Appear at the Potboilers [Art Theatre]," *Los Angeles Times*, April 14, 1926, Part 2:9.
6. "Battling Butler: A Musical Knockout" ad, *New York Herald Tribune*, October 5, 1923, 12.
7. "New Plays Bring Stars Back Home," *Los Angeles Times*, October 25, 1925, 30.
8. "Talmadge Girls Soon to Resume," *Los Angeles Time*, November 16, 1925, Part 2:9.
9. "Keaton's Next Is Prize-Fight Comedy Feature," *Los Angeles Times*, December 16, 1925, Part 2:9.
10. *Ibid.*
11. "'Battling Butler' Is a Real Champ," *New York Evening Telegraph*, October 9, 1923, 14.
12. Gerald Mast, *The Comic Mind: Comedy and the Movies* (Indianapolis: Bobbs- Merrill, 1973), 128.
13. Laura Collins-Hughes, "Thorton Wilder in

the Trump Era," *New York Times*, February 19, 2017, Theatre section: 21.

14. "Machine Movies Dwarf Real Art, 7 Stars Declare," *New York Daily News*, February 23, 1923, 25.

15. James Baldwin, *The Devil Finds Work* (1976; reprint. New York: Vintage, 2011), 3–4.

16. See the author's *Film Clowns of the Depression: Twelve Defining Comic Performances* (Jefferson, NC: McFarland, 2007); and *Forties Film Funnymen: The Decade's Great Comedians at Work in the Shadow of War* (Jefferson, NC: McFarland, 2010).

17. "Death Ends Valentino's Career at 31," *New York Sun*, August 23, 1926, 1.

18. "'We Are Engaged,' Lisps Pola, As Charlie Blushes and Nods," *New York Tribune*, January 29, 1923, 4.

19. "Dempsey on Way Back to New York," *New York America*, April 3, 1922, 8.

20. See the author's *Leo McCarey: From Marx to McCarthy* (Lanham, MD: Scarecrow Press, 2005), 3.

21. Harry Brand, "They Told Me to Stick to It," *Motion Pictures Classics*, June 1926, 32, 80, 89.

22. *Ibid.*, 80.

23. Leonard Maltin, ed., *Leonard Maltin's 2011 Movie Guide* (New York: New American Library, 2010), 95.

24. David Robinson, *Buster Keaton* (1969; rpt. Bloomington: Indiana University Press, 1970), 136.

25. Mast, *The Comic Mind: Comedy and the Movies*, 135.

26. Kevin J. Hayes, ed., *Martin Scorsese's Raging Bull* (New York: Cambridge University Press, 2005).

27. Richard Cohen, *She Made Me Laugh: My Friend Nora Ephron* (New York: Simon & Schuster, 2016), 275.

28. Edwin Schallert, "Playroom: Keaton Clever," *Los Angeles Times*, August 30, 1926.

29. *Ibid.*

30. "The Current Cinema: Comical Manna from Buster Keaton," *New York*, August 28, 1926, 36.

31. *Ibid.*

32. Creighton Peet, "'Battling Butler'—MGM," *Cinema Art*, September 1926, 32, 56.

33. Edward Albee, *The Goat or Who Is Sylvia?* (New York: Overlook Duckford, 2000), 95.

34. "'Battling Butler' [Review]," *Variety*, August 25, 1926.

35. Jason Baker's "Introduction," to Franz Kafka's *The Metamorphosis and Other Stories*, trans. Donna Freed (1915; rpt. New York: Barnes and Noble Classics, 2013), xvii.

36. See the author's *Robert Wise: Shadowlands* (Indianapolis: Indiana Historical Society, 2012).

37. David Cronenberg, "Introduction" to *The Metamorphosis*, trans. Susan Bernofsky (1915; New York: W. W. Norton, 2014), 9.

38. It first appeared in book form in the humorist's *My World and Welcome to It* (New York: Harcourt, Brace,, 1942), 72–81.

39. Author's conversation with Plimpton and other writers after the Midwest Writers' 2002 summer conference, Roberts' Hotel Bar, downtown Muncie, Indiana.

40. Robert E. Sherwood, "The Silent Drama: 'Battling Butler,'" *Life*, September 16, 1926, 26.

41. Robert E. Sherwood, "The Silent Drama: "The Celluloid Crop of 1926,'" *Life*, January 6, 1926, 26.

42. Mordaunt Hall, "The Screen: Mr. Keaton Again," *New York Times*, August 23, 1926, 9.

43. Mordaunt Hall, "Phlegmatic Mr. Keaton Is a Stylist as Jester," *New York Times*, August 29, 1926, Section 7:5.

44. Irene Thirer, "Buster Keaton, Directing Self, Does Good Job," *New York Daily News*, August 26, 1926, 6.

45. "'Battling Butler' [Review]," *Screenland*, November 1926, 49.

Chapter 8

1. Wilella Waldorf, "New Photoplays: Buster Keaton in 'The General' at the Capitol [Theatre]," *New York Evening Post*, February 7, 1927, np.

2. *Ibid.*

3. Gertrude Chase, "Buster Keaton Can Smile and Yawn, Too, If He Wishes," *New York Telegraph*, October 8, 1922.

4. Malcolm H. Oettinger, "Tumbling to Fame," *Picture-Play Magazine*, December 1920.

5. Grace Kingsley, "Buster Bursts Into Stardom," *Los Angeles Times*, May 16, 1920.

6. Buster Keaton, *My Wonderful World of Slapstick* (with Charles Samuels) (Garden City, NY: Doubleday, 1960), 95.

7. Buster Keaton, "Why I Never Smile," *Ladies Home Journal*, June 1926, 173.

8. "Famous Comedian Sees Own Picture for Fourth Time," *Los Angeles Herald*, February 6, 1921, PA-20.

9. Keaton, "Why I Never Smile," 174.

10. Roger Cohen, "The Age of Distrust," *New York Times*, September 20, 2016, A-23.

11. Fatty Arbuckle, "Nothing to Laugh At," *Picture and Picturegoer*, July 15, 1919, 76.

12. *Ibid.*

13. *Ibid.*

14. Keaton, *My Wonderful World of Slaptstick*, 94.

15. Rudi Blesh, *Keaton* (1966; rpt. New York: Collier Books), 253.

16. See the author's *Screwball Comedy: A Genre of Madcap Romance* (Westport, CT: Greenwood Press, 1986); and *Romantic vs Screwball Comedy: Charting the Difference* (Lanham, MD: Scarecrow Press, 2002).

17. Marquis Busby, "Locomotive with a Soul," *Los Angeles Times*, March 13, 1927, Part 3:19.

18. "Keaton's Co-Workers Are from Broadway," *Variety*, March 24, 1927, 27.

19. See the author's chapter on *Chinatown* in his *Genre-Busting Dark Comedies: Twelve American Films* (Jefferson, NC: McFarland, 2016), 122–138.

20. Mordaunt Hall, "New Vitaphone Features: Mr. Keaton's Face Overpowers This Film," *New York Times*, February 13, 1927, Part 7:7.

21. David Thomson, *The New Biographical Dic-

tionary of Film (New York: Alfred A. Knopf, 2003), 459. (There have been earlier installments of this text, but Thomson so reinvents each one I prefer to list this as a new text.)

22. Robert Benchley, "Johnny-on-the-Spot," in *From Bad to Worse or Comforting Thoughts About the Bison* (New York: Harper & Brothers, 1984), 255–259; also see the author's *"Mr. B" Or Critical Biography of Robert Benchley* (Westport, CT: Greenwood Press, 1992).

23. Benchley, "Johnny-on-the-Spot," 255.

24. See the author's *"Mr. Be" or Comforting Thoughts About the Bison: A Critical Biography of Robert Benchley*.

25. See the author's *Parody as Film Genre* (Westport, CT: Greenwood Press, 1999).

26. See the author's *Chaplin's War Trilogy: An Evolving Lens in Three Dark Comedies, 1918–1947* (Jefferson, NC: McFarland, 2014).

27. Charlie Chaplin, *My Trip Abroad* (New York: Harper & Bros., 1922), 77–78.

28. "Reshowing of Chaplin Comedy Scores Success," *Los Angeles Times*, March 13, 1927, Part 3:19.

29. Mordaunt Hall, "The Screen: A Civil War Farce," *New York Times*, January 18, 1926. 26.

30. "'Hands Up' [Review]," *Variety*, January 20, 1926.

31. "'The General'—United Artists," *Photoplay*, March 1927, 52.

32. Katherine Lipke, "Comedy Is Lost in War Incidents," *Los Angeles Times*, March 12, 1927, Part 1:7.

33. Marquis Busby, "Locomotive with a Soul."

34. *Ibid.*

35. *Ibid.*

36. *Ibid.*

37. Ernst Lubitsch, "Mr. Lubitsch Takes the Floor for Rebuttal," *New York Times*, March 29, 1942, Section 8:3.

38. *Ibid.*

39. Eileen Creelman, "Carole Lombard's Last Picture, the Somber 'To Be or Not to Be,'" *New York Sun*, March 7, 1942.

40. Lubitsch, "Mr. Lubitsch Takes the Floor for Rebuttal."

41. *Ibid.*

42. Gehring, *Genre-Busting Dark Comedies of the 1970s: Twelve American Films*.

43. "'The General' [Review]," *Variety*, February 9, 1927.

44. Regina Cannon, "Keaton Comedy Grips Fans," *New York American*, February 8, 1927, 9.

45. "New Films: 'Comedians' and 'Hamlet' Complex Again," *New York Sun*, February 8, 1927, 23.

46. *Ibid.*

47. Mordaunt Hall, "The Screen: A Civil War Farce," *New York Times*, February 8, 1927, 21.

48. *Ibid.*

49. "A Costly Joke," *Picture-Play Magazine*, May 1927, 72.

50. "A Confidential Guide to Current Releases," *Picture-Play Magazine*, September 1927, 119.

51. "'The General'—with Buster Keaton," *Harrison's Report*, February 9, 1927, 27.

52. Robert Sherwood, "The Silent Drama: 'The General,'" *Life*, February 24, 1927, 26.

53. Keaton, *My Wonderful World of Slapstick*, 132.

54. *AFI 100 Greatest American Movies of All Time* (10th Anniversary Edition), originally broadcast on CBS, June 20, 2007.

55. François Truffaut (with Helen G. Scott), *Hitchcock: Revised Edition* of *Hitchcock/Truffaut* (1966; rpt. New York: Simon & Schuster, 1983), 202–203.

56. Gerald Mast (revised by Bruce F. Kawin), *A Short History of the Movies* (1971; rpt. New York: Macmillan, 1992, 5th ed.).

57. *Ibid.*, 126–130.

58. "The Current Cinema: Buster Keaton," *The New Yorker*, February 12, 1927, 51.

59. See the author's *Personality Comedians As Genre: Selected Players* (Westport, CT: Greenwood Press, 1997).

60. Leonard Maltin, ed., *Leonard Maltin's 2011 Movie Guide* (New York: New York American Library, 2010), 512.

61. John Kennedy Toole, *A Confederacy of Dunces* (New Orleans: Louisiana State University Press, 1980).

62. Burke Davis, *Our Incredible Civil War* (New York: Holt, Rinehart and Winston, 1960).

63. *Ibid.*

64. "By the Book: Philip Meyer," *New York Times*, April 2, 2017, Book Review Section: 8.

65. Ernest Hemingway, *A Farewell to Arms* (1929; rpt. New York: Charles Scribner's Sons, 1957), 185.

Chapter 9

1. "Buster Keaton Latest to Go Rah-Rah on Screen, *New York Evening News*, September 12, 1927, 22.

2. Milfred Spain, "Harold Lloyd as 'Freshman' Sure Cure for Grouchy Mood," *New York Daily News*, September 22, 1925, 27.

3. *College* ad, *Los Angeles Daily Times*, July 25, 1927, Part 2:7.

4. Edwin Schallert, "Playdom: College Life Spirit Fills Grange Feature," *Los Angeles Times*, September 10, 1926, Part 2:11.

5. "Norma Talmadge Hailed as Chaplin Counterpart By Clarence Brown, Director," *Los Angeles Times*, May 23, 1926, Part 3:26.

6. *Ibid.*

7. Charlie Chaplin, *My Trip Abroad* (New York: Harper & Bros., 1922), 86.

8. Rudi Blesh, *Keaton* (1966; rpt. New York: Collier Books, 1971), 268.

9. Sam Roberts, "Masha Leon, Columnist Who Fled Nazi, Dies at 86," *New York Times*, April 10, 2017, D-8.

10. "Perfectly Good Train Is Wrecked: Spectacular Finale for 'Signal Tower' Filmed at Universal," *Los Angeles Times*, January 12, 1924, Part 2:7.

11. *Ibid.*

12. Will Rogers, "Will Rogers Names Chaplin as His Lieutenant Mayor" (January 4, 1927, syndicated

daily telegram), in *Will Rogers' Daily Telegrams, vol. 1, The Coolidge Years, 1926–1929*, ed. James L. Smallwood (Stillwater: Oklahoma State University Press, 1978), 43.

13. See the previous chapter, especially the article by Marquis Busby, "Locomotive with a Soul," *Los Angeles Times*, March 13, 1927, Part 3:17.

14. Will Rogers, "Will Rogers Explains One Joke Is on Him" (August 26, 1927, syndicated daily telegram), in *Will Rogers' Daily Telegrams, vol. 1, The Coolidge Years, 1926–1929*, 121.

15. Will Rogers, "Will Rogers Studies Effect of a Million" (September 16, 1927, syndicated daily telegram), in *Will Rogers' Daily Telegrams, vol. 1, The Coolidge Years, 1926–1929*.

16. "Athletes Take Part in New Keaton Film," *Los Angeles Times*, August 1, 1927, Part 2:7.

17. "Studio Flashes," *Los Angeles Times*, February 13, 1927, Section 7:7.

18. "Keaton Is Shown in New Role: Comedian Turns Athlete in College," *Los Angeles Times*, July 31, 1927, Part 3:13.

19. "Keaton's Nose Is Broken," *New York Times*, July 31, 1927, 25.

20. Chaplin, *My Trip Abroad*, 32–33, 149–150.

21. *Ibid.*, 32–33.

22. *Ibid.*, 6–7.

23. John M. Blum, "Retreat from Responsibility," in *The National Experience: A History of the United States*, Blum, ed. (New York: Harcourt, Brace, 1968), 617.

24. Carl Sandburg, *The Chicago Race Riots: July 1919* (New York: Harcourt, Brace and Howe, 1919).

25. Mordaunt Hall, "The Screen: 'College,'" *New York Times*, September 12, 1927, 29.

26. *Ibid.*

27. John S. Cohen, Jr., "The New Photoplay: Buster Keaton Appears in a College Film," *New York Sun*, September 12, 1927, 17.

28. Regina Cannon, "'College' [Review]," *New York America*, September 13, 1927, 14.

29. "The Current Cinema: And Buster Keaton," *The New Yorker*, September 17, 1927, 79.

30. Marquis Busby, "'College' Needy of Education," *Los Angeles Times*, July 30, 1927, Part 2:7.

31. *Ibid.*

32. *Ibid.*

33. "'College' [Review]," *Variety*, September 14, 1927.

34. *Ibid.*

35. "Blacks But Not Blue: Our Comedians Struggle in the Dark for Laughs," *Photoplay*, October 1927, 100.

36. "'College—United Artists," *Photoplay*, December 1927, 8.

37. "'College' [Review]," *Harrison's Reports*, September 17, 1927.

38. Luis Buñuel, "Buster Keaton's College," in Francisco Aranda's *Luis Buñuel: A Critical Biography* (1969; rpt. New York: Da Capro Press, 1975), trans. and ed. David Robinson, 272–273.

39. Robert E. Sherwood, "Silent Drama: 'College,'" *Life*, October 6, 1927, 26.

40. Robert E. Sherwood, "Silent Drama: Young Mr. Keaton," *Life*, November 16, 1922, 24.

41. Robert Benchley, "Drama," *Life*, April 16, 1925, 18.

42. Busby, "'College' Needy of Education."

43. *Ibid.*

44. James Baldwin, *The Devil Finds Work* (1976; rpt. New York: Vintage, 2011), 39–40.

45. See the author's *Genre-Busting Dark Comedies of the 1970s: Twelve American Films* (Jefferson, NC: McFarland, 2016).

46. Ellen Bryant Voigt, "*Chinatown* [Thoughts]," in *Writers at the Movies*, ed. Jim Shepard (New York: HarperCollins, 2000), 266.

47. Charles Simic, "[Thoughts on] 'Cops,'" in *Writers at the Movies*, ed. Jim Shepard, 245.

48. *Ibid.*, 248.

49. *Ibid.*, 247.

50. Paul Vitello, "Robert Pirsig, 88, Author of 'Zen and the Art of Motorcycle Maintenance,' Dies," *New York Times*, April 25, 2017, B-12.

51. Anthony Channell Hilfer, *The Revolt from the Village: 1915–1930* (Chapel Hill: University of North Carolina Press, 1969), 5.

52. Carl Van Doren, "The Revolt from the Village," *Nation*, October 12, 1921, 407.

Chapter 10

1. Charlie Chaplin, *Steamboat Bill, Jr.* ad, *Los Angeles Times*, June 5, 1928, Part 2:11.

2. Douglas Fairbanks, *Steamboat Bill, Jr.* ad, *Los Angeles Time*, June 5, 1928, Part 2:11.

3. "Ernest Torrence to Become Free Lancer," *Los Angeles Times*, May 6, 1926, Part 2:9.

4. Alma Whitaker, "Torrence Feels 'King of Kings' Role Responsibility," *Los Angeles Times*, September 5, 1926.

5. "'Fighting Coward' Star, Praises Actor's Make-Up," *Los Angeles Evening Herald*, March 14, 1924, B-6.

6. "Ernest Torrence, Film Actor, Dead," *New York Times*, May 16, 1933, 17.

7. "Rites Held for Torrence," *Indianapolis News*, May 17, 1933, 7.

8. Marquis Busby, "Villain Tired of Cussedness," *Los Angeles Times*, July 6, 1927, Part 2:8.

9. "Torrence Surprised Again," *Los Angeles Times*, July 8, 1928, Part 3:11.

10. Edwin Schallert, "'Steamboat Bill' Stormy Fun Special," *Los Angeles Times*, June 8, 1928, Part 2:11.

11. *Ibid.*

12. Robert E. Sherwood, "The Silent Drama: 'Steamboat, Jr.,'" *Life*, May 31, 1928, 23.

13. Philip K. Scheuer, "What Makes Laughter, Asks Comic," *Los Angeles Times*, June 3, 1928, Part 3:11.

14. R. Tripp Evans, *Grant Wood: A Life* (New York: Alfred A. Knopf, 2010), 61.

15. Leonard Maltin, ed., *Leonard Maltin's 2011 Movie Guide* (New York: New American Library, 2010), 1312.

16. Schallert, "'Steamboat Bill' Stormy Fun Special."
17. Will Cuppy Papers, William Steig letter to Will Cuppy, Box 9:Folder 24 (William Steig correspondence), undated letter (circa 1941); also see the author's *Will Cuppy, American Satirist: A Biography* (Jefferson, NC: McFarland, 2013).
18. Jeanne Steig, "Clowning Around," in *The Art of William Steig* (New Haven: Yale University Press, 2007), 73, 75, 78.
19. Joe Keaton, "The Cyclone Baby," *Photoplay*, May 1927, 98, 125.
20. "Keaton Says Success and Name Linked," *Los Angeles Times*, July 22, 1928, Part 3:11.
21. *Ibid.*
22. David Robinson, *Buster Keaton* (1969; rpt. Bloomington: Indiana University Press, 1970), 164.
23. "The Shadow Stage," *Photoplay*, September 1927, 6.
24. "Keaton Gets All Wet in River Film," *Los Angeles Times*, June 10, 1928, Part 3:12.
25. *Ibid.*
26. Buster Keaton (with Charles Samuels), *My Wonderful World of Slapstick* (Garden City, NY: Doubleday, 1960), 199–215.
27. Wes D. Gehring, "Conversation Notes with Eleanor Keaton," Piqua, Kansas' Annual Keaton Festival, early 1990s. (My main focus was on Keaton's mentoring of Red Skelton, for the first of three books I was to do on the younger comedian, but we ended up covering many topics.)
28. "'Steamboat Bill, Jr.' [Review]," *Variety*, May 16, 1928.
29. *Ibid.*
30. Schallert, "'Steamboat Bill' Stormy Fun Special."
31. Mordaunt Hall, "The Screen: 'Steamboat Bill, Jr.,'" *New York Times*, May 15, 1928, 17.
32. "'Steamboat Bill, Jr.'—Buster Keaton," *Harrison's Reports*, May 12, 1928, 83.
33. Laurence Reid, "The Celluloid Critic: 'Steamboat Bill, Jr.,'" *Motion Picture Classic*, August 1928, 83.
34. Robert E. Sherwood, "The Silent Drama: 'Steamboat Bill, Jr.,'" *Life*, May 31, 1928, 23.
35. Rose Pelswick, "'Steamboat Bill, Jr.' [Review]," *New York Evening Journal*, September 15, 1928.
36. John S. Cohen, Jr., "The New Photoplays: Buster Keaton in 'Steamboat Bill, Jr.,'" *New York Sun*, May 15, 1928, 21.
37. "'Steamboat Bill, Jr.' [Review]," *Time*, May 28, 1928, 19.
38. "Georgie Harris Adds Comedy to 'Flood' Film," *Los Angeles Times*, June 19, 1926, Part 1:7.
39. "'Talkies' Just Fad, Says Joseph Schenck: Producer Thinks They Will Lose Popularity," *New York Times*, August 22, 1928, 25.
40. "Harold Lloyd Picture Sets New Records," *Los Angeles Times*, June 9, 1928, Part 2:9.
41. "'Steamboat Bill, Jr.' [Review]," *Variety*.
42. Sherwood, "The Silent Drama: 'Steamboat Bill, Jr.'"
43. Hall, "The Screen: "Steamboat Bill, Jr."
44. Robert E. Sherwood, "The Movies: The Celluloid Crop of 1928," *Life*, December 28, 1928, 25.

Chapter 11

1. "'Cameraman' [Review]," *Variety*, September 19, 1928.
2. *Ibid.*
3. See the author's *Personality Comedians As Genre: Selected Players* (Westport, CT: Greenwood Press, 1987); and *Groucho & W. C. Fields: Huckster Comedians* (Jackson: University of Mississippi Press, 1994).
4. *AFI's 100 Years ... 100 Movies—10th Anniversary Edition*, originally aired on CBS on June 20, 2007.
5. See the author's award-winning *Red Skelton: The Mask Behind the Mask* (Indianapolis: Indiana Historical Society Press, 2008); and also his *I, Red Skelton: Exit Laughing or, A Man, His Movies and Sometimes His Monkeys*, a novelized memoir (Albany, GA: BearManor Fiction, 2011).
6. Buster Keaton (with Charles Samuels), *My Wonderful World of Slapstick* (Garden City, NY: Doubleday, 1960), 130.
7. Rudi Blesh, *Keaton* (1966; rpt. New York: Collier Books, 1966), 302.
8. Irving Thalberg, "New Goals to Achieve," *Los Angeles Times*, "Pre-View Magazine" insert, April 23, 1929, 6.
9. Many sources. For example, see the documentary *So Funny It Hurts: Buster Keaton and MGM*, a Film By Kevin Brownlow and Christopher Bird (Turner Classic Pictures, 2004).
10. Keaton (with Charles Samuels), *My Wonderful World of Slapstick*, 262.
11. Jane Ellen Wayne, *Clark Gable: Portrait of a Misfit* (New York: St. Martin's Press, 1993), 158–159.
12. Regina Cannon, "Buster Keaton Seen in 'The Cameraman,'" *New York American*, September 17, 1928, 15.
13. Irene Thirer, "*Cameraman* Focuses Fun Only in Last Two Reels," *New York Daily News*, September 16, 1928, 64.
14. "Shadow Stage: 'The Cameraman,'" *Photoplay*, October 1928, No. 5.
15. "'Hot News' [Review]," *Variety*, July 25, 1928.
16. Mordaunt Hall, "The Screen: More on Newsreels," *New York Times*, July 23, 1928.
17. "'The News Parade' [Review]," *Variety*, May 30, 1928.
18. See the author's "The House That Buster Built," *USA Today Magazine*, March 2016, 55.
19. Robert E. Sherwood, "The Movies: 'The Cameraman,'" *Life*, October 5, 1928, 28.
20. See the author's *Mr. Deeds Goes to Yankee Stadium: Baseball Films in the Capra Tradition* (Jefferson, NC: McFarland, 2004).
21. *Baseball: The Fifth Inning: Shadow Ball* (covering 1930–1940), a Film by Ken Burns (PBS, 1994).
22. Will Rogers, untitled column (October 21, 1928), in *The Autobiography of Will Rogers*, ed. Donald Day (Boston: Avon, 1975), 183.

23. Thirer, "*Cameraman* Focuses Fun Only in Last Two Reels."
24. Charles Bukowski, *Love Is A Dog from Hell* (1977; rpt. New York: New York: HarperCollins, 2003).
25. Charles Bukowski, *Factotum* (1975; rpt. New York: HarperCollins, 2002), 104.
26. Barry Miles, *Charles Bukowski* (London: Virgin, 2005), 61.
27. See the author's *I, Red Skelton: Exit Laughing or A Man, His Movies and Sometimes his Monkeys* (Albany, GA: BearManor Fiction, 2011).
28. Mordaunt Hall, "The Screen: Chaplin of Hollywood," *New York Times*, January 9, 1928, 20.
29. Norman Lusk, "The Screen in Review: Mr. Keaton at His Best," *Picture-Play* Magazine, December 1928, 72.
30. "'The Cameraman'—with Buster Keaton," *Harrison's Reports*, September 15, 1928.
31. "Buster Keaton's Bicycle," *Variety*, May 9, 1928, 5.
32. Feg Murray, "Ernie Orsatti: He Doubles For Buster Keaton in the Movies—But He Can Sock a Mean Double for Himself, As Well!" *Los Angeles Times*, January 16, 1929, Part 3:1,2.
33. "Keaton's Bungalow Really Star's Gymnasium," *Metro-Goldwyn-Mayer Picture Newspaper*, in *The Cameraman* file, New York Performing Arts Library at Lincoln Center, New York.
34. Gene Fowler, *Minutes of the Last Meeting* (New York: Viking Press, 1954), 172. Also see the author's: *W. C. Fields: A Bio-Bibliography* (Westport, CT: Greenwood Press, 1984).
35. Fowler, *Minutes of the Last Meeting*, 170.

Chapter 12

1. Mordaunt Hall, "Poor Comedy," *New York Times*, March 31, 1929, Part 8:7.
2. Conversation with the actress, "The Movies: D. W. Griffith and Lillian Gish: Broken Blossoms" (Bloomington: Indiana University Auditorium Program, March 15, 1981).
3. John S. Cohen, Jr., "The Photoplay: 'Spite Marriage' with Mr. Keaton, Quickly Displaces 'The Great Power,' a Talkie," *New York Sun*, March 25, 1929, 18.
4. *Ibid*.
5. Mordaunt Hall, "The Screen: Silence Wins," *New York Times* March 25, 1929, 32.
6. *Ibid*.
7. Bruce D. Haynes and Syma Solovitch, *Down The Up Staircase* (New York: Columbia University Press, 2017).
8. "Keaton Silent and Funny," *Los Angeles Times*, June 1, 1929, Part 2:9.
9. *Ibid*.
10. See the author's *The Marx Brothers: A Bio-Bibliography* (Westport, CT: Greenwood Press, 1987); and *Groucho & W. C. Field: Huckster Comedians* (Jackson: University Press of Mississippi, 1994).
11. "The Shadow Stage: 'Spite Marriage,'" *Photoplay*, April 1929, 54.
12. "'Spite Marriage' [Review]," *Variety*, March 27, 1929.
13. Harry Evans, "Movies: 'Spite Marriage,'" *Life*, April 19, 1929, 40.
14. "'Spite Marriage (SD) —with Buster Keaton," *Harrison's Reports*, April 6, 1929.
15. Malcolm Cowley, "Introduction" to Sherwood Anderson's *Winesburg, Ohio* (1919; rpt. New York: Viking Press, 1960), 11.
16. "Mr. Keaton's Film at the Empire," *London Times*, October 11, 1939, 10.
17. Edwin Schallert, "Silents Withstand Onslaught," *Los Angeles Times*, September 8, 1929, Part 3:11.
18. *Ibid*.
19. Edwin Schallert, "Rogers' Star Shines Brightly," *Los Angeles Times*, September 20, 1929, Part 2:9.
20. *Ibid*.
21. Grace Kingsley, "Films Made in Many Tongues," *Los Angeles Times*, August 30, 1929, Part 1:10.
22. Buster Keaton (with Charles Samuels), *My Wonderful World of Slapstick* (Garden City, NY: Doubleday, 1960).
23. *Ibid.*, 199–215.
24. Mordaunt Hall, "Mr. Keaton in Khaki," *New York Times*, September 30, 1929, 19.
25. Jhan Robbins, *Inka Dinka Doo: The Life of Jimmy Durante* (New York: Paragon House, 1991), 97.

Epilogue

1. Malcolm H. Oettinger, "Low Comedy as a High Art," *Picture-Play Magazine*, March 1923.
2. Grace Kingsley, "Buster Bursts Into Stardom," *Los Angeles Times*, May 16, 1920.
3. *Ibid*.
4. Justin Spring, *The Essential Hopper* (New York: Harry N. Abrams, 1998), 22.
5. Rolf G. Renner, *Hopper* (San Diego: Thunder Bay Press, 1997), 65.
6. Rudi Blesh, *Keaton* (1966; rpt. New York: Collier Books, 1971), 253.
7. Robert Sherwood, "Silent Drama: Young Mr. Keaton," *Life*, November 16, 1922, 24.
8. Luis Buñuel, "Buster Keaton's 'College,'" in Francisca Aranda's *Luis Buñuel: A Critical Biography* (1969; rpt. New York: Da Capro Press, 1975), trans. and ed. David Roginson, 272–273.
9. See George Orwell's *1984* (1949; rpt. New York: Signet Classics, 1961); and Aldous Huxley's *Brave New World* (London: Chatto & Windus, 1932).
10. Ron Padgett, *How Long* (Minneapolis: Coffee House Press, 2011), 21.
11. "Is God Dead?" cover, *Time*, April 8, 1966.

Bibliography

Books

Albee, Edward. *The Goat or Who Is Sylvia?* New York: Overlook Duckford, 2000.
Baldwin, James. *The Devil Finds Work*. 1976; rpt. New York: Vintage, 2011.
Becket, Samuel. *Waiting For Godot*. 1953; rpt. New York: Grove, 1989.
Benny, Jack, and daughter Joan Benny. *Sunday Night at Seven: The Jack Benny Story*. New York: Warner Books, 1990.
Ben-Zvi, Linda. *Samuel Beckett*. Boston: Twayne, 1986.
Blesh, Rudi. *Keaton*. 1966; rpt. New York: Collier Books, 1966.
Bukowski, Charles. *Factotum*. 1975; rpt. New York: HarperCollins, 2002.
Bukowski, Charles. *Love Is a Dog from Hell*. 1977; rpt. New York: HarperCollins, 2003.
Camus, Albert. *The Plague*. 1948; rpt. New York: Vintage, 1975.
Camus, Albert. *The Stranger*. 1946; rpt. New York: Vintage, 1989.
Camus, Albert (trans. Philip Thody). *Notebook: 1935–1942*. 1962; rpt. Chicago: Ivan R. Dee, 2010.
Capra, Frank. *Frank Capra: The Name Above the Title*. New York: Macmillian, 1977.
Chan, Jackie (with Jeff Yang). *I Am Jackie Chan: My Life in Action*. New York: Ballantine, 1998.
Chaplin, Charles. *My Autobiography*. 1964; rpt. New York: Pocket Books, 1966.
Chaplin, Charlie. *Charlie Chaplin's Own Story*. Indianapolis: Bobbs-Merrill, 1916.
Chaplin, Charlie. *My Trip Abroad*. New York: Harper and Brothers, 1922.
Christopher, Milbourne. *Houdini: The Untold Story*. New York: Thomas Y. Crowell, 1969.
Cohen, Richard. *She Made Me Laugh: My Friend Nora Ephron*. New York: Simon & Schuster, 2016.
Cuppy, Will. *How to Be a Hermit*. 1929; rpt. New York: Liveright, 1987.
Davis, Burke. *Our Incredible Civil War*. New York: Holt, Rinehart and Winston, 1960.
Edmonds, Andy. *Frame-Up!: The Untold Story of Roscoe "Fatty" Arbuckle*. New York: William Morrow, 1991.
Edwards, Larry. *Buster: A Legend In Laughter*. Bradenton, FL: McGuinn & McGuire, 1995.
Evans, R. Tripp. *Grant Wood: A Life*. New York: Alfred A. Knopf, 2010.
Eyman, Scott. *Ernest Lubitsch: Laughter in Paradise*. New York: Simon & Schuster, 1993.
Fairbanks, Douglas. *Laugh and Live*. New York: Britton, 1917.
Foote, Lisle. *Buster Keaton's Crew*. Jefferson, NC: McFarland, 2014.
Fowler, Gene. *Minutes of the Last Meeting*. New York: Viking Press, 1954.
Gehring, Wes D. *American Dark Comedies: Beyond Satire*. Westport, CT: Greenwood Press, 1996.
Gehring, Wes D. *Carole Lombard: The Hoosier Tornado*. Indianapolis: Indiana Historical Society Press, 2003.
Gehring, Wes D. *Charlie Chaplin: A Bio-Bibliography*. Westport, CT: Greenwood Press, 1983.
Gehring, Wes D. *Film Clowns of the Depression: Twelve Defining Comic Performances*. Jefferson, NC: McFarland, 2007.
Gehring, Wes D. *Forties Film Funnymen: The Decade's Great Comedians at Work in the Shadow of War*. Jefferson, NC: McFarland, 2010.
Gehring, Wes D. *Genre-Busting Dark Comedies of the 1970s: Twelve American Film*. Jefferson, NC: McFarland, 2016.
Gehring, Wes D. *Groucho & W. C. Fields: Huckster Comedians*. Jackson: University Press of Mississippi, 1994.
Gehring, Wes D. *I, Red Skelton: Exit Laughing or, A Man, His Movies and Sometimes His Monkeys*, a novelized memoir. Albany, GA: BearManor Fiction, 2011.
Gehring, Wes D. *Leo McCarey: From Marx to McCarthy*. Lanham, MD: Scarecrow Press, 2005.
Gehring, Wes D. *The Marx Brothers: A Bio-Bibliography*. Westport, CT: Greenwood Press, 1987.
Gehring, Wes D. *Movie Comedians of the 1950s: Defining a New Era of Big Screen Comedy*. Jefferson, NC: McFarland, 2016.

Gehring, Wes D. *"Mr. B" or Comforting Thoughts About the Bison: A Critical Biography of Robert Benchley*. Westport, CT: Greenwood Press, 1992.
Gehring, Wes D. *Mr. Deeds Goes to Yankee Stadium: Baseball Films in the Capra Tradition*. Jefferson, NC: McFarland, 2004.
Gehring, Wes D. *Parody as Film Genre: "Never Give an Even Break."* Westport, CT: Greenwood Press, 1999.
Gehring, Wes D. *Personality Comedians As Genre: Selected Players*. Westport, CT: Greenwood Press, 1997.
Gehring, Wes D. *Red Skelton: The Mask Behind the Mask*. Indianapolis: Indiana Historical Society, Press, 2008.
Gehring, Wes D. *Robert Wise: Shadowlands*, Indianapolis: Indiana Historical Society Press, 2012.
Gehring, Wes D. *Romantic vs. Screwball Comedy: Charting the Difference*. Lanham, MD: Scarecrow Press, 2002.
Gehring, Wes D. *Screwball Comedy: A Genre of Madcap Romance*. Westport, CT: Greenwood Press, 1986.
Gehring, Wes D. *Steve McQueen: The Great Escape*. Indianapolis: Indiana Historical Society Press, 2003.
Gehring, Wes D. *W. C. Fields: A Bio-Bibliography*. Westport, CT: Greenwood Press, 1984.
Gehring, Wes D. *Will Cuppy: American Satirist: A Biography*. Jefferson, NC: McFarland, 2013.
Gresham, William Lindsay. *Houdini: The Man Who Walked Through Walls*. New York: Henry Holt, 1959.
Griffith, John. *Charlotte's Web: A Pig's Salvation*. 1980; rpt. New York: Twayne, 1993.
Haynes, Bruce D. and Syma Solovitch. *Down the Up Staircase*. New York: Columbia University Press, 2017.
Hays, Kevin J., ed. *Martin Scorsese's Raging Bull*. New York: Cambridge University Press, 2005.
Hemingway, Ernest. *A Farewell to Arms*. 1929; rpt. New York: Charles Scribner's Sons, 1957.
Hilfer, Anthony Channell. *The Revolt from the Village: 1915-1930*. Chapel Hill: University of North Carolina Press, 1969.
Hope, Bob, and Bob Thomas. *The Road to Hollywood*. Garden City, NY: Doubleday, 1977.
Huxley, Aldous. *Brave New World*. London: Chatte & Windus, 1932.
Keaton, Buster (with Charles Samuels). *My Wonderful World of Slapstick*. Garden City, NY: Doubleday, 1960.
Kendall, Paul Murray. *The Art of Biography*. 1965; rpt. New York: W. W. Norton, 1985.
Knopf, Robert. *The Theatre and Cinema of Buster Keaton*. Princeton: Princeton University Press, 1999.
Knowlson, James. *Damned to Fame: The Life of Samuel Beckett*. New York: Simon & Schuster, 1996.
Lelyveld, Joseph. *His Final Battle: The Last Months of Franklin Roosevelt*. New York: Alfred A. Knopf, 2016.
Lindsay, Vachel. *The Art of the Moving Picture*. 1915; rpt. New York: Liveright, 1970.
Lloyd, Harold (with Wesley W. Stout). *American Comedy*. 1928; rpt. New York: Dover, 1971.
Loos, Anita. *The Talmadge Girls: A Memoir*. New York: Viking Press, 1978.
Maltin, Leonard, ed. *Leonard Maltin's 2011 Movie Guide*. New York: New American Library, 2010.
Marx, Arthur. *Red Skelton*. New York: E. P. Dutton, 1979.
Masters, Edgar Lee Masters. *Spoon River Anthology*. 1915; rpt. New York: Macmillan, 1962.
Mast, Gerald (revised by Bruce F. Kawin). *A Short History of the Movies*. 1971; rpt. New York: Macmillan, 1992, 5th ed.
Mast, Gerald. *The Comic Mind: Comedy and the Movies*. Indianapolis: Bobbs-Merrill, 1973.
McPherson, Edward. *Buster Keaton: Tempest in a Flat Hat*. 2004; rpt. New York: New Market Press, 2005.
Meade Marion. *Buster Keaton: Cut to the Chase*. 1995; rpt. New York: Da Capo Press, 1997.
Meyer, Edward C., M. D. *Houdini: A Mind In Chains*. New York: E. P. Dutton, 1976.
Miles, Barry. *Charles Bukowski*. London: Virgin, 2005.
Milton, Joyce. *Tramp: The Life of Charlie Chaplin*. New York: HarperCollins, 1996.
Moews, Daniel. *Keaton: The Silent Features Close Up*. Los Angles: University of California Press, 1977.
Montgomery, John. *Comedy Films: 1894-1954*. 1954; rpt. London: George Allen & Unwin, 1968.
Orwell, George. *1984*. 1949; rpt. New York: Signet Classic, 1961.
Padgett, Ron. *How Long*. Minneapolis: Coffee House Press, 2011.
Paris, Barry. *Louise Brooks*. 1989; rpt. New York: Anchor Books, Doubleday, 1990.
Renner, Rolf G. *Hopper*. San Diego: Thunder Bay Press, 1997.
Robbins, Jhan. *Inka Dinka Doo: The Life of Jimmy Durante*. New York: Paragon House, 1991.
Schmitz, Neil. *Huck and Alice: Humorous Writing in American Literature*. Minneapolis: University of Minnesota Press, 1983.
Schulberg, Budd. *The Disenchanted*. New York: Random House, 1950.
Sherwood, Robert, E., ed. *The Best Moving Pictures of 1922-1923*. Boston: Small, Maynard, 1923.
Sherwood, Robert E. *Roosevelt and Hopkins: An Intimate Biography*. New York: Harper and Brothers, 1948.
Seldes, Gilbert. *The 7 Lively Arts*. 1924; rpt. New York: Sagamore Press, 1957.
Silverman, Kenneth. *Houdini: The Career of Ehrich Weiss*. New York: HarperCollins, 1996.
Smith, David. *Hoosiers In Hollywood*. Indianapolis: Indiana Historical Society, 2006.
Spring, Justin. *The Essential Hopper*. New York: Harry N. Abrams, 1998.
Talmadge, Margaret L. *The Talmadge Sisters: Norma, Constance, Natalie: An Intimate Story of the World's Most Famous Screen Family By Their Mother*. Philadelphia: J. B. Lippincott, 1924.

Tisserand, Michael. *Krazy: George Herriman, a Life in Black and White*. New York: HarperCollins, 2016.
Thurber, James and E. R. White. *Is Sex Necessary?* 1929; rpt. New York: Harper & Row, 1975.
Toole, John Kennedy. *A Confederacy of Dunces*. New Orleans: Louisiana State University Press, 1980.
Truffaut, François. (with Helen G. Scott). *Hitchcock: Revised Edition of Hitchcock/Truffaut*. 1966; rpt. New York: Simon & Schuster, 1983.
Twain, Mark. *The Adventure of Huckleberry Finn*. 1884 rpt. New York: Barnes & Noble Classics, 2003.
Vonnegutt, Kurt. *A Man Without a Country*. New York: Seven Stories Press, 2005.
Wayne, Jane Ellen. *Clark Gable: Portrait of a Misfit*. New York: St. Martin's Press, 1993.
Wiley, Mason, and Damien Bona. *Inside Oscar*. 1986; rpt. New York: Ballantine, 1993.
Wister, Owen. *The Virginian*. 1902; rpt. New York: New American Library, 1979.
Yallop, David. *The Day the Laughter Stopped*. New York: St. Martin's Press, 1976.

Shorter Works

Agee, James. "Comedy's Greatest Era." *Life*. September 3, 1949. See also. *Agee on Film, Volume* 1. 1958, rpt. New York: Grossett & Dunlap, 1969.
Agnes, Smith. "The Screen in Review: 'The Kid.'" *Picture-Play*. October 1921, 62.
Arbuckle, Fatty. "Nothing to Laugh At." *Picture and Picturegoer*. July 19, 1919, 76.
"At the Capitol: Buster Keaton in 'Go West.'" *New York World*. October 26, 1925, 11.
"At the Capitol: Buster Keaton in 'Seven Chances.'" *New York World*. March 16, 1925, 13.
"At the Rialto: Buster Keaton in 'Our Hospitality.'" *New York World*, December 10, 1923, 9.
"Athletes Take Part in New Keaton Film." *Los Angeles Times*. August 1, 1927, Part 2:7.
"Auditorium—'Funnyland,'" *Chicago Tribune*. October 11, 1914, Part 8:2.
Baker, Jason. "Introduction." In Franz Kafka's *The Metamorphosis and Other Stories*, trans. Donna Freed. 1915; New York: Barnes and Noble Classics, 2013.
"Battling Butler: A Musical Knockout" ad. *New York Herald Tribune*, October 5, 1923,12.
"'Battling Butler' Is a Real Champ." *New York Evening Telegraph*. October 9, 1923, 14.
"'Battling Butler' [Review]." *Variety*. August 25, 1926.
Benchley, Robert. "Drama." *LIFE*. April 16, 1925, 18.
Benchley, Robert. "Drama: A General Readjustments." *LIFE*, March 5, 1925, 18.
Benchley, Robert. "Fascinating Crimes 1." In *The Early Worm*. New York: Henry Holt, 1927.
Benchley, Robert. "The Passing of the Cow." *LIFE*. July 14, 1927, 9.
Bisch, Louis E., M.D., Ph.D. "What Makes You Laugh?" *Photoplay*. June 1928, 34.
"Blacks But Not Blue: Our Comedians Struggle in Dark for Laughs." *Photoplay*. October 1927, 100.
"'The Blacksmith' Review." *Moving Picture World*. December 16, 1922, 672.
Blum, John M. "Retreat from Responsibility." *The National Experience: A History of the United States*, ed. Blum. New York: Harcourt, Brace, 1968.
Brand, Harry. "They Told Buster to Stick to It." *Motion Picture Classics*. June 1926, 80.
Brantley, Ben. "A Playwright Intent on Naming, and Goading, the Beast Within." *New York Times*. September 19, 2016, C-2.
"Brief Reviews of Current Pictures: 'The Navigator.'" *Photoplay*. May 1925, 11.
"Brief Reviews of Current Pictures: 'Three Ages.'" *Photoplay*. November 1923, 102.
Buñuel, Luis. "Buster Keaton's 'College.'" In Francisco Arenda's *Luis Buñuel: A Critical Biography*, trans. and ed. David Robinson 1975; rpt. New York: Da Capo Press, 1976.
Busby, Marquis. "'College' Need, of Education." *Los Angeles Times*. July 30, 1927, Part 2:7.
Busby, Marquis. "Locomotive with a Soul." *Los Angeles Times*. March 13, 1927, Part 3:17.
Busby, Marquis. "Villian Tired of Cussedness." *Los Angeles Times*. July 6, 1927, Part 2:8.
Busch, Charles. "I Performed in Drag." *New York Times*. December 25, 2016, Arts & Leisure Section: 6.
"Buster Gets Along Without Flabbers." *Los Angeles Times*. October 3, 1924, Part 2:9.
"Buster Keaton Gets Grins At Symphony." *Los Angeles Times*. April 9, 1923, Part 2:15.
"Buster Keaton Has First Call With Navy Men." *Los Angeles Times*. September 30, 1923, Part 3:33.
"Buster Keaton." In *The Blue Book of the Screen*. Hollywood: Blue Book of the Screen, Inc., 1923.
"Buster Keaton Latest To Go Rah-Rah On Screen." *New York Evening News*. September 12, 1927, 22.
Buster Keaton telegram. November 14, 1921. In Babe Ruth Scrapbook, Volume 1, Part 3:61. Baseball Hall of Fame, Cooperstown, New York.
"Buster Keaton's Bicycle." *Variety*. May 9, 1928, 5.
"Buster Prefers To Smoke Tailor-Made." *Los Angeles Times*. November 26, 1925, Part 2:11.
"Buster to Build If He Can Find a Hill." *Los Angeles Times*. May 4, 1924, Part 3:21.
"Buster Would Write Book on 'How to Smile.'" *Los Angeles Times*. May 11, 1923, Part 2:9.
"By the Book: Phillip Meyer." *New York Times*. April 2, 2017, Book Review Section: 8.

"'Cameraman' [Review]." *Variety*. September 19, 1928.
"'The Cameraman'—with Buster Keaton." *Harrison's Reports*. September 15, 1928.
Cannon, Regina. "Buster Keaton Seen in 'The Cameraman.'" *New York American*. September 17, 1928, 15.
Cannon, Regina. "'College' [Review]." *New York America*. September 13, 1927, 14.
Cannon, Regina. "Keaton Comedy Grips Fans." *New York American*. February 8, 1927, 9.
Chaplin, Charlies. *Steamboat, Jr.,* ad. *Los Angeles Times*. June 5, 1928, Part 2:11.
Cohen, John S. "The New Photoplay: Buster Keaton Appears in a College Film." *New York Sun*. September 12, 1927. 17.
"'College [Review]." *Harrison's Reports*. September 17, 1927.
"'College' [Review]." *Variety*. September 14, 1927.
"'College—United Artists." *Photoplay*. December 1927, 8.
"The Current Cinema: And Buster Keaton." *The New Yorker*. September 17, 1927, 79.
"Certainly Mr. Keaton Believes." *Los Angeles Times*. April 15, 1923, Part 3:1.
"Chaplin Shows Art of Pictures Century Hence." *Los Angeles Times*. February 7, 1924, Part 3:11.
"Charlie Chaplin, as a Comedian, Contemplates Suicide." *Current Opinion*. February 1922, 209–210.
Charlie Chaplin files. Lincoln Center's New York Public Library of the Performing Arts.
Chase, Gertrude. "Buster Keaton Can Smile and Yawn, Too, If He Wishes." *New York Telegraph*, October 8, 1922.
Chicago White Sox telegram. November 14, 1921. In Babe Ruth Scrapbook, Volume 1, Part 3:50, Baseball Hall of Fame, Cooperstown, New York.
"'Clansman' Revival." *Los Angeles Times*. March 25, 1923, Part 3:33.
C. O. "The Current Cinema: 'Battling Butler.'" *The New Yorker*. August 28, 1926, 36.
Cohen, John S. "The New Photoplay: Buster Keaton in 'Steamboat Bill, Jr.'" *New York Sun*. May 15, 1928, 21.
Cohen, Roger. "The Age of Distrust." *New York Times*. September 20, 2016, A-23.
College ad. *Los Angeles Daily Times*. July 25, 1927, Part 2:7.
Collins-Hughes, Laura. "Thorton Wilder in the Trump Era." *New York Times*. February 12, 2017, Theatre Section: 21.
"Comedian Has to Be [an] Athlete." *Los Angeles Times*. June 17, 1923, Part 3:34.
"A Confidential Guide to Current Release." *Picture-Play Magazine*. September 1927, 119.
"A Confidential Guide to Current Release": 'The Navigator'—Metro-Goldwyn." *Picture-Play Magazine*. May 1925, 60.
Connie Mack telegram. November 15, 1921. In Babe Ruth Scrapbook, Volume 1, Part 3:46. Baseball Hall of Fame. Cooperstown, New York.
"Coolridge to Press Dry Law to Limit, Watson Declares." *New York Times*. May 20, 1925, 1, 12.
"'Cops' [Review]." *Moving Picture World*. March 11, 1922, 198.
"A Costly Joke." *Picture-Play Magazine*. May 1927, 72.
Cowley, Malcolm. "Introduction" to Sherwood Anderson's *Winesburg, Ohio*. 1919, rpt. New York: Viking Press, 1969, 11.
Creelman, Eileen. "Carole Lombard's Last Picture, the Somber 'To Be or Not to Be.'" *New York Sun*. March 7, 1942.
Cronenberg, David. "Introduction." In Franz Kafka's *The Metamorphosis*, trans. Susan Bernofsky. 1915; New York: W. W. Norton, 2014.
Crowther, Bosley. "In 'The Great Dictator Charlie Chaplin Reveals Again the Greatness in Himself.'" *New York Times*. October 20, 1940.
"The Current Cinema: Buster Keaton." *The New Yorker*. February 12, 1927, 51.
"The Current Cinema: Comical Manna From Buster Keaton." *The New Yorker*. August 28, 1926, 36.
"Death Ends Valentino Career At 31." *New York Sun*. August 23, 1926, 1.
"Death of John Bunny." *London Times*. April 29, 1915, 5-D.
"Deep Sea Comedy: Buster Keaton Collecting Shipload for Next Comedy." *Los Angeles Times*. May 11, 1924, Part 3:23.
"Deluge Buster with All Kinds of Kid Stuff. *Los Angeles Times*. January 3, 1924, Part 2:11.
"Dempsey on Way Back to New York." *New York American*. April 3, 1922, 8.
Doren, Carl Van. "The Revolt from the Village." *Nation*. October 12, 1921.
"'Electric House' Is Worth Laughing At." *Los Angeles Times*. October 22, 1923, Part 2:9.
"Ernest Torrence Film Actor, Dead." *New York Times*. May 16, 1933, 17.
"Ernest Torrence to Become Free Lancer." *Los Angeles Times*. May 6, 1926, Part 2:9.
Evans, Harry. "Movies: 'Spite Marriage.'" *Life*. April 19, 1929, 40.
"Famous Comedian Sees Own Picture for Fourth Time." *Los Angeles Herald*. February 6, 1921, PA-20.
Fairbanks, Douglas. "Films for the Fifty Million." *Ladies Home Journal*. April 1924, 27.
Fairbanks, Douglas. *Steamboat Bill, Jr.* ad. *Los Angeles Times*. June 5, 1928, Part 2:11.
"'Fighting Coward' Star, Praises Actor's Make-Up." *Los Angeles Evening Herald*. March 14, 1924, B-1.

"Film Star Goes in for New Style." *Los Angeles Times*. February 9, 1926, Part 2:11.
"Films Will Tell Story of Keatons." *Los Angeles Times*. October 8, 1924, Part 2:9.
"Flashes: Metro Hums." *Los Angeles Times*. February 28, 1924, Part 2:12.
Franklin, Robert, and Joan Franklin. "Interview with Buster Keaton." In *Buster Keaton Interviews*, ed. Kevin W. Sweeney. Jackson: University Press of Mississippi, 2007, 90.
Friedman, Alan W. "Samuel Beckett Meets Buster Keaton: Godeau, Film, and New York." *Texas Studies in Literature and Language*. Spring 2009, 41–46.
Gallaway, Stephen. "No, Woody Allen Won't Read This Interview." *Hollywood Reporter*. May 13, 2016, 73–74.
Gehring, Wes D. "Bunny to Buster: Beyond Just Bookends to Silent Film Comedy." *USA Today Magazine*. September 2016, 72–74.
Gehring, Wes D. Conversation with Buster Keaton's third wife and widow, Eleanor Norris Keaton. Pique, Kansas. Annual Buster Keaton Festival, early 1990s.
Gehring, Wes D. "Conversation with Lillian Gish." At "The Movies: D. W. Griffith and Lillian Gish: 'Broken Blossoms.'" Bloomington: Indiana University Program, March 15, 1981.
Gehring, Wes D. Conversation with George Plimpton. Muncie, Indiana: Midwest Writers, Summer Conference, 2002.
Gehring, Wes D. "John Bunny: America's First Important Comedian." *Literature/Film Quarterly* 25, No. 2 (1995).
Gehring, Wes D. "Hope & Crosby: The Road to Bali. In *Movie Comedians of the 1950s: Defining a New Era of Big Screen Comedy*. Jefferson, NC: McFarland, 2016.
Gehring, Wes D. "Martin & Lewis: Artists and Models." In *Movie Comedians of the 1950s: Defining a New Era of Big Screen Comedy*. Jefferson, NC: McFarland, 2016.
Gehring, Wes D. "*Some Like Hot* chapter." In *Movie Comedians of the 1950s: Defining a New Era of Big Screen Comedy*. Jefferson, NC: McFarland, 2016.
Gehring, Wes D. "The House That Buster Built." *USA Today Magazine*. March 2016, 55.
Gehring, Wes D. Unpublished Interview with Sam Gill. Los Angeles, California, Summer 1975.
"'The General' [Review]." *Variety*. February 9, 1927.
"'The General'—United Artists." *Photoplay*. March 1927, 52.
"'The General'—with Buster Keaton." *Harrison's Report*. February 9, 1927, 27.
Genzlinger, Neil. "With Good Timing, a Look Back at Comedy." *New York Times*. February 9, 2017, C-4.
"Georgie Harris Adds Comedy to 'Flood' Film." *Los Angeles Times*. June 19, 1926, Part 1:7.
Gill, Sam. "John Bunny: A Filmography Compiled by Sam Gill." In *The Silent Picture*. Summer 1972, 8–15.
Goldbeck, Willis. "Only Three Weeks." *Motion Picture*, October 1921.
Gopnik, Adam. "Magic in a Web." *New York Times*. November 13, 2016, Book Review Section: 24.
"'Go West'—Metro-Goldwyn." *Photoplay*. May 1926, 12.
"'Go West' [Review]." *Screenland*. January 1926, 42.
"'Go West' [Review]," *Variety*. October 28, 1928.
"'Go West'—with Buster Keaton." *Harrison's Reports*. November 1, 1925, 174.
"'Grandma's Boy' to Show at Miller's [Theatre]." *Los Angeles Times*. April 6, 1923, Part 2:7.
Griffith, Richard. "Introductory Note." In Harold Lloyd and Wesley W. Stout's *An American Comedy*. 1928; rpt. New York: Dover, 1971.
Grimes, William. "William Trevor, Who Rendered Ordinary Extraordinary, Dies at 88." *New York Times*. November 23, 2016, A-27.
Hall, Mordaunt. "Mr. Keaton in Khaki." *New York Times*. September 30, 1930, 19.
Hall, Mordaunt. "New Vitaphone Features." *New York Times*. February 13, 1927, Part 7:7.
Hall, Mordaunt. "New Vitaphone Features: Mr. Keaton's Face Overpowers This Film." *New York Times*. February 13, 1927, Part 7:7.
Hall, Mordaunt. "Phlegmatic Mr. Keaton Is a Stylist as Jester." *New York Times*. August 29, 1926, Section 7:5.
Hall, Mordaunt. "Poor Comedy." *New York Times*. March 31, 1929, Part 8:7.
Hall, Mordaunt. "The Screen: Chaplin of Hollywood." *New York Times*. January 9, 1928, 50.
Hall, Mordaunt. "The Screen: A Civil War Farce." *New York Times*. February 8, 1927, 21.
Hall, Mordaunt. "The Screen 'College.'" *New York Times*. September 12, 1927, 29.
Hall, Mordaunt. "The Screen: More on Newsreels." *New York Times*. July 28, 1928.
Hall, Mordaunt. "The Screen: Mr. Keaton Again." *New York Times*. August 23, 1926, 9.
Hall, Mordaunt. "The Screen: Silence Wins." *New York Times*. March 25, 1929, 32.
Hall, Mordaunt. "The Screen: Steamboat Bill, Jr." *New York Times*. May 15, 1928, 17.
Hall, Mordaunt. "A Slump in Fun." *New York Times*. March 17, 1925, 18.
"'Hands Up' [Review]." *Variety*. January 20, 1926.
"Harold Lloyd Does Marathon to Studio." *Los Angeles Times*. August 18, 1923, Part 2:7.
"Harold Lloyd Football Costume From the 'Freshman' [1925] Free to the Fan Who Writes the Best Harold Letter." *Screenland*. February 1926, 37.

"Harold Lloyd Offers $500.00 in Prizes for Your Letters: He Wants to Know Which of His Films You Liked Best." *Screenland*. December 1924, 38–39.
"Harold Lloyd Picture Sets New Records." *Los Angeles Times*. June 9, 1928, Part 2:9.
"Harold Lloyd's Latest At Brooklyn Strand." *Brooklyn Eagle*. August 29, 1926, Part E:3.
Helen Keller telegram. November 14, 1921. In Babe Ruth Scrapbook Volume 1, Part 3:47. Baseball Hall of Fame. Cooperstown, New York.
"He Likes Picture Better Than Stage." *Los Angeles Times*. April 19, 1923, Part 2:9.
"Hick-Town Censors—Look Out! Buster Keaton on War Path with New Comedy, Showing Gang at Work." *Los Angeles Times*. January 28, 1924, Part 2:8.
"'The High Sign' [Review]." *New York Times*. March 22, 1922, 10.
"Hilarious Troubles of a 'Freshie' at the Colony." *New York Sun*. September 21, 1925, 22.
"His Play [Film] Rends [Removes] Veil of Comedy." *Los Angeles Times*. October 21, 1923, Part 3:28.
"'Hot News' [Review]." *Variety*. July 25, 1928.
"Houdini's Latest Act Is Unique." *Los Angeles Times*. April 22, 1923, Part 3:30.
"Is God Dead?" cover. *Time*. April 8, 1966.
"John Bunny Again." *Indianapolis Star*. January 10, 1915, 12.
"Keaton and Durante a Riot in New Farce." Loew's Weekly. August 27, 1932.
Keaton, Buster. "Why I Never Smile." *Ladies Home Journal*. June 1926.
"Keaton Fills Capitol [Theatre] with Laughter." *New York Sun*. October 13, 1924, 18.
"Keaton Finds Real Comedy Troubles." *Los Angeles Times*. May 4, 1924, Part 3:27.
"Keaton Frolics in Historic Costumes." *Los Angeles Times*. September 6, 1923, Part 2:11.
"Keaton Gets All Wet in River Film." *Los Angeles Times*. June 10, 1928, Part 3:12.
"Keaton Has [Discovered] New Leading Woman for 'Go West.'" *Los Angeles Times*. May 30, 1925, Part 2:7.
"Keaton Is Shown in New Role: Comedian Turns Athlete in College." *Los Angeles Times*. July 31, 1927, Part 3:13.
Keaton, Joe. "The Cyclone Baby." *Photoplay*. May 1927, 124.
"Keaton Next Is Prize-Fight Comedy Feature." *Los Angeles Times*. December 16, 1925, Part 2:9.
"Keaton Says Success and Name Linked." *Los Angeles Times*. July 22, 1998, Part 3:11.
"Keaton's Ship Was Lure for Whole Family." *Los Angeles Times*. October 26, 1924, Part 3:24.
"Keaton Silent and Funny." *Los Angeles Times*. June 1, 1929, Part 2:9.
"Keaton's Bill for Expenses Rouses [Lou] Anger." *Los Angeles Times*. November 25, 1923, Part 3:33.
"Keaton's Bungalow Really Star's Gymnasium." *Metro-Goldwyn-Mayer Picture Newspaper*. In *The Cameraman* File. New York Performing Arts Library at Lincoln Center, New York.
"Keaton's Comedy Has New Wrinkles." *Los Angeles Times*. April 25, 1924, Part 2:9.
"Keaton's Co-Workers Are from Broadway." *Variety*. March 24, 1927, 27.
"Keaton's Nose Is Broken." *New York Times*. July 31, 1927, 25.
"Kennedy, Randy. "Donald Judd, Unexpected Philosopher." *New York Times*. December 26, 2016, C-6.
"The Kid Brother." *Time*. February 7, 1927, 44.
Kingsley, Grace. "Buster Bursts Into Stardom." *Los Angeles Times*. May 16, 1920.
Kingsley, Grace. "Buster Keaton's Tumbling to Success." *Picture Show*. August 5, 1922, 21.
Kingsley, Grace. "Films Made in Many Tongues." *Los Angeles Times*. August 30, 1929, Part 1:10.
Kingsley, Grace. "Flashes: Didn't Ask to See License." *Los Angeles Times*. October 10, 1924, Part 2:9.
Kingsley, Grace. "Great Comedy: Buster Keaton Triumphs in "Go West.' *Los Angeles Times*. November 23, 1925, Part 2:9.
Kinglsey, Grace. "'Navigator' Great." *Los Angeles Times*. October 6, 1924, Part 1:7.
Kingsley, Grace. "Which Shall It Be? Syd Chaplin Is Undecided Between Star Offers." *Los Angeles Times*. February 8, 1924, Part 2:11.
Klumph, Helen. "Highbrows Are for It." *Los Angeles Times*. October 7, 1928, Part 3:33.
Lane, Anthony. "Seeing Things." *The New Yorker*. October 17, 2016, 108.
Lanier, Henry Wysham. "The Coquelin of the Movies." *World's Work*. March 1915, 566–577.
"Laugh Bill Still Showing at Rialto." *Los Angeles Times*. December 11, 1923, Part 2:18.
Lipke, Katherine. "Comedy Is Lost in War Incidents." *Los Angeles Times*. March 12, 1927, Part 1:7.
Lloyd, Harold. "Don't Be Discouraged!" *Picture-Play*. December 1925, 19, 105.
"Lloyd Staff in Team Work." *Los Angeles Times*. November 2, 1924, Part 3:26.
"Lloyd's Clean Film Wins." *Los Angeles Times*. December 14, 1924, Part 3:24.
"Lloyd's New Gag Man. *Los Angeles Times*. April 4, 1925, Part 1:7.
Lubitsch, Ernst. "Mr. Lubitsch Takes the Floor for Rebuttal." *New York Times*. March 29, 1942, Section 8:3.
Lusk, Norman. "The Screen in Review: Mr. Keaton at His Best." *Picture-Play Magazine*. December 1928, 72.
"Lyceum—John Bunny, Himself." *Indianapolis Star*. November 10, 1914, 15.
"Lyceum—John Bunny." *Indianapolis Star*. January 15, 1915, 15.
"Machine Movies Dwarf Real Art, 7 Stars Declare." *New York Daily News*. February 23, 1923, 23.

"'Mark of Zorro' [Review]." *Variety*. December 3, 1920.
Martin, Quinn. "At the Capitol: Buster Keaton In 'The Navigator.'" *New York World*. October 13, 1924, 9.
Mencken, H. L. "Notes on Journalism." *Chicago Daily Tribune*. September 19, 1926.
"Mr. Keaton's Cow." *New York Times*. October 26, 1925, 25.
"Mr. Keaton's Film at the Empire." *London Times*. October 11, 1930, 10.
Mosher, John. "The Current Cinema: Charlie's Hitler." *The New Yorker*. October 26, 1940, 78.
"Motion Pictures: 'Go West.'" *The New Yorker*. October 31, 1925, 19.
"A Movie Without Headlines [Titles]." *Literary Digest*. February 28, 1925, 26.
Murrey, Feg. "Ernie Orsatti: He Doubles for Buster Keaton in the Movies—But He Can Sock a Mean Double For Himself, as Well!" *Los Angeles Times*. January 16, 1929, Part 3:1, 2.
"'The Navigator' [Review]." *Variety*. October 15, 1924.
"'The Navigator'—with Buster Keaton." *Harrison's Reports*. October 13, 1924.
Nelson, George. "Invincibly Black." *New York Times*. January 15, 2017, Book Review Section: 14–15.
"New Disease Hits Harold Lloyd Fans." *Los Angeles Times*. June 7, 1923, Part 2:11.
"New Films: Comedians and 'Hamlet' Complex Again." *New York Sun*. February 8, 1927, 23.
"'The New Parade' [Review]." *Variety*. May 30, 1928.
"The New Photoplay: Harry Langton Tries a Tragic-Comedy." *New York Sun*. October 3, 1927, 17.
"The New Picture: 'Sherlock Jr.'" *Time*. June 2, 1924, 17.
"The New Picture: *The Navigator*." *Time*. October 20, 1924, 13.
"New Play Bring Stars Back Home." *Los Angeles Times*. October 25, 1925, 30.
"Newest Reviews and Comments: 'The Saphead.'" *Moving Picture World*. February 1926, 1091.
"Norma Talmadge Hailed As Chaplin Counterpart by Clarence Brown, Director." *Los Angeles Times*. May 23, 1926, Part 3:26.
"Noted Comic Artist Leads a Strenuous Life." *Los Angeles Evening Herald*. May 12, 1924, B-7.
Oettinger, Malcolm H. "Love Comedy as a High Art." *Picture-Play Magazine*. March 1923.
Oettinger, Malcolm H. "Low Comedy as High Art." *Picture-Play* Magazine. March 1923, 59.
Oettinger, Malcolm H. "Tumbling to Fame." *Picture-Play Magazine*. December 1920.
"On a Drifting Vessel." *New York Times*. October 13, 1924, 24.
"On the Screen in City Theatres: Buster Keaton at Rialto." *New York Sun*. May 28, 1924, 20.
Our Hospitality ad. *New York Herald Tribune*. December 11, 1923, 12.
"'Our Hospitality' [Review]." *Moving Picture World*. November 24, 1923, 405.
"'Our Hospitality' [Review]." *New York Times*. December 10, 1923.
"'Our Hospitality' [Review]." *Picture-Play Magazine*, December 1923.
"'Our Hospitality' [Review]." *Screenland*. January 1924.
"'Our Hospitality [Review]." *Variety*. December 13, 1923.
"'Our Hospitality'—with Buster Keaton." *Harrison's Reports*, November 19, 1923.
Palmer, John. "Mr. Bunny." *London Saturday Review*. April 1914, 466.
Parsons, Louella O. "'Go West.' Keaton Comedy At Capitol." *New York American*. October 26, 1925, 8.
Parsons, Louella O. "New Films Reviewed: Capitol Showing Buster Keaton Comedy." *New York American*. October 14, 1924, 11.
Parsons, Louella O. "'Sherlock Holmes, Jr.' Feature at Rialto." *New York Sun*, May 27, 1924, 11.
Pearson, David B. "Playing Detective: Possible Solutions to the Production Mysteries of Sherlock, Jr." In *Buster Keaton's Sherlock Jr.*, ed. Andrew Horton. Cambridge: Cambridge University Press, 1997, 140–157.
Peet, Creighton. "'Battling Butler'—MGM." *Cinema Art*. September 1926, 32, 56.
Pelswick, Rose. "'Steamboat Bill, Jr. [Review]." *New York Evening Journal*. September 15, 1928.
Pemberton, Ralph Brock. "A Man Seen Daily by Millions." *American Magazine*. August 1914, 60.
"Perfectly Good Train Is Wrecked: Spectacular Finale for 'Signal Tower' Filmed at Universal." *Los Angeles Times*. January 12, 1924, Part 2:7.
Price, Guy. "Guy Price's Gossop [sic] of the Silverscreen." *Los Angeles Evening Herald*. May 19, 1924, B-8.
"Public Demand Puts Beery Back in Villain Class." *Los Angeles Times*. June 3, 1923, Part 3:28.
Quirk, James R. "Speaking of Pictures." *Photoplay*. August 20, 2015.
"Rites Held for Torrence." *Indianapolis News*. May 17, 1933, 7.
"Real Arts of Chaplin Revealed." *Los Angeles Times*. January 27, 1924. Part 3:19.
Reid, Laurence. "The Celluloid Critic." *Motion Picture Classic*. December 1924, 49.
Reid, Laurence. "The Celluloid Critic: 'Steamboat Bill, Jr.'" *Motion Picture Classic*. August 1928, 53.
"Reshowing of Chaplin Comedy Scores Success." *Los Angeles Times*. March 13, 1927, Part 3:19.
"'Rocket' Gets Into Comedy." *Los Angeles Times*. September 2, 1923, Part 3:21.
Roberts, Sam. "Harry Mathews Dies 86; Writer Who Experimented." *New York Times*. February 3, 2017, A-22.
Roberts, Sam. "Masha Leon, Columnist Who Fled Nazis, Dies at 86." *New York Times*. April 10, 2017, D-8.
Rogers, Will. "We Save Money, Egypt Loses It." December 14, 1924. Syndicated weekly newspaper article. In

Will Rogers Weekly Articles, vol. 1 the Harding/Coolidge Years:1922:1925, ed. James M. Smallwood. Stillwater: Oklahoma State University Press, 1980.
Rogers, Will. "Will Rogers Explains One Joke Is On Him." August 26, 1927, Syndicated daily telegram. In *Will Rogers' Daily Telegram, vol.1, The Coolidge Years, 1926–1929,* 121.
Rogers, Will. "Will Rogers Names Chaplin as His Lieutenant Mayor." January 4, 1927. Syndicated daily telegram. In *Will Rogers' Daily Telegrams, vol. 1, The Coolidge Years, 1926–1929.*
Rogers, Will. Untitled column. October 21, 1928. In *The Autobiography of Will Rogers,* ed. Donald Day. Boston: Avon, 1975.
"'Rosita [Review].'" *Variety.* September 6, 1923.
Russell, Frederick. "The Life Story of Carole Lombard." *Film Pictorial.* July 4, 1936, Part 2:17.
St. Johns, Adela Rogers. "Can a Genius Be a Husband." *Photoplay.* January 1927, 116.
St. Johns, Adela Rogers. "A Gallant Lady ... Carole Lombard." *Liberty,* March 7, 1942: Part 2:25.
St. Johns, Adela Rogers. "Interviewing Joseph Talmadge Keaton." *Photoplay.* October 1922, 51, 93.
Sandburg, Carl. "Limited." In *Chicago Poems.* New York: Henry Holt, 1916.
Sandburg, Carl. "The Navigator [Review]." *Chicago Daily News.* November 18, 1924.
Sandburg, Carl. "'Seven Chances' [Review]." *Chicago Daily News.* April 16, 1925.
Sandburg, Carl. "The Three Ages' [Review]." *Chicago Daily News.* November 14, 1923.
Sandomir, Richard. "Rodney Smith, 68, Photographer of Surrealistic Whimsy." *New York Times.* December 17, 2016, A-19.
Schallert, Edwin. "Chaplin Opens New Epoch." *Los Angeles Times.* September 27, 1928, Part 2:9.
Schallert, Edwin. "The Comedian's Hour of Triumph." In *The Pre-View: A Week Film Magazine.* Insert In *Los Angeles Times,* November 24, 1924, 2.
Schallert, Edwin. "Harold on Rampage." *Los Angeles Times.* October 1923, Part 2:11.
Schallert, Edwin. "Pathos Mood in Prospect." *Los Angeles Times.* March 25, 1928, Part 3:13.
Schallert, Edwin. "Playdom: College Life Spirit Fills Grange Feature." *Los Angeles Times.* September 10, 1926, Part 2:11.
Schallert, Edwin. "Playdom: Keaton Clever." *Los Angeles Times.* August 30, 1926.
Schallert, Edwin. "Playdom: Title Is Settled." *Los Angeles Times.* July 18, 1923, Part 2:2.
Schallert, Edwin. "Rogers Star Shines Brightly." *Los Angeles Times.* September 20, 1929, Part 2:9.
Schallert, Edwin. "The Scene Stealers." *Picture-Play.* November 1924, 65.
Schallert, Edwin. "Silents Withstand Onslaught." *Los Angeles Times.* September 8, 1929, Part 3:11.
Schallert, Edwin. "'Steamboat Bill's Stormy Fun Special." *Los Angeles Times.* June 8, 1928, Part 2:11.
Scheuer, Philip K. "What Makes Laughter, Asks Comic." *Los Angeles Times.* June 3, 1928, Part 3:11.
"The Screen: 'The Mark of Zorro." *New York Times.* November 29, 1920, 20.
"Second Chance [Category]." *Picture-Play Magazine.* May 1925, 60.
Sennett, Mack. "Two Reels Are Enough For Comedy." *Los Angeles Times.* February 22, 1925. Part 3:19–20.
"'Seven Chances' [Review]." *Time* magazine. March 23, 1925.
"'Seven Chances' [Review]." *Variety.* March 18, 1925.
"'Seven Chances'—with Buster Keaton." *Harrison's Report.* March 21, 1925.
"The Shadow Stage. 'Go West.'" *Photoplay.* January 1926, 49.
Simic, Charles. "[Thoughts on] 'Cops.'" In *Writers at the Movies,* ed. Jim Shepard. New York: HarperCollins, 2000, 245.
"The Shadow Stage." *Photoplay.* September 1927, 6.
"The Shadow Stage: 'Spite Marriage.'" *Photoplay.* April 1929, 54.
"'Sherlock, Jr.'—Metro." *Photoplay.* July 1924, 46.
"'Sherlock, Jr.' [Review]." *New York Times.* May 26, 1924, 21.
"'Sherlock, Jr.' [Review]." *Variety.* May 28, 1924.
Sherwood, Robert E. "Life of the Silent Drama: 'The Chaser.'" *Life.* April 26, 1928, 19.
Sherwood, Robert E. "The Movies: 'The Cameraman.'" *Life.* October 5, 1928, 28.
Sherwood, Robert E. "The Movies: The Celluloid Crop of 1928." *Life.* December 28, 1928.
Sherwood, Robert E. "The Perils of Monotony." *Photoplay.* November 1925, 70, 123.
Sherwood, Robert E. "'Seven Chances' [Review]." *Life.* April 19, 1925, 26.
Sherwood, Robert E. "'Sherlock, Jr." *Life.* June 19, 1924, 28.
Sherwood, Robert E. "Short Subjects." In *The Best Moving Pictures of 1922–1923.* Boston: Small, Maynard, 1923, 121.
Sherwood, Robert E. "The Silent Drama: 'A Woman of Paris.'" *Life.* November 29, 1923, 24.
Sherwood, Robert E. "The Silent Drama: 'Battling Butler.'" *Life.* September 16, 1926, 26.
Sherwood, Robert E. "The Silent Drama: 'The Circus.'" *Life.* February 2, 1928, 26.
Sherwood, Robert E. "Silent Drama: 'College.'" *Life.* October 6, 1927, 26.
Sherwood, Robert E. "The Silent Drama: 'The General.'" *Life.* February 24, 1927, 26.
Sherwood, Robert E. "The Silent Drama: 'Go West.'" *Life.* November 19, 1925, 26.

Sherwood, Robert E. "The Silent Drama: 'The Navigator.'" *LIFE*. November 6, 1924, 26.
Sherwood, Robert E. "The Silent Drama: 'Our Hospitality.'" *LIFE*. January 3, 1924, 24.
Sherwood, Robert E. "The Silent Drama: 'Speedy.'" *LIFE*. May 10, 1928, 30.
Sherwood, Robert E. "The Silent Drama: 'Steamboat Bill, Jr.'" *LIFE*. May 31, 1928, 23.
Sherwood, Robert E. "The Silent Drama: 'Steamboat Bill, Jr.'" *LIFE*. May 31, 1928, 23.
Sherwood, Robert E. "The Silent Drama: 'Three Ages.'" *LIFE*. October 25, 1923, 24.
Sherwood, Robert E. "The Silent Drama: "Young Mr. Keaton.'" *LIFE*. November 16, 1922.
"Sinclair Lewis Hornest." *Literary Digest*. May 29, 1926, 27.
Smith, Agnes. "The Screen in Review: 'A Woman of Paris.'" *Picture-Play*. January 1924, 52.
Smith, Agnes, "The Screen in Review: 'Pay Day.'" *Picture-Play*. June 1922, 57.
Smith, Frederick James. "The New Screen Plays in Review: 'Go West.'" *Motion Picture Classic*. January 1926, 81.
"Snitz Edwards to Appear at the Potboilers [Art Theatre]." *Los Angeles Times*. April 14, 1926, Part 2:9.
Spain, Mildred. "Buster Keaton Provides 82 Laughs in Chase for Bride." *New York Daily News*. March 17, 1925.
Spain, Mildred. "Harold Lloyd as 'Freshman' Sure Cure for Grouchy Mood." *New York Daily News*. September 22, 1925, 27.
"'Spite Marriage' [Review]." *Variety*. March 27, 1929.
"'Spite Marriage' (SD)—with Buster Keaton." *Harrison's Reports*. April 6, 1929.
Stanley, Jason. "My Parents' Mixed Message on the Holocaust." *New York Times*. August 21, 2016, Sunday Review Section: 9.
"'Steamboat Bill, Jr.'—Buster Keaton." *Harrison's Reports*. May 12, 1928, 83.
"'Steamboat Bill, Jr.' [Review]." *Time*. May 28, 1928, 19.
"'Steamboat Bill. Jr.' [Review]." *Variety*. May 16, 1928.
Steig, Jeanne. "Clowning Around." In *The Art of William Steig*. New Haven,: Yale University Press, 2007.
Steig, William. Letter to Cuppy. Will Cuppy Papers. Box 96: Folder 24. Undated letter (circa 1941). University of Chicago.
"Studio Flashes." *Los Angeles Times*. February 13, 1927, Section 7:7.
"Swelled Head Not Funny." *Los Angeles Times*. April 8, 1923, Part 3:27.
"'Talkies' Just Fad Says Joseph Schenck: Producer." *New York Times*. August 22, 1928, 25.
Taylor, Kenneth. "And Now the Comedian Seen to Have Succumbed to the Costume Vogue." *Los Angeles Times*. August 5, 1923, Section 4:27.
Taylor, Kenneth. "Keaton Comic in Latest Picture." *Los Angeles Times*. April 28, 1924, Part 2:9.
"Talmadge Girls Soon to Resume." *Los Angeles Times*. November 16, 1925, Part 2:9.
Thalberg, Irving. "New Goals to Achieve." *Los Angeles Times*. Pre-View Magazine. April 23, 1929, 6.
"'Thief of Bagdad' [Review]." *Variety*. March 26, 1924.
Thirer, Irene. "Buster Keaton, Directing Self, Does Good Job." *New York Daily News*. August 26, 1926.
Thirer, Irene. "Cameraman Focuses Fun Only in Last Two Reels." *New York Daily News*. September 16, 1928, 64.
Thomson, David. "Harold Lloyd." In *The New Biographical Dictionary of Film*. New York: Alfred A. Knopf, 2003.
"'Three Ages' High Stepping Burlesque." *Los Angeles Times*. September 10, 1923, Part 2:5.
"'Three Ages' [Review]." *Moving Picture World*. September 8, 1923, 155.
"'Three Ages' [Review]." *Variety*. October 4, 1923.
"'Three Ages'—with Buster Keaton." *Harrison's Reports*. September 24, 1923.
"Torrence Surprised Again." *Los Angeles Times*. July 8, 1928, Part 3:11.
"Three-Reeler One of Buster's Best." *Los Angeles Times*. April 16, 1923, Part 2:7.
Thurber, James. "The Secret Life of Walter Mitty." In *My World and Welcome to It*. New York: Harecourt, Brace, 1942, 72–81.
Underhill, Harriette. "On the Screen." *New York Herald Tribune*. May 27, 1924, 10.
Underhill, Harriette. "On the Screen: Buster Keaton Is Just Himself in 'The Navigator.'" *New York Herald Tribune*. October 13, 1924, 10.
Underhill, Harriette. "On the Screen: 'The Three Ages.'" *New York Tribune*. October 1, 1923, 9.
Verongos, Helen T. "Shirley Hazzard, 85, Writer Who Shared Life's Cruelties." *New York Times*. December 14, 2016, B-14.
Vitella, Paul. "Robert Pirsig, 88, Author of 'Zen and the Art of Motorcycle Maintenance' Dies." *New York Times*. April 25, 2017, B-12.
Voigt, Ellen Bryant. "'Chinatown' [Thoughts]." In *Writers at the Movies*, ed. Jim Shepard. New York: Harper-Collins, 2000, 266.
Vreeland, Frank. "Chaplin Seeths with Revolutionary Plans." *Los Angeles Times*. October 21, 1923, Part 3:24.
Waldorf, Wilella. "New Photoplays: Buster Keaton in 'The General' at the Capitol [Theatre]." *New York Evening Post*, February 7, 1927, n.p.

Waterbury, Ruth. "Why Women Like Sophisticated Men." *Photoplay*. May 1926, 32.
W. E. "Melancholy Monarchs of Mirth." *Picture Show*. November 25, 1922, 20.
"'We Are Engaged,' Lisps Pola, As Charlie Blushes and Nods." *New York Tribune*. January 29, 1923, 4.
Webber, Bruce. "Edwin Albea, Trenchant Playwright of Desperate Era." *New York Times*. September 18, 2016, Part 1:23.
Wertheimer, Ron. "Irwin Corey, Comedian, Dies at 102. Posed as World's 'Foremost' Authority." *New York Times*. February 8, 2017, B-11.
Whitaker, Alma. "Buster Smiles for This Scribe." *Los Angeles Times*. August 29, 1926, Part 3:19.
Whitaker, Alma. "Torrence Feels 'King of Kings' Role Responsibility." *Los Angeles Times*. September 5, 1926.
Woolcott, Alexander. "Preface." In *Beggar on Horseback*. New York: House Liveright, 1924.
Wooldridge, A. L. "Yes Men Need Not Apply." *Picture-Play*. September 1926, 24.
Werner, Margaret. "How Buster Keaton Got That Way." *Movie Weekly*. November 10, 1923, 12.
"W. S. Hart Tells of Wit Shown by Wild Bill Hickok." *Los Angeles Times*. October 7, 1928, Part 3:38.
York, Cal. "Studio News & Gossip East and By West." *Photoplay*. April 1926, 49.
"Youngest Keaton Baby Names Bob." *Los Angeles Times*. March 19, 1924, Part 2:11.
Zinoman, Jason, "Once Too Raw, a Carlin Special Resurfaces." *New York Times*. September 5, 2016, C-4.

Documentaries

AFI 100 Greatest American Movies of All Time. (10th Anniversary Edition). Originally broadcast on CBS, June 20, 2007.
Baseball: The Fifth Inning: Shadow Ball. A film by Ken Burns, PBS, 1984.
Documentary on The Three Ages. A Bonus Feature on Kino's Blue-Ray Edition of *The Three Ages*. A Film Written and Directed by John Bengtson, 2010, 10 minutes.
"Seeing Green." By Charles Drazin (1949). Bonus material on 1949's *The Third Man*, DVD. New York: Criterion Collection, 2007.
So Funny It Hurts: Buster Keaton and MGM. A film by Kevin Brownlow and Christopher Bird. Turner Classic Pictures, 2004.

Index

Numbers in ***bold italics*** indicate pages with illustrations

The Adventures of Huckleberry Finn 19, 24, 30
Aesop's Fables 109
Agee, James 3, 4, 6, 7, 145, 202
Albee, Edward 49, 105, 106, 129
Allen, Woody 60, 62, 90, 94, 105, 106, 188
An American Comedy 1, 13
American Gothic 30, 164
An American in Paris 34–35; comedy theory 37, 40–41
Anderson, Sherwood 14, 188
Androcles and the Lion 109, 112
Anne Hall 106
Arbuckle, Fatty 26–28, 30, ***32***, 33, 41, 77, 162; comedy theory 37, 40, 41, 132–134; scandal of 33, 43, 51, 59, 72, ***107***, 108; *Sherlock, Jr.* and 60, 62, 66–67, ***68***, 69, 71–73
Arrowsmith 16
Automat ***197***

Baldwin, James 122, 158
The Bank Dick 63
Barnes, Lee 151, 156
Battling Butler 14, 22, 32, 91, 118–131, ***123***, 135, 137, 138, 174
Beckett, Samuel 1, 6, 12, 13, 15, 20, 29, 49, 78, 178, 198
Beery, Wallace 46, 48, 193
Being John Malkovich 35
Being There 62
Bellows, George 126
Ben Hur: A Tale of Christ 45
Benchley, Robert 57–58, 59, 110–111, ***139***–140, 157
Benny, Jack 17
Bergman, Ingmar 95
Berra, Yogi 178, 203
The Birth of a Nation 27, 39, 45, 82, 135
"Black Sox Scandal" 43, 51
The Blacksmith 34, 47, 110, 134
Blazing Saddles 110

The Boat 46, Damfino and 35, 155
Bringing Up Baby 63, 134–135
Broken Broken Blossoms 113
Brooks, Louise 50
Brooks, Mel 110
Brown, Joe E. 22
Bruce, Lenny 116
Bruckman, Clyde 17, 97, 98, 149
Bukowski, Charles 181
Bunny, John 27, 28, 60, 63–64, ***65***, 163
Bunny in Funnyland 64–66
Buñuel, Luis 21, 28, 157, 160, 201
Burns, Ken 179
The Buster Keaton Story 5
The Butcher Boy 27, 28, 30

The Cameraman: 172–183, 185; "shadow ball" 22, 47, 75, 155, 178
Camus, Albert 12, 15, 20; *The Stranger* and 13, 62, 90
Candy, John 54
Capra, Frank 3, 7
Carlin, George 25, 44
Carson, Johnny 124
Cassavetes, John 7
The Catcher in the Rye 19
Chan, Jackie 57, 110
Chaplin, Charlie ***68***, ***111***; author and 7, 13, 15, 18, 49, 85, 112, 153–154; comparison with Keaton 192–204; comedy god 7, 13, 18, 49, 85, 112; greatest auteur 1, 3, 192; see also *The Circus*; *City Lights*; *Easy Street*; *The Gold Rush*; *The Great Dictator*; *The Immigrant*; *The Kid*; *Limelight*; *Modern Times*; *Monsieur Verdoux*; *Pay Day*; *Shoulder Arms*; *A Woman of Paris*
Chaplin, Sydney (brother of) 83–84

Chariots of Fire 151
Charlie Chaplin's Own Story 15
The Chaser 7
Chicago Race Riots: July 1919 154
The Circus 8, 13, 42, 117, 181–182
City Lights 17, 124, 126, 130, 151, 164, 174, 181, 190
Cobb, Ty 152, 156
College 21, 28, 35, 44, 47, 76, 83, 90, 101, 106, 147–160, ***152x***, 163; *Battling Butler Close* and 91, 125, 136
"Comedy's Greatest Era" 1, 145, 202
Coney Island 30
A Confederacy of Dunces 147
Convict 13 30
Cooke, Alistair 1
Cops 1, 30, 31–32, 34, 35, 44, 56–57, 90, 91, 97, 105, 130, 137, 146, 152, 159
Corbett, Jim 21, 127
Costeau, Jean 90
Crawford, Sam 151, 154
Cronenberg, David 129
Cuomo, Mario 179
Cuppy, Will 39, 101, 125, 165–166, 170

Dalí, Salvador 20, 24, 28, 34; *The Navigator* 82, 94, 157
Daniels, Bebe 177
Davies, Marion 66, 72, 97, 171, 176
Davis, Burke 147
Day Dream 29, 44, 47, 105
Day for Night 1
Death of a Salesman 87
DeMille, Cecil B. 44–45, 57
Dempsey, Jack 126, 128, 152
Dempsey & Firpor 126
The Devil Finds Work 122, 158
Dickens, Charles 15, 16, 30, 186
The Disenchanted 74–75
A Dog's Life 43

231

Doughboys 12, 189, 190
Duck Soup 143, 173
Dupont, Richard 95
Durante, Jimmy 189, 191

Easy Street 28, 83, 125
Edwards, Snitz **88**, 91, 118–131, 155, 159, 174, 193, 199; high profile character actor 118–119; Keaton and 118
The Electric House 34, 35, 79
Eltinge, Julian 94

Factotum 181
Fairbanks, Douglas 33, 39, 40, 41, 42, 48, 63, 81, 83, 119, 125, 151, 161, 166; books 75–76
Feldman, Marty 94, 140
Ferguson, Otis 202
Fields, W.C. 27, 63, 78, 117, 155, 173, 183
Film 1, 6, 12, 13, 29, 178
Fitzgerald, F. Scott 74–75, 102
Fleischer, Max 46
For Heaven's Sake 10
Ford, John 59, 102, 107, 110
Free and Easy 186
Freeman, Morgan 171
The Freshman 47, 85, 98, 101, 148, 150, 153, 156; rare pan 117
The Frozen North 13, 25, 30, 32–33, 44, 67–68, 73, 103

Gable, Clark 175, **176**
The General 6, 21, 25, 32, 40, 42, 51, 52, 54, 75, 76, 117, 127, **128**, **135**, 131–147, 148, 152, 156, 159, 160; death/dark comedy 137, 142, 145; *Our Hospitality* and 56–57
Genre-Busting Dark Comedy of the 1970s 144
Gertie the Dinosaur 46
Gish, Lillian 113, 184
Go West 34, 38, 47; Albee and 49, 98–99, 102–117, **104**, 129, 157
The Goat, or Who Is Sylvia 49, 105, 106, 129
Going Around By Passing Through 95
Goldberg, Rube 34, 76, 79
The Gold Rush 8, 9, 25, 57, 67, 85, 101, **111**, 112, 117, 145–146, 181; "Oceana Roll" 66
Grandma's Boy 8
Griffith D.W. 39, 41, 42, 44–45, 57, 82, 107, 166; cruelest spoof 113
Griffith, Raymond 142
Grange, Red 126, 148
The Great Dictator 25, 115–116, 130–131, 142

The Great Escape 61
The Great Locomotive Chase 135, 149
Greene, Graham 111
Grey, Zane 102–103, 110

Hale, Georgia 19, 112
Hall, Charlie 155
Hands Up 142–143
A Hard Day's Night 31
Hard Luck 30, 31
"Harlem Renaissance" 153
Harold and Maude 30, 96
Harriman, George 44, 97–98, 101, 106
Hart, William S. 13, 32–33, 67, 75, 103
The Haunted House 34
Hawks, Howard 61
Hays, Will 18, 33, 43, 51
Hearst, William Randolph 72, 106, 176, 180
Hellman, Lillian 94
Hemingway, Ernest 20, 74, 130, 147
The High Sign 30, 33, 35, 146
Hitchcock, Alfred 29, 91, 141, 145, 198
Hoosiers [especially "cowboys"] in Hollywood 108
Hope, Bob 3–4, 5, 17, 105, 173
Hope & Crosby 173
Hopper, Edward 177–178, 196–197; *Automat* 197
Houdini, Harry 23, 24, 61, 62, 76, 89–90, 95, 167, 169
"Hurray for Captain Spalding" 1

I Was a Male War Bride 61
The Immigrant 28, 35
Intolerance 39, 44, 48, 107, 109, 166
The Iron Mule 59, 67; Arbuckle and 59–60; Keaton cameo 60
It's a Gift 27, 63, 78

Johnson, Noble 82

Kael, Pauline 87, 90–91, 165
Kafka, Franz 15, 20, 29, 35; "The Metamorphosis" and 129–130, 141
Kaye, Danny 124
Keaton, Bob (son) 80, 92, 93
Keaton, Buster **5**, **44**, **51**, **53**, **64**, **71**, **80**, **81**, **89**, **93**, **95**, **104**, **106**, **123**, **128**, **135**, **144**, **152**, **163**, **175**, **180**, **187**; author and 15, 18, 142, 149, 153–154; close comparison with Chaplin 192–204; postcard script and 1, 37, 132–133, 164, 165, 166,
173, 185, 188; surrealism and 3, 18, 20, 24, 23, 33–35, 54–55, 57, 78, 82, 86, 87, 90, 94, 96, 98, 110, 114, 116, 158, 159, 165, 171, 177, 178–179, 181, 183, 198; see also *Battling Butler*; *The Blacksmith*; *The Boat*; *The Butcher Boy*; *College*; *Coney Island*; *Convict 13*; *Cops*; *Day Dreams*; *Doughboys*; *The Electric House*; *Free and Easy*; *The Frozen North*; *The General*; *Go West*; *Hard Luck*; *The Haunted House*; *High Sign*; *My Wife's Relations*; *One Week*; *Our Hospitality*; *Parlor, Bedroom and Bath*; *The Playhouse*; *The Saphead*; *The Scarecrow*; *Seven Chances*; *Sherlock, Jr.*; *Spite Marriage*; *Steamboat Bill, Jr.*; *The Three Ages*; *What, No Beer?*
Keaton, Eleanor (third wife) 169, 188
Keaton, Joe (father of) **11**, 20–21, 22–23, 25, 80, 167
Keaton, Joseph (son) 52, 55, 80, 92, **93**
The Kid 17, 41, 42
Krazy Kat 44, 97, 101, 106, 108

Lane, Anthony 61
Langdon, Harry 3, **4**, 7, 97, 116, 202
Laurel & Hardy 29, 54, 63, 110, 155, 202
Leahy, Margaret 47–48
Levant, Oscar 34–35
Lewis, Jerry 75, 84, 124, 173
Lewis, Sinclair 16, 18, 68
Limelight 4
"Limited" 87
Lindsay, Vachel 64
Little Big Man 106–107
Lloyd, Harold **9**; consistency 7, 8, 49, 85, 148; "glasses character" 9, 16, 19, 88; PR machine and 3, 9–10, 16, 17, 24, 107, 182; see also *The Freshman*; *Grandma's Boy*; *The Kid Brother*; *Safety Last*; *The Sin of Harold Diddlebock*; *Speedy*; *Welcome Danger*; *Why Worry?*
Lombard, Carole 108
Long Pants 7
The Lovable Cheat 12
Love and Death 188
Love Is a Dog from Hell 181
Lubitsch, Ernst 8, 17, 105, 119, 143–144, 145, 173
Lynd, Helen 16
Lynd, Robert 16

Index

Maher, Bill 32
Main Street 16
Maltin, Leonard 146
Man with a Movie Camera 177
Man's Genesis 39, 45
Martin, Steve 54
Marx Brothers (Groucho, Harpo Chico, and sometimes Zeppo) 105, 143, 172–173, 174, 175, 186, 191
Masters, Edgar Lee 14, 160
Mayakovsky, Vladimir 57
McCarthyism 17, 18, 19, 105
McKay, Claude 153–154
McQueen, Steve 21, 61
Mencken, H.L. 40, 107
MGM, smothering comedians 172–176, 180, 181, 182, 184, 185–186, 188, 189
Middletown: A Study in Contemporary Culture 16
The Milky Way 124, 126
Miller, Arthur 87
Mix, Tom 33, 108, 115
Modern Times 29, 130–131, 137
Monsieur Verdoux 19, 25
Most, Gerald 98, 107, 121, 145–146
Murphy, Gerald 21, 22
The Music Box 29
My Autobiography 15
My Trip Abroad 18, 149, 153–154
My Wife's Relations 35–36, 43, 89
My Wonderful World of Slapstick 5, 12, 15, 24, 60, 73, 87, 133, 134, 145, 169, 190
The Mysterious Stranger 20
"Myth of Sisyplaus" 29

Nanook of the North 13, 60
National Advancement of Colored People (NAACP) 82
The Navigator 39, 70, 74–87, **80**, 91, 117, 118, 128, 133, 134, 138, 146, 147, 161, 174, 177, 197, 198
A Night at the Opera 172, 174, 186
1941 134
"Nowhere to Run" 1
Number, Please 30
Nurse Betty 171

Oakie, Jack 78
Oliver Twist 15
One Week 21, 24, 29, 35, 46, 121, 146, 181
Orsatti, Ernie 182
Our Hospitality 20, 21, 28, 37, 52–58, **53**, 59, 70, 101, 105–106, 134, 138; *The General* and 56–57; high praise 115, 117, 140, 165; *The Navigator* and 77
Our Incredible Civil War 147

Pan's Labyrinth 95
Paramount 173, 186, 191
Parker, Dorothy 32
Parlor, Bedroom and Bath 35, 188
Parsons, Louella O. 86, 115
Pay Day 13
Pearson, David 8, 67, 69
Penn, Arthur 106
Persistence of Vision 94
Pittenger, William 135
The Plague 12
Planes, Trains & Automobiles 54
Plimpton, George 130
The Playhouse 34, 35, 92, 144
Poe, Edgar Allan 25
The Purple Rose of Cairo 60, 62

Raskin, David 90
The Red Mill 66, 72, 97
Renoir, Jean 106, 111, 121
"Revolt from the Village" 14, 107, 160
The Road to Hollywood 3–4
Rogers, Roy 105, 150
Rogers, Will 19, 150, 179, 189
Ruggles, Charles 121
Rules of the Game 106, 111, 121
Ruth, Babe 50, 51, 75, 152, 156, 167, 179

Sacco and Vanzetti 31–32, 34, 105
Safety Last 10, 16, 183, 187
Sailor Beware 124
St. Rodgers, Adela 8, 24, 108
Salinger, J.D. 19
The Sand Pebbles 21
Sandburg, Carl 55, 79, 87; "Limited" 100, 153–154
The Saphead 38–39, 61, 70, 74, 93, 118, 131, 165, 173
Sarris, Andrew 90–91
The Scarecrow 33–34
Schenck, Joseph M. 28, 37, 55, 68, 69, 80, 88, 148; mentor making mistakes 43, 47–48, 89, 168–170, 198, 200, 201
Schulberg, Budd 74–75
"Scopes Monkey Trial" 107
Scott, Randolph 104
Sebastian, Dorothy 79, 185, 186, **187**, 188
Seldes, Gilbert 97
Sellers, Peter 62
Semon, Larry 8, 98
Sennett, Mack 7, 26, 29–30, 31, 38, 39

The Set-Up 129
Seven Chances 1, 38, 39, 83, 84, 88–101, **89**, **95**, 114, 190
The Seven Lively Arts 97
Shanghai Noon 110
Sharkey, Jack J. 21, 127
Shaw, George Bernard 8, 32, 109
The Sheriff 33
Sherlock, Jr. 13, 24, 28, 29, 34, 47, 59–73, **71**, 75–76, 84, 88, 92, 111, 130, 147, 171; Arbuckle and 60–69, 71–73; highest praise of 44, 87, 115
Sherwood, Robert E. 7, 9, 14, 22, 37, 38, 42, 44, 49, 52, 71, 86, 87, 100–101, 103, 115, 130, 143; key insights of 44, 87, 115, 157, 162, 169, 178–179, 201
Shoulder Arms 41, 84, 142, 168
Signal Tower 149–150
The Sin of Harold Diddlebock 24, 47
Skelton, Red 85, 99, 173, 174, 175, 181
Slaughterhouse-Five 157
"Smile" 1
Smith, Dave 108
Smith, Rodney 90
Some Like It Hot 56
Son of Paleface 105
Speedy 13, 16, 170, 180
Spite Marriage 79, 173, 184–191
Spoon River Anthology 14, 160
Steamboat Bill, Jr. 23, 40, 99, 143, 161–171
Steig, William 165–166
"Stephenson Rocket" 52–53
Stevens, Cat 30
The Stranger 13, 62, 190
Stroheim, Eric von 57
The Strong Man 7
Sturges, Preston 24, 47
A Submarine Pirate 84
Sullivan, John L. 21, 127

"Take Me Out to the Ball Game" 22
Talmadge, Constance (sister-in-law) 24, 28, 36, 43, 48, 55, 66, 79, 88, 92, 122, 149
Talmadge, Margaret L. (mother-in-law) 36, 43, 50, 66, 80, 92
Talmadge, Natalie (first wife) 20, 28, 36, 43–44, 55, 66, 80, 88, 92, **93**, 189
Talmadge, Norma (sister-in-law) 24, 28, 36, 43, 47–48, 50, 66, 79, 88, 92, 122, 149
Thalberg, Irving 174
"Theatre of the Absurd" 1, 43
Thomson, David 17, 137
Thorpe, Jim 103

The Three Ages 5, 20–21, 44–52, 46, 54, 107, 109
"The Three Keatons" 11, 22, 23, 25, 26, 46, 62, 127, 169
Three Stooges 11, 178
Three's a Crowd 116
Thurber, James 39, 121; "The Secret Life of Walter Mitty" and 130–137
To Be or Not to Be 17, 143–144
Tom Sawyer 16, 19
Too Hot to Handle 175, **176**
Toole, John Kennedy 147
Torrence, Ernest 143, **163**, 161–170, 193, 201
Tramp, Tramp, Tramp 7
The Trial 29
Truffaut, François 1, 92, 145

Turner, Florence **152**
Twain, Mark 16, 19, 30, 159
Twilight Zone 6, 78

Valentino, Rudolph 125–126
Vertov, Diziga 177
The Virginian 103
Vonnegut, Kurt 116, 157

Waiting for Godot 1, 12, 29, 62, 87, 90, 178, 186, 203
Wallace, Lew 45
Warner, Andy 147
The Watch 21, **22**
Watch the Birdie 175
Welcome Danger 187
What, No Beer? 109, 190
White, E.B. 39, 74

Why Worry? 8, 101
Wild and Woolly 39
Wild Strawberries 95
Wilder, Bill 56
Wilder, Gene 105
Williams, Robin 44
Wilson, Edmund 117
Wister, Owen 103, 112, 113
Wood, Grant 30, 164
Woollcott, Alexander 70
A Woman of Paris 8, 18, 41, 42–43, 57, 59, 101, 117, 129, 133; working title *Public Opinion* 41, 105

Yeats, William Butler 26

www.ingramcontent.com/pod-product-compliance
Lightning Source LLC
Chambersburg PA
CBHW081551300426
44116CB00015B/2843